MONDO CANUCK

GEOFF PEVERE · GREIG DYMOND

MONDO CANUCK

**A CANADIAN
POP CULTURE
ODYSSEY**

PRENTICE HALL CANADA INC.,
SCARBOROUGH, ONTARIO

Prentice-Hall Canada Inc.
1870 Birchmount Road
Scarborough, Ontario
M1P 2J7

First edition

Canadian Cataloguing in Publication data

Pevere, Geoff
Mondo Canuck: a Canadian pop culture odyssey

Includes index.
ISBN 0-13-263088-5

1. Popular culture - Canada. I. Dymond, Greig. II. Title.

FC95.4.P48 1996   306'.0971   C96-931424-8
F1021.P48 1996

Printed and bound in the United States

Acknowledgements

When we agreed to write a book on Canadian pop culture we knew we had taken on a daunting yet necessary task: the very future of the country was at stake, and there was no margin for error. What if we misstepped in our analysis of Tim Horton's Donuts? Or, even worse, underestimated the cultural significance of Loverboy's spandex? Make no mistake, we knew that the fate of the Dominion was riding on every word. Fortunately, we've had wonderful support from our very own Team Canada, an all-star roster of super-Canucks. We gratefully acknowledge their contributions, and if this volume fails to halt the breakup of the country, it's our fault, not theirs.

First and foremost, we wish to acknowledge the team at Prentice Hall. We owe a huge debt to our extraordinarily hard-working and enthusiastic editor, Sara Borins: quite simply, she made the writing of this book possible, and we're most grateful for her incisive comments, unwavering support and generosity of spirit. A special thanks also to Paula Thiessen, who – with truly inspirational good cheer – tirelessly tracked down many of the photos in this volume. As well, Marijke Leupen gave us much helpful advice in the photo search. Anne-Marie Sorrenti served admirably as an eleventh-hour research reinforcement. Jan Coughtrey and Julie Preston offered their production expertise and skilful coordination. Thanks also to our publicist, Susan Baldaro, and the delightfully rambunctious Prentice Hall sales squad.

We were most fortunate to work with the ultra-funky hipsters at Concrete Design in Toronto: thanks to John Pylypczak, Diti Katona and Nick Monteleone. Our top-notch copy editor, Liba Berry, made countless helpful corrections and suggestions, which were greatly appreciated.

Thanks also to several friends and relatives who lent us their ears and support while we were writing the book: Stephen Brooke, Bill Carr, Alice Hopton, Linda Hunter, Andrew Lundy, Jonathan Mills, Robert Pevere and Steve Pevere. Cathie James deserves a special debt of gratitude: she introduced us to our editor, and served as a constant source of encouragement. We also gratefully acknowledge the Focus brothers, Dave Downey and Anton Leo. Thanks to Lynda Barnett at Toronto's CBC Still Photo Collection for her diligence, and to Fiona Conway at CTV for her patience. Dean Cooke, the redoubtable CanCon enthusiast, served nobly as our agent.

Geoff wishes especially to thank Claire Davey, who lives with a man who does things like this for a living, and Emma Davey, who is proof that evolution is still possible.

Finally, thanks to our parents, Beverley and Glenn Pevere, Jean Dymond and the late A.T. Dymond. By taking both of us to Expo '67, they inadvertently sowed the seeds for the writing of *Mondo Canuck*. This book is dedicated to them, with love.

Contents

Introduction

To grow up in those parts of this country called "English Canada" is to grow up with a peculiar certainty of the in-betweenness of things. It is to come to define yourself more readily as what you aren't than what you are, and to learn to register constant equivocation merely by the simple rhetorical attachment of a tentative 'eh' to the end of otherwise declarative statements, as in "Hey, give back my damned wallet, eh?" Because neither your measuring nor monetary systems correspond with the most influential cultural, political and economic presence on your continent, as a Canadian you learn to do metric and financial conversions almost as early as you learn to skate. Though your background may be Chinese, Romanian, Ojibway or Haitian, you know the proper French phrase for things like "high in dietary fibre," and "now enriched with six essential vitamins" from staring daily at bilingual cereal boxes. You grow up psychically strafed by the relentless barrage of American media, yet every time you reach for change you realize you still share a queen with the tiny, distant island which was once your colonial master. To be Canadian is to live in the space between certainties, to dwell in the gap that separates conviction from speculation. To be Canadian, in other words, is to exist in a state of constant becoming.

This explains why there may be no other country which has managed to turn the process of self-definition into

René Simard & Bruno Gerussi | Knowlton Nash & Barbara Frum | Casey & Finnegan

such an industrious national pastime: next to hockey, watching TV and making long-distance phone calls, Canadians seem to enjoy nothing more than sitting around and fretting about who they are. And even more so lately: what with the unsettling prospect of Quebec separation, the continued depletion of the public sector and the post-multicultural distrust of nationalism generally, the process of anxious self-examination has reached a feverish pitch. Indeed, so much of our indigenous cultural activity – from *Morningside* panel discussions to *Maclean*'s readers' polls – seems preoccupied with the question of defining Canada, one wonders if we'd have any indigenous cultural activity without the question to ask. Imagine it: if Canada *were* actually defined to the satisfaction of everyone involved what would Canadians do for rhetorical amusement? After all, it may only be uncertainty, but it's *our* uncertainty. The fact is, in the absence of any other unanimously endorsed cultural characteristic, it's all we've got. Without doubt, we're nothing.

On one hand, this book belongs firmly to that tradition of obsessive Canadian self-examination. It is motivated by questions of identity and distinction, and it is rooted in a conviction that somehow, in some way, Canadians are different. Moreover, it is convinced that the difference is important: that knowing how and why we are distinct is somehow vital to our cultural health and well-being, if not survival. (Far as we know, no Canadians have yet died from a lack of cultural identity.) Where we break with tradition is over the arena of cultural reflection. While the vast bulk of national self-scrutiny has been circumscribed geographically – "Canadian" being what

Canadians do in Canada – or limited in interest to activities and practices which are so unmistakably Canuck as to verge on national clichés, we'd like to suggest another approach. It's an approach which to us, as a pair of Anglo-Canadians who grew up between strip malls and TV screens, is obvious, but which has nonetheless only rarely been invited on the voyage of national self-definition.

Not that there's anything wrong with studying Canada through the Group of Seven, CanLit, politics, canoe trips or regional folk music heard on CBC-Radio. (Tiresome, redundant and mind-numbingly dull maybe, but not wrong.) Just that, for us, such things merely doubled that deeply Canadian sense of alienation: while we knew beyond doubt we were "Canadian" – and, as children of Expo and Trudeau, were unquestioningly *proud* to be so – we also knew that our "Canadian" experience wasn't necessarily reflected in the icy phallic peaks of Lawren Harris, the textured verse of Earle Birney, the spiritually cleansing act of portaging or, god knows, the foreign policy of Lester Pearson. Nope, it was right there, right in front of our little suburban faces: on TV. To be told that being Canadian meant sapping trees or digging documentaries amounted to being told one was not Canadian at all. On the other hand, to kick back after an invigorating game of road hockey by watching *The Forest Rangers* while eating packaged butter tarts off the back of the first Guess Who LP cover was to just know you were up to something culturally distinct. If it didn't make you feel proud to be Canadian, it left you with absolutely no doubt that you were one.

The fact was, if, like several million

Canadians by this point, you grew up transfixed in the high beams of popular culture, much of the anxiety over national self-definition could just seem downright irrelevant. While the various gatekeepers of national identity would clasp hands and moan skyward over Canada's imminent cultural obliteration, we who watched too much TV knew better. We could spot "Canadian" in an instant, simply with a flick of the channel, and we knew it was different. We knew *The Forest Rangers*, an "adventure" show with a polite emphasis on collective problem-solving, was different from *Lost In Space*, and we knew that *Don Messer's Jubilee* would never be confused with *The Dean Martin Show*. As for The Guess Who, well, try to find a top-40 band across those entire fifty states down there which was quite so arrogantly indifferent to fashion and diet as Canada's first genuine hoser-rock superstars.

In pop culture at least there was no doubt: Canadian was distinct. Indeed, because the country was otherwise largely dominated by various forms of American media, the contrast was all the more stark: in the noisy din of U.S. network programming, the Canadian stuff stuck out like a stunned moose in the middle of the trans-Canada highway.

Our point is, it still does, perhaps now more than ever. Certainly, there is more Canadian popular culture now than ever, but it's also more *popular* than it ever was. Indeed, when one begins to list the names of Canadians who have made an impact on global entertainment over just the past few years, the results are nothing short of staggering: Bryan Adams, James Cameron, Jim Carrey, Doug Coupland, Celine Dion, Atom Egoyan, David

David Cronenberg & Norman Jewison

Norhern Lights for Africa: Gordon Lightfoot, Bryan Adams, Burton Cummings, Anne Murray

Foster, k.d. lang, Pamela Anderson Lee, Alanis Morissette, Mike Myers, Matthew Perry, Shania Twain, Steve Williams. And we repeat: that's just the past few years.

Here's our suggestion. What if, for a moment, we were to drop that conventional Canadian middlebrow disinclination toward popular culture – a disinclination which is still very much alive and well – to suggest that Canada is every bit as distinct in its approach to schlock as it is to art, and that the former may indeed reveal vastly more of a national distinction than the latter. That it's possible to see as much of ourselves (if not more) in Mike Myers as it is in Margaret Atwood. That The Tragically Hip have as much to tell us (if not more) about the experience of living in post-Mulroney Canada as Peter Gzowski does. Moreover, what if, contrary to the established Canadian tradition of disowning anyone who dares to seek and find success elsewhere, we were to expand and ventilate our notion of what's Canadian to include what Canadians are doing on the global pop-culture stage? If one agrees first

that there is something distinct about the way Canadians view and engage with the world, then why not allow for the possibility that our sensibility is a portable, flexible and resilient one, which influences what Canadians do no matter where we do it? Moreover, what is revealed about living in this strained Confederation when you examine Canada's parallel but distinct pop-cultural strains – the domestic (*Singalong Jubilee, King of Kensington*) and the international (*Ghostbusters*, Alanis Morissette) – side by side? If one *does* begin to think about Canada in terms of the pop culture it produces, both nationally and internationally, one not only begins to move away from the us-verses-them national-victimhood model of the past, one in fact starts to see something so different as to be strikingly so: a "Canada" which is not only sly, dynamic, intelligent and resourceful, but one that's also a helluva lot more fun than the old one.

In deciding what to include in the book, we applied what for us were the most reasonable of criteria. For the culture we were discussing to truly qualify as popular, it had to be both familiar and accessible to people across the country: while there have been a number of enormously successful regional TV and radio shows, for example, we have decided only to address those popcult products which were easily and affordably available to

Canadians nationally. Partly this was a matter of convenience, partly it was because we wanted to consider Canadian pop in the context of its impact on national experience. This approach also accounts for what might otherwise be perceived as the most egregious oversight in the book: the fact that there's so much more English-than French-Canadian pop culture in it. While one could easily have done an entire volume on Quebecois pop culture, our primary interest in forms of pop that had a national profile or impact. Right or wrong, much of even the most popular forms of culture in Quebec are virtually unknown outside the province, and therefore fell outside our field of interest and expertise. (Basically, if it reached our rec rooms, it's here.) That being said, if you grew up anywhere in the country over the past half century, you ought to find something in here to remind you just how hopelessly Canadian you really are. So put on your galoshes, strap on your toques, button up your flannel, plunge in, and break the ice…

Geoff Pevere
Greig Dymond
Summer 1996

← Jean Beliveau & Pierre Trudeau

Lorne Greene & William Shatner
Julius Caesar, Stratford, 1955 →

With A Bullet Bryan Adams Aims to Please

For a certain echelon of successful rock musician, making it means no longer having to work much. These are the artists whose successes have long since passed into such perpetually heavy rotation on Middle-of-the-Road (M.O.R.) pop radio that their back catalogue of greatest hits virtually sustains a career which can be lucratively maintained by the occasional tour, maybe an "Unplugged" release (a.k.a. Acoustic Greatest Hits), a recycled box set and an album of new material once every four, five or even six years. It helps that very often these are artists whose followings have aged well beyond musical fervency; who'd just as soon keep listening to old stuff on the minivan stereo as bother to orient themselves to something new. These are the so-called "classic rock" artists, and their glory days are usually two decades to a full generation gone: The Stones, Pink Floyd, Elton John, Rod Stewart, The Eagles, James Taylor, Dire Straits, Boston. For still-passionate rock fans, this is the virtual Mount Rushmore of rock, the all-star roll call of the living dead.

For Bryan Adams, the Kingston, Ontario–born son of a British army officer-turned-diplomat, many of these people would probably qualify as heroes, which probably explains why, in his mid-thirties, Adams seems already to have joined their leisurely company. Inarguably Canada's most successful rock artist of the eighties – 16 million albums sold internationally by 1991 – and arguably Canada's most successful *ever* – his 1991 ballad "Everything I Do (I Do It For You)" was so successful it merited entry into the *Guinness Book of World Records* – Adams had, by the mid-nineties, slowed down his output to a carefully managed megastar trickle – of such movie-soundtrack treacle as "All For Love" (1993) and "Have You Ever Really Loved a Woman" (1995). Following the global register-jingling success of 1991's

Waking Up the Neighbours, Adams has released only the inevitable greatest-hits package (in 1993, with the revealingly list-less title of *So Far So Good*) and his 1996 tribute to arrested adolescence, *18 Til I Die*. He has also made the requisite carefully selected superstar personal appearances: in 1995, Adams was performing live alongside such a paragon of rock credibility as Luciano Pavarotti. If few else were, one imagines Paul Anka, whose "My Way" had already been "interpreted" by Pavarotti, must have been impressed.

In many ways, Adams's career cuts to the crux of the Canadian popcult condition. An army and diplomatic brat whose family moved around the world – England, Austria, Portugal, Israel – before settling in North Vancouver, with his mother, after

his parents separated in 1975, Adams apparently grew up with a passion for only the most widely available kinds of pop and rock. Repeatedly, he has cited his greatest formative musical influences as the thoroughly generic combination of the Beatles and Led Zeppelin. Yet, as easy as it is to ridicule Adams's M.O.R. inclinations – and it is almost impossible to find a positive critical appraisal about the guy *The Village Voice* once called "a generic American hunk, only whiter because he's Canadian" – there's something in his precise, upward navigation of the radio-friendly, rock-and-roll middle which fits into a noteworthy, if hardly proud, Canadian popcult tradition. Like Anka, another prodigal musical superstar and first-generation Canadian with an appetite for mainstream success, Adams

Waking Up the Neighbours album cover

has a pronounced talent for precision without passion, and for personification without personality. (In other contexts, one might say the same about Jim Carrey, Celine Dion or Lorne Greene.)

With his ear for a killer hook and his jeans 'n' T-shirt faux-rebel pose, and with his career-long determination to be seen in the company of fiscally, if not aesthetically, endowed rock stars, Adams seems less an individual artist than a computer-generated cluster of slightly diluted influences: a bit Springsteen, a bit Mellencamp, a bit Stewart, a bit Sting, a bit U2. His first solo single, 1979's disco-flavoured "Let Me Take You Dancin'," now seems like the first example of Adams's situational artistry – he's shown no interest in taking anybody dancing with his music since.

In the mid-eighties, when it was the height of rock-star vogue to appear cause-committed, the stadium-friendly Adams not only appeared prominently at such events as Live Aid and Amnesty International's Conspiracy of Hope Tour, he, along with manager Bruce Allen, then-songwriting partner Jim Vallance and West Coast Canadian M.O.R.-mogul David Foster, was instrumental in the organization of the Canadian version of Band Aid, 1985's veritable Canuckpop cheesefest "Tears Are Not Enough." When asked to contribute a song to the latently homoerotic mid-eighties military-recruitment movie *Top Gun*, Adams refused, saying, "There's no way I'm putting my song into this piece of war propaganda." (A comment one is tempted to imagine must have been at least subliminally directed at Adams's father, who'd always hoped his golden-haired eldest would join the army.)

There's something in his precise, upward navigation of the radio-friendly, rock-and-roll middle which fits into a noteworthy, if hardly proud, Canadian popcult tradition.

Now that the commitment vogue has passed, and it's back to business as usual for most of the superstar rock centre, Adams appears to have let his politics take an indefinite leave. It probably didn't help on the world-betterment front that Adams's only flop so far, 1987's *Into the Fire*, was also his only release to take social and political issues as their lyrical inspiration. As he told *Saturday Night* in 1992, "I'm getting less political the older I get. I've realized you just can't change anything without becoming part of the system and having the system change you in the process." Which sounds odd coming from as unchanging an embodiment of the nonthreatening "system" rock & roller as Bryan Adams. But it's also worth noting that, if there's been a conspicuous absence of any trace of raw, visceral passion in Adams's music, and if political commitment

seems to him something one grows out of, the one thing he's capable of getting real fired up about is the protection of the same free-market system that brought him the Beatles and Zeppelin in the first place.

In 1992, after building a career on a combination of insanely catchy hooks and polite Canadian self-effacement, Adams went publicly ballistic when the Canadian Radio-television and Telecommunications Commission (CRTC), Canada's federal broadcasting regulation agency, ruled that the singer's most successful album yet, 1991's *Waking Up the Neighbours*, did not qualify under current regulations as "Canadian content." You knew the situation cut like a knife through Adams, as he usually left any public expressions of sourness to his gregarious manager (and formerly Loverboy's and BTO's), Bruce Allen.

Since it was cowritten with British producer (and future husband of Canadian country-babe Shania Twain), Robert John "Mutt" Lange, the non-CanCon status of *Waking Up the Neighbours* stood to severely restrict its rotation, and theoretically its royalty-making potential, on Canadian radio. (Though one has a hard time imagining anything, let alone government leglislation, restricting Adams's rotation on commercial radio anywhere.) What with all the ensuing mud-slinging that went on – most of it slung CRTC-ward by Adams – it was difficult to discern which was more offensive to the multimillionaire balladeer: the aspersion cast on his nationality, or the impeded cash flow the regulation might potentially represent. Whatever, his ire was most piqued: "If anyone came up to me and asked me for advice," Adams told the *Globe and Mail* in 1992, "I'd tell them to stay away from the Canadian music business. It's full of politics and bureaucracy. It's trouble. Don't sign to a Canadian company. Don't sign to a Canadian publisher. Go south of the border. You'll get a better deal." At a press conference in Nova Scotia, he railed: "I think it's a disgrace and I think it's a shame that we have to deal with this kind of stupidity all the time." And when asked about the issue during an interview with Dublin's *Hot Press* in 1992, he finally sounded more punk than pop: "Fuck you! That's all I've got to say to those guys. Fuck you man!"

Sound familiar? This is a voice one encounters often in the echo chamber of Canadian popcult: the border-transcendent superstar, successful beyond wildest childhood dreams, now firmly peered with their greatest idols, yet still raging against the provincial, narrow-minded and success-hating Canadian mind-set. It's a voice which can be heard in the early interviews of Paul Anka and Lorne Greene, and of Ivan Reitman and Norman Jewison. And, cranky as that value tends to be, we should heed it, for it tells us something about the experience of starstruck detachment which may well be a defining one for many super-successful Canadian performers. Like many

With his ear for a killer hook and his jeans 'n' T-shirt faux-rebel pose, Adams seems less an individual artist than a computer-generated cluster of slightly diluted influences.

Canuck superstars who have turned their infatuation with imported entertainment into international M.O.R. success, Adams has processed the national experience of outside observation into a clinically precise, eminently marketable and finally hollow form of replication: they are the entertainment version of *Invasion of the Body Snatchers'* pod people. Immaculate reproductions of the most popular entertainment products of the moment, they're almost impossible to distinguish from the real thing. Except for this: mention Canadian bureaucracy, or challenge their commitment to Canadian culture, and they grow horns.

- -

Recommended Listening
Reckless (1984). Featuring: "Run To You," "Summer of '69" and "Somebody." All the monster hooks, hackneyed sentiments and borrowed poses. As irresistibly catchy as it is insubstantial, every song on this album is perfect for a corporate beer commercial. Everything he does, he does best here.

Royal summit: Bry meets Di →

King of Cartoons
Canada's Animated Empire

In November 1995, the Canadian domination of international animation was certified. At a press conference in Toronto, a pair of executives from the Walt Disney Company announced that Disney would be opening new animation studios in Toronto and Vancouver. The reasoning behind the multimillion-dollar branch plants was obvious.

For years, Disney studio scouts – like animation-studio scouts the world over – had been coming regularly to Canada to pick the most promising sprouts from the country which was renowned as the world's most fertile seedbed of cartoon talent. As far as Disney was concerned, the opening of the two Canadian studios, which would specialize in direct-to-video features, was simply an acknowledgement of reality. If you wanted chocolate, you went to Belgium. If you wanted coffee, you went to Brazil. And if you wanted cartoons, you had to go to Canada. "There's a substantial number of creative people who don't want to leave Canada," said Tom Ruzicka, senior vice-president of production for Disney TV animation, at a press conference, "so we're coming to them."

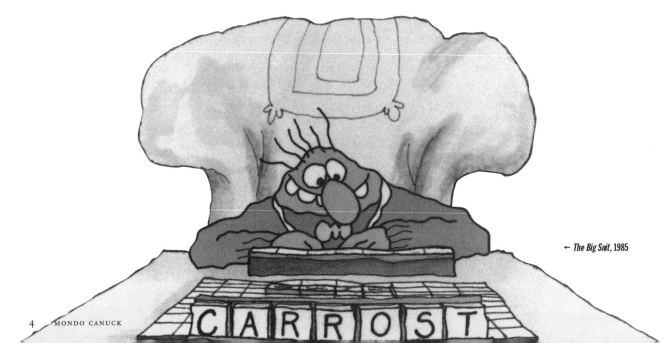

← *The Big Snit*, 1985

The End, 1995

Norman McLaren, animation pioneer

Along with newsreading, comedy writing and sketch performance, animation is one of those peculiar cultural activities that Canadians practice so well they are constantly being scanned and plundered by powerful outside interests. Indeed, at the annual screening of student projects at Oakville, Ontario's Sheridan College – which has been called by James Strauss, a prominent alumnus, "the best animation school in the world" – up to 40 representatives from animation studios around the globe watch the screen with pens poised over their chequebooks. "If you are capable of doing computer graphics for film and you're a graduate of Sheridan College," Halifax film-maker Paul Donovan told *Maclean's* magazine, "you will be offered a $50,000 to $70,000-a-year job – one year before you graduate."

A $150-million-a-year domestic industry, the Canadian cartoon game may be the highest-stakes home-grown pop-cultural activity of the nineties. Which is no wonder when you consider that the Canuck mastery of animation isn't limited to one or two areas of the medium: we rule it *all*. From mass-produced TV kidstuff like *The Care Bears*, to slam-bang computer-generated small-screen action series like *Reboot*, from hip gross-out fare like MTV's *The Brothers Grunt*, to multi-million-dollar Disney features like *The Lion King*, there is no aspect of contemporary animation practice that isn't conspicuously overpopulated by current or former citizens of the Dominion.

The Canadian cartoon influence isn't limited by forms of animation either. Whether it's classical, computer or experimental, Canada boasts major players. When it comes to computer animation, easily the most prestigious, lucrative

There is no aspect of contemporary animation practice that isn't conspicuously overpopulated by current or former citizens of the Dominion.

and influential area – creating and applying special-effects software for big-budget Hollywood features – Canadians also exert a disproportionate influence. If it weren't for key contributions by Canadians, the following films might not have been as remotely successful as they were: *Who Framed Roger Rabbit?*, *Jurassic Park*, *Forrest Gump*, *Terminator 2: Judgment Day*, *True Lies*, *Apollo 13*, *Toy Story*. As Robert Burgess, president of Toronto-based software developer Alias/Wavefront has said: "There are no significant players in computer graphics that are *not* Canadian-based."

Whether one ascribes this peculiar Canadian cultural inclination to institutional factors (e.g., the National Film Board's animation unit) or to temperament (Canadians being veteran technerds who happily spend countless hours performing fussy tasks by themselves in the dark), the end result remains the same: when it comes to cartoonery, the world comes to Canada.

And here are 22 reasons why:
Alias/Wavefront: Formerly Alias Research, this Toronto-based computer-graphics firm is renowned for developing the software that made morphing possible in *Terminator 2: Judgment Day* (1991). Alias Research was purchased for $440 million U.S. by California's Silicon Graphics in 1995, and merged with Santa Barbara's Wavefront Technologies. Eight of the ten

top-grossing American movies in 1995 used Alias software.

a.k.a. Cartoons inc.: A small Vancouver-based company with a large reputation. Founded primarily on its grotesquely entertaining gross-out cartoons like *Lupo the Butcher* (1986) and the notorious *The Brothers Grunt* (1994-1995), created and animated by Danny Antonucci, a Sheridan College alumnus. The latter cartoon, about a group of wheezing, cancer-ridden pustules who sit around and excrete various liquids, was so repulsive MTV dropped it.

BLT Production Inc.: The computer-animation house responsible for the ground-breaking, internationally successful all-computer cartoon *Reboot* (1994-present). In 1996 BLT announced the production of *Beast Wars*, another all-computer animation series about animal characters that can shape-shift into badass robots. According to *Reboot* producer and BLT president Christopher Brough, his company has created "more computer-generated images than all of the computer companies in the world."

Cinar: This Montreal-based TV animation house, primarily devoted to TV kidstuff has successfully produced television series which have been distributed in 100 countries. Best known for: *Little Lulu*, *The Busy World of Richard Scarry*, *Madeline*, *Smoggies*, *Young Robin Hood*.

C.O.R.E. Digital Pictures: This Toronto-based computer-effects company developed in 1993 out of a team originally assembled for William Shatner's *TekWar* TV series. In 1996, the company collaborated with Salter Street Films Ltd. (producers of *This Hour Has 22 Minutes*) on *LEXX: The Dark Zone Stories*, described by its creators as "the most ambitious hybrid of live-action and computer-generated animation ever attempted for television."

Discreet Logic: Based in Montreal, Discreet Logic is the computer-animation software developer responsible for the seamless photographic pastiche evident in 1994's *Forrest Gump*, 1995's *The Indian In the Cupboard* and the *Rolling Stones*' 1994 *Love is Strong* video.

Gray Matter: A leading designer of animation for computer games, based in Toronto. Titles include "Ren and Stimpy Show – Veediots!," "Adventures of B.O.B." and "Sega Game Gear Hockey." In 1995, the company began working with Oakville's Sheridan College to implement courses in gaming animation.

Haidar, Joe: Canadian-born animator, best known for work on Disney features. Key collaborator on *Beauty and the Beast* (1991), *Aladdin* (1992) and *Pochahontas* (1995).

Hume, Lenora: Vice-president of international animation for the Walt Disney Company, a graduate of the University of Waterloo.

International Rocketship Productions: Vancouver-based animation company headed by Marv Newland, animator of the legendary cartoon *Bambi Meets Godzilla* (1969), described by *Maclean's* magazine as "the definite 90-second statement about naivete and fate."

Kricfalusi, John: Canadian expatriate who rejuvenated cartoonery with anarchic Nickelodeon network's smash *Ren & Stimpy* (1991-1995). The deliriously scatological show tracked the antics of a manic-depressive Chihuahua, Ren, and his moronic feline friend, Stimpy. Kricfalusi briefly studied animation at Sheridan College. Random quote: "Asking why *Ren & Stimpy* is popular is like asking why

The NFB's current doldrums cannot dampen its incalculable historical significance. Without the Board, we would simply have no animation industry.

fucking is popular. It's fun to do." Halfway through *Ren & Stimpy*'s second season, Nickelodeon dumped Kricfalusi over content disputes. In the mid-nineties, he developed several projects featuring "Jimmy the Hapless Boy."

Lacewood Productions: Ottawa-based animation company. Best known for animating TV specials based on Lynn Johnston's *For Better or For Worse* comic strip.

Marjoribanks, Duncan: This former student of Sheridan College is the Disney animator responsible for supervising animation of key characters in *The Little Mermaid* (1989) and *Aladdin* (1992).

National Film Board of Canada: This institution, founded by an act of Parliament in 1939, is the mother of all Canadian cartoonery. Norman McLaren, a soft-spoken Scot and one of the country's most innovative animators (1949's *Begone Dull Care* and 1952's *Neighbours*) became the NFB's first animation head in 1942, and worked at the Board until his retirement in 1984. McLaren wooed the best from around the world: Kaj Pindal (Denmark), Gerald Potterton (Britain), Paul Driessen (Netherlands). Encouraging innovation and artistry, the NFB became renowned as the planet's leading noncommercial animation house. Toronto-born George Dunning (*Yellow Submarine*, 1968) apprenticed at the NFB, as did Richard Williams

(*Who Framed Roger Rabbit*?, 1988), also from Toronto. After introducing the world's first computer controlled animation system in 1968, the NFB released the first fully computer-animated short – *La Faim/Hunger* in 1974. Today, the NFB has been weakened considerably by extensive and relentless cuts to its budget. However, the NFB's current doldrums cannot dampen its incalculable historical significance. Without the Board, we would simply have no animation industry.

Nelvana Ltd.: One of the most established and successful of Toronto-based animation houses, generating $50 million a year and specializing in conventional TV animation for kids. Founded in 1971, it is Canada's largest cartoon studio, with markets in 140 countries. Nelvana's *The Magic School Bus* was the first animated series to be broadcast regularly by PBS in the U.S. Best known for these TV shows: *Care Bears*, *Tintin*, *Babar*, *Beetlejuice*.

Ranieri, Nik: Former Sheridan College student, now Disney animator. Best known for animating the character of Lumiere (the singing candlestick) in *Beauty and the Beast* (1991).

Reeves, Bill: Canadian-born computer animator who oversaw the production of Disney's *Toy Story* (1995), the first fully computer-animated feature. Graduate of (where else?) Sheridan College in Oakville, Ontario.

Bob's Birthday, 1993 →

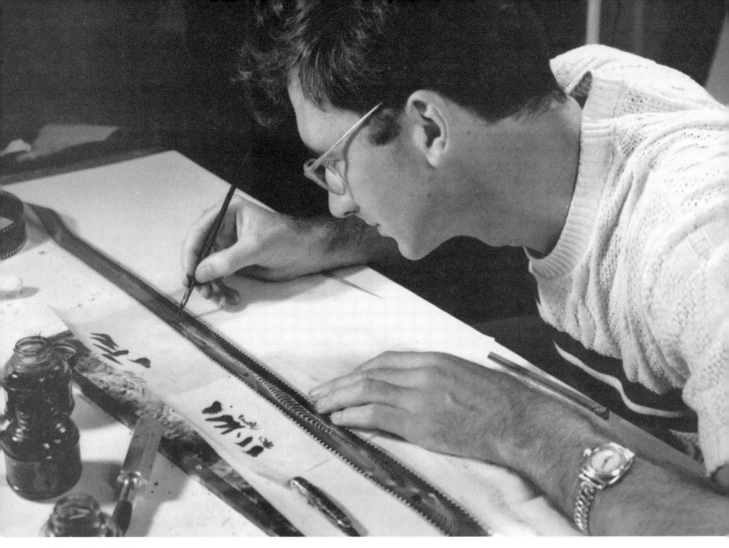

Norman McLaren at work

Sheridan College: Located in the Toronto suburban bedroom community of Oakville, Ontario, this community college houses the most influential animation school in the world. Founded in 1969 by Sheridan president Jack Porter and dean of arts William Firth, the school's track record for turning out such blockbuster-enhancing talents as Steve (*Jurassic Park*) Williams has made it what Nelvana chairman Michael Hirsh called "the Harvard of animation schools." A pioneering institution in every way, Sheridan introduced its first computer-animation program as early as 1980. Given its rep for turning out Hollywood-ready talent, each year it's graduates are scouted, scrutinized and courted by up to 40 animation-studio representatives from around the world. This accounts for the fact that the school receives up to 2,500 applications for its three-year classical animation program, which has a capacity of 110 spaces.

Softimage: This Montreal-based computer-graphics firm, purchased by Microsoft Corporation for $176 million (Cdn.) in 1994, was founded by Daniel Langlois, originally trained at the National Film Board. These days, Langlois's Softimage supplies software to the NFB.

Side Effects: The Toronto software firm that supplied programs for special effects in 1994's *True Lies* and 1995's *Apollo 13*.

Surrey, Mike: Disney animator, Sheridan College alumnus and senior animator on both 1994's *The Lion King* and 1996's *The Hunchback of Notre Dame*.

Williams, Steve: a.k.a. "Spaz" This Toronto-born Sheridan College dropout and former Alias employee is the innovative, top-flight computer-graphics whiz most famous for work on 1993's *Jurassic Park*, 1994's *The Mask* and 1995's *Jumanji*. Originally, *Jurassic Park* was to have used fairly conventional stop-motion animation techniques for its dinosaurs, until Steven Spielberg saw what Williams and his computer could do. After that, it was digital all the way. For his work animating the T-Rex in the film, Williams received an Oscar nomination. Currently employed by George Lucas's Industrial Light and Magic effects firm, along with fellow Canadian James Strauss, who supervised creature animation in 1996's *Dragonheart*.

Paul Anka Highway to My Way

In coming to terms with Paul Anka, certainly one of the most successful and savagely attacked of expat-Canadian celebrities, it seems important to note the geographical location of his father's restaurant: right across the street from the Parliament Buildings in Ottawa. It was there that Anka worked during those fleeting moments of pre-celebrity teenhood – he'd be an international pop sensation at age 15 and many times a millionaire before turning 20 – and it must have been there, virtually on the doorstep of distilled official Canadiana, that the idea struck him: if he was going to make it anywhere, it wasn't gonna be here.

And boy, did he make it. By all accounts a ferociously ambitious and single-tracked teenager, Anka's early life abounds with stories of a most un-Canadian chutzpah: the time he told promoter Irvin Feld, who had nabbed the baby-faced teenager sneaking backstage to have a white jacket autographed at a Fats Domino gig, to write down Anka's name before throwing him out, because someday Feld was going to want to hire him, which Feld eventually did; the time Anka went to Los Angeles at age 14, alone, and worked as an usher before being signed as RPM Records' only white artist, where he cut his first single, a flop; the time he talked his father into reluctantly loaning him 100 bucks (Andy Anka roundly disapproved of his son's pop-star dreams) for the trip to New York during which Anka would convince Don Costa at ABC/Paramount Records to record a tune the boy had written in 20 minutes called "Diana." An instant international smash hit in 1957, the song – ostensibly about Anka's Ottawa "babysitter," Diana Ayoub, who refuted the job description in 1991:

"How could I be? We're only a year apart" – had become by 1962 the second biggest-selling single in history, trailing only Bing Crosby's "White Christmas."

The late fifties were delirious years for the kid from Fisher Park High. In Japan, 2,000 teenagers withstood a typhoon waiting outdoors for tickets to an Anka show, and in Puerto Rico, his only way out of a throng of autograph-seekers was up, airlifted by helicopter. In Algiers, a dozen armed paratroopers were required to move him through hysterical crowds. Meanwhile, the hits just kept on coming: "You Are My Destiny" (1958), "Lonely Boy" (1959), "Put Your Head on My Shoulder" (1959) and "Puppy Love" (1960), the future Donny Osmond smash, originally inspired by Anka's infatuation with voluptuous Mouseketeer Annette Funicello. In Hollywood, Milton Berle attended an Anka show at the Cocoanut Grove, and leapt onstage, apparently less out of spotlight-envy than sheer excitement. Grabbing the microphone from the singer, Uncle Miltie yelled: "You're a sensation!" In the French paper, *Aux*

Ecoutes, one reviewer was moved by Anka somewhere near poetry: "He is no beauty, but his voice has the fullness of the Canadian forests." In 1962, Irvin Feld, no longer acting as Fats Domino's bouncer, proclaimed his diminutive client the "greatest international star in the history of show business."

Rocket-fuelled as the ascent was, it hit turbulence in orbit. At his first post-"Diana" hometown concert, in an early demonstration of the uniquely Canadian resentment of what Stompin' Tom Connors would later call "border jumping," Anka was pelted by flashbulbs and booed by an audience made up at least partly of friends, schoolmates and family. (It would be 1974 before he'd play there again: nine sellout shows, much adula-

The late fifties were delirious years for the kid from Fisher Park High. In Japan, 2,000 teenagers withstood a typhoon waiting outdoors for tickets to an Anka show.

The Prodigal Son Returns, 1965

With "Diana" Ayoub

tion, no flying flashbulbs. By the way, in 1995, the sudden pop superstardom of fellow Ottawan Alanis Morissette would generate hometown hostility of similarly Ankaesque proportions.)

By the early sixties, when the era of the clean-cut crooner had been flattened by the British Invasion, Anka abandoned performing altogether, rechanneling his energies into the equally lucrative, but less ego-fulfilling, process of penning monster hits for others. For Buddy Holly, he'd written "It Doesn't Matter Anymore" in 1958, and at Johnny Carson's request, he penned the long-running theme for *The Tonight Show* in 1962. Tom Jones had a huge hit in 1971 with Anka's gender-insensitive strutter, "She's A Lady." But, in terms of hits-for-hire, nothing approaches the highball heights attained by the song Anka wrote specifically for idol Frank Sinatra, that lion-in-autumn lounge standard, "My Way." "I sat there and wrote the song in two hours after living with it for months," he once said of "My Way"'s immaculate conception. "As a songman I knew I had hit gold and I started to cry."

Even during the mid-1970s when, along with other aging popthrobs Neil Sedaka, Bobby Vinton and Frankie Valli, Anka was riding high on the charts again, the comeback came with lumps. His deliriously sexist "(You're) Havin' My Baby" (which *Newsweek* called "a musical miscarriage") might have rocketed to number one, but it also drew howls of feminist scorn, and even landed Anka the National Organization for Women's Keep-Her-In-Her-Place Award for 1974. Nonplussed and stubbornly unenlightened, he followed "Baby" with "One Man Woman" and "I Don't Like to Sleep Alone" in 1975. By the late 1970s, the golden-oldie pop-

idol resurgence was over, and Anka slipped off the charts again.

Today he lives in Las Vegas, the desert monument to megawatt artifice he has called home since the 1960s, and which has historically proven a haven for many off-the-chart teen sensations, from Frank Sinatra to Elvis Presley, both of whom sang "My Way" in various glitterdomes there. Anka himself first played Vegas at age 16, opening for Sophie Tucker. Now a very wealthy and well-tanned fiftysome-thing father to five daughters – proof, perhaps, that God is a woman with a cruel sense of humour – he continues to tour and perform, though not with nearly the front-and-centre visibility of the past. He has attempted to maintain a connection to his distant hometown of Ottawa but, in keeping with tradition, it hasn't really worked out as planned. In the early nineties, he owned a major piece of the Ottawa Senators hockey franchise, then became embroiled in a nasty legal squabble with the team's owners, and besides, the team kept losing. Maybe, like Paul Anka, they should get the hell out of Ottawa.

Essential Listening:

21 Golden Hits (1963) All the early hormonal hits are here, including "Puppy Love," "Lonely Boy" and "Put Your Head on My Shoulder." Anka explores the world of overheated teenage infatu-ation with the kind of emotional overstatement usually reserved for grand opera.

Anka (1974) Perhaps it's fitting that Anka made his musical comeback in the middle of an energy crisis. By the mid-seventies he was no longer the horny "lonely boy," but the mellowed-out king of his domestic castle, taking the time to thank his wife for having his baby. Although it sounds like just another easy-listening album, *Anka* is a seminal text of the "me" decade, a handbook to the culture of narcissism.

Essential Viewing:

Lonely Boy (1961) The still-riveting, slyly critical 1961 NFB documentary chronicling Anka at the height of success, and mere moments before the British Invasion blew him right off the charts. Watching the 19-year-old Anka schmooze portly, cigar-sucking Atlantic City club owners is a spectacle worthy of a Martin Scorsese movie.

Ottawa street sign →

Having His Babies
Five Totally Weird Cover Versions of
Paul Anka's "My Way"

As we all know, Paul Anka took the French song "Comme d'Habitude," and turned it into a musical cash cow. "My Way" became Frank Sinatra's signature tune, and in a just world, it would have ended there. Of course, it didn't. Like lemmings, all kinds of Sinatra acolytes lined up to assault Anka's ode to self-aggrandizement. Wayne Newton, Jerry Vale, Steve Lawrence and Andy Williams all did it "their way." But their wooden versions of "My Way" just don't compare with the following; listening to these covers is the musical equivalent of stopping to gawk at the scene of a brutal car accident:

1. Sid Vicious (1978) Anka's opening line, "*And now, the end is near,*" held a special meaning for Mr. Vicious, who expired shortly after completing his spirited punk reading of the ultimate showbiz anthem. Coming at the end of the Sex Pistols documentary *The Great Rock n' Roll Swindle*, Sid's version gleefully careens out of control as he improvises lines such as, "*To think, I killed a cat/And may I say not in a shy way.*" As the song ends, this rather disturbed individual pulls out a gun and gives new meaning to the term "killing an audience." It's the final musical legacy of Johnny Rotten's best pal: transforming the Anka tune into a vision of a showbiz apocalypse.

2. Elvis Presley (1977) Come to think of it, the end was also near for the heavily tranquillized Elvis by the time he turned his attention to "My Way." The King took a break from his strict regimen of karate, fried food and shooting TV sets to re-interpret Anka's tune in June 1977. The musical result is a lot like Elvis himself at that stage: flabby, pathetic and pretty well incoherent.

3. Hugo Montenegro (1969) For sheer weirdness, this version of "My Way" from Montenegro's *Moog Power* LP will probably never be equalled. A truly delectable musical stew, featuring these

tasty ingredients: out-of-tune doodlings on a primitive Moog synthesizer, an obtrusive horn section and a vocalist named Gene Morford who seems blissfully unaware of the mess unfolding around him. Probably not what our Ottawa homeboy had in mind when he wrote the song.

4. Sammy Davis, Jr. (1970) From his optimistically titled Motown album *Something for Everyone*, Sammy gives "My Way" his traditional bombastic workout. The big-horn sound, tambourines and funky guitar turn the song into something that sounds like an early run-through of the "Theme From Shaft." Things get completely out of control near the end, when the Candy Man starts doing his trademark rap/scat singing.

5. The Three Tenors: Domingo, Carreras and Pavarotti (1994) Domingo, Carreras and Pavarotti were definitely doing a little musical slumming when they decided to perform "My Way" during their L.A. concert in 1994. They probably figured it would be one of the few songs the audience would recognize. However, there are a couple of major problems with their version: most importantly, none of these guys really speaks English very well. This proves to be quite an obstacle for those listeners who might actually want to understand the lyrics. The tenors do their best to sing phonetically (à la Abba or Ace of Base), but wind up sounding like Al Pacino in *Scarface*. Of course, there's also the basic insanity of having voices this gifted tackle a musical trifle like Anka's: it's like enlisting Einstein to figure out the sum of two plus two.

Orphan Annie Green Gables, Inc.

Even for a woman as optimistic by nature as 29-year-old Lucy Maud Montgomery, things were getting depressing by 1904. Living in the tiny Prince Edward Island village of Cavendish (population today: 94), Maud – as she liked to be called – was single-handedly caring and keeping house for the aged Lucy Macneill, her stern, recently widowed Calvinist grandmother, who had taken the young girl in after her mother died and her father moved west. After obtaining a hard-earned college degree and a job as a rural schoolteacher, Maud learned that her grandfather, Alexander Macneill, had died. Consequently, she gave up teaching to care full-time for Mrs. Macneill. This she did for 13 years – that is, when she wasn't required to execute her duties operating the Cavendish post office.

At the same time, Maud was trying to keep afloat a surprisingly successful career as a freelance writer. An aspiring writer since the age of nine, by 1904 Maud was the author of dozens of stories and poems published both in Canada and the United States. In fact, it must be considered a measure of the degree of her unhappiness that although her $600 annual income was more than double the contemporary working woman's average, Maud was still unhappy. To the journal she had unfailingly maintained since girlhood, she confided the reason: "I am so horribly *alone*. I have *no* real friends near me."

← Anne of Green Gables

Anne welcoming tourists

As she often did, Maud sought respite from loneliness and sadness in the act of writing. Like many writers, she jotted down ideas constantly, later transferring them into her journal for future reference. One day that grey year, searching for literary inspiration, she came across the shard of a narrative idea she'd written in her journal a few years before: "Elderly couple apply to orphan asylum for a boy; by mistake a girl is sent them." And that is how *Anne of Green Gables*, the most widely read Canadian book ever written, and the basis of one of the most popular and enduring Canadian pop-cultural phenomena ever, came to be.

Nearly a century after Lucy Maud Montgomery rediscovered that scant story kernel in her journal, her creation, the freckle-faced, red-haired and verbosely romantic orphan dreamer, Anne Shirley, has become the closest any Canadian literary equivalent can get to Mickey Mouse. Recognized and loved around the world, *Anne of Green Gables* is the nexus of a multimillion-dollar tourist trade, and – perhaps the true certification of contemporary popcult success – the object of vigorous litigation concerning merchandising rights. As recently as 1994, in fact, disputes for the ownership of Lucy Maud Montgomery's lucrative legacy were still being fought between Montgomery's Ontario-based heirs and the province of Prince Edward Island, which makes millions of dollars annually from the pigtailed orphan girl. (These disputes have since been resolved.)

Each year, the tiny province of Prince Edward Island, population 130,000, draws 700,000 tourists largely on Anne's allure alone. Approximately 120,000 of these visitors venture to Province House

The freckle-faced, red-haired and verbosely romantic orphan dreamer, Anne Shirley, has become the closest any Canadian literary equivalent can get to Mickey Mouse.

in Charlottetown, where the Canadian Confederation was devised in 1864, but three times as many go to Cavendish, where Anne Shirley was devised in 1905. The province boasts no less than five museums which preserve the artefacts of Maud Montgomery's life, and the likeness of Anne's freckle-sprinkled face appears on every provincial licence plate. By 1985, the year the CBC would first air a four-hour adaptation of Maud's book that was viewed by almost six million Canadians, there were so many cars travelling to Montgomery's Cavendish grave, a traffic light had to be installed. As the owner of the "Anne of Green Gables Store," which stocks $300 Anne figurines, told *Reader's Digest* with true Maritime understatement, "Her character is very important to our economy."

Without question, however, the centre of Annemania is Japan, where *Anne* and its sequels have been read by more than 13 million Japanese since 1954, and where a national travel-magazine survey determined in 1992 that the only destinations its readers wanted to visit more than Prince Edward Island were New York, Paris and London. Japanese travel agencies book a staggering 10,000 package trips to Prince Edward Island annually. In 1991, the same *Anne* musical which has been selling out in Charlottetown since

1965 had 54 performances in Japan. According to historian Douglas Baldwin, each night following the performance, the cast were "mobbed following the show by Japanese girls wanting to touch them… like North American rock stars." Meanwhile, back in North America, one-half million new copies of *Anne of Green Gables* are sold each year. Evidently, Lucy Maud Montgomery unleashed a bona fide

- -

And Then There's Maud
The Novels of Lucy Maud Montgomery

Lucy Maud Montgomery was nothing if not prolific: she could churn out sequels faster than Sylvester Stallone. When *Anne of Green Gables* became an instant best-seller in 1908, there was huge demand for a follow-up. The very next year, *Anne of Avonlea* was released. Montgomery revisited the character of Anne Shirley several times in her writing career, and also struggled valiantly to come up with other franchise characters. Alas, *Rilla of Ingleside* and *Pat of Silver Bush* just didn't have the same impact as Anne. Herewith, the complete list of Montgomery's novels.

1908 *Anne of Green Gables*
1909 *Anne of Avonlea*
1910 *Kilmeny of the Orchard*
1911 *The Story Girl*
1912 *Chronicles of Avonlea*
1913 *The Golden Road*
1915 *Anne of the Island*
1917 *Anne's House of Dreams*
1919 *Rainbow Valley*
1920 *Further Chronicles of Avonlea*
1920 *Rilla of Ingleside*
1923 *Emily of New Moon*
1925 *Emily Climbs*
1926 *The Blue Castle*
1927 *Emily's Quest*
1929 *Magic for Marigold*
1931 *A Tangled Web*
1933 *Pat of Silver Bush*
1935 *Mistress Pat*
1936 *Anne of Windy Poplars*
1937 *Jane of Lantern Hill*
1939 *Anne of Ingleside*

"Thwack! Anne had brought her slate down on Gilbert's head."

Illustration from a 1911 edition of *Anne of Green Gables*

Canadian monster on the world. With pigtails, no less.

Yet, as global cultural viruses go, you could ask for a lot worse than Anne Shirley. Let's face it, Anne is one of the most confident, intelligent, independent and credible young female heroines found in kidlit anywhere. In fact, no less prominent a Montgomery fan than Mark Twain himself made note of this when shortly after the book's initial, best-selling publication he wrote that Anne was "the dearest and most lovable child in fiction since the immortal Alice." She is both, but what makes her so dear and lovable is also what makes it so hard to argue with her international star status; as literary role models for girls go, Anne is one of the most inspirational and positive around.

Using the sometimes painful material of her own life, Montgomery fashioned in Anne a young woman whose cheerful inability to conform to a restrictive and repressive semi-rural community is presented as vital and liberating. In her hopelessly romantic, bombastic and often stumbling way, she is a veritable whirlwind of nonconformity. Early in *Anne of Green Gables*, after Anne is unwisely mocked by Gilbert Blithe about the colour of her hair (an extremely sensitive issue with our Anne), she walks over and cracks a chalk slate against the back of the boy's skull. In an essay called "L. M. Montgomery's 'Anne of Green Gables': The Japanese Connection," historian Baldwin contends that this prefeminist precociousness partly explains the fervour of the Anne cult in Japan, where females of all ages are thrilled by the girl's refusal to knuckle under to the many forms of repressive authority surrounding her. Baldwin also reports that many Japanese

Recognized and loved around the world, *Anne of Green Gables* is the nexus of a multimillion-dollar tourist trade, and the object of vigorous litigation concerning merchandising rights.

women reread the book for motivational inspiration before taking on a new job.

Anne's endurance and international popularity become even more remarkable in the context of other prominent serial heroines in children's literature. Compared to that of Dorothy Gale, for example, the gingham-dressed midwestern protagonist of L. Frank Baum's *Oz* books, Anne's fictional life would seem rather dull: no tornado-fuelled trips to magical lands, no talking scarecrows or tin woodmen, no witches of the good or evil variety whatsoever. Same with Astrid Lindgren's also-freckled and pigtailed Pippi Longstocking, who lives in a literary realm where she is blessed with superpowers of almost Paul Bunyanesque proportions. No, the appeal of Anne becomes even more noteworthy when one considers the comparatively docudramatic ordinariness of her world, a quality which arguably not only makes her even more compelling and vivid to young female readers, it's also what qualifies her as a distinctly Canadian literary sensation.

As a rule, Canadian literature has demonstrated an abiding wariness of the fantastic, preferring to find its metaphors and lessons in carefully re-created simulations of tangible and familiar worlds. Which also explains the mass pilgrimage to Lucy Maud Montgomery's childhood stomping grounds every year, wherein

hundreds of thousands of tourists visit the sites so vividly described by the author in the Anne books. They go there because they *can* go there, which is not something you can say about Oz.

As for Lucy Maud Montgomery, despite the enormous amount of fame and fortune Anne brought her during her lifetime (she died in 1942), she never quite found her way out of the loneliness she was feeling when she first stumbled across that nearly forgotten story snippet in her journal. After her grandmother died, Maud moved to Ontario and married a Presbyterian minister named Ewan MacDonald, who was by all accounts a stern and joyless man convinced of his own damnation and deeply resentful of his wife's imagination, talent and success. As she once told a friend, "Those whom the gods wish to destroy, they make ministers' wives."

Schwing Time
The Great Canadian Babewatch

You've got to love the fact that Pamela Anderson Lee, the platinum blond *Baywatch* ultrababe, was born in Ladysmith on Vancouver Island on July 1, 1967. That's right, while the rest of the country observed the 100th birthday of Confederation by barbecuing Maple Leaf weenies and, in both official languages, singing along with Bobby Gimby's "Ca-na-da," the birthday nation's greatest gift to base masculine impulses was being ushered into the world. This seems an important coincidence to note, particularly considering that those who feel compelled to besmirch the global cultural contribution of Ms. Lee (the subject of 7,000 Internet Web sites and easily one of the planet's most famous, um, faces) often dismiss her on the grounds that she's somehow not Canadian.

To this we say yeah, right. Let's face it, if she was put on God's earth, she was put here for a purpose, and if she was put here on the very day that Canada marked its first century of existence, God's purpose is as clear as spring runoff in the Rockies: first Pamela Anderson was God's gift to Canada, and now Pamela Anderson Lee is Canada's gift to the world.

Juliette →

Linda Evangelista   Pamela Anderson Lee

Furthermore, Ms. Lee is not alone in the made-in-Canada spectacle she so generously offers to the world. In the mid-nineties, the babes of Confederation were drawing the prurient focus of eyes around the planet: cat-eyed superdupermodel Linda Evangelista, born and raised in St. Catharines, Ontario; Timmins-born, navel-flashing new country blockbuster Shania Twain; supermodel-turned-alien-killer-bombshell Natasha Henstridge of the movie *Species*, born in Springdale, Newfoundland; Ottawa-born pop-chart stormer Alanis Morissette, reigning babe of the alternative-rock set.

Once, Canada, if thought of at all, was most likely thought of as a place of snow, syrup, Mounties and ice hockey. Now it's just as likely to be thought of as a place great-looking chicks come from. Whether this marks progress will obviously depend on your notion of the proper form our international image ought to take. (Though, as form goes, what's wrong with 36-24-36?) One thing's certain: as a Canadian image, it sure is different.

Yet, it's not as though the country hasn't made contributions to the international babe arena in the past. Fay Wray, the woman who caused King Kong's giant hairy palms to sweat, was born in Alberta. During the late sixties and early seventies, Montreal-born Genevieve Bujold was one of the most alluring and enigmatic women on screen anywhere. And the babeness factor cannot be ruled out when pondering the early impact made by Joni Mitchell. Margot Kidder's Lois Lane was easily Clark Kent's sexiest co-worker, and veteran women's movement supporter, Hugh Hefner, has demonstrated a willingness to enhance the visibility of gifted Canadian women,

In the mid-nineties, the babes of Confederation were drawing the prurient focus of eyes around the planet.

which compels sober consideration of the *Playboy* publisher for the Order of Canada.

Yet, when it comes to taking stock of the country's role in the development of overall global wellness, rarely if ever is this precious national resource cited. Perhaps it has to do with the traditional forms the national self-image has taken, which taken collectively – let's face it – hasn't left much room for sex. (Show us an oxymoron and we'll show you Canadian sex.) Canada tends to pride itself precisely on its lack of passion: its ability to remain calm, polite, diplomatic and reasonable under even the most steamy circumstances. For decades, Canadians have seemed to insist if it's sex as national identity you want, go to France, or the States, or one of those hairy-chested Latin countries, but for Pete's sake don't look here.

Yet clearly this is wrong. In the same way that so many of our movies percolate with weirdly displaced forms of erotic obsession – à la David Cronenberg, Atom Egoyan or Guy Maddin – so the culture at large throbs with barely contained sensuality. After all, the country had to boost its population by several million since Pamela Anderson Lee's 1967 birthday somehow. Not that we're trying to project any sexually progressive or liberating value onto the expanses of Ms. Lee and other Canadian babes. No, our point is this: having erected – so to speak – a national identity based on unflappable propriety,

Canadians haven't left much room for sex in the country's collective self-image. Maybe it's time we did. Maybe it's time we realized that 7,000 Internet Web sites can't be wrong, and maybe it's time we took pride in the fact that it was a woman from Ottawa – Alanis Morissette – who first took the notion of going down on someone in a theatre to the top of the pop charts. Geez, maybe it's time to change Canada Day to Pamela Anderson Lee Day. One thing's for sure, in Canada, and in the world at large which ogles her, it's definitely schwing time.

Here, arranged *purely* in scientific categorical terms, are some of Canada's most watched women:

Runway Babes

Canadian women have made impressive incursions into the aesthetically demanding world of modelling unaffordable designer clothing. Maybe that's because it's a profession where blank indifference is definitely an asset.

Linda Evangelista: Suburban-mall-rat-turned-superdupermodel from St. Catharines, Ontario. The ultimate hair-colour chameleon.

Eve Salvail: Skinheaded, scalp-tattooed strutter from Montreal.

Shalom Harlow: Deadhead neo-hippie bombshell from Oshawa, Ontario. This waif has replaced uber-babe Cindy Crawford as host of MTV's *House of Style*.

Yasmeen Ghauri: Full-figured, fur-shilling runway denizen from Montreal.

Veejay Babes

In the interest of making the broadcast arena a progressive forum for the free exchange of ideas about sexual politics, MuchMusic mogul Moses Znaimer sure has paraded a lot of primo babeage before those uqibuitous shakycams. Maybe that's why they're shaking. At any rate, thanks, Moses – you man of the future, you.

Monika Deol: Statuesque ex-disco anchorperson from Winnipeg. Delivered dance-music news with the studied gravitas of Walter Cronkite.

Erica Ehm: Fiercely upbeat, fearlessly guileless former video traffic cop from Montreal.

Natalie Richard: Endearingly overaccented francophone clip-flipper from Montreal.

Big-Screen Babes

Since Mary Pickford first strapped on the bonnet of silent-movie superstardom, Canadian women have popped the corn of millions.

Natasha Henstridge: Supermodel-turned-alien-killer-bombshell, from Springdale, Newfoundland. (*Species*)

Genevieve Bujold: Alluring, intelligent and sadly underused Canadian proto-babe, from Montreal. (*Anne of a Thousand Days, Coma, Dead Ringers, Earthquake, Kamouraska, La guerre est finie*)

Carole Laure: Dark-eyed, drop-dead gorgeous chanteuse/actor, from Shawinigan, Quebec. (*L'Ange et la Femme, Get Out Your Handkerchiefs, Maria Chapdelaine*)

Pascale Bussières: Flawless and talented almond-eyed camera magnet, from Montreal. (*When Night Is Falling, Eldorado*)

Rachael Crawford: Perfectly featured performer with traffic-stopping smile, from Toronto. (*When Night Is Falling, Rude*)

Mia Kirshner: Raven-haired post-teen temptress, from Toronto. (*Exotica, Love and Human Remains*)

Margot Kidder: Sandpaper-voiced siren to the Man of Steel, from Yellowknife, N.W.T. (*Superman, Black Christmas, Gaily, Gaily, The Amityville Horror*)

Classical Babes

Karen Kain: Primo prima ballerina and middle-brow pinup, from Hamilton, Ontario.

Ofra Harnoy: Mermaid-maned cellist based in Toronto, born in Israel.

Liona Boyd: Classical string–strumming ex-date of Pierre Trudeau, from London, England.

Natasha Henstridge

Hugh Hefner and Kimberley Conrad Hefner

Northern Exposure
Hugh Hefner and the Women of Canada

It's difficult to think of a septuagenarian more obsessed with beautiful, young CANADIAN women than the pipe-smoking, silk-pyjama-loving founder of the *Playboy* empire, Hugh Hefner. (Except for, perhaps, Pierre Trudeau.)

Truly, Hef is a champion of buxom Canadians. Although he spends most of his time espousing the decision he made over 40 years ago to reject Diefenbaker-era, er... make that Eisenhower-era sexual mores, he has always found the time to feature well-proportioned northern lovelies both in *Playboy* and his personal life.

Canadians who have received the airbrush treatment:

Pamela Anderson Lee: Easily the most famous *Playboy* centre-fold since Marilyn Monroe, but the similarities with Norma Jean end there. Case in point: Monroe married legends Joe DiMaggio and Arthur Miller; Pamela married tattooed love boy/Motley Crue drummer Tommy Lee. Her video, *The Best of Pamela Anderson*, is *Playboy*'s number-one tape of all time, apparently selling even more copies than their *Art of Sensual Massage*. The posters for her 1996 big-screen bomb, *Barb Wire*, screamed "Don't Call Me Babe," but the B.C. native practically defines the term.

Shannon Tweed: Before her romantic alliance with Kiss front-man/tongue-wiggler Gene Simmons, this Newfoundland knockout was Hefner's number-one lady at the Playboy Mansion. Talk about a stepping stone! Tweed's tenure as 1982 Playmate of the Year led to acting gigs in the nighttime soap *Falcon Crest* and the daytime soap *Days Of Our Lives*. Today she's the queen of straight-to-video "erotic thrillers," starring in cultural flotsam like *Model By Day, Vegas Vice* and *Cannibal Women in the Avocado Jungle of Death*. Shannon once posed for *Playboy* with her equally Canadian sister, Tracy.

Public-Broadcasting Babes

Your tax dollars at work.

Wendy Mesley: Meech Lake wave-maker and parliamentary pulse-pounder, from Toronto. (*Sunday Report, Undercurrents*)

Cynthia Dale: Button-cute *Street Legal* brief-bearer, from Toronto. Also starred in 1985 aerobic movie disaster, *Heavenly Bodies.*

Juliette: CBC's original songbird and Canada's first lady of lite, from Winnipeg. Her show, *Juliette*, ran on Saturday nights from 1956 to 1966, right after *Hockey Night in Canada.*

Adrienne Clarkson: Bracing visual contrast to Gordon Sinclair, from Hong Kong. (*Take 30*)

Chart Babes

Schwingalong jubilee.

Mitsou: Pulchritudinous pouter from Trois Pistoles, Quebec.

Alanis Morissette: Bad girl from next door. Well, actually Ottawa.

Deborah Cox: Silken-voiced soul-stirrer, from deepest suburban Scarborough, Ontario.

Shania Twain: Ultra-perky new country knockout, from Timmins, Ontario.

Lee Aaron: Stud-bearing main mama of Canadian metal, from Belleville, Ontario.

Susan Aglukark: Ebony-eyed aboriginal belter, from Arviat, N.W.T.

k. d. lang: Velvet-voiced vegetarian vixen, from Consort, Alberta.

Prime-Time Babes

Along with the immortal Pamela Anderson Lee, just Canada's way of saying thanks to the American TV industry for the endless hours of culturally corroding, identity-crushing entertainment it has so generously buried us under over the years. Don't mention it.

Jill Hennessy: Former pouty prosecutor on *Law & Order*, from Waterloo, Ontario. (Also had small film roles in *Dead Ringers* and *I Shot Andy Warhol*)

Gloria Reuben: Heart-stopping *ER* temperature-taker, from Toronto.

Kathleen Robertson: Undeniably gifted student on *Beverly Hills 90210*, from Hamilton, Ontario.

Neve Campbell: Lovable orphan on Fox Network's *Party of Five*, from Toronto. (Also starred in 1996 teenage witch movie, *The Craft*.)

Carrie Leigh: After living with Hefner for four years at the Mansion, things turned quite nasty between this native of Richmond Hill, Ontario, and her older paramour. In 1988 she slapped a $35 million palimony suit on the *Playboy* figurehead, claiming that Hefner had reneged on a promise to "medically and scientifically store a sufficient amount of his own sperm in a sperm bank in order to impregnate (Leigh) in case he became too old to father children. Hefner soon launched a countersuit accusing Leigh of extortion and "flagrant" infidelity. Her suit was eventually dropped, and she has dropped out of the public eye despite being referred to once in *Playboy* as "dark, flashy, with a wide sensuous mouth, brown eyes burning with ambition and the kind of body men see in their most ambitious dreams." Phew!

Kimberley Conrad Hefner: Yes, it's true! It took a Canadian to tame Hef, the "world's most ineligible bachelor." Her *Playboy* data sheet told us that she loved "Levi 501 Jeans, sexy lingerie, and midnight walks on the beach." After his relationships with Tweed and Leigh, perhaps it was inevitable that Hef would marry a Canadian. Certainly, he was sensitive to Conrad's northern needs, getting hitched, in true hoser fashion, on Canada Day in 1989.

Dorothy Stratten: After Stratten was brutally murdered in 1980 by her estranged husband, Paul Snider, the British Columbia–born Playmate of the Year predictably went supernova in the world of pop culture. Her death inspired a myriad of product, including the film *Star 80* (directed by Bob Fosse, with Mariel Hemingway, and Eric Roberts in a sublimely creepy turn as Snider), the TV-movie *Death of a Centerfold: The Dorothy Stratten Story* (starring Jamie Lee Curtis), the book *The Killing of the Unicorn – Dorothy Stratten 1960-1980* (by her lover, the director Peter Bogdanovich, who went on to marry Dorothy's sister, Louise) and even a Bryan Adams song, "The Best Was Yet To Come." Bogdanovich's book sparked an intense feud with Hefner, as the director criticized *Playboy*'s treatment of Stratten. In turn, Hefner labelled the book "pathological."

Mitsou

Shania Twain

Alanis Morissette

Man Alive!
The Export Boom in Canadian Beefcake

A funny thing happens to Canadian men when they leave this country. Their looks improve.

Weird but true. When combing the nation's pastures for Grade-A domestic beefcake, one discovers the vast bulk of the best-looking stud material has already been exported out of the country. Not that what's left isn't perfectly good beef, it just isn't perfectly good-*looking* beef. While the occasional prime hunk can still be found grazing on this side of the pasture – stickman Doug Gilmour, TV-throbs Art Hindle and Paul Gross – there's literally tons more on *that* side: prime-time tube steaks Jason Priestley, David James Elliott and Matthew Perry, newshunks John (J.D.) Roberts, Peter Jennings, Keith Morrison and Arthur "Scud Stud" Kent, skating product-endorser Wayne Gretzky, screen-dreams Keanu Reeves and Kiefer Sutherland, and ageless rock-slab Robbie Robertson. All Canadian. All hunks. All elsewhere.

Moreover, there's the high percentage of prime domestic hunkage that wasn't recognized as such until it was displayed outside of the country: singer Roch Voisine's superstardom was clinched in France, and it took American network exposure before *Due South*'s Paul Gross, who'd been kicking around Canadian movies and TV shows for years, started showing up on anybody's to-die-for list. Similarly, the timeless and indisputable masculine magnetism of Leonard Cohen and Pierre Trudeau cannot be extricated from their high international profiles. They drew chicks with passports.

← Gino Vanelli

What gives here? How does one account for the fact that, while the great Canadian gene pool is eminently capable of producing heart-pounding specimens of weather-resistant masculinity, most of them have to leave home to hear any whistling? For let's face it, whatever generalization one wishes to make about Canada's more prominent males, it's unlikely to require variations on the phrase "drop-dead gorgeous." Peter Gzowski? Don Cherry? Jean Chrétien? Peter Mansbridge? Garth Drabinsky? Moses Znaimer? Talented and powerful though each may be, is there a one you'd like to see sprawled naked over a bearskin rug?

Didn't think so. On the one hand, this can be interpreted as positive; as yet further proof, along with the fact that we're clean and courteous, of Canada's firm dominion over North America's highest moral ground. No cruel tyranny of the image for us, folks: we're a content country. Leave the image obsession to lesser, more shallow cultures than ours. Indeed, no country has had more tolerance of portly, sloppy and generally unbecoming rock stars than this one. (Just check out the industrial-strength tonnage in BTO.) To that fact we hoist a doughnut in salute.

But is there more to it? Perhaps there's something to that old joke about Canadian sex being a contradiction in terms. Maybe it's true that we are made profoundly uncomfortable by too-conspicuous displays of physical beauty, perhaps because it rubs some deep-seated, residual vestige of Protestant stoicism the wrong way. Could be it's just easier for Canadians to admire homely people, because it's obvious homely folk had to work for their notoriety; unlike some unfairly famous folk from some less spiri-

Where American culture has woven ruggedly virile and individualistic masculinity into the very fabric of its self-image, Canada has stubbornly resisted stooping to any such impulse.

tually enlightened country, they earned it. One look at Farley Mowat, and you just know he's got to be a talented writer. In the same way that Knowlton Nash must be one helluva journalist. Which comforts us, as it's our variation on the American Dream. In Canada, even the dowdiest hoser can grow up to be famous. Which is better than being shallow and sexy any day, isn't it? Well, *isn't* it?

Another explanation for the export boom in Canuck beefcake might be the historically persistent absence of conventionally heroic figures in Cancult. Where American culture has woven ruggedly virile and individualistic masculinity into the very fabric of its self-image, a fact which in turn informs every aspect of its culture, Canada has stubbornly resisted stooping to any such impulse. Instead of celebrating the achievements of lone heroes, we're far more comfortable promoting group, team or institutional achievements. Heck, even our national sport tells you something about the Canadian relationship to masculine beauty. In pre-helmet-regulation days anyway, when players picked splinters from toothless gums to pass time in the penalty box, hockey players were easily the plug-*ugliest* athletes this side of pro-wrestling. (Which, come to think of it, was another disproportionately popular sport in Canada.)

In U.S. culture, for better or worse, heroism is pretty well inseparable from physical attractiveness. Indeed, hunkiness is a virtual shorthand for moral virtue. Here in Canada, with our inverse national mythology based on the celebration of the mundane and the elevation of the ordinary, to be too handsome is to court suspicion and hostility, to risk banishment even. To its more conspicuously attractive citizens, Canada says: So you want to be good-looking, do you? Be world-famous, enjoy tons of exciting sex and make pantloads of cash in the process? Be shallow, beautiful and happy? Fine, just don't do it here!

And so the beefcake stampede southward.

For your dietary amusement, a meateater's guide to Canada Grade-A No. 1 Beef.

Domestic Beef

Corey Hart: Proof of our thesis that Canada crushes its cutest. In the mideighties, this doleful-eyed pop balladeer – a teendream mingling of James Dean's pout and Sting's pipes – seemed primed for neck-and-neck superstardom with Bryan Adams. Never happened. Corey stayed home.

René Simard: In 1971, this button-cute, preteen pop singer was bigger in Quebec than Elvis. His fame had spread to Japan by 1974, where he was awarded the Frank Sinatra Award at the International Song Festival in Tokyo. There, no less an expert on pop-star longevity than Francis Albert Sinatra himself offered Simard the best advice of the former teen star's long-faded career: "Never grow up."

Gino Vanelli: During the 1970s, this raven-ringleted, fuzzy-chested macho singer from Montreal stuck out of the drab and doughy Canadian pop-music

Leonard Cohen   Pierre Trudeau

landscape like prosciutto in an egg salad sandwich.

Paul Gross: As the earnest-as-a-corpse Mountie in the CBS/CTV action-comedy series *Due South*, Paul Gross comes across like Dudley Dooright with genitals. Possibly this is progress.

Export Beef

Arthur Kent: It says something about the moral climate of North America in the early nineties that, as George Bush's Scud missiles were pounding away at Baghdad during the creepy ratings blockbuster called The Gulf War, this Canadian NBC correspondent – sprung from the same journalistic gene pool as former CBC anchor Peter Kent – was declared positively hunkalicious by female viewers. Nickname: The Scud Stud. Moral: Carnage is much easier to take if it's covered by someone cute.

Matthew Perry: This likeable cast member of the product-endorsement machine disguised as a sitcom called *Friends* has some truly eyebrow-raising Canuck credentials: his mother is Suzanne Perry, former press aide to Pierre Trudeau, and current spouse of

As the earnest-as-a-corpse Mountie in the CBS/CTV action-comedy series *Due South*, Paul Gross comes across like Dudley Dooright with genitals

border-crossing newshunk Keith Morrison. Plus, he is the second Canadian, after Kiefer Sutherland, to claim legitimate squeezehood with Julia Roberts. Coincidence? We think not.

Jason Priestley: Like Perry, the operative word for this slab of well-coiffed, blue-eyed beefcake, star of the once-mighty prime-time teen soap *Beverly Hills 90210*, is "likeable." It's a perfect Canadian quality, the nicer way of saying "inoffensive."

Keanu Reeves: This Beirut-born, Toronto-raised Hollywood hunk has limited range but infinite appeal, and a self-punishing tendency to take on roles that emphasize the narrow parameters of his range. If anybody shouldn't be doing accents in period movies, it's this guy, who's done it about a dozen times. Early in his career, Reeves guested on the CBC comedy *Hangin' In*. Random quote: "How do I play stupid people so incredibly well? It's easy. I guess I'm not the most intelligent person in the world." Random note: *Speed*, his biggest

hit to date, was written by fellow Canuck Graham Yost.

Kiefer Sutherland: The son of actors Donald Sutherland and Shirley Douglas, this blond, aging bratpacker makes up for all the bland roles in formula movies by looking and sounding eerily like his dad. In other words, the direct-to-video Donald.

Prime Rib (edible in Canada and abroad)

Leonard Cohen: Poet, novelist, popsinger, raconteur, fashion-plate, knee-wobbling hunk. All this and over 60. Couldn't you just kill the guy?

Pierre Trudeau: The international babe-lure of a former prime minister, and the only person in the history of this country who managed to inject a little sex into Canadian politics. No one did it before Pierre, and no one has since. We're not sure if this reveals more about sex or Canadian politics, but it says a lot about Pierre Trudeau.

Roch Voisine: His music as M.O.R. bland as he is M.O.R. handsome, this bilingual New Brunswicker with the cola-commercial good looks has become a huge international star in French-speaking markets. His success with the North American English market has proven much harder to attain, perhaps because they already have enough blandly handsome M.O.R. stars of their own.

← Arthur Kent

Jason Priestley

National Dreamer **Pierre Berton**

Canada has always been the perfect place to be good at many things without excelling at any. This is particularly true of work in journalism and entertainment, where the species of the Great Canadian Generalist has thrived for decades. When one considers some of the more prominent Canadians in the postwar boom years and beyond, one invariably conjures up a list of hyphenates – Lorne Greene: broadcaster/actor; Arthur Hailey: TV dramatist/pulp novelist; Peter Gzowski: journalist/broadcaster; Don Harron: actor/comedian/radio host; Norman Jewison: actor/TV director/film-maker; Robert Fulford: journalist/critic/broadcaster. But of all the generalists at large coughed up by this country, none has loomed larger than Pierre Berton: journalist/historian/columnist/children's author/TV host/radio personality/professional Canadian.

A virtual colossus of Canuck generalism, for almost a half century the unfailingly outspoken Berton straddled just about every area of popular discourse the country has to offer. In the process of doing so very many things, he has, of course, become many things: a one-man living museum of Canadian broadcasting history, a hugely successful popularizer of Canadian history, a militant nationalist, a brashly opinionated and fearless liberal, a ubiquitous windbag, and – along with fellow megageneralists Farley Mowat and Peter C. Newman – one of the linchpins of the postwar Canadian publishing industry. To even attempt to imagine the past half century of Canadian mainstream media without imagining Berton is quite simply impossible. It's like hockey without Howe or politics without Trudeau. Big as the country is, Pierre Berton's pockets always seemed big enough to fit it inside.

← Pierre Berton: Multi-media man

Two Canadian icons: The CPR and Pierre Berton's sideburns

Young Pierre

To examine Berton's career, which includes 38 years as a panelist on the warhorse *Front Page Challenge* and over 40 published books, is in some ways to trace the history of postwar Canadian generalism itself. For, as well as being generalism's most successful and popular practitioner, he is also its archetype.

Born in Whitehorse, Yukon, in 1920, Berton was of an age and inclination that happened to land him at exactly the right place at the right time in mainstream Canadian media history. He became a Vancouver newspaperman just as that city's local press was entering its most adventurous and fiercely competitive period (1942-1947); a staffer at *Maclean's* during the so-called golden era of Canadian magazine journalism in the forties and fifties; a scrappy investigative columnist for the *Toronto Star* when scrappy investigative columnists were a novelty (1958-1962); a radio personality just before television took over, and a TV personality precisely when it did. He became a hugely successful pop-history author during the intensely nationalistic sixties and seventies, an outspoken opponent of racism and sexism at the moment such issues were beginning to seep into the mainstream, and an erudite and confrontational television interviewer when idle chat was the norm.

Indeed, one might call him Lucky Pierre if it

Berton was of an age and inclination that happened to land him at exactly the right place at the right time in mainstream Canadian media history.

weren't for the fact that luck apparently had so little to do with his success. While Berton's timing has always been good, it also helped that he may be one of the most tireless workhorses in Canadian media history. In his seventies, despite the fact that the demand for his product seems to be on the wane, he continues – like a Canuck version of Bob Hope – to threaten never to retire. Nor even to slow down: according to at least one source, Berton wrote 60,000 words of memoirs in a head-spinning five days.

However, even if Berton's omnipresent, cross-media generalism wasn't sufficient to warrant his inclusion in this volume, his Midas-like knack for producing pop-literary history would clinch him quicker than you can uncap a Golden. For if there is a single area of Pierre Berton's sprawling career in which he has made a truly significant and singular contribution to distinctly Canadian popular culture, it is in the series of enormously popular books he has written about events in Canadian history. Not surprisingly, the same thing that

Berton's Coming An Erotic Misadventure

She raises her whip.
"On your knees, worm," she says, coldly. "And do not dare to speak again until I give you leave."
He grovels, the sweat pouring from his brow. He licks the toe of her polished boot. She raises her whip.
His jacket, she notes, is splendidly tailored. He cannot see the single tear rolling down her cheek.

From Lara's Theme
by Lisa Kroniuk, a.k.a. Pierre Berton

In late spring 1985, McClelland and Stewart, the proudly Canadian publishing stable which once counted Peter C. Newman, Farley Mowat and Pierre Berton as its most prized literary horseflesh, published a volume of erotic short stories called *Masquerade: 15 Variations on a Theme of Sexual Fantasy*. The first work of English fiction by an obscure Eastern European immigrant named Lisa Kroniuk, the book was published by M&S on the recommendation of Kroniuk's agent, Elsa Franklin. (Who also happened to be the long-serving agent of bestseller machine Pierre Berton.)

The title's promise of forbidden delights notwithstanding, *Masquerade* stiffed. The only daily newspaper in the country even to bother reviewing it was the *Globe and Mail*, and its

response was, well, flaccid: "Entertaining," allowed reviewer Laszlo Buhasz, "but somewhat flawed in execution." No one paid attention to the publisher's press releases about the author, and only a scant 1,300 copies of the book's 5,000-unit run were purchased by indifferent retailers.

Seven weeks after its publication, as nearly all 1,300 copies *of Masquerade* continued to gather dust on bookstore shelves, certain select members of Hogtown's prominent literati, including publisher Jack McClelland himself, received invitations to a mysterious event to be held at Toronto's King Edward Hotel. When they arrived, they were greeted by a strange spectacle that seemed designed to resemble some kind of mock-literary variation on *Front Page*

clinched their popularity is precisely what's left them open to ridicule from critics and historians alike: their chatty approachability. Not that Berton seems ever to have cared much about his lack of scholarly credibility. He knows for whom he writes, and in mainstream publishing, sales figures tend to speak louder than footnotes.

In favouring character over event, and in adopting a prose style so plain-spoken it verges on campfire storytelling, Berton's pop-historical project has not only single-handedly challenged the widely held notion of Canadian history as dull, he has just as single-handedly worked at the erection of a communal national mythology. Like the building of the CPR he so lovingly recounts in the best-selling two-volume epic *The National Dream* (1970) and *The Last Spike* (1971), Berton's literary efforts can be seen as an attempt to find a way of binding national experience together. While the two-volume CPR history, which also inspired a hugely successful CBC miniseries, remains his most beloved and enduring work, Berton has applied his beer-and-shirtsleeves approach to Canadian history to a number of other key domestic events: *The Dionne Years* (1977), the War of 1812 in *Flames Across the Border* (1981), World War I in *Vimy* (1986), the settling of the Canadian West in *The Promised Land* (1984), among many others. Whether you buy his vision of a heroic

Canada or not – and his work seems to permit no middle ground – there's no denying its influence and popularity, and thus its significance as domestic pop culture.

Recently, both Berton's sales and his visibility have slipped somewhat. *Niagara*, his published pop history of the great cataract was a tank by Bertonian standards, and his Saturday column in the *Toronto Star* was dropped by the paper in 1994, only a year before the CBC would finally pull the plug on the wheezing *Front Page Challenge*. Still, in terms of making Canadian history irresistible to Canadians, nothing can diminish what he accomplished with his series of pop histories of the country. While the literary quality of these volumes is open to debate, their popular impact is not.

Like it or not, for many thousands of Canadians, Berton was the voice of our past: the campfire orator spinning colourful folk tales out of the grey fabric of Canadian history. That he has done so almost single-handedly merely makes the marking of his achievement that much more necessary. For the fact is, as the influence of our national dreamer appears to decline, there is no one standing at the campfire's edge to take his place. As a literary popularizer of Canadian history, Berton has left no apparent heirs, no one to keep those home fires burning.

Challenge. With veteran TV personality Paul (the voice of Spiderman) Soles as host, a panel of three celebrities – author William Kilbourn, actor Dinah Christie and no less a bona fide "challenger" than Pierre Berton himself – were charged with the responsibility of guessing which of three masked women at the front of the room happened to be the real Lisa Kroniuk. After a thorough grilling of all three women failed to establish which of them was indeed the real item, Berton abruptly stood up to declare that he was in fact Lisa Kroniuk. Or, if not Lisa, then the real author of *Masquerade: 15 Variations on a Theme of Sexual Fantasy*. Jack McClelland, who'd been sitting near the front was, according to the *Toronto Star*'s Beverley Slopen, "visibly shaken." He'd been completely suckered by Berton's hoax.

The roots of what the *Globe and Mail*'s William French somewhat overexcitedly called "the most ingenious publicity stunt in the history of Canadian publishing" apparently began with a novel Berton had finished two decades prior to *Masquerade*, but which McClelland, presumably highly unimpressed, had strongly advised his best-selling author against publishing. *Masquerade* was thus Berton's revenge: a way of showing Jack McClelland that not only was he a good novelist – he was good enough even for Jack McClelland to publish!

Ingenious or otherwise, the hoax didn't help *Masquerade*. It continued to sit briefly on a very few Canadian bookstore shelves before being dumped ignominiously into the remainder bins. Apparently, few Canadian readers really cared that Lisa Kroniuk was actually Pierre Berton, and fewer still cared to know about Pierre Berton's idea of erotica.

Not that Berton could have been that surprised by the nation's indifference. He had, after all, had a foretaste of it in his own home. Before the party, he deliberately left the book lying around his house (which, incidentally, happened to be next door to Jack McClelland's), in hopes that one of his seven children or their spouses might pick it up and offer some spontaneous response. Which one of them did. Not knowing it had been written by her famous father, Berton's daughter Perry spotted *Masquerade* on the coffee table, picked it up and read a few pages. Moments later, she put it down and looked at her father. "Boy," she said, "is it ever boring." Berton's wife, Janet, then walked over, looked down at the book, dusted it off and walked away without even picking it up.

Pierre partying

The Man Who Fell to Earth
Jim Carrey Beams Down

In attempting to describe the otherworldly comic gifts of Jim Carrey, the toothy kid from Toronto's satellite suburbs who rocketed from cult obscurity to A-list Hollywood superstardom over the course of 1994, the oft-evoked comparison to an alien leaps to mind. Which is handy, as the analogy allows the user to both name the phenomenon – for that is what Carrey and his immense, sudden popularity amount to – while admitting they've never seen anything quite like it before. And since few self-interested professional journalists would risk credibility by fessing up to actual extraterrestrial contact, the comparison works, because few of us have ever seen the likes of Carrey, let alone an alien, before, either.

If there's a region of Canada which might be likened to a geographical satellite dish, it's Southern Ontario, many nondescript suburbs of which Jim Carrey grew up in: Scarborough, Jackson's Point, King City, Aurora, Burlington. Traditionally both the centre of Canada and one of the most densely populated and media-saturated regions on the continent, Southern Ontario therefore embodies one of those paradoxes that may well define the English-Canadian experience. As a prominent media centre, it tends to set the agenda for national identity, yet as a prominent media receptacle has precious little identity of its own. Case in point: Southern Ontario may be the only part of Canada that never speaks of having a "regional identity." When the regions are thus referred to, it means anywhere but the area roughly contained between Ottawa and Windsor, the area from which Jim Carrey, and most of Canada's major comic exports, sprung.

Born in 1962 just outside of Metro Toronto in the much-malled community of Newmarket, Jim Carrey was the youngest of four children born to accountant Percy Carrey and his wife, Kathleen. As a result of professional setbacks experienced by his father, Jim's family moved around a lot, but never out of Southern Ontario. What this most likely meant to young Carrey who, at a precociously early age, exhibited an extraordinary knack for mimicry and classroom disruption, was an almost pathological identification with television: while friends, teachers, schools and even homes were constantly changing, TV offered a degree of comforting constancy. It was, in other words, the glass eye at the centre of the hurricane. No matter where he lived and no matter how few friends he found there, he could always tune in *Star Trek*, *Hollywood Squares* or *The Tonight Show*.

By 1981, Carrey had begun making a name for himself on the regional standup circuit. Not yet 20 years old, the Grade 10 dropout would leave audiences dumbfounded by the range, accuracy and sheer surrealistic bravado of his impressions. ("I have the face of John-Boy Walton," he told *Saturday Night* just before the *Ace Ventura* shuttle took off, "and the brain of Salvador Dali.") He didn't just do Gandhi, for example, he did Gandhi sneaking potato salad on a hunger strike. And not Elvis, but "Post-Armageddon Elvis," with flippers for arms. And for every Vegas-approved impression – John Wayne, Henry Fonda, Katharine Hepburn, Frank

Finally, after more than ten years whooping on the fringes of fame, notoriety hit Carrey with the force of a neutron bomb.

Carrey's first movie, *Introducing... Janet* (1981)　　　　The *Masked* man (1994)

Sinatra – he'd mimic someone – Bruce Dern, The Amazing Kreskin, Alan Thicke – whose iconic power was evident primarily to people who, like Jim Carrey, had access to far too many television channels for far too many unsupervised hours. (The Thicke impression apparently once so stunned Canadian mimic Rich Little he begged the young comic to explain how he'd done it.)

After he'd made a name for himself as a killer impressionist, and counted no less than comic luminary Rodney Dangerfield as a supporter and fan, Carrey moved to the city from which most of the sounds and images colliding in his subconscious had first emanated: Los Angeles. In 1984, he landed his first TV series, a short-lived, midseason flop called *Duck Factory*. Carrey had decided to put his impressions on the back burner and focus on comic acting.

It could have been that meeting with Rich Little that did it: maybe Carrey saw nothing in an impressionist's future but the desert beyond Vegas; more likely it was what he didn't see. After all, how many professional mimics have attained anywhere near the notoriety or enduring popularity of those they mimic? And Jim Carrey has never been anything less than ambitious about showbiz: at age ten he mailed off his résumé to *The Carol Burnett Show*, and by his early twenties he'd moved his parents to L.A. where he hoped to support them. Which he did, but not for much longer than the aborted run of *Duck Factory*. (Both Carrey's parents have since passed on.)

Finally, after more than ten years whooping on the fringes of fame, notoriety hit Carrey with the force of a neutron bomb. By 1994 Carrey was a regular lunatic presence on the Fox Network sketch comedy *In Living Color*, where he

once did a horny Bill Clinton struttin' to the tune of Bobby Brown's "Humpin' Around." Carrey was teetering on the brink of genuine celebrity. That's when *Ace Ventura, Pet Detective*, a movie that features Carrey talking through his butt and beating the tar out of a man in a chicken suit, became '94's sleeper blockbuster, and that's when Carrey began a run of megahits which, for their consecutive success, were rivalled only by the unstoppable Tom Hanks. In each film he did a slight variation on the extraterrestrial loon he'd been doing since imitating all Three Stooges in Grade 3: in *The Mask*, a libidinous, green-skinned shapeshifter; in *Dumb and Dumber*, a man so stupid he thinks he's outsmarted everyone; in *Batman Forever*, a hypercaffeinated Riddler; Ace again in *Ace Ventura: When Nature Calls*. He is one of the most famous and highly paid performers in the world, but that doesn't mean his gradual takeover of human civilization has been completely snagless. In 1996, his winner's streak snapped with the *The Cable Guy*, a daringly dark – perhaps *too* dark – comedy about a deranged renegade cable installer with a pathological fixation on bad TV.

As a Canadian, and as a very funny and very popular Canadian, Carrey compels our attention. His comedy stresses the extent to which a certain segment of the Canadian sensibility, and particularly the comic sensibility, is forged in the electronic-age identity gap between where you live and what you watch. While he is the first contemporary Canadian comic star not to spring from the *Saturday Night Live/SCTV* stable, his work can be seen as both a continuation and a radical extension of that school: like Dan Aykroyd, Martin Short or

Catherine O'Hara, he is less a comedian than fully camouflaged chameleon – an uncanny and ruthless impersonator of comic characters. How long Carrey's popularity will last is anyone's guess, entertainment vogues being the commercial equivalent of afternoon breezes in summer. What matters is that he attained a position of public recognition higher than that of any other Canadian movie star since Mary Pickford, and that it all began with a distinctly Canadian, if not Southern Ontarian, tradition: with a kid sitting at home watching way too much TV beamed in from somewhere else.

- -

Recommended Viewing:

Ace Ventura, Pet Detective (1994) The one that started it all, the movie with the guy whose butt talks and whose hair looks like it was licked by King Kong. Also the first to introduce a curiously recurring theme in Carrey's early star vehicles: single men who live in small apartments with precocious animals. Ph.D. thesis to follow.

The Mask (1994) An otherwise by-the-numbers comic-book scenario – magic whatzit makes weird superhero out of mild-mannered dweeb – is punched into entertainment overdrive by the heaven-made match of Carrey's natural morphing skills with Industrial Light and Magic's eye-popping computer animation. God save us if the formula should ever fall into the wrong hands.

Dumb and Dumber (1994) No movie presents the case for boneheadedness as a subversive force more strongly, or stupidly, than this. Accessorized by a geeky pageboy 'do and a dental gap, Carrey bounds through this movie wielding his idiocy like a sledgehammer in a shopping mall. So this is how Canada takes its revenge.

The Rock's Revenge
CODCO and This Hour Has 22 Minutes

In attempting to account for the conspicuous, vibrant and durable presence of Newfoundlandian satirical comedy on the Canadian public television airwaves since the mid-1980s, consider the following fact: on April 1, 1949, when the citizens of Newfoundland started their day for the very first time as part of the Dominion of Canada, nearly half of them were pissed off. It's true: when the second referendum on the self-governing British colony's possible confederation with Canada was held on July 22, 1948, 48 percent of Newfoundlanders voted against it. Any way you cut it, that's a lot of reluctant Canadians.

The fact is, many Newfoundlanders have never really felt a part of the country (in local terms, "the mainland") whose westernmost point is farther away from the provincial capital of St. John's than Ireland is. Separated from the rest of Canada by a combination of factors which include geography, history, politics, economics and culture, Newfoundland represents the virtual and actual outer limits of the Canadian experience. If one of the defining characteristics of Canadian popular culture is a sense of continental marginality, then the Newfoundland experience exists on the margins of marginality. The outsiders' outsider. Alienation squared.

It's fitting that residents of the province call it "The Rock," a reference to the unyielding chunk of earth protruding from the Atlantic Ocean, first spotted by Viking explorers seven centuries ago. The image of the windswept, wave-lashed rock has a natural metaphoric mate in the idea of hardship, an idea which has become endemic to the popular conception of the province. Beset since Confederation by industrial collapse, unemployment, population depletion and the cruel irony of an economy dependent on the same federal government half the province wanted no part of, in no other province in Canada has hardship managed to seep quite so deeply into the regional soul than Newfoundland. Were one to count the number of times the word "Newfoundland" has appeared grafted to the phrase "Canada's poorest province," it would probably outnumber the reluctant province's own population.

Newfoundland's sheer distance and difference from Canadian mainstream society has taken a toll both on how the culture defines itself and how it is defined by others. Encouraged since 1949 to view the latest addition to the family as a chronic economic liability – the helpless foundling dumped on Canada's doorstep – the rest of Canada has felt utter impunity at regarding Newfoundland with indifference. For decades, the only images of Newfoundland seen by the rest of the country were those dictated purely by the public obligation to so-called "regional representation": NFB documentaries on fishing and the occasional musical TV show which featured lots of Irish reels.

Moreover, the phenomenon of the "Newfie joke" served to make matters worse. Something of a national craze during the sixties, the Newfie joke used the

The rest of Canada finally got an opportunity to see just how wickedly smart and funny the former butt of their childhood bullying had grown up to become.

myth of the stupid, chronically luckless Newfoundlander as the butt of the same kind of derisive humour the French reserve for Belgians, the Americans for hillbillies, and Australians for New Zealanders. In this context, already feeling insecure and unworthy next to its dashing overachiever of a southern neighbour, Canadians could vent their own insecurity against Newfoundland. Thus, the real cultural purpose of the Newfie joke becomes apparent: to make the rest of us hosers feel smart.

Only in the last decade has it become apparent that the real joke has been on the rest of the country. Remarkably, perpetual hardship in Newfoundland has not produced a culture defined by despair, stoicism or even resignation. Instead, it has produced a wealth of scathing, fearless and pointed satire. This is something of a Canadian cultural talent, but in Newfoundland it's intensified by the province's status as the edge-dweller of an already marginal country.

For theatregoing Canadians, this satirical revelation was no secret, as the various members of the St. John's–based CODCO troupe, founded in 1973, had been taking their distinctive brand of bird-flipping humour on the road for years. But we're talking *popular* culture here, and the fact is the number of theatregoing Canadians probably wouldn't fill the bleachers in Ottawa's Frank Clair

Stadium. That's why it wasn't really until the mid-1980s, when the CBC (doubtless in response to that grim bureaucratic summons of regional representation) began to intermittently broadcast an uproariously ill-tempered sketch program called *CODCO*, that the rest of Canada finally got an opportunity to see just how wickedly smart and funny the former butt of their childhood bullying had grown up to become. Even if Newfie jokes hadn't already passed into cultural history by that point, one gets the feeling *CODCO* would have killed them right quick.

Consisting of a number of performers, St. John's residents all, who in some cases had not only known each other since childhood but had joined the troupe at its inception, *CODCO* was a deft and often disorienting mix of regionally rooted colour and mass-culture parody: a skit called "Anne of Green Gut" one moment, a wicked impersonation of Barbara Frum the next. Watching *CODCO,* as performed by siblings Andy and Cathy Jones, Greg Malone, Tommy Sexton and Mary Walsh, was like finding a chili pepper in your potato salad: a bracing burst of bitterness. As *CODCO* director David Acomba noted in a 1993 *Globe and Mail* interview, "They have a strong personal and social sense of politics. When *SNL's* Dana Carvey does George Bush, it's all effect, there's no politics in it. When Greg Malone does George Bush, in one sketch he used golf as a metaphor for the Gulf War. It's far more effective, biting and scathing." And did someone ask for regional? *CODCO* thrust regional in your face on the end of a sharp stick. It skewered the Catholic clergy at the time the nation was beginning to learn the extent of the sexual abuse at Catholic schools in Newfoundland, and traded in characters so starkly (and hilariously) specific to life on The Rock they made any outside attempts at stereotyping seem either redundant or lame. (Truly, characters like perennial shut-ins the Friday Night Girls and loudmouth landlords the Budgells could only have come from Newfoundland.)

Initially, the program was buffeted by what seemed to be that lingering sense of central Canadian antipathy. Having checked off the regional requirement to air the show, the CBC seemed little interested in doing anything to promote or develop it. While the Lorne Michaels–produced *Kids in the Hall* – a less pointed, more polished, downtown-Toronto kind of show – enjoyed heavy promotion and a fixed time slot, *CODCO* was not only denied a full season slot until 1989, it was bounced mercilessly around the programming schedule for most of its seven-year run. Chances were, if you saw and liked *CODCO* one week, it was often hard to find the show the next.

Unlike *Kids in the Hall*, which rarely drew its humour from public figures or events, *CODCO* was also plagued by network censorship problems: skits like "Blaming Africa for AIDS" and "Madonna, Penis Teaser, Media Pleaser" were either banned or run in expurgated form. This eventually led to the angry and public 1990 departure of one of the group's mainstays – Andy Jones – over the network's pulling of a screamingly funny sketch about barely sublimated clerical lust called "Pleasant Irish Priests in Conversation." (A taste of what these pleasant Irish priests converse about?: "I'd sure like to have a go at them buttocks, Father!") Regardless of Jones's departure

22 Minutes **would amount to nothing less than a satirical stake driven through that most vaunted of Canadian public broadcasting institutions – the national network news program.**

and the endless noggin-knocking with the CBC, the program carried on without Jones until 1993, at which time the group wisely decided to voluntarily call it quits – wisely because they did it before quits were called for them.

Any fears, however, that the end of *CODCO* might also mark the end of Newfoundland's triumphant comedic revenge on the mainland were quickly allayed by the announcement of a new program called *This Hour Has 22 Minutes*. The brainchild of Mary Walsh, *22 Minutes* would amount to nothing less than a satirical stake driven through that most vaunted of Canadian public broadcasting institutions – the national network news program. Deriving its name from the legendary 1960's Canadian current affairs program *This Hour Has Seven Days*, the show came to air in 1993 featuring Walsh, fellow *CODCO* alumnus Cathy Jones and two profoundly talented but relatively unknown sons of St. John's, Rick Mercer and Greg Thomey.

Far more focused and tightly formatted than *CODCO*, *22 Minutes* adapted the seamlessly slick look and structure of a CBC news broadcast, only to use this familiar and nationally beloved format as a means of taking on some of Canada's more ridiculously respected elite institutions. Not since *SCTV* has any Canadian

comedy program derived such savage pleasure in taking the piss out of the practice of TV journalism, and none have gone quite so far in the systematic perforation of displays of arrogance and hypocrisy on the part of Canada's political and economic elite. Roughly half of each episode consists of the mock newscast; the other half is a series of on-location commentaries by various "experts," including: Babe Bennett (Cathy Jones), the tough-talking, forties movie dame/"sexual affairs correspondent"; Marg Delahunty (Mary Walsh), the political candidate-at-large; and Dakey Dunn (Walsh), a macho nightmare. The satire can be scathing. Shortly after the 1995 Quebec referendum, Rick Mercer offered these thoughts on Lucien Bouchard: "He's like a ten-year-old having a temper tantrum in the middle of Toys "R" Us. And instead of hauling him out and putting him in the car, Jean Chrétien is starting to fill up the cart. Distinct culture, constitutional veto … whatever it takes. Nothing is good enough for Lucien. Hey Jean, if you don't watch it, you're gonna spoil that youngster and we're gonna have to live with it." About Preston Manning, Delahunty once observed, "I've always enjoyed [his] speeches, and I'm sure they're even more edifying in the original German."

Compared to the equally headline-fixated but vastly more middle-of-the-road *Royal Canadian Air Farce*, *22 Minutes'* brand of tooth-and-nail political satire is utterly subversive: the difference between a tickle and a slap.

The sheer pointedness of the program's political attacks, combined with its clear affinity for the Canadian powerless over the powerful has predictably left it open to

The cast of *This Hour Has 22 Minutes*: (left to right) Cathy Jones, Greg Thomey, Mary Walsh, Rick Mercer

criticism, particulary from conservative corners which charge *22 Minutes* with being too obviously left-wing. (Yawn. Yeah. Sure. Whatever.) One can't help suspecting, however, that the criticism is rooted as much in resentment as content: *22 Minutes'* real crime against conservatism isn't that's it's too left, but that it's too funny and popular: in its third season, the mock news program was not only drawing higher numbers than *CODCO* did, but occasionally more viewers than the real national news. At a time when no elected officials seem capable of addressing the mendacious lunacy of those in power,

Not since *SCTV* has any Canadian comedy program derived such savage pleasure in taking the piss out of the practice of TV journalism.

the job is left to satire. And no one seems up to that job quite so indisputably as *This Hour Has 22 Minutes*.

Moreover, the damn-the-consequences brazenness of the program couldn't have been more bracingly timely. As provincial governments in Alberta and Ontario were swinging mightily rightward, as the ultra-

conservative Reform party was gaining ground in the federal government, as the debate over Quebec sovereignty tore open wounds which had never really had an opportunity to heal and as the Liberal government under Jean Chrétien skipped away from campaign promises with the frightened deftness of a skittish welterweight, no one was speaking up more loudly, fearlessly or hilariously than *22 Minutes*. One shouldn't be surprised, really. After nearly half a century of throwing rocks at the mainland, one's aim would have to get pretty damned good.

emergent evolution. *n. Philosophy.* the doctrine that, in the course of evolution, some entirely new properties, such as life and consciousness, appear at certain critical points, usually because of an unpredictable arrangement of the already existing entities.

– COLLINS ENGLISH DICTIONARY

Emergent Evolutionary
David Cronenberg Breaks with Form

It's likely that David Cronenberg, the best-known and most widely admired movie-maker English Canada has ever produced, doesn't look back on 1977 fondly. Among other things, it was the year that, indirectly anyway, he was booted out of his apartment by columnist-critic, middle-brow-at-large Robert Fulford.

In 1975, the 32-year-old Cronenberg invited the influential editor of *Saturday Night* magazine, a Canadian general-interest periodical established during the reign of Victoria, to a screening of his first commercial feature, then called *The Parasite Murders*. (Its Canadian title has since been changed to *Shivers*.) Fulford, who for some reason also wrote as a movie critic under the nom de plume Marshall Delaney, had previously seen and written favourably about one of the young Torontonian's short experimental features, *Stereo*. Believing that Fulford might also respond positively to the new movie, which was about how a scientifically generated out-break of undulating, wormlike parasites turns an exclusive Montreal apartment building into a veritable orgy of predatory bloodlust, Cronenberg arranged a private pre-release screening for the man who was arguably the most important cultural voice in English Canada.

← Gynecological tool from *Dead Ringers*

Scanners

A lifelong science enthusiast, Cronenberg had written the script for *The Parasite Murders* while his father was dying of a bone-weakening condition which had started as colitis. "He would turn over in bed and break ribs," the film-maker told one interviewer many years later. To another, he recalled: "His body was sick; he said he wanted to have my body." The story of the outbreak of the sexual parasite, which is triggered by a scientist's doomed effort to liberate the libido by injecting his mistress with a parasite comprising equal parts aphrodisiac and venereal disease, would be the first of many to demonstrate the film-maker's fascination with the post-Darwinian theory of "emergent evolution," or the principle that evolutionary development is as much a matter of genetic accident as environment.

For Cronenberg, a largely self-taught

Like viral horror itself, a flurry of op-ed activity broke out in the national press, and the propriety of cultural-funding policies was debated in the House of Commons.

film-maker who'd graduated from the University of Toronto in 1967, there was much at stake. It was his first straight commercial feature and, after waiting two hungry years for the agency to make up its mind, he had finally been granted considerable financial support by the federal funding body, the Canadian Film Development Corporation (CFDC, now called Telefilm Canada). Cronenberg knew the success or failure of the film might make a difference between a career as a movie-maker or a return to jobs like

clerking at Sam the Record Man.

During the two-year wait for the CFDC to come through with its funding, Cronenberg decided to go to L.A. to try to sell the script in Hollywood. But the trip there, with future *Dead Ringers* collaborator Norman Snider, proved fruitless.

Legendary B-movie mogul Roger Corman had read and liked the script, but was unavailable for a meeting when the two eager but callow Canadians turned up. Canuck Lorne Michaels (who would later become executive producer of *Saturday Night Live*) advised the boys to face facts, forget Canada and move to Lotusland forever: "We thought we were going to be the first generation that was going to be able to stay home," Snider later recalled Michaels telling them, "and do it ... but it didn't happen. You're going to have to come down here and so

Recommended Viewing:

Shivers (a.k.a The Parasite Murders) (1975) The one that convinced Robert Fulford the country was going down the drain. Actually, based on the evidence on-screen, it was coming up the drain.

Rabid (1976) After surgery following a motorcycle accident, Marilyn Chambers develops a killer phallus in her armpit. Call it what you will, but don't call it derivative.

Scanners (1981) The exploding-head movie. Need we say more?

The Dead Zone (1983) Cronenberg's elegant, understated adaptation of Stephen King's novel is undoubtedly the best version of the author's work since Kubrick's *The Shining*.

M. Butterfly (1993) Diplomat Jeremy Irons falls in love with a Chinese opera singer who turns out to be a man played by John Lone. Although based on a true story and far and away the least icky Cronenberg movie ever, it's also one of his most eccentric and purely romantic.

Essential Viewing:

Videodrome (1983) Cronenberg meets McLuhan in a highbrow splatterfest. Deliriously strange.

The Fly (1986) This intensely visceral, AIDS-conscious remake of a cheesy 1950s programmer is one of the most intelligent and strangely heart-wrenching monster movies of recent decades.

Dead Ringers (1988) The twin-gynecologist movie with Jeremy Irons in both roles. A masterful study of male dread and dysfunction, elegantly made and honestly creepy.

Naked Lunch (1991) Cronenberg's career-long dream of adapting William S. Burroughs's seminal free-form drug novel plays something like a narcotized Woody Allen movie, with pharmaceutically generated hallucinations standing in for dull urban neurosis. Which is meant as a compliment.

will your kids." Cronenberg and Snider also had an L.A. run-in with Toronto's Citytv honcho Moses Znaimer which proved to be equally disappointing. As accounts have it, he told Cronenberg and Snider that making movies was simply a waste of time. (Later, Cronenberg ruthlessly parodied Citytv 's mix of sleaze and self-importance as Civictv in 1983's *Videodrome*.)

By 1974 Cronenberg's endurance paid off: the CFDC finally announced it was in for $75,000 of the movie's $185,000 total, and the relatively inexperienced director, who didn't even know that A.D. stood for assistant director, shot the movie in 15 days in the summer. *The Parasite Murders* went on to become the most commercially successful movie the federal funding agency had yet supported, mopping up a tidy $5 million worldwide.

For Cronenberg, however, the bad news came first — in the September 1975 issue of *Saturday Night*. After screening *The Parasite Murders*, Fulford went off to tell his readers about how he had not only disliked the movie, he had hated it to the depths of his being, calling it (among other unambivalent things) "an atrocity, a disgrace" and, in case the point was too subtly conveyed, "the most repulsive movie I've ever seen." Using Cronenberg's movie as the cudgel, he proceeded to pound away mercilessly at the funding policies of the CFDC itself, which he called "hopeless" and "mired in discredited practices," before adding "only very desperate people would put public money, and some part of their reputations, behind a film like *The Parasite Murders*."

Yee-owch. The repercussions were as

Cronenberg was radically breaking the rules of proper artistic conduct in this country, more so than any English-Canadian film-maker had before or since.

immediate as they were widespread. Like viral horror itself, a flurry of op-ed activity broke out in the national press, and the propriety of cultural-funding policies was debated in the House of Commons. While at first the hitherto obscure Cronenberg seemed to bask in the negative notoriety, its true effects were soon felt — funding for his next viral horror movie *Rabid* was initially refused by the CFDC, and *Shivers* was rudely excluded from eligibility in the Canadian Film Awards.

Two years later, the fallout from Fulford's diatribe was still cascading down on Cronenberg's head. In the process of divorcing his first wife, Margaret, whose child-custody battle with Cronenberg would influence the extreme nuptial horror of *The Brood*, he was living with future wife, Carolyn Zeifman, in an apartment on Toronto's Cottingham Street. In early 1977, Cronenberg's landlady, an antipornography activist and an acquaintance of Fulford's who lived elsewhere in the home, was reading an article in the *Globe and Mail* on the forthcoming release of a Canadian movie called *Rabid*.

The article not only mentioned the fact that *Rabid*'s director, one David Cronenberg, had generated no small amount of controversy with his previous outrage, but that Cronenberg's new star was no less than the notorious mid-sev-

Dawn of the David: Young Cronenberg →

enties porno superstar Marilyn (*Beyond the Green Door*) Chambers. Moreover, Fulford was quoted extensively therein. This was how Cronenberg's landlady discovered, to her profound mortification, that her tenant was not only the man who'd perpetrated the dread *Shivers* on the world, he was the guy who'd just spent a few months in dangerously close proximity to Ms. Chambers. Faster than you can say "exorcism," Cronenberg and Zeifman were purged from the property.

In spite, Cronenberg not only wrote to the *Globe*, the newspaper which had revealed the identity of the evil Cronenberg to his erstwhile landlady, he bought a house directly across the street from his former landlady. As he explained in the *Globe*, the forces of Canadian propriety knocked there too. An "anonymous" complaint had been filed that Cronenberg was running a commercial pornography business in a residential neighbourhood.

Despite all the pressure Cronenberg felt after releasing *The Parasite Murders*, he stayed put. It was, after all, his town, or at least as much his as his fellow Toronto native Fulford's. He'd been born there in 1943 – father Milton Cronenberg was a freelance writer who wrote a stamp-collecting column in the *Toronto Telegram* and mother Esther a pianist who'd accompanied the National Ballet of Canada – grown up there, become smitten with science fiction, racing cars and watching movies there, and even went to university and made his first experimental movies in the same city.

Cronenberg's inspiration to make movies came from movies themselves, and particularly a little, barely seen made-in-Toronto movie made while Cronenberg was a student of honours

English at the University of Toronto. (He'd originally enrolled in science, but bailed after his sophomore year.) Directed by David Sector, the film was called *Winter Kept Us Warm*, and the effect of seeing its familiar locations and faces was, as Cronenberg recalled years later, a catalytic event for the nascent film-maker: "It takes someone your own age or someone close to you to suddenly say, 'My god, I can do this – it's exciting!' And that's exactly what happened."

Not only did Sector's film convince the future film-maker that he too could make movies, it convinced him it was possible to do it in Toronto, a principle that Cronenberg, a lifelong resident of the city, has clung to even as his star has risen to one of the distinctive brand-name auteurs working in the world today.

In the two decades since the Fulford episode, Cronenberg has mutated from the Canadian film industry's most notorious pariah to its most vital and visible exponent of uncompromising artistic independence. (His 1996 film, *Crash*, was awarded a special prize for "audacity" at that year's Cannes Fim Festival.) While many of the film-makers held up by Fulford as exemplifying virtuously Canadian artistic tendencies, such as Peter Pearson, Don Shebib and Allan King, have long since receded almost entirely from public consciousness, David Cronenberg, like it or not, stands at the forefront of the way Canada must now think of itself culturally. As a model for successful and stubborn independence, he is arguably the most important figure in the recent history of English-Canadian cinema: in terms of acting as a positive role model of home-grown, grassroots resistance, it is impossible to consider the careers of Atom Egoyan,

Bruce McDonald, Guy Maddin, Patricia Rozema, David Wellington and Clement Virgo, just to name a few, without him.

Perhaps without even knowing it, Cronenberg was radically breaking the rules of proper artistic conduct in this country, more so than any English-Canadian film-maker had before or since. He was self-taught when most aspiring film-makers were paying institutional dues at the NFB or CBC. He was working in genre – horror and science fiction – when it was considered an act of national virtue not to do anything resembling Hollywood-style "schlock." He was making money when the pantheon-approved film-makers weren't. From an unapologetically masculine point of view, he was addressing issues of sex, gender and dread when it was becoming increasingly perilous to stray from the model of liberal-feminist middle-class moralism. And, worst of all, he refused to do the decent thing, the Ivan Reitman thing, and just go away to L.A.

Proof as well as an adherent of the principle of "emergent evolution," Cronenberg represents both a rupture with Canada's conventional cultural identity and a sensibility so Canadian it could not have emerged anywhere else. Which he knows, of course, or he wouldn't have dug in his heels and endured the vitriol being spewed his way for as long as he did.

Why, therefore, we like Cronenberg, why we think he may be the single most inspiring figure in unmistakably Canadian popular culture today: you can attack him, you can evict him and you can deny him funding and awards, but you can't ignore him, and you sure as hell can't make him stop or disappear. A real Canuck hero.

David Cronenberg directing Jeremy Irons in *Dead Ringers*

Don't Forget to Flush
The Nine Ickiest Moments from David Cronenberg's Movies

Shivers (1975) A naked woman in a bathtub is, er, infiltrated by a pulsating penile parasite. Note the sound of legs crossing when it happens: they're your own.

Rabid (1976) In the midst of performing surgery, a freshly infected doctor goes berserk and slices off the top of a colleague's finger with a scalpel. As if operating rooms weren't creepy enough.

The Brood (1979) As the vengeful mother of all mothers in this cerebral perversion of *Kramer vs. Kramer*, Samantha Eggar wolfs down her own afterbirth. Cronenberg has said this movie was inspired by his own divorce and subsequent custody struggle. One hopes he exaggerates, for effect.

Scanners (1981) While being "scanned" by telekinetic supercreep Michael Ironside, Louis Del Grande's head blows up (real good!) like a watermelon left in a microwave. The kind of scene where you go "yuck!" and then play it over, in slow motion, about six times.

Videodrome (1983) James Woods's kinky date (Deborah Harry) likes to have her ears pierced and breasts burned during sex. Woods is only too happy to oblige. At this point, one abandons hope they'll settle down and raise children.

The Dead Zone (1983) A small-town cop (Nicholas Campbell) is discovered to be a murderous pedophile, so he goes home to off himself in a most novel if unpleasant fashion: by sitting in a bathtub and forcing his head down on a pair of sharp, open scissors. Probably just observing regulations about firearm use off-duty.

Dead Ringers (1988) Because this is a movie about a pair of creepy twin gynecologists (both played by Jeremy Irons) who take turns posing as each other for kinky kicks, any of the scenes involving internal examinations have a decidedly unwholesome punch to them.

Naked Lunch (1991) Among the many charming hallucinations experienced by junkie protagonist Peter Weller in this adaptation of William S. Burroughs's drugcult classic is a throbbing typewriter which not only speaks, it speaks through an orifice which looks unmistakably like an anus. Just say no to drugs, kids.

M. Butterfly (1993) Disgraced diplomat Jeremy Irons, made up in full white-faced geisha drag, slits his own throat in front of an audience at the prison where he has been sent as a convicted spy. The cruel, mocking indifference etched on the face of his fellow cons, combined with a kimono running crimson with blood, makes for a deeply queasy moment.

Cronenberg's Brood
The Next Generation of Canadian Film

At the same time that David Cronenberg's grim and gory vision was drawing howls of middle-brow outrage during the seventies, (Robert Fulford's *Saturday Night* review of 1975's *Shivers* was titled "You Should Know How Bad This Movie Is: You Paid For It"), he was nevertheless clearing a path that the following generation of Canadian film-makers would charge up with gusto, and for much the same reasons the culturati were squealing.

To understand the extent of Cronenberg's independence during the seventies and influence during the eighties, we have to take a look at the film-making climate in which he began. He was making speculative fiction shockers in the mid-seventies when the dominant Canadian model was based in documentary realism. His films were blatantly commercial when most critic-approved Canadian movies were aimed squarely (if not often successfully) at the art-house. He was largely self-taught at a time when most film-makers had trained at public institutions like the National Film Board and the CBC, a circumstance which pretty well made his radical break with the prevailing realist mode in Anglo-Canuck movie-making possible. He was dealing overtly, if controversially, with sexuality at a time when sex was far less visible in our movies than the prairies were. Finally, perhaps most significantly, he never sacrificed control for scale: by acting as writer-director on his movies, and by working with an ensemble crew on a low budget, he made the movies he wanted to make with a minimum of compromise. Cronenberg is the most influential English-Canadian film-maker of his generation. How can we know this? By looking at some of the people he influenced, and whose work might well not have been possible without him:

Sheila McCarthy in *I've Heard the Mermaids Singing* →

Scenes from: *Exotica*   *Roadkill*

Atom Egoyan

Like Cronenberg, this Egyptian-born, Toronto-based international-festival fixture is fascinated with sex, technology, identity and the perverse manner in which they intersect. He's also an inveterate hyphenate, acting as writer and director on most of his deliberately scaled-down productions. As well, he brings a degree of brand-name eccentricity to his work that is also a cult-building hallmark of Cronenberg's. Finally, though Egoyan has scored one bona fide box-office hit – *Exotica* being Canada's most successful movie export since Bob Clark's blockbusting no-brainer *Porky's* – the film-maker, like Cronenberg, insists on using Toronto as his base of operations.
Recommended Viewing: *The Adjuster* (1991), *Exotica* (1994).

Mike Hoolboom

While the influence of Cronenberg on this prolific, uncompromising and deeply gifted Toronto experimental film-maker is not immediately apparent (Hoolboom will most certainly never make movies for Twentieth Century Fox), close scrutiny of Hoolboom's work reveals some compelling parallels between the two. Obsessed with the same mind/body duality that enriches Cronenberg's most resonant work, Hoolboom's approach suggests a route the older film-maker might have taken had he followed the experimental path pointed to in such early short films as *Stereo* and *Crimes of the Future*. Plus, they both take conspicuous satisfaction from showing their audiences things most people just don't want to look at: for Cronenberg, it's Jeff Goldblum peeling off his own diseased fingernails in *The Fly;* for Hoolboom, a clown eating his own faeces in *Shiteater.*

Moreover, Hoolboom's own controversial, nonpurist status in the Canadian experimental community suggests someone just as willing to court ostracism in pursuit of the muse as Uncle Dave is.
Recommended Viewing: *Kanada* (1993), *Frank's Cock* (1993), *Valentine's Day* (1994).

Jean-Claude Lauzon

Quebec's most internationally celebrated film-maker, apart from *Jesus of Montreal's* Denys Arcand, represents a break with his province's cinematic tradition almost as stark as Cronenberg's own flight from Anglo-Canadian movie orthodoxy. Where much pre-Lauzon Quebec cinema is insular in both aesthetic and dramatic terms, his movies feed, and feed heartily, from a global feast of influences. Lauzon is a former street kid turned highly accomplished commercial director, whose films – the Michael Mann-ish *Night Zoo* and the Felliniesque *Léolo* – are both feverishly fantastical affairs: nakedly allegorical, intensely personal, opulently art-directed and baldly nonrealistic.
Recommended Viewing: *Léolo* (1992).

Bruce McDonald

At first glance the least Cronenbergian in temperament and practice of any listed here, this former film editor (for Egoyan and Patricia Rozema among others) is nevertheless a key figure in the development and visibility of the English-Canadian independent scene in the post–tax shelter 1980s. An active organizer of independent screenings and film-making cooperatives, and cagey promoter of independent work, he has come to embody the so-called "outlaw" spirit of DIY movie-making practice in Canada, a spirit in no small way made possible by Cronenberg. Thus, while the quality of

his work is inconsistent, his impact has been solid.
Recommended Viewing: *Roadkill* (1989), *Highway 61* (1991).

Guy Maddin

Arguably Canada's most weirdly gifted director, this Winnipeg Film Group alumnus – of Icelandic extraction – is another aggressively independent writer-director with a singular sensibility. Feverishly cramming his movies – which boast plots drawn from a psychic universe where Gilbert and Sullivan collide with *Eraserhead* – with images, sounds and editing techniques found in a forgotten attic of cinematic prehistory, Maddin is a prime example of a post-Cronenberg Canadian auteur.
Recommended Viewing: *Tales From the Gimli Hospital* (1988), *Careful* (1992).

Patricia Rozema

After working as an assistant director on Cronenberg's *The Fly*, this Calvinist-reared Ontarian, who wasn't permitted to see movies as a child, went on to make her own ultra-low-budget, self-written debut feature, *I've Heard the Mermaids Singing*, a widely watched and celebrated account of a Walter Mittyish everywoman (Sheila McCarthy) whose fantasy life is vastly richer and more interesting than her real one. Although response to Rozema's subsequent work (1990's *White Room* and 1995's *When Night is Falling*) has been decidedly mixed, and although her sensibility is considerably sweeter than Dave's, she's stuck to her guns and weathered the criticism, undoubtedly a lick or two learned from Cronenberg.
Recommended Viewing: *I've Heard the Mermaids Singing* (1987), *When Night is Falling* (1995).

Baby Boom The Dionne Quintuplets

During the Great Depression, there were few spectacles more likely to rivet people's attention, or separate them from their few pennies, than those that offered the commodity of hope. While the movies and radio did their best to exploit and assuage people's dread, they did so with fiction: family comedies, super-heroics, gangster sagas, urban musicals, urbane mysteries. Effective and necessary as these temporary escapes were, the fact is they *were* fictional, and what people really craved were stories of hope and survival drawn from something resembling the real world they lived in.

Invariably, the biggest stories of the thirties traded in the spectacle of individuals bucking tremendous odds: the fearless solo flights of Amelia Earhart and Howard Hughes; the doomed romance of the antifascist struggle against Franco in Spain; the transcendent athleticism of Jesse Owens; the rash of heartland Robin Hoods like Dillinger, Bonnie and Clyde and Baby Face Nelson. But of all these stories, none would compel the attention of a hope-hungry world more than the one that began in the small farming community of Corbeil, about eight miles from the hitherto largely unheard-of town of North Bay, Ontario. It was there, in a tiny log house on May 28, 1934, that a 25-year-old, French-speaking farm wife named Elzire Dionne literally gave birth to what was arguably the North American pop-cultural event of the decade, and certainly the biggest story to come out of Canada since Mary Pickford. Elzire Dionne, already a subsistence-level mother of five children, gave birth to five more. All girls, all sickly and premature, and all at the same time.

"Quintuplets' Lullaby" sheet music →

Emilie   Annette   Marie

In today's era of medically assisted reproductive miracles, when the birth of quintuplets seems an only slightly less likely event than winning a lottery, it is hard to comprehend the impact at the time of the birth and survival of Elzire and Oliva Dionne's five daughters – Annette, Cécile, Yvonne, Emilie and Marie. But the fact was, the birth did seem nothing short of miraculous in 1934: five identical girls born from the same egg, collectively weighing a scant 13 pounds six ounces (a nurse on hand likened the babies' cries to "the mewing of kittens"), and delivered on what first looked very much like death's doorstep. So tiny and frail they had to be fed with eyedroppers, the Dionne Quints were the decade's most unlikely, irresistible and heart-wrenching heroes. Prior to their birth, no complete set of quintuplets had survived childbirth and infancy. The odds these mewing preemies bucked were enough to shame Superman: the chances against their surviving more than a day or two were estimated at 57 million to one.

When news of the quints' birth first broke out of North Bay, the reaction was immediate. Suddenly, there was a miraculous, human-interest story of hope and survival which not even the most cynical tabloid editor could dream up: dirt-poor farmer's wife gives birth to five identical girls in log cabin! Within 24 hours, North Bay and nearby Callandar were teeming with reporters from across the continent. What they found there apparently touched the hearts of even the most seasoned of big-city scribes. One Chicago reporter, stunned to learn that the babies were being kept warm in a wood-slatted basket next to the cabin stove, flew in with a kerosene-heated incubator for the quints. Others

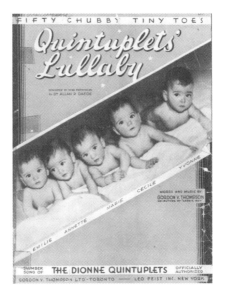

Quints-inspired music cover

began a public campaign for the donation of breast milk. The *Toronto Star* sent a nurse to Corbeil along with its team of reporters and photographers.

Needless to say, if North Bay was knocked sideways by the combined impact of the quints' birth and subsequent press swarm, the effect on Elzire and Oliva Dionne was nothing short of cataclysmic. Having lived hard but quiet lives as farmers, the Dionnes were already struggling financially by the time the quints were born. As the tiny home and property began to teem with reporters and photographers, it's entirely likely the young father began to feel a clammy sense of imminent fiscal doom: how, in the middle of this terrible Depression, was he going to feed a family that had doubled overnight? That's probably why Oliva decided to accept the offer, made by a promoter within 24 hours of the quints' birth, to have them exhibited at the Chicago World's Fair.

Dionne's decision would prove devastating indeed, the precise moment when the Dionne saga would shift irrevocably from a tale of human triumph to an account of heartbreaking tragedy. Not that it was a decision Oliva made lightly. A devout Catholic, he first sought the advice of Father Daniel Routhier, the local parish priest. According to some accounts, Father Routhier's blessing was conditional. If Oliva would donate part of the money being offered for the Chicago appearance to the construction fund of the local church, Oliva could accept the offer with the church's full approval. Feeling secure in the priest's permission, he said yes to the World's Fair.

Within two months, the life of the Dionnes was changed forever. Claiming Oliva's decision to exhibit the children for profit proved the Dionnes were unfit parents, the Ontario government under Premier Mitchell Hepburn removed the children from their parents' custody, replacing familial care with a phalanx of doctors and nurses. The quints never were exhibited at the Chicago World's Fair. With the almost unanimous support of the press, they were made wards of the state under the supervision of the same doctor, Allan Roy Dafoe, who had delivered them. Their parents were under strictest orders to have only minimal contact with their five baby girls. Ostensibly in the interest of their daughters' survival, Elzire and Oliva were not only forbidden to kiss or handle them, they were required to make appointments just to see their girls.

One can only imagine how Oliva, publicly demonized by the accusations of seeking to exploit his children for profit, must have felt when he realized the government was turning his family into one

Cécile   Yvonne

of the biggest tourist attractions the country had ever seen. As he and Elzire stood and watched, the government built a compound-cum-theme-park across the road from their tiny farmhouse. Quintland was replete with public washrooms, a souvenir stand and a horseshoe-shaped glass observatory where people could gawk at the quints at play in their nursery four times a day. The attraction proved a staggering success, the biggest natural tourist magnet the province had seen since Niagara Falls. Due to the blanket exposure the babies received in newsreels, newspapers and magazines – appearing on the covers of *Time, Look* and *Life* – people from around the world flocked to the tiny community of Corbeil to see the miraculous brood.

Decades on, the figures remain truly jaw-dropping. At the height of Quintmania a few years later, as many as 6,000 people a day turned up to ogle the darling Dionnes, numbers which included such luminous visitors as Clark Gable and Bette Davis. In 1936, Quintland saw half a million people pass through its doors. By 1938, the government of Ontario, which had earlier taken such moral umbrage over Oliva's acceptance of the Chicago World's Fair offer, was making a cool $20 million a year from the business generated by the quints, whose total profits from endorsements, souvenirs, public appearances and Quintland itself has been estimated at $500 million in Depression-era dollars.

The Dionnes were the most photographed children on the planet. Quint dolls were actually outselling Shirley Temple dolls at one point, and the girls were the subject of no less than three Hollywood movies: *The Country Doctor, Reunion* and *Five of a Kind*. They were even summoned to greet the touring King George VI and Queen Elizabeth in Toronto. Their gorgeous, ringletted faces were used to peddle just about any product that could afford the official endorsement: cereal, syrup, cleaning flu-

Quint-endorsed product

ids, even typewriters and automobiles. By the early 1940s, when Oliva had finally managed to regain custody of his girls, nearly three million people had made the pilgrimage to Quintland.

By the time the quints were returned to their parents in 1943 – a development which, it should be noted, is probably explained less by belated judicial fairness than the fact that the kids were outgrowing their tourist-attracting cuteness – the damage done to the Dionnes' family solidarity was so extensive the wounds continue to bleed 60 years later. Raised by professionals and used to being treated like tiny princesses, the sisters had little in common with either their siblings or their parents, who had continued to farm the land. Moreover, many of the quints' brothers and sisters couldn't help blaming

the girls, whom they had been barely permitted to know, for the pain and suffering endured by the rest of the family. Some of the children had been sent to live with relatives as a result of the quints' birth, and the long struggle to regain custody of the five girls was a constant source of anxiety and suffering to Oliva and Elzire. Despite the fact that the five girls had been brought up just across the road from the rest of their family, a chasm of experience separated them from their siblings. Understandably, the resentment between the quints and the rest of the Dionne children – of which there were now eight – was therefore profound, prompting the girls to move out when they turned 18.

Impossible as it seems, the Dionne saga grew uglier as the quints entered adulthood. The family discovered that the same trust fund that had been set up for them had also been used to pay for the construction of the playroom-observatory, the travel expenses and fees of the state-appointed guardians and even the public toilets at Quintland. Even the large brick home ostensibly built for the Dionne family by the government had been paid for by funds generated by the quints' endorsements and public display. By the time they grew up, there was practically nothing left: the $1 million the girls were supposed to receive on their twenty-first birthday had dwindled to $800,000, and that was eventually eaten up by such matters as the legal fees incurred by some of the quints' divorces. Not surprisingly, things like marriage, along with other conventions of a so-called "normal" life, proved difficult for these children raised as sideshow attractions.

Today, only three of the Dionne Quintuplets survive: Emilie died as the

Singing on CBC-Radio

result of an epileptic seizure in 1954, and Marie of a blood clot – possibly alcohol-related – in 1970. (Their father died in 1979 and their mother in 1986.) Notoriously wary of contact with the press, Cécile, Yvonne and Annette have nevertheless stepped back into the spotlight recently. Their reason for doing so reveals much about the climate of mendacity and resentment in which they were reared: to try to get some payback for the lives they believe were taken from them by both their parents and the Ontario government. To this end, they have published two books of scathing memoirs, 1963's *We Were Five*, and 1995's *Family Secrets*, the more recent of which dropped the explosive allegation that their father had sexually molested the quints on a regular basis. As vehemently as the surviving quints make the charge, the other siblings deny their father could have done any such thing. In 1995, Cécile, Yvonne and Annette sued the government of Ontario for compensation

to the tune of $10 million. (The suit remains unsettled.) Moreover, they demanded and received a form of profit share from the Dionne Museum in North Bay, which is still visited by 13,000 Quint-crazy tourists each year.

In 1993, when the CBC announced the production of a miniseries about the Dionnes called *Million Dollar Babies*, the sisters agreed to take part in the program's promotion, but only after being offered six-figure fees. In 1994, on the occasion of the Dionnes' sixtieth birthday, the sisters agreed to give only one interview – to *The National Enquirer*, the publication which also happened to offer the most money. When *The New York Times* came along offering nothing but prestige and responsible journalism, the Dionnes turned down America's most respected newspaper: no cash, no comment. Asked in 1994 why they seemed so hellbent on selling the stories of their lives to the highest bidders, Cécile responded in a way which might well

stand as the epitaph for the entire Dionne tragedy: "We need the money," she said.

The pain, resentment and heartbreak of the Dionne saga are far from subsiding. If anything, the remaining quints seem more determined than ever to exact justice over what was done to them by their family and government. Still, in the context of a pop-cultural phenomenon so fraught with irony it often seems more fictional than actual, this one cuts through like an axe: in 1995, while promoting *Family Secrets*, Cécile Dionne confessed at a press conference that the ordeal she had endured had robbed her of the capacity to dream, a condition which both Yvonne and Annette subsequently admitted they also suffer. This, one supposes, is the price paid by the Dionnes for giving everyone else in the world something to dream about at a time when hope was such a hard thing to find.

Rock of Ages The Endurables

Curious thing, this sixties legacy. On the one hand, it feels like nostalgia by gunpoint, a self-mythologizing legacy force-fed by one generation to all others. For many people older or younger than the media-dominating boomer generation, which has turned its formative decade into a kind of theme park of selective memory, the dissonance is inescapable. On the other hand, we're asked to accept that the era was a benchmark of activism and consciousness-raising, and yet the evidence of belligerent, intolerant conservatism, often embodied by boomer-aged politicians, has never been as distressingly epidemic. But in no hallowed arena are we asked to take the divine right of the sixties on faith more than with music.

If the mythology is to be believed, the music of youth culture has never been, and by implication can never be, better than it was then. More dissonance here, too: while radio relentlessly spurts the decade's "solid gold" "classic rock," and while the Beatles vs. Stones rivalry is as intense as ever, if only as a merchandising legacy, it's been so long since anything of current value has come from most of that generation's most cherished musical icons that, for young people today, many of them must represent what ubiquitous lounge dinosaurs like Sinatra, Bing or Dino were to their counter-culture-era predecessors. Truly, folks, how can we expect kids to see in the Dylans, Jaggers, McCartneys or Pink Floyds of today anything other than the aging, complacent, irrelevant bores that they have insisted on becoming? Never mind the marketing cynicism behind the term "alternative rock" – the explosion of the very idea should tell us something about the size of the icebergs in the mainstream.

Robbie Robertson

Description: singer-songwriter, former Band focal point and enduring low-key hunk. **Career kickoff:** Bob Dylan asks Robertson and Band, then known as The Crackers, to join him as backup musicians for ground-breaking "electric" tour in 1965. **Career peak:** The Band's first two albums, *Music From Big Pink* and *The Band,* still maintain the reputation of being two of the most original, influential works in rock history. His 1987 album, *Robbie Robertson,* is a wonderful collaboration with Canadian knob-twiddling wunderkind, Daniel Lanois. **Career not-so-peak:** After an awesomely impressive farewell concert performed on American Thanksgiving in 1976, filmed by director Martin Scorsese as 1978's *The Last Waltz,* and featuring fellow endurables Neil Young and Joni Mitchell, The Band regroups without Robertson for uninspired, obligatory reunion during the early 1980s. Acrimony and despair abound: drummer Levon Helm starts accusing Robertson of taking full credit for songs he allegedly only partially wrote, and singer-pianist Richard Manuel commits suicide after a Florida concert in 1986. **Unlikely collaboration:** Robertson produced Neil Diamond's 1976 album *Beautiful Noise.* **Signs of durability:** Robertson's recent decision to go highly public with his mixed Mohawk heritage has put him at the forefront of a sure-fire pop music growth industry: Native American music. In 1994, he not only composed the soundtrack for Turner Broadcasting's six-hour documentary *The Native Americans,* the then over-50 musician was described by the *New York Times* as "drop-dead handsome."

Joni Mitchell

Description: avant-pop singer-songwriter, inspirational as pioneering woman artist in heavily guy-oriented business. **Career kickoff:** One year after dragging Leonard Cohen into the spotlight, apparent Canuckophile Judy Collins has a top-ten hit in 1968 with Mitchell's "Both Sides Now." **Career peak:** Mitchell's fourth recording, *Blue,* is released in 1971, and is still considered one of the definitive folk albums of its era. **Career not-so-peak:** The influential mainstream rock bible *Rolling Stone* dismisses Mitchell's ambitiously innovative *Hissing of Summer Lawns* LP as the worst album of 1975. In 1986, she performs as last-minute replacement for Pete Townshend at Amnesty International concert, and is booed by an audience who seems to have no idea who she is. **Unlikely collaboration:** Sings duet with unenduring punk Billy Idol on 1988 album *Chalk Mark in a Rainstorm*; collaborates brilliantly with dying jazz giant Charles Mingus on *Mingus* in 1979. **Signs of durability:** They abound. Chelsea Clinton, daughter of non-inhaling boomer President Bill, is named after Mitchell's "Chelsea Morning." Moreover, it's hard to think of a contemporary woman singer–songwriter, from Alanis Morissette and Sarah McLachlan, to Courtney Love and P. J. Harvey, who doesn't bear some trace of Mitchell's influence. Also, no other pop artist demonstrated an interest in so-called "World Music" earlier than Joni Mitchell. World-class eccentric/hieroglyph "artist formerly known as Prince" is a major fan, as is British multiplatinum crooner Seal.

Leonard Cohen

Description: poet, singer, songwriter, novelist, ageless chick magnet. **Career kickoff:** In 1966, Judy Collins records Cohen's haunting "Suzanne." At a Central Park concert in 1967, she invites the poet on-stage. Later the same year, he performs solo at Newport Folk Festival and records his first album. **Career peak:** Cohen's 1969 album, *Songs From a Room,* is still considered one of the best examples of pop as poetry. *Songs of Love and Hate* (1971) comes a close second. The latter was released the same year film-maker Robert Altman used Cohen's music as melancholy, end-of-frontier backdrop in *McCabe and Mrs. Miller.* **Career not-so-peak:** While recording 1977's *Death of a Ladies' Man* with world-class eccentric Phil Spector, Cohen was approached by the producer who put a gun to the poet's neck, telling him, "I love you, Leonard." Years later, Cohen allowed that the incident "wasn't much fun." **Unlikely collaboration:** While studying at McGill University in Montreal, Cohen formed a country-and-western band – The Buckskin Boys – which at one point included future redneck anthemist Charlie ("The South's Gonna Do It Again") Daniels on bass guitar and fiddle. **Signs of durability:** Mentioned by name in Nirvana's "Pennyroyal Tea," and the subject of no less than three English-language tribute albums. Based on recent relationship with actress Rebecca De Mornay, still a chick magnet in his sixties.

Neil Young

Description: singer-songwriter, punk prototype, professional chameleon, godfather of grunge, hoser godhead. **Career kickoff:** Moving to Los Angeles from Toronto in 1966, Young runs into Stephen Stills and Richie Furay, whom he'd met earlier on the Canadian folk circuit. The two Americans ask Young to join in the formation of Buffalo Springfield, along with fellow Canadians Bruce Palmer and Dewey Martin. The seeds of legend are sown. **Career peak:** Take your pick: 1970's *After the Gold Rush*? 1974's *On the Beach*? 1975's prepunk double-header *Zuma* and *Tonight's the Night*? How about 1979's *Rust Never Sleeps*? 1990's *Ragged Glory*? **Career not-so-peak:** In 1982, Young records an album called *Trans* on which he sings all vocals through an electronic voice-distorting device called a vocoder. As if that weren't sufficient, he takes the album, vocoder and all, on tour. In concert, he substitutes instruments and vocals with various synthetic devices, tape loops, video, electronic keyboards, and sings duets with projected video images of himself. **Unlikely collaboration:** Before leaving Toronto for apparently permanent stardom in Los Angeles, Neil Young appeared in a band called the Mynah Birds with – we kid you not – future "funk punk" Rick "Superfreak" James. **Signs of durability:** Veteran noisemeister Young, riding a wave of alt-rock credibility after the so-called grunge explosion of the early nineties, records album *Mirror Ball* with superstar upstarts Pearl Jam in 1995. Also, there seems to be no busker in any major North American centre who cannot play most of the *Harvest* album in the quest for spare change.

Young Neil Young　　　　　　Young Joni Mitchell　　　　　　Young Leonard Cohen

And yet, as infuriatingly bankrupt as the contemporary legacy of love-generation music now seems, one would be ill-advised to dismiss it entirely. Particularly if one holds any interest in the infinitely strange phenomenon of Canadian popular culture. For the fact is, not only have certain musical careers remained inspirationally vital well beyond their sixties origins, a surprising number of them happen to belong to Canadians.

Take these four endurables, in declining order of age, if most certainly not influence: Leonard Cohen (born 1934, Montreal, Quebec), Joni Mitchell (born 1943, Ford Macleod, Alberta), Robbie Robertson (born 1944, Toronto, Ontario) and Neil Young (born 1945, Toronto). While each rose to prominence during the 1960s, and while each enjoys almost mythic status as an icon of the period, each has also transcended the living-dinosaur syndrome by exerting a continuing and vital influence on generations of fans and musicians for whom the sixties are little more than the decade the first *Star Trek* series went on the air. As recently as 1996, Ottawa-born rookie chart-topper Alanis Morissette was warmly citing Mitchell as an influence and inspiration, and the despairing postmodern cool of film-maker Atom Egoyan's art-house smash *Exotica* was in no small way embellished by the generous use of Cohen on its soundtrack. Young is the flannel-and-feedback godhead for a generation of noisemakers who weren't even born when "Heart of Gold" hit number one, and Robertson's pivotal role in the legendary, enigmatically brilliant outfit The Band ensures his continuing status as one of rock music's few genuine visionaries.

Is there any way to account for this concentration of abiding musical influence in nationalistic terms? Or are we merely looking at one of those provocative coincidences (like the fact that Johnny Wayne and David Cronenberg went to the same Toronto high school) that pop culture likes to hurl in your face every now and then? Impossible as that may be to answer definitively, an examination of what these four artists share might tilt the argument in the direction of some kind of national condition. Here are the reasons we think so.

Pop Poetics

Each of the four endurables is a singer as well as writer of their own material, a circumstance that places them squarely and prominently at the enormously influential intersection where poetry crosses pop (don't forget that Cohen was already well-established as a poet and novelist before he ever embarked on a recording career) and at a time when the post-Dylan singer-songwriter explosion was just taking off. And as singer-songwriters, each has managed to find an artistic position from which that solid Canadian tendency to stand outside and observe has yielded a wealth of lyrical treasures. The ability, that is, to see things from "both sides now."

Raising Their Voices

Each of the singers, and none more so than Neil, has faced a considerable amount of resistance concerning their eccentric vocal stylings, an early liability that would evolve into an inspirational asset as their credibility as artists grew. Then there's the fact that three of them, Cohen, Mitchell and Young, were tagged early on as folksingers, which meant much dues-paying and craft-honing before reaching anything like a broad audience: they had all grown into something distinct on their own by the time fame found them.

Canadian Chameleons

There is a chameleonic quality that all of the endurables share. Among other things, Mitchell has swung from diaphanous, cloud-watching flower-folkie to avant-garde jazz fusion artist, while Robertson and his mostly Ontario-reared Band compatriots, Rick Danko, Garth Hudson and the late Richard Manuel, forged a form of contemporary roots Americana so eerily precise that it might only have been made possible by people who'd experienced the country from the outside. For Young, who may be the most recklessly unpredictable rock icon of his, or arguably any, generation, the changing of perspectives, personas and musical technique has been as central to the notion of artistic vitality as songwriting itself.

As for Cohen, well, his endurance is equally revealing, if for the opposite reason. Of the four, he has demonstrated the least tendency to reinvention – and he quickly dismissed his most experimental album, the 1977 Phil Spector–produced *Death of a Ladies' Man*, "a catastrophe" – but his irresistibly sexy attitude of erudite, world-weary romantic stoicism has meant that he seems to stand impervious while an increasingly restless world inevitably returns its attention to him. By now, how many generations of chain-smoking dorm residents have been seduced by, or to, the deliciously hedonistic melancholy of Cohen? Besides, he was one of the first artists of his generation to favour a wardrobe dominated by black and, as everyone knows, as an accessory to artistic distinction, black is always in fashion.

Young Robbie Robertson with Band mates

"Expo '67 is an outrageous, lunatic, wondrous dream come to reality."

— THE MONTREAL STAR, APRIL 28, 1967: OPENING DAY

When We Were Fab Expo '67

The great Canadian Centennial love-in was definitely a top-down affair: an officially legislated, publicly sponsored, impeccably choreographed national debutante ball. Compulsory attendance notwithstanding, we loved it anyway: it was probably the most fun the country ever had doing something it was told to do. It was the year marking the 100th anniversary of Canadian Confederation, and it was to be nothing less than Canada's opportunity to strut its stuff for the planet.

The centrepiece was Expo '67: a six-month-long, billion-dollar world's fair held on two islands – one built for the occasion – in the St. Lawrence River at Montreal. Over 60 countries would agree to participate in the good-natured architectural showdown called (ahem) "Man and His World," and over 50 million people from around the world would come to gawk at this glittering, high-modernist birthday cake baked in our honour. Make no mistake, it was a dream come true for a gangly, self-conscious adolescent of a country: *everybody* came, and everybody left impressed.

For many Canadians, however, it turned out to be more than a good party. Much more. You know this by the dreamy, melancholy way in which Expo is evoked by people who were there. In the same way that phenomena like Haight-Ashbury and the Monterey Pop Festival are unavoidably embroidered by nostalgia for those who experienced them, Expo looms as large as a dream as it does an event: magnificent yet somehow sad. While it might have lacked the counter-cultural cachet of its American counterpart, Expo '67 was Canada's Summer of Love.

In 1987, on the twentieth anniversary of Expo '67's opening, Robert Fulford remembered the first day of more than 100 he would spend covering the event for the *Toronto Star*. "In memory," he

mused, "the sun is always bright, the St. Lawrence River sparkling blue, and the breeze gentle." On the twenty-fifth anniversary, Emil Sher, writing for the *Globe and Mail*, returned to the now-dilapidated site of the fair which had wowed him when he was eight. The dream remained potent even in the evidence of ruin: "That summer lingers, its pleasant aftertaste sweetened by time.

Memories are distilled into a nectar of nostalgia." Four years later, again in the *Globe*, the potency of the dream showed no signs of abating. "It seems a long ago time now," wrote Alanna Mitchell, "but there was a moment, a shining moment, when Canada felt good about itself."

That's it, of course: a shining moment when Canada felt good about itself. This is why the memory of Expo lingers so long and sweetly for those who lived through it: it is a symbol of what memory insists was a simpler, brighter and possibly better time for Canada, when an entire nation was capable of setting aside all its differences in the interest of raising a toast and a hoot to Confederation's centenary, when there were millions of public dollars around to throw into something as fundamentally nonessential

Expo '67: Man and His World

as a national birthday party. Even our greatest threat to national unity at the time – the growing separatist movement in Quebec – seemed allayed by the mere situation of Expo at Montreal.

As an internationally transmitted symbol of Canadian federalism transcending internal discord, the event was as potent as propaganda as it was as situational showbiz. Indeed, after Expo, there wasn't anything we couldn't do: "The more you see of it," wrote the *Toronto Star*'s Peter C. Newman on opening day, "the more you're overwhelmed by a feeling that if this is possible, that if this little subarctic, self-obsessed country of 20,000,000 people can put on this kind of show, then it can do almost anything." In 1968, in his book called *This Was Expo*, Robert Fulford reiterated the vision of Expo as the dawn

of a glorious new day for Canada: "Expo '67 was the greatest birthday party in history, but for those willing to learn it was also an education. For one beautiful and unforgettable summer, Expo took us into the future that can be ours."

"The future that can be ours." That we can no longer feel that way – that the country has never felt less like a "country" than it does 30 years after Expo – is what accounts for the sentimental mist the event still generates so generously. While one must always approach nostalgia with nothing less than extreme prejudice, evidence does suggest Expo was, if not a better time, certainly a different one. The proof is that so many people *did* dig on the idea of celebrating Canada's birthday: countless towns, cities and villages gladly tackled the official

challenge of executing some kind of "Centennial Project"; hundreds of thousands of Canadians eagerly greeted the arrival of the "Centennial Train" and "Centennial Caravan," and it was almost a matter of civic obligation that one made the pilgrimage to Expo. (One of this book's authors acquired a pet turtle that summer, whom there seemed no choice at the time but to name "Expo.") Bobby Gimby's high-stepping, government-sponsored Centennial song "Ca-na-da" found its way into 300,000 Canadian homes: the highest-selling Canadian single in history.

Amazingly, Expo '67 nearly didn't happen. As late as 1963, press and politicians alike were suggesting the whole thing be flushed. The day he ceremoniously dumped the first few yards of Expo soil

Centennial antics on Parliament Hill

onto Ile Ste Hélène that year, Prime Minister Lester Pearson was still voicing grave misgivings in public. "I would be less than frank if I did not add that I feel we all have cause for concern over the magnitude of the tasks that must be accomplished if the fair is to be the success it must be." *The Toronto Star* agreed: "The simplest thing is to call the whole thing off." It was a sentiment shared even by Expo director George Hees. Hees, once a Conservative cabinet minister in John Diefenbaker's government, also thought the Expo situation hopeless by 1963: "It was my opinion that there wasn't the slightest chance for Expo. Our chances were zero, nil."

Pearson's public reservations were doubtless the result of pressures from his Liberal cabinet to kill Expo. Pearson's government had inherited the mammoth

Pearson's government had inherited the mammoth project from Diefenbaker's Conservatives, and it was nothing short of an unholy mess when they did.

project from Diefenbaker's Conservatives, and it was nothing short of an unholy mess when they did. The idea of holding an international exposition in Canada during its Centennial year had first occurred to Conservative senator Mark Drouin in 1958. Returning from the Brussels World's Fair that year, Drouin thought it was precisely the kind of event Canada needed for an appropriately splashy international coming-out. Since the epochal New York World's Fair in 1939, the international exposition had

evolved into a chic and popular national-vanity showcase: any country that had one instantly became the beneficiary of global attention and visibility. Diefenbaker's Conservatives liked the idea, and applied to the International Exhibitions Bureau in Paris for permission to hold nothing less than a "first-category exhibition." Defined by the I.E.B. as an event which "constitutes a living testimony to the contemporary epoch," each country putting forth its candidacy had to demonstrate that it had the financial, the political and organizational wherewithal to pull off such an exhibition.

Canada apparently didn't. We were turned down. The same year we were to turn 100, the Soviet Union was to turn 50, and the I.E.B. unsurprisingly gave them the nod to host the 1967 exhibition.

Then, in 1962, the Soviet Union backed out, presumably upon taking a closer look at the assembling such an exhibition might actually involve. This might well be what gave so many Canadians pause at the possibility of holding a first-category exhibition on home soil. An event *too big for the Soviet Union*? At the height of the testosterone-charged Cold War? Yet Canada, which had not so much as put a gerbil in orbit, was going to pull off the very *first* first-category international exhibition in the history of the West?

Behind all the practical concern facing the country there lurked a more primal form of national terror. What if, having invited the world to our coming-out party, we blew it – and this time with the whole world watching? Or, what if, having invited the world, it couldn't be bothered to show up? Small wonder that perennial conservative voice in the Canadian national psyche was telling the country to call it off: having set out to storm heaven, what if we slipped in the muddy St. Lawrence instead?

The skepticism around Expo's potential for success didn't abate soon either. Rumours abounded that the site wouldn't be ready, and that Edward Churchill, the seasoned military construction chief brought in as director of installations, was threatening to bulldoze pavilions into the river if they were found lagging behind the whip-cracking construction schedule. Even before that, back in 1963, there was the surreal news that, in order to create more offshore space for Expo close to the heart of Montreal, Mayor Jean Drapeau – whom many suspected of building Expo as a monument to his own ego anyway – had actually commissioned the building of an *artificial island* in one

What if, having invited the world to our coming-out party, we blew it – and this time with the whole world watching?

of the largest countries in the world. Drapeau created the artificial island of Ile Notre Dame by dumping 25,000 tonnes of soil into the St. Lawrence.

The griping did not stop until April 1967, when the gates of Expo opened and warm tides of international applause finally began to wash away our national insecurity. A spectacular monument to the potential of space-frame architecture – a principle that involves covering the greatest area possible with the lightest and most flexible forms of building material – the park was sheer visceral pleasure to experience firsthand: inviting, eye-popping and intensely pedestrian friendly. Accompanied by the constant sound of outdoor concerts and performances, one walked from exhibit to exhibit virtually agog: at the minirail trundling overhead, at Buckminster Fuller's unforgettable geodesic dome, at the state-of-the-art cinematographic technology on display, and sometimes just at the sheer star power the event generated. Each day drew another star or two from the international firmament, and each made Expo shine that much brighter. (On the day that one of this book's authors – then nine years old – made the family pilgrimage to Expo, so did Maurice Chevalier and Senator Robert F. Kennedy, although not in the same station wagon.)

Yes, the whining stopped dead at opening day. (Well, not entirely. In the pages of the *New York Review*, the profes-

sionally malcontent Mordecai Richler, heaping insult on injury because he was a *Montrealer* yet, called Expo a "good-taste Disneyland.") Indeed, the tone of the Canadian press was almost bullying in its enthusiasm, as though anything less than fulsome praise was a national security risk. Certainly there seemed to be an *insecurity* risk. On April 28, opening day, Peter C. Newman wrote in the *Toronto Star*: "The cannonade of fireworks which marked the opening of Expo... may in retrospect turn out to have been one of those rare moments that change the direction of a nation's history... This was the greatest thing we have ever done as a nation and surely the modernization of Canada – of its skylines, of its styles, of its institutions – will be dated from this occasion and from this fair." On the same day, after calling Expo "the most staggering Canadian achievement since this vast land was finally linked by a transcontinental railway," the *Montreal Star*'s Frank Moritsugu declared, "It will change us. The Canadian's image of himself and his country – an ambivalent one even when it reflects pride – will never be the same. To those exposed to Expo, and, of course, those who worked on it, the traditional national inferiority complex is becoming a foolish anachronism."

Anachronistic perhaps, but not extinct, as was made clear once it got down to reaping one of Expo's most substantial harvests: the good opinion of others. Across eight columns, the *Globe and Mail* announced the knee-wobbling news: "IMPACT OF EXPO; EVERYONE IN PARIS IS TALKING ABOUT IT." In Ottawa, the *Citizen* breathlessly added, "EXPO – IT'S A SOLID HIT IN THE U.K."

Centennial medallions

"Vive le Quebec libre": Charles de Gaulle's Expo visit

Paris, London, New York, Rome: *everybody* was talking about Canada's birthday fair, and everybody seemed to love it. Buckminster Fuller's U.S. pavilion, the stunning geodesic dome, made the cover of both *Life* in the U.S. and *Match* in Paris. The *New Yorker* ran several cartoons with Canadian punchlines. The *London Evening Standard* proclaimed: "There has never been any other show of its kind that has ever come near it," while the same city's *Observer* added this swooner: "Expo '67 isn't just a world fair, it has glitter, sex appeal, and it's given impact and meaning to a word that had neither: Canadian."

"You had to be a pretty cool Canadian to read those words without a certain pleasure," wrote Fulford in 1968. Indeed, if it was possible for a country like Canada to stroke itself into a frenzy,

these were the words that would do it. Finally, for the first time ever, "Canadian" was appearing in the same sentence with phrases like "sex appeal." In what might rank as the most satisfying and apt confirmation of the national ego, Canadians could tune in American TV and see… *Canadians*! NBC ran an hour-long documentary on Expo, and Perry Como hosted a special musical theme show inspired by Canada. For once, instead of inviting Canadians – like his beloved Wayne and Shuster – to New York, Ed Sullivan came to Canada to do a show from here. From Expo!

It was, quite simply, successful beyond this painfully self-conscious confederation's wildest dreams. Not only had the event been pulled off in an unspeakably short amount of time, it had brought back the gold in Canadian cultural-

Not only had the event been pulled off in an unspeakably short amount of time, it had brought back the gold in Canadian cultural-identity terms.

identity terms. They liked us. They *really*, really liked us! We had done it. We had done it and, squinting through sunlight the morning after, it was easy to believe we would never be the same again. Among the thousands who believed a new era had dawned was William Thorsell, the future editor-in-chief of the *Globe and Mail* who spent the summer working at the Western Canada Pavilion. "Expo '67 changed the world, for Canada at least, or so we thought," Thorsell wrote in the twenty-fifth anniversary year

Pop Goes The Country Bobby Gimby's Centennial Song

For a great many Canadians who lived through it, the mere mention of the 1967 Centennial brings two things immediately to mind: Expo '67 and Bobby Gimby's Centennial song "Ca-na-da."

Long a record-holder for the best-selling Canadian single in history – 300,000 copies sold when the country's population was, as you'll recall, "twen-ty mill-i-on" – the story of the song begins in the Toronto offices of the publicity firm of Vickers and Benson in the spring of 1966. Hired by the Centennial Commission as the event's official (i.e., government-endorsed) publicist, it had been left to the firm to come up with a sure-fire kick-off gimmick for the

upcoming Centennial bash.

While the government had already made the commissioning of some sort of Centennial anthem part of the firm's responsibilities, none of the executives at V&B believed anything as potentially deadly as a "Centennial anthem" would qualify as kick-off material. "What we needed," recalled V&B vice-president Al Scott in 1967, "was a grabber. A stirring flag-waver that would make everybody feel 'Gee, this is a real good country.'" They still hadn't found their grabber the day Bobby "Nimble Lips" Gimby walked through the door.

They knew who he was, of course. A trumpet player and bandleader (who bore

an uncanny resemblance to kiddie-TV host Mr. Dressup) who'd apprenticed with Mart Kenney and his Western Gentlemen, the 45-year-old Saskatchewan native was already about as well known as Canadians get: after leaving Kenney, Gimby spent a decade as a regular performer on CBC-Radio's popular *The Happy Gang* show, and then worked as musical director of the equally popular *Juliette* show on CBC-TV. In addition, Gimby was a prolific composer of jingles (*Stay away from snacks, chew a Chiclets and relax!*), novelty tunes ("The Cricket Song") and even had a track record with hit pop national anthems: in 1962, Gimby had a smash-hit song on

Queen Elizabeth cuts the Centennial cake

of 1992: "We were terribly naive and ide-alistic… Maybe we were just young."

Maybe. For if there was one national characteristic Expo clearly failed to change, it was the country's abiding yearning for world attention. We still seek and covet the global gaze as avidly as we ever did. Nothing, however, seems to satisfy our need for confirmation through flattering attention the way Expo did: neither the 1976 or 1988 Olympics, not the back-to-back World Series wins of the Toronto Blue Jays, not the 1986 Expo in Vancouver. We've witnessed the corro-sion of the ideal of national cohesion which made the dream of Expo so vivid. Back then it was still possible to imagine that there might be some kind of pan-provincial experience which we could call Canadian, and that this experience not only included the distinction between

what was then called English and French Canada, it needed it. Today, after the rav-ages to the national dream perpetrated by factors as wide ranging as separatism, recession, government cutbacks, aboriginal politics, free trade and multiculturalism, it is not only more difficult to speak with any assumption of consensus about "Canadian" experience, it's almost absurd. Canada has never seemed more like an arbitrary assortment of defensive tribal interests than it does today. Which is precisely why little national pride is taken anymore even from the most "world-class" achievements: the World Series wins were *Toronto*'s, Expo '86 was *Vancouver*'s coming-out party, and the still unpaid-for 1976 Montreal Olympics have become the national standard for municipal folly.

In 1967, it was widely thought that

Expo might be a moment that changed Canada forever. The fact is Canada *has* changed significantly since that distant spring day the gates opened on, as Emil Sher wrote, "two small islands that held the world." Just not in the way Expo – that monument to national idealism – suggested it might. It was a dream of something better, a playground of global utopianism in Canada's own backyard, a fantasy of social perfection. A dream, in other words, but a helluva nice one, with mem-ories destined to last much longer than most of the pavilions would. Anybody who was anybody made the pilgrimage to Expo at least once, thus fulfilling the national fantasy of certification by associa-tion in another essential way: if you're only as good as your guest list, we were good beyond dreams at Expo. We were *great*.

- -

Singapore radio with a snappy, kid-sung tune called "Malaysia Forever." It was in Asia that he'd first been called "Canada's Pied Piper."

On the day he walked into Vickers & Benson's offices, Gimby had in his hand a song he'd worked on for nine months. It was inspired by a St. Jean-Baptiste cele-bration he'd seen in La Malbaie, Quebec, in 1964. Nothing if not an ardent nation-alist, Gimby was inspired by the spectacle of 50 kids marching through the streets singing in French. "Wouldn't it be won-derful," he recalled thinking at the time, "if the French and English kids of this great country could pull together and sing a song in their own language?"

Preparing to audition the song to V&B executives with no more accompa-niment than a tapped pencil, Gimby

Nothing if not an ardent nationalist, Gimby was inspired by the specta-cle of 50 kids marching through the streets singing in French.

explained that what they were about to hear was really designed to be sung by kids: it was a children's martial march in both official languages. This understood, Gimby sang "Ca-na-da."

"It had real gut feeling," Al Scott told an interviewer after the song had gone through the national roof. "And when I realized the catchphrases were between French and English, to be sung by *chil-dren*, I really flipped. We needed the bilingual-togetherness angle in our mar-keting campaign, and even the wise guys

in the communications dodge can't knock kids. So I knew immediately I had found my grabber."

Recorded in Toronto and Montreal, originally the song was to be used only once; as the opening to a Centennial kick-off program on the CBC called *Preview '67*. The plan was to film Gimby doing the Pied Piper bit with some kids lip-synching in a Toronto park. This was to be the opening of *Preview '67*.

When the lights went up after the pro-gram was screened for Centennial officials, all anybody was talking about was that opening – they were bowled over by it. Realizing they had their kick-off anthem, the Centennial organiz-ers ordered the Pied Piper scene cut into a commercial-length promo clip for the big event. Eventually, it was shown for 26

"Canada's Pied Piper": Bobby Gimby

Centennial Caravan

weeks on TV stations across the country. The response was again electric: television stations were swamped with requests for recordings and sheet music, neither of which existed due to the somewhat predictable absence of any expectations on the part of the government that the song would chart with a bullet. It is not often, after all, that the Canadian government got involved in the business of selling hit singles. Moreover, the proportion of requests from teachers outflanked any other group, proving that Gimby's idea of a national anthem for kids was a stroke of something approaching genius. "It was the schoolteachers who did it," Gimby told the *Globe and Mail* in 1987.

Realizing also that the TV clip – in which Gimby led the children playing his long, gaudily festooned trumpet – had made the composer almost as familiar as the song, Centennial organizers quickly hired him to do the same thing coast to coast during the Centennial year. Riding in the rear car of the Centennial Train and Caravan, Gimby's job was to play Pied Piper wherever the train or caravan stopped. Dressed in his unmistakable red-and-green cape, Gimby was to spring forth and lead local kids in a real live version of the commercial.

Knowing somewhat belatedly that they had a very big hit on their hands, Centennial organizers finally released a recording of the bilingual song by

Secretary of State Judy LaMarsh admitted that "Ca-na-da" was very likely "the only Centennial project that will make money for the government."

Gimby's Song

"Ca-na-da: A Centennial Song"
Ca-na-da,
(One little, two little, three Canadians…)
we love thee,
(Now we are twenty million)
Ca-na-da,
proud and free.
North! South! East! West!
there'll be happy times;
Church bells will ring, ring, ring.
It's the hundredth anniversary of
Con-fed-er-ation,
Everybody sing together!

- WORDS AND MUSIC BY BOBBY GIMBY

- -

"Bobby Gimby and the Young Canada Singers." "After this record hit stores," Gimby said, "you couldn't stop it with a train. It just exploded." With one side in blue (opening in French, swinging to English and ending in French) and one side in red (with the song in reverse order), the demand was overwhelming. By year's end, "Ca-na-da" had not only sold in excess of 300,000 copies, it would become the biggest-selling Canadian single in history, a record it would hold by a wide margin until "Tears Are Not Enough" almost broke it in 1985.

When it started to become clear that Gimby had created nothing short of a feel-good monster, Secretary of State Judy LaMarsh admitted that "Ca-na-da" was very likely "the only Centennial project that will make money for the government." Ed Lawson, the promotion

manager for the song's label, Quality Records, proudly beamed at the time that "On some radio stations, it's even running ahead of the Monkees." Eventually, there would be more than 30 versions of the song recorded, including one in which impressionist Rich Little sang the song à la John Diefenbaker and Lester Pearson.

Today, 1967 must seem something of a blur to Bobby Gimby as he looks back on it from his home in North Bay, Ontario. (Taking a flat salary of $35,000 for his Pied Piper gig, Gimby donated all proceeds from sales of the record to the Boy Scouts of Canada.) His public appearances and media interviews numbered in the hundreds, and there were few days that year in which Bobby Gimby, now in his seventies, wasn't either playing Pied Piper or packing up his horn and cape to play Pied Piper. "I spent most of 1967 between planes," he said 20 years later. For years following the Centennial, he continued to perform the song for children, and once estimated he'd led a quarter of a million kids singing along to "Ca-na-da."

In 1992, troubled by mounting apparitions of discord in the country, Gimby again assembled a group of children to sing a national-togetherness anthem called "Let's Get Together, Canada Forever." However, what worked for Canada in 1967 wasn't cutting it in the surlier national climate of 1992. The song sank and disappeared. "They were happier times, 25 years ago," Gimby said not too long ago. "Canadians were ready to celebrate. They were a-hooping and a-hollering. They were ready for a song. You don't see many smiling faces today."

Rage of Aged Front Page Challenge

It was a split between outrage and indifference, fury and a shrug, a yell and a yawn. In the first flush of spring 1995, as the zeroes on Jim Carrey's paycheck multiplied and Alanis Morissette was putting the finishing touches on the *Jagged Little Pill* album, as referendum acrimony was building on both sides of the linguistic divide, the Canadian Broadcasting Corporation announced what for many people – but not that many – was unthinkable: the cancellation of the 38-year-old "institution," *Front Page Challenge.*

For institution-boosters like the *Globe and Mail,* the removal of the low-rated, middle-aged quiz show, which "challenged" a veritable Canadian Rushmore of journalistic experts to guess the identity of newsworthy mystery guests, was a terrifying rent in the fraying quilt of national unity. Another sign the country was going to the dogs, the private sector, or worse, the dread Yanks. This is because *FPC*, particularly for those ever-dwindling numbers who loved it, was an example of a Canadian institution which was, like *Morningside*, Wayne and Shuster or the *Globe* itself, both noteworthy and distinctly Canadian on the basis of a certain fundamental drabness. As Michael Valpy put it in the *Globe and Mail*: "Like Canadians of mythology, *Front Page Challenge* was almost unrelentingly nice. Talk shows, panel shows, across the border or in the United Kingdom could be glib, cheeky or, in Canadianese, 'stepping over the line' of politeness and decency. Not *FPC.*"

Front Page Challenge host, Fred Davis →

Saucy challenger

Not good, in other words, but good for you. This no doubt explains why, for every Canadian outraged or saddened by the demise of the show, whose regulars (Fred Davis, Betty Kennedy, Pierre Berton, Jack Webster and Allan Fotheringham) by then had a combined age of 355 years, there were many more who were probably more surprised to learn that the show was still on the air in the first place. Said the *Toronto Star*'s Antonia Zerbisias: "So, while *Front Page Challenge* will be missed by many of its half million loyal fans, 26 million other Canadians, more than a third of whom weren't around when *FPC* first aired, won't even notice it's gone."

FPC can not be ignored, if only because its' stubbornly anticommercial longevity tells us much about the role of institutions, particularly publicly supported ones, within Canadian popular culture. *FPC* was one of those institutions whose very imperviousness to commerce, evolution and, arguably, to entertainment itself was in certain corners a certifier of national worth: it may be earnest, low-rated and hopelessly out-of-date, but it's distinctly Canadian! It would be a refrain heard often in the budget-balancing nineties, as the CBC's fading institutions underscored the uneasy sense of a public broadcaster with a past but not a future, and as the once-dominant middle-class Anglo audience of the fifties dwindled in numbers and influence. As the operative programming philosophy seemed to favour preservation over evolution, the disappearance of an institution like *Front Page Challenge* was doubly frightening to its constituency because there was nothing to replace it. Thus it was possible to entertain the notion of national

Beginning as a summer replacement series, *FPC* combined the built-in suspense of live TV with the deeply Anglo-Canadian obsession with current events.

Armageddon in the wake of the aging quiz show's cancellation. No more *Front Page Challenge*. No more Canada? Not likely. How about one less intransigent Anglo-WASP institution? How about one less haven for curmudgeons?

It began in 1957, before either of the almost-middle-aged authors of this volume were born. And, to be fair, it was hot at the time. Beginning as a summer replacement series, *FPC* combined the built-in suspense of live TV with the deeply Anglo-Canadian obsession with current events. (Here's one of those definitive Yank-Canuck differences: while America's best-loved game shows featured celebrities or average folk, Canada's most enduring example of the form boasted… journalists.) The premise was so ingeniously simple that *60 Minutes*' Mike Wallace actually once tried to get a Hollywood version going with himself as host. (And Andy Rooney as the Yank answer to ubercurmudgeon Gordon Sinclair? *That* might've worked.) Four panelists – originally, broadcasters Alex Barris and Gordon Sinclair, actress Toby Robins, and occasionally author-broadcaster Pierre Berton or Neil Young's journalist father Scott – were given a limited time to guess the identity of a person integrally connected with a past or present news event.

The early appeal of the show, which had more than two million regular viewers

at its height, was generated by the combination of the ticking clock, the often surprising "challengers" (everyone from Malcolm X and Pierre Trudeau, to Eleanor Roosevelt and Jayne Mansfield made appearances) and, of course, the feisty but deferential chemistry of the panelists themselves. By 1962, *FPC* had settled on the combination – Sinclair, Berton, broadcaster Kennedy and announcer Davis – which came to define the show itself: Davis, the blandly obliging ringleader; Berton, the erudite hypernationalist; Kennedy, the calmly intelligent voice of reason; and Sinclair, the bekilted, crotchety loose cannon. (Sinclair's most famous on-air outrages included asking Olympic swimmer Elaine Tanner if menstruation dulled her championship performance, lecturing feminist Kate Millett on circumcision and wondering why radical priest Daniel Berrigan wore a crucifix around his neck instead of a noose or an electric chair: "Why not use a similar symbol to start a new religion?" That indelicate tongue was stilled by death, and only by death, in 1984.)

The problem was, once installed as a prime-time public broadcasting institution in the mid-sixties, *FPC* ossified. Only the Reaper could pull Sinclair from the seat he'd held since 1957, and Kennedy, Davis and Berton remained in place until the 1995 cancellation. Sinclair was replaced by the similarly sensitive Allan Fotheringham in 1984, and Jack Webster was added shortly thereafter. Thus, as the panelists aged and the format froze, so did the audience. At the time it went off the air, the audience had fallen to a half-million or so loyal viewers. And, as it was by then long an "institution" or a "tradition," the CBC

Malcolm X stumps the panel, 1965

The Fab Four: (left to right) Sinclair, Berton, Kennedy, Davis

was more likely to drop *Mr. Dressup* than dick with *Front Page Challenge*. It was this fundamental paradox of "institutionalism" – the self-strangulating contradiction between evolution and preservation in electronic media – which, according to one *FPC* programmer, eventually sealed the show's demise.

In a hilarious article published in *Saturday Night* a few months after its cancellation, Terry Gould recalled the attempts made by certain *FPC* staffers to juice up and age down the show – which had a premise that could easily still be kept cooking – by changing the panelists.

Sinclair's most famous on-air outrages included asking Olympic swimmer Elaine Tanner if menstruation dulled her championship performance.

"Quite simply terrified of risking a grey-power boycott," wrote Gould, the CBC left *FPC* to simply sink into the tar pits of institutional broadcasting. Gould recalls one latter-day incident where Pierre Berton began blasting country-and-western singer Lisa Brokop, who the seventysomething author had clearly never heard of before that day, for changing "a good Canadian accent to a Tennessee accent" when she sang. "You do it because you're down in Nashville listening to those guys talk in that phoney accent!," Berton inexplicably railed at the stunned 21-year-old Brokop. Wrote Gould of the incident: "Anyone between eighteen and thirty-four who might have been watching the show would probably never tune in again."

No more *Front Page Challenge*? No problem.

The Toughest Challenge Winston Churchill's Kids Drop In

Although hundreds of "challengers" appeared on *FPC* during its 38 years, there is unanimous consent as to which mystery guest was the worst. Absolutely and unequivocally, this distinction goes to Randolph Churchill: insufferable son of Winston, columnist of London's *Evening Standard* and boozehound extraordinaire. It was 1958, very early in the show's record-setting run. After showing up 20 minutes late for his taping, the wobbly, scotch-soaked Churchill was ushered into a backstage press conference.

Randolph: "I was told that I'd have a chance to get a drink before we went on the air. Where is it?"

Producer: "We're having it brought in, sir."

Randolph: "It's taking a long time."

Producer: "Well yes, sir, it is, but the liquor laws in this part of the world just don't permit you to carry a glass out of a bar and into..."

Second Producer (chiming in): "It's on the way from my house, sir. My wife's bringing a bottle."

Randolph: "What are all these people doing here? Aren't they the press?"

Producer: "Well yes, sir, this is a press conference. You said..."

Randolph: "Well, this is hardly the place for this sort of thing. Don't you think they could leave while we discuss this?"

After pinching a female production assistant, Churchill ultimately stumbled onto the set to tape his segment. The panelists guessed his identity in two minutes, but at the four-minute time limit they still hadn't guessed his "headline" about the 1943 Teheran Conference: "Big Three Guarantee Victory." After the show, Churchill addressed the hastily reconvened press conference backstage:

Randolph: "Those were dull questions. If the panel had only asked the right questions, I'd have given them some news."

Reporter: "Why don't you tell us now?"

Randolph: "No. I'll save it for my column back home. You had your chance. I think I will leave this place, signing myself, 'Yours truly, disgusted.'"

Producer: (as Randolph was leaving the press conference to catch his 10:20 p.m. plane to London) "Never again. Never. Never."

Just how lame was Churchill? Well, let's put it this way: Fred Davis's ulcers started to bleed. Yes, that's right. Anglo-Canada's king of cool, the unflappable king of conciliation, the guy who could smooth over Gordon Sinclair's worst breaches of etiquette, started bleeding internally during Randolph Churchill's segment.

Chances are good that the genial host's tummy started to churn again in 1975. That's when Randolph's equally soused sister, Sarah, was booked to appear on *FPC*. As Gordon Sinclair so diplomatically put it, she "wasn't much better. Just before airtime, we found her outside the hotel directing traffic in the pouring rain." After several pots of coffee, Sarah had sobered up enough to go on the air. Ironically, her front-page story was "World Commemorates 100th Anniversary of Winston Churchill's Birth." It was the last time one of Sir Winston's kids appeared on *Front Page Challenge*. Fred Davis's ulcers just couldn't handle another Churchill.

The Sixty-Four Dollar Question
Canadian Game Shows

In the grand pantheon of Canadian achievements in pop culture, it's an oft-overlooked but telling fact that Canucks make most excellent game-show hosts. Indeed, of the three men whom many would cite as the most popular U.S. game-show hosts of the last 30 years – *The Price is Right*'s Bob Barker, *Let's Make a Deal*'s Monty Hall and *Jeopardy!*'s Alex Trebek – two (Hall and Trebek) were born in the Dominion; moreover, Canuck quizmasters Art Linkletter, Mike Darow and Al Hamel each had several U.S. gigs.

It's no coincidence that Canucks have achieved such exalted status in the realm of buzzers and bouncing contestants. Step back and consider the idea of the Canadian as game-show host, and it begins to make sense. The game-show host's role comprises certain characteristics Canadians have long tended to demonstrate. Like the professional newsreader, a field in which Canadians excel, the game-show host's role is to be the unflappably calm, professionally disinterested guide through otherwise chaotic events: think of Peter Mansbridge's glacial demeanour as he delivers the day's daily carnage, then think of Monty Hall's imperial cool as he points his mike squarely at a shrieking woman dressed as a giant gourd. Moreover, the game-show host's role is basically

that of an impartial diplomatic conciliator: someone who reminds us what the rules are, who never loses his cool and who facilitates the fun to be had by others. Who takes selfless professional satisfaction out of knowing his guests had a good time. In that context, Canadian success in the field of hosting game shows is less surprising than the fact that anyone from anywhere else ever bothered. Canada is, after all, the peacekeeping conciliator of the postwar world: the line to be drawn between Lester Pearson and Alex Trebek may be straighter than you think.

In addition to producing a disproportionate number of genial hosts, Canadian have also displayed a voracious appetite for home-grown game/quiz shows. Even though the genre has always been consigned to the production-values bargain bin in this country, viewers have loyally tuned in. While prime-time game shows in places like Italy, Japan and the U.S. may regularly draw viewers in the millions, those numbers can't be divorced

from the fact that these countries tend to have the resources available to produce the slickest schlock possible: as pure show, in other words, these programs deliver. In Canada, on the other hand, game shows have not only been notoriously cheap, many have involved practically no sense of "show." It's hard to imagine a more static game show than, for instance, *Front Page Challenge*, in which an unchanging panel of professional contestants guessed the names of hidden guests for 38 consecutive seasons. Or, how about *This Is The Law*, in which another unchanging panel of professional contestants attempt to identify arcane misdemeanours? Even the jackpot-fantasy allure of the splashier foreign game shows cannot account for Canadians' long-running interest in our home-grown versions: one of the things no reasonably sentient Canadian couch spud could fail to notice was the often hilarious discrepancy between what you stood to win on something like *The Dating Game* – an all-expenses-paid, chaperoned trip to

← Winnipeg tribute to home-town host

Monty Hall on *Let's Make a Deal*

Honolulu, for example – versus the booty at stake on *Headline Hunters*, where even the winning of an electric toothbrush was considered a rare and impressive event. Most were lucky to win a $25 Loblaws gift certificate.

The quaint but paltry nature of Canadian game-show hauls can't help coming to mind when one looks back on one of the more fascinating minor chapters in Canadian game-show history. Call it the movie Robert Redford will never make – *Quiz Show 2: Exile in Canada*. It was the late 1960s, and Screen Gems Canada had brought Jack Barry and Dan Enright, deposed host and producer, respectively, of the infamously scandalized *Twenty-One* program, north to produce game shows. (The two men had fallen into disrepute after giving answers in advance to popular contestant Charles Van Doren, in order to prolong his stay on the show.) Enright had been forced to appear before a congressional subcommit-

Canada is the peacekeeping conciliator of the postwar world: the line to be drawn between Lester Pearson and Alex Trebek may be straighter than you think.

tee, and Canada was the only place the two – once high-profile players in American network television – could work after *Twenty-One* went down in disgrace. Working alternately in Toronto and Montreal, Enright and Barry collaborated on such assembly-line game-show enterprises as *The Little People* and *Photo Finish*. Imagine what it must have been like for Jack Barry, who once could offer up to $64,000 to contestants as host of one of the highest-rated game shows in American broadcasting history, to find himself stranded north of the 49th Parallel, trying to whip up some semblance of in-studio frenzy over *Photo Finish*'s top jackpot of

$256. Imagine, too, how he felt when he realized that these eager Canuck contestants considered themselves lucky to get it. He must have felt a long way indeed from his home in Pacific Palisades, California.

The point is, contestants on low-budget Canadian game shows not only appeared to feel lucky if they won half of this week's grocery money, they were perfectly content. As much as one watched *Headline Hunters* or *Definition* or the ultra-low-rent Canadian version of *Beat the Clock*, one never heard an expression of disappointment or dismay over the dimestore nature of the prizes. No, if Canadians played and watched game shows – and no matter how cheap or silly the show, Canadians watched anyway – they seemed to do so for the sheer pleasure of it. Leave it to other countries to use greed, gluttony, sex and exhibitionism as dressing to beef up a game show's allure. Canadians needed no such excuse: we watched our own game shows for the pure, simple love of them.

Alex Trebek on *Jeopardy!*

A Comparative Guide to Canadian Game-Show Hosts

Monty Hall

Born: Winnipeg, Manitoba, 1925.

Game-Show Specialty: Wheeling and dealing with contestants dressed as carrots and other forms of produce. (*Let's Make A Deal,* 1963-1976, 1980-1981, 1984-1986.)

Brush With Greatness: In 1962, Hall was coproducing a U.S. game show called *Your First Impression.* Richard Nixon, then campaigning for governor of California, had taped a mystery-guest appearance. Hall had to phone Tricky Dick to inform him that NBC was going to delay airing the segment, in order to avoid appearing to favour one of the candidates. Nixon went ballistic.

Personal Trademark: His ability to generate hysteria in contestants. Guests on *Let's Make A Deal* would occasionally forget their names or wet their pants.

Literary Effort: Hall wrote his autobiography, *Emcee Monty Hall,* in 1973. In one rather poignant chapter, he describes his ill-fated attempt to become a Las Vegas song-and-dance man. In an exceptionally pathetic scene, Danny Thomas consoles Hall after the ex-Winnipegger has played to an almost empty house.

Game-Show Résumé: U.S.: *Let's Make A Deal, Split Second, It's Anybody's Guess, Keep Talking, Strike It Rich, Video Village.* (Hall was also a substitute host on *Twenty-One,* the famous "scandal show" featured in the film *Quiz Show.*)

Signs of Superstardom: Parodied by fellow Canadian Tommy Chong in the immortal Cheech and Chong skit "Let's Make A Dope Deal." As the most popular game-show host of the seventies, Hall made numerous guest appearances on dreck like *The Odd Couple, The Flip Wilson Show* and *The Dean Martin Show.*

Honest Self-Appraisal: "Look, don't judge me against *Jane Eyre* or the New York City Ballet. Just judge me as to how I do as an entertainer. And I do entertain. Don't give me an Oscar, Emmy or Pulitzer Prize. Just give me respect as an outstanding performer in my field."

Jim Perry

Born: Camden, New Jersey, 1933.

Game-Show Specialty: Low-rent Canadiana (*Headline Hunters,* 1972-1983, *Definition,* 1974-1990)

Brush With Greatness: During the fifties, Perry briefly worked in New York as Sid Caesar's straight man.

Personal Trademark: During his peak years on the air, Perry changed his hair colour (from black to grey to black, etc.) with puzzling regularity.

Literary Effort: In 1991, Perry became the first-ever game-show host to write a memoir of "spiritual awakening." It was called *The Sleeper Awakes: A Journey to Self-Awareness.* During a promotional tour for the book, Perry would recite ancient haiku.

Game-Show Résumé: Canada: *Headline Hunters, Definition, Fractured Phrases, Words and Music, Money Makers, It's Your Move, Eye Bet.*

U.S.: *Card Sharks, Sale Of The Century.*

Signs of Superstardom: Frequently called upon to host the Miss Canada pageant.

Honest Self-Appraisal: "I'm a great believer in human dignity.

I try to bring out the best in the contestants, not try to make a fool of them."

Alex Trebek

Born: Sudbury, Ontario, 1940.

Game-Show Specialty: High-end egghead quiz shows. (*Jeopardy!,* 1984 to present)

Brush With Greatness: In 1973, fellow Canuck Alan (*Growing Pains*) Thicke, asked his pal Trebek to move to California to host a new game show he had developed: it was called *The Wizard of Odds.* Trebek accepted the invitation, and the rest is game-show history.

Personal Trademark: Looking mildly perturbed on *Jeopardy!* when Yanks screw up questions about Canadian geography.

Literary Effort: In 1990, Trebek cowrote *The Jeopardy! Book: The Answers, the Questions, the Facts, and the Stories of the Greatest Game Show in History.*

Game-Show Résumé: Canada: *Reach For The Top, Strategy, Pitfall.*

U.S.: *Jeopardy!, Battlestars, Classic Concentration, Double Dare, High Rollers, The $128,000 Question,*

Alex Trebek on *Reach for the Top* →

REACH FOR THE TOP

Party Game home team

Jim Perry and the *Definition* crew

The Wizard of Odds, Wheel of Fortune (occasional substitute host).

Signs of Superstardom: Jeopardy! is watched by between 15 and 20 million people each evening. As an instantly recognized cultural reference point, Trebek is in demand for tongue-in-cheek cameos in Hollywood product like *Cheers, White Men Can't Jump, Short Cuts, Dying Young* and *Rain Man.*

Honest Self-Appraisal: "If you're interested in opera you want to wind up at La Scala or at the Met in New York. If you're interested in show business, you have to wind up in Hollywood. I'm where I want to be."

Canadian Game-Show Hall of Fame

Reach For The Top (CBC, 1961-1985)
The high-school-brainiac quiz show debuted in Vancouver in 1961, and was eventually produced in several locales across the country. In the late sixties, a young Alex Trebek hosted the Toronto version. After one unruly taping session, the host was confronted by a disgruntled group of high schoolers who felt that he had somehow stiffed their team. "I was genuinely frightened," Trebek recalled in 1971. "They were like a lynch mob. But one of their teachers moved in and brought them to heel."

Party Game (Syndicated, 1969-1980)
A daily charades show produced at CHCH-TV in Hamilton, Ontario, featuring host Bill Walker and the "home" team of Dinah Christie, Billy (*Hilarious House of Frightenstein*) Van and "Captain" Jack

Duffy. Each week the regulars would take on a different team of three celebrity guests. The set was a prototypical seventies rumpus/rec room, with a couch for each squad. Compared to other stodgy Canadian game shows, *Party Game* was a veritable Bacchanalian revel, a cauldron of barely repressed sexual tension. Awash in a sea of impossibly loud polyester, the boisterous players would climb all over the couches, throw cushions and double entendres at each other and have fun in an exuberant, distinctly un-Canadian manner. Definitely sexier than *Front Page Challenge.*

Beat the Clock (CTV, 1969-1974)
A made-in-Montreal version of the long-running American game show, which featured contestants trying to perform a variety of goofy stunts within an allotted time limit. These stunts invariably involved props like breakable dishes or exploding balloons. During its Canadian incarnation, *Beat the Clock* introduced a weekly celebrity guest – usually an American – to help liven up the proceedings. Thus we were treated to the sight of people like Cab Calloway, Frankie Avalon and ubiquitous Canadian game-show presence Marty ("Hello 'dere!") Allen doing wacky things like tossing tennis balls into a basket. Hosted by Jack Narz (1969-1972) and Gene Wood (1972-1974), two enthusiastic Americans who never seemed to grow weary of the inane high jinks.

This Is The Law (CBC, 1971-1976)
While the Yanks were giddily handing out dream homes and luxury automobiles on greed-fests like *Let's Make A Deal,* Canadians were producing dreary, civics-lesson shows like *This Is The Law.* Yes, only in authority-loving Canada would you find a game show based on arcane legal trivia. *This Is The Law* was moderated by Austin

Willis, and featured a panel consisting of Larry Solway, Susan Keller, Bill Charlton and Hart Pomerantz (a lawyer himself, and Lorne Michaels's former comedy partner). Every week they looked at three short, silent films featuring Paul Soles as the goofy "Lawbreaker." In each hammy scenario, he would commit some incredibly obscure misdemeanour, like building a six-foot fence in Regina when the limit in that city was five feet. The panel would spend a couple of minutes trying to figure out what minor law Soles had broken, and then move on to the next film. A responsible time was had by all.

Headline Hunters (CTV, 1972-1983)
Long-running CTV game show hosted by Jim Perry. A bargain-basement version of *Front Page Challenge, Headline Hunters* attracted 1.5 million viewers a week in the mid-seventies. This made it the third most-watched Canadian show on CTV, behind *Stars On Ice* and *The Bobby Vinton Show.* (How's that for a frightening prime-time lineup?)

Definition (CTV, 1974-1990)
Basically, a TV version of the old Hangman game. Hosted by Canadian game-show stalwart Jim Perry, *Definition* featured a pair of two-player teams (one celebrity/one contestant) involved in a languid battle for word-puzzle supremacy. Over the years, notables ranging from Kitty Carlisle to Martin Short made guest appearances. Although the prizes were definitely low-rent (Hanes panty hose, Shaeffer pen-and-pencil sets, lady shavers), the show produced one important cultural legacy: in 1991, Toronto rappers Dream Warriors sampled the show's Quincy Jones–penned theme song on their hit single "My Definition of a Boombastic Jazz Style."

Life is a Highway to Hell
Goin' Down the Road

The best-known English-Canadian movie of its era is about a couple of guys who drive from Cape Breton to a grim destiny in Toronto. It's no surprise that the road holds such allure for North American story-tellers. Considering that the first several chapters of the continent's colonized history are largely accounts of white people moving uncertainly through a strange and threatening landscape, one understands why the open road would become such an enduring narrative concern.

This preoccupation applies not only to literature, but also to movies, both American and Canadian. Which lands us smack at the intersection where, in terms of Canadian/American cultural identity, things get real interesting. While American road movies, from *Stagecoach* and *The Wizard of Oz*, to *Easy Rider* and *Thelma and Louise* – even *Star Trek* and *Natural Born Killers* – reflect the country's fundamental faith in its destiny by promoting the idea of the road as a pathway to enlightenment, the Canadian counterpart looks at the map rather more skeptically. In Canadian movies (as opposed to Canadian road songs, which tend to be upbeat), the road tends to be a pipeline to disappointment; a confirmation that, in Canada, there's lots of space but nowhere to go. This idea had been kicking around in Canadian literature for over a century (Susanna Moodie's *Roughing It in the Bush*, 1852), and in movies for a decade (Don Owen's *Nobody Waved Goodbye*, 1964), but it was never as clearly or distinctly articulated as

in August 1970, when a raw, low-budget little Canadian movie called *Goin' Down the Road* was released in Toronto, the city where it was made. Directed by Donald Shebib, Hogtown-born UCLA grad and a film-school classmate of Francis Ford Coppola's, *Road* is regarded less as a movie than a primordial national cultural text. Yet, ask most Canadians of a certain age if they've seen it, and they're more likely to remember the hilarious *SCTV* parody of the movie than the movie itself. (That's the one where hosers-deluxe John Candy and Joe Flaherty leave the East, hooting for "doctorin' and lawyerin'" jobs in Toronto.) The story of Joey and Pete, two luckless Cape Bretoners (parts impeccably rendered by actors Paul Bradley and Doug McGrath) whose dreams of fiscal and sexual nirvana in Toronto are lost in the grey canyons of the city, *Road* not only became a paradigm of a certain kind of home-brewed docudramatic pessimism, it paved the way for English-Canadian cinema of the decade to follow. During the 1970s,

working-class losers would take Joey and Pete's lead and hit the road, the skids or both, in virtual droves: *The Far Shore*, *Wedding in White*, *Paperback Hero*, *Why Shoot the Teacher*, *Montreal Main* – English-Canadian movies of the seventies comprised what amounted to a rush-hour turnpike of despair.

In pop-cultural terms, *Road* deserves a hearty Red Cap salute for other reasons, as well. Despite its lack of overt hockey references, it remains the ultimate hoser-cult primer, the wellspring from which all other artifacts of English-Canadian hoser culture, in movies, music and comedy, can be traced. The film represents the first hoser-buddy team, and establishes the dumb-and-dumber dynamic that would characterize all subsequent hoser and hoser-derivative buddy teams, from Bob and Doug, to Wayne and Garth, to Ren and Stimpy and, yes, *Dumb and Dumber* itself. It established the Canadian male as one of the most persistently impotent and unappealing characters in world cinema – a trait which endures to

Goin' Down The Road: Doug McGrath (Pete) and Paul Bradley (Joey)   Pete and Joey: Beer-Loving Proto-Hosers

this very day, and which has probably taken an incalculable toll on the collective national ideal of masculinity. Moreover, in stark contrast to the Hollywood model of holy heroism, it promoted losing as a distinctive national right (if not rite), thus helping to distinguish Us from Them in unmistakable terms: they're winners, we're wieners. Perhaps most importantly, however, *Road* represented a particularly visible affirmation of the low-budget, gritty independent movie as the standard of Canadian movie production – a standard which still defines the industry's best nearly three decades later.

In any other country but this, the movie might have ignited some long-smouldering careers: Shebib continues to work in Toronto, but mostly in television. Doug McGrath, who played Pete, after appearing in Bob Clark's 1975 proto-slasher *Black Christmas*, has appeared on the periphery of a number of Clint Eastwood productions, most visibly in 1985's *Pale Rider*. Jayne Eastwood, who played Bradley's gum-chewing waitress wife, and who employs such state-of-the-art hoserisms in the movie as "samwidges," "Kraft Dinner" and "Jeez," continues to work in TV drama and commercials, and is probably most affectionately remembered for her truly sporting appearance parodying herself in *SCTV's Road* takeoff. As for Paul (Joey) Bradley, who spent his brief moment of hometown celebrity being squired around Toronto in a rented limo (a moment Shebib himself recorded in the sadly funny 1972 documentary *Born Hustler*) – by 1995, when the *Globe and Mail* attempted to seek him out for an article on the film's twenty-fifth anniversary, the actor couldn't be found. Hit the road apparently, and never came back.

A Selective Guide to English Canada's Coolest Movies

Goin' Down the Road (1970) Don Shebib's shaggy, bargain-basement 1970 account of two hopeless Cape Bretoners (Paul Bradley, Doug McGrath) hitting the mean streets of Toronto is as close to an archetypal-Canadian viewing experience the English half of this country has to offer. Essential, if you can find it.

Black Christmas (1975) Shot on the University of Toronto campus in the dead of a Canadian winter, this Bob (*Porky's*) Clark–directed account of a sorority house under psycho siege may be pure formula on one level – and, with its faceless killer offing promiscuous girls, it anticipates the entire dreary *Friday the 13th* cycle – yet it's directed with a perverse verve and intelligence which hasn't dimmed a wit in the ensuing decades. A movie that enjoys toying with you and knows how. With a cast made in CanCon heaven: Art Hindle, Andrea Martin, Margot Kidder and Doug McGrath.

Videodrome (1983) In retrospect, this open-and-shut commercial bomb now seems one of the key Canadian movies of the 1980s. A deliberately indecipherable and disorienting attempt to fuse the body/media meld of McLuhan with the post-Watergate conspiracy thriller, David Cronenberg's wildest movie is also his most outrageous and intellectually ambitious. We've watched it a dozen times, and we still have no idea what goes on at the end. Moreover, we consider that a good thing.

Dead Ringers (1988) After the deliciously icky, blockbuster excesses of *The Fly*, David Cronenberg shifted into an altogether other realm of visceral creepiness with this one. Based loosely on the true story of twin gynecologists who died violently and mysteriously in New York in the 1970s, *Dead Ringers* is as much a study in the pathology of male desire as it is a horror movie of almost chilling beauty.

The Falls (1991) Former journalist Kevin McMahon's feature documentary profile of his hometown of Niagara Falls, Ontario, certainly ain't no sunshine sketch. McMahon's mesmerizing study of the toxic decay of the Honeymoon Capital is nothing less than a harrowing indictment of western civilization's suicidal arrogance over nature. Disturbing, powerful and beautiful.

Careful (1992) Winnipegger Guy Maddin's third feature may be his most narratively straightforward, but that's like saying this Jackson Pollock painting is a little more representational than that one. Set on a ridiculously remote and precarious Alpine village where, among other bizarre things, the vocal cords of sheep are severed to prevent avalanche, it's really a hysterically overwrought study in sexual repression. Roughing it in the bush indeed.

Clearcut (1992) Made by the expatriate Polish film-maker Richard Bugajski, this is a flawed but still devastating account of the limits of white liberalism in the arena of Native land claims. Graham Greene, as the violent and possibly spectral trickster figure who kidnaps and tortures white people, is here playing the nightmare *doppelgänger* to his Native nice guy in *Dances With Wolves*.

Exotica (1994) Atom Egoyan's most successful movie is hardly your conventional crowd-pleaser. Set largely in an opulently overdecorated strip club patronized by some of the saddest-looking men this side of death row, the movie is a veritable minefield of subterranean motivation, repressed desire and angular relationships. As compelling as it is perplexing, and thoroughly original, to boot.

The Suburbanators (1995) Seven guys, divided into three groups, try to fill up a typically vacant suburban afternoon in Calgary with quests of varying banality: three Iranian-Canadians attempt to liberate some gear from a really pissed ex-girlfriend's apartment, two others go for a haircut, and the others try vainly to score some reefer without benefit of a car. Calgarian Gary Burns's debut feature is the most promising first feature by a Canadian director to come along in years.

Doom Daddy Lorne Greene

As Pa Cartwright, the benevolent patriarch of the Ponderosa, Lorne Greene became the most popular father figure in TV history. In effect, *Bonanza* (1959–1973) taught the world what Canadians already knew.

Before becoming possibly the most famous Canadian on the planet at the show's mid-sixties peak (*Bonanza* was watched weekly by a quarter-billion viewers around the world), Greene was already one of the most famous in the Dominion. Greene was born in Ottawa in 1915, the only son of a Russian-born shoe repairman. He enrolled in chemical engineering at Queen's University in Kingston in 1933, switched to modern languages, and upon graduation won a scholarship to attend New York's renowned Neighborhood Playhouse School of Theatre. He returned to Canada in 1939, just in time for his career to be catapulted by the Second World War. Unable to find acting jobs, he took a newsreading job at the CBC, and within three months the impossibly oaken-toned, 24-year-old Greene was reading the national news. Arguably, Greene was the first of Canada's long and distinct line of celebrity anchors, and his ubiquitous daily dispatches, which were transmitted over movie-theatre loudspeakers as well as radios, earned him two weighty nicknames: The Voice of Canada, and The Voice of Doom.

Soon, neither his notoriety nor ambitions could be contained by wireless transmissions over the public airwaves, leaving him poised to become one of our few national celebrities to successfully cross over from institutional to commercial notoriety. After leaving the CBC over a nasty dispute concerning extra-curricular voice-over work with the National Film Board, Greene went quite successfully private.

He opened a short-lived but influential school of radio broadcasting on Jarvis Street across from the old CBC building in Toronto, voiced the first Canadian-television test broadcast from the same city's Exhibition Stadium and eventually devised a stopwatch for newsreaders which, by running backwards, let them know how much airtime was left. It was on a trip to peddle the gadget, while walking through New York's Rockefeller Center, that Greene ran into Canada's most successful ex-pat TV producer Fletcher (*Front Row Center)* Markle. The latter, a former instructor at Greene's radio academy, thought his old boss would be perfect for a couple of roles on the anthology series *Studio One*, and thus was Lorne Greene's path to the Ponderosa paved.

Like many TV totems of his era, Greene was not much of an actor, but that mattered far less to the medium at that moment than being an archetype, which Greene, with an effortlessly authoritarian aura much in demand during the Eisenhower era, was capable of being in spades. ("The only way I can work as an actor," he told *Maclean's* in 1967, "is by being me. I happen to be Lorne Greene.") During the pre-Ponderosa years, on Broadway and television and in the movies (where he debuted alongside a callow Paul Newman in the legendary 1954 sword 'n slipper stinker *The Silver Chalice*), he prepared for Pa Cartwright by playing a series of men firmly in control: Oliver Cromwell, Sir Walter Raleigh, Ludwig van Beethoven.

In 1959, for the reasons cited above, Lorne Greene, who'd never ridden a horse or fired a gun in his life, landed the part of Ben Cartwright on *Bonanza*. A show whose global popularity (as television popularity tends to do) flew in the face of taste, intelligence and dramatic logic – it was, after all, a wholesome drama about a wealthy, middle-aged widower with three grown but dependent sons from three separate dead mothers – *Bonanza* made Lorne Greene one of the most famous people in the global village by the early 1960s. Curiously, it was a fame that would stubbornly refuse to expand outside the Ponderosa's studio corral or the square confines of the tube itself. Apart from the fluke chart-topping success of the spoken-word cowboy-kitsch hit "Ringo" in 1964, none of Greene's subsequent movies or TV appearances, as fatherly figures facing Armageddon in disaster-movie disasters like 1974's *Earthquake* and 1975's *Tidal Wave*, or behind the bridge of the *Star Wars/Trek* clone *Battlestar Galactica* (1979), would match the totemic identification sparked by the comfortingly patriarchal figure of Ben Cartwright.

Before he died in 1987, at the age of 72, a very wealthy man, Lorne Greene's most successful latter-day vehicle returned him to a variation on the role which had made him the Voice of Canada in the first place. And no, we're not referring to the Alpo commercials, but to *Lorne Greene's New Wilderness*. On that syndicated television program, which ran from 1982 to 1987, the eat-or-be-eaten world of TV nature was presided over by the majestically stentorian tones of the same man who once commanded the attention of his fellow citizens so profoundly he left them unsure whether to call him Pa, Doom or the country itself.

The Delegate from Ponderosa
How Pa Cartwright Rustled the U.N.

It was a sombre day in the United Nations in June 1967. The U.N. Security Council had been in intense emergency deliberation all the previous night about an event in the Middle East that would come to be called the Six Day War.

That's why there wasn't much talking when Pa Cartwright walked in and moved toward a reserved front-row seat in the visitors' gallery. Accompanied by Sidney Freifeld, then serving at Canada's mission to the United Nations, Pa – known less widely as Lorne Greene – was making a visit to the U.N.

Freifeld, who was accustomed to doing things like passing the commissary salt to Sir Anthony Eden and chatting up Fidel Castro in the lounge, had expected that His Deep-Voiced Charge would pass quietly through the United Nations, particularly considering the grave implications of the global emergency at hand. But as he escorted Greene to his seat, a buzz started to ripple through the chamber like an electric current carried through the ubiquitous, U.N.-issue headphones. Delegates began to look up and point at the visitor, their normally taciturn expressions beaming in starstruck recognition. Locked in their soundproof glass booths, the ranks of translators started frantically gesticulating to each other about the new arrival in the balcony. U Thant, the secretary-general of the United Nations, whom many suspected was a man utterly unburdened by emotion, was actually seen to grin like a kid when he spotted the patriarch of the Ponderosa.

Soon the visitors' gallery was swarmed with delegates who'd left their seats in order to get Pa Cartwright's autograph on their Security Council agendas. Freifeld was asked by fellow Canadian delegates whether the Ottawa-born cowboy star might join them on the chamber floor, until Freifeld reminded them that the suggestion violated one of the strictest rules of U.N. protocol. Later, in the commissary, the world's most famous cowboy father figure was surrounded by even more delegates desperate to get Greene's signature on any piece of paper they could grab. Waiters, hostesses and busboys closed in with copies of the menu for the actor to sign. Many years later, Freifeld noted that he'd never enjoyed such immaculately attentive service in the U.N. commissary "before or since."

After lunch, Freifeld finally managed to pull the besieged actor to a quiet corridor, where two men happened to be heading their way: Nicolai Federenko, the Soviet ambassador to the U.N., and his boss, no less a personage than the USSR's unsmiling foreign minister Andrei Gromyko. Seeing Greene, Federenko just about fainted on the spot, but recovered and bounded toward the silver-haired actor with his Security Council agenda outstretched before him.

"My dear Mr. Bonanza, my dear delegate from Ponderosa," Federenko gushed as the astonished Gromyko stood by. "I want you to know that for years you have been one of my own family. You are with us in our family living room in New York. You are one of our very own. You must sign something for my children."

Greene obliged of course, and the two prominent Soviets proceeded to the council chamber. Freifeld then escorted the actor from the building, and it was back to business at the U.N. As for the war in the Middle East, it was over in six days, perhaps in time for the delegates to enjoy an evening at home watching *Bonanza*.

"The Voice of Doom" →

Pure Prairie League
The Guess Who/BTO Legacy

To be among the countless thousands of radio-addicted Canadian suburban-mall rats during the first half of the 1970s was to be convinced that Canada had secured a place on the pop airwaves which was only exceeded by its international dominion – spectacularly certified by '72's catalytic Russkie-stomping – of hockey. And this conviction, naive or premature though it might have been, was facilitated in no small part by the seemingly unstoppable singles juggernaut that was the legacy of Winnipeg's aggressively nationalistic, hoser-rock prototype The Guess Who and its riff-churning, industrial-strength spawn, Bachman-Turner Overdrive. From 1970 through 1975, a period roughly bracketed by the release of The Guess Who's jingoistic anthem "American Woman" and BTO's last top-ten album release *Four Wheel Drive*, Canadian rock not only acted the two-fisted heavyweight global contender, it never seemed more Canadian.

BTO with gold records

The story begins in Winnipeg in the early 1960s, when Randy Bachman, a Chet Atkins–worshipping teenage guitarist, joined Chad Allan's hot local group, Allan's Silvertones. (As Bachman would sing with ex-'Pegger Neil Young nearly 30 years later, on the solo single "Prairie Town": "*Portage and Main, Fifty below/ You stay inside and rock and roll!*"). When Allan left to attend university in 1966, his co-pilot status was assumed by a Jim Morrison wannabe named Burton Cummings who had recently joined the group, and the die was cast. Its name originally designed to spark speculation that this was some incognito British supergroup, The Guess Who spent 1967 and 1968 gaining national recognition on CBC's after-school show *Let's Go* before scoring chart success with the smash single "These Eyes" in 1969. This was followed by the serial hits "Laughing," "Undun" and "No Time." Then came the fuzz-toned riff-monster "American Woman," whose misogynistically framed anti-Yank stance ("*American woman stay away from me/American woman mama let me be*") in no way hindered its fuel-injected flight up the American charts; on the contrary, this slick slice of hosehead chauvinism cracked the U.S. market wide-open for the band, which would maintain an unprecedented hold on it for at least three years, right about when Bachman-Turner Overdrive was ready to muscle in and take over. In the meantime,

If you listened to pop radio in the early seventies, it was easy to believe that Burton Cummings was the voice of Canada.

if you listened to pop radio in the early seventies, it was easy to believe that Burton Cummings was the voice of Canada.

It was after the 1970 release of the *American Woman* LP that Bachman, a practising Mormon who has traded cat-calls with Cummings for more than three decades, decided to leave the band and go solo. The impact of this move was twofold: first, it allowed Cummings to take over The Guess Who, which prospered temporarily by shifting from hard rock to radio-friendly pop balladry; second, it allowed Bachman to build the no-frills, meat'n spuds rock machine he'd always dreamed of fronting. The timing, as it turned out, was fortuitous. After a failed solo album and two stiffs from the Chad Allan/Bachman–fronted Brave Belt, Bachman, with portly bellower C. F. "Fred" Turner, formed Bachman-Turner Overdrive. After being rejected by no less than 25 labels, BTO, as it was inevitably monikered, finally found a happy home with Mercury, where it hit big-time paydirt in 1974 with a single from its second album, "Takin' Care of Business." With serendipitous symmetry, and no small degree of spiteful irony, this success poised BTO to take over as Canada's leading singles band just as The Guess Who found itself in sharp radio freefall, no doubt thanks to such odious novelty tunes as "Clap for the Wolfman." For the next two years, BTO's brand of hook-heavy, badly sung blue-collar raunch blared out of discerning eight-track car stereos across the continent: "Gimme Your Money Please," "Let it Ride," "You Ain't Seen Nothing Yet," "Roll on Down the Highway." With its incessant trucker imagery and heavy-metal sonic gear-crunching, BTO didn't so much as lay down tracks as pour hot asphalt.

By the end of the decade, both bands were long past their glory days, yet, betraying an authentic hoser impervi-ousness to fashion and popular opinion,

Recommended Listening:

The Guess Who: Best of the Guess Who, Volume I (1971), Best of the Guess Who, Volume II (1974)
The Guess Who was the greatest AM hit machine in Canadian history, and their tastiest prairie tunes are available on these two volumes. Volume I basically documents the Bachman-Cummings years, culling sublime chart-toppers like "These Eyes," "Undun," "Laughing" and "No Sugar Tonight." Volume II is weaker, but still contains some downright impressive vocal work by Cummings on "Sour Suite," "Albert Flasher" and "Runnin' Back to Saskatoon."

Bachman-Turner Overdrive: Best of BTO (So Far) (1976)
BTO took their name from a trucking magazine called *Overdrive*. It's appropriate, then, that this compilation contains all the hoser truckin' hits one could ever want: "Roll on Down the Highway," "Four Wheel Drive" and "Let It Ride." Not to mention the twin peaks of their chart ascent, "Takin' Care of Business" and "You Ain't Seen Nothing Yet."

Randy Bachman: Any Road (1993)
A return to form for Bachman, worthwhile simply because of "Prairie Town," a blistering exercise in Winnipeg nostalgia with ex-'Peg pal Neil Young.

TCB: The King Meets BTO

After Elvis Presley's Memphis Mafia, inspired by the BTO song "Takin' Care of Business" took the acronym TCB as its motto, the boys from Winnipeg were actually summoned to Las Vegas for a royal audience in 1975. Although Randy Bachman didn't attend, the rest of the boys enjoyed their two-hour visit with the King. Naturally, the conversation revolved around the standard Presley themes of cars, girls and firearms.

neither had refused to go away completely. Original member Jim Kale re-formed and toured extensively with a Bachman and Cummings–less Guess Who, while Randy and Burton briefly put aside their squabbling for a 1983 reunion, after which they resumed squabbling. Meanwhile, the same kind of litigious battles have also marred the post-glory years for BTO, with Randy (who toured under the name Bachman-Turner Overdrive) at one point suing brother Robbie (who toured under the name BTO) for rights to use the band's wheel logo. Fortunately for all involved, most of the music of the past is still good enough to crank up and drown out the bickering in the present.

Reviewing The Guess Who's atrocious *Flavours* album in 1974, the *Village Voice*'s Robert Christgau summed up the passing of the inspirational torch from Cummings to Bachman with characteristic laser precision: "The Burton Cummings part of this group always wanted it to be the Doors, Santana and Gary Puckett and the Union Gap all rolled into one. This rather monstrous goal has finally been realized. Personally, I always preferred the part that wanted to be Bachman-Turner Overdrive." Astoundingly, this was written a full decade before Cummings started recording such easy-listening atrocities as "Stand Tall" and "My Own Way To Rock."

American Woman, Stay Away From Me
Six Reasons Why The Guess Who Was the Ultimate Canadian Band

1. Rabid Anti-Americanism: Let's face it, "American Woman" is probably the most blatant dis of our southern neighbour in recording history. Who knows what prompted this misogynistic anti-Yankee *cri de coeur*? Perhaps it was the Vietnam War, maybe it was just an annoying American groupie. In 1996, Burton Cummings recalled writing the song on the spot during a concert at an Ontario curling rink. Looking out at the sea of "refreshingly innocent" female faces, he claims to have been thinking, "Canadian woman, I prefer you." Whatever the case, it went to number one in both Canada AND the States, and proved once and for all that Canadians don't want "war machines" or "ghetto scenes." Incidentally, the band was strongly advised not to perform the tune when they played their White House gig for renowned *Wheatfield Soul* enthusiast, Richard Nixon.

2. Promoted Canadian Products: The band's album titles – *Canned Wheat* and *Wheatfield Soul* – helped to raise the international profile of our popular prairie product.

3. Understood Canadian Iconography: Album cover for *Best of The Guess Who, Vol. 2* features a variety of hoser accoutrements, such as a flannel shirt, a Montreal Canadiens jersey (Ken Dryden's #29) and short-stubbed beer bottles. Moreover, the band's logo proudly displayed a beaver superimposed on our maple leaf flag.

4. Supported Fellow Canadian Artists: In Canada's Centennial year, the band recorded "Flying on the Ground is Wrong," a song by future grunge hero, Neil Young. Later on they recorded a tribute song called "Lightfoot," in which they argue that Gordon Lightfoot is an artist "painting Sistine masterpieces of pine and fir and backwoods." Lightfoot wasn't inspired to return the musical favour, and has yet to write a song praising The Guess Who or Bachman-Turner Overdrive.

5. Enjoyed Canadian Cuisine: Once recorded a song called "Maple Fudge." It just doesn't get any more Canadian than that.

6. Obsessed with Canadian Geography: In the middle of cutting a live album at Seattle's Paramount Theater, The Guess Who displayed their knowledge of Canadian place names in "Runnin' Back to Saskatoon." During the same concert, they also performed an homage to Cape Breton called "Glace Bay Blues." The band even released an album called *So Long Bannatyne – Hello My Chevrier Home*, a reference to band member Kurt Winter's move from a Bannatyne Avenue apartment in gritty downtown Winnipeg to a home on Chevrier Boulevard in the comparatively posh middle-class suburb, Fort Garry. In an era when many Canadian singers are loath to mention anything even remotely specific to Canada, you've got to admire The Guess Who: they were the hottest band in North America, yet they kept peppering their material with references to places like Medicine Hat.

Canadian Shield Who Asked Peter Gzowski To Save This Country, Anyway?

For several years now, in late summer, in certain corners of the Canadian media, the annual cliffhanger kicks in. Well, *curbhanger*, really, for the level of concern is, in public terms, actually pretty low. It is the time of year that CBC-Radio uberhost Peter Gzowski – who may be the only nonlegislative entity in the country to be so often called "a national institution" – is to renew his contract as host of the show *Globe and Mail* writer Bronwyn Drainie once called a "Canadian cultural miracle," *Morningside*. And each year, every year, there is some question as to whether the bearded, and gravel-voiced Gzowski will sign. That's when the nail-biting begins. For if there is any doubt that Gzowski, whose program consumes 20 hours of Canadian public airtime per week – three hours each weekday morning, plus one each evening – might not continue, then there is apparently ample reason to believe that the country itself, like Humpty Dumpty in a stiff breeze, will certainly teeter and smash.

This highly dubious assertion deserves close scrutiny. If *Morningside,* which is listened to by less than 15 percent of the entire nation each day, is all the glue we've got, we might as well be trying to bind the *Titanic* with Bondfast. But if the Galt, Ontario-raised former *Maclean's* editor is in fact the national linchpin, the semi-annual panic is then justified. If Gzowski, who in interviews annually seems to grow more wearied (as the broadcaster said after the 1995 contract-signing curbhanger, "The job wears you down... I was tired... It's hard work.") by the single-handed task of keeping Confederation together, were to actually sign off, then Canada must surely slip over the roaring abyss into chaos, obliv-ion or (*the horror, the horror*) the dark heart of America itself.

Born on a Friday the thirteenth in Toronto in 1934, Peter Gzowski is the great-grandson of a Russian civil engineer, Sir Casimir Stanislaus Gzowski, who designed much of Montreal's harbour. Which makes one wonder if bridge-building and support structures might not run through the family genes. His parents, Margaret MacGregor Young and Harold Edward Gzowski, were divorced when he was five, and he was raised, partly by grandparents, an only child in the small Ontario town of Galt. His mother, who worked in the Galt library, died when Gzowski was 15, leaving, according to the *Montreal Gazette* in 1988, "a gap that all his later successes, friends and lovers have never quite filled." If true, this might explain not only the Canada-as-cozy-family orientation of *Morningside*, but Gzowski's reluctant-but-determined role in holding the national family together.

He attended Ridley College, a private boys' school in St. Catharines, Ontario,

If Gzowski were to actually sign off, then Canada must surely slip over the roaring abyss into chaos, oblivion or *(the horror, the horror)* the dark heart of America itself.

and then the University of Toronto. Barely past his teens, the precociously talented Gzowski, nicknamed "Boy Wonder," worked on newspapers in Timmins, Moose Jaw and Chatham, and was then hired by the Canadian-to-the-marrow *Maclean*'s. He became the magazine's youngest managing editor ever at 28. In 1964, he left *Maclean*'s and worked the editorial trenches in Toronto, at the *Star* and the *Star Weekly*, finally winding up at the venerable institution of CBC-Radio in the early seventies. There he became the first host of *This Country in the Morning*, the precursor to what would evolve into *Morningside*, and the program which, by becoming an institution itself, began to pave the way for Gzowski's own national institutionhood.

In 1976, disaster – or at least its Canadian institutional counterpart – struck. Gzowski left radio to develop what would become one of the CBC's most high-profile failures of the seventies, a doomed attempt to Canadianize the late-night talk show called *90 Minutes Live*.

The program featured the nontelegenic former radio and print man as host of a show which almost immediately had its wheels spinning in the bog of an archetypical CBC quandary: while the program's time slot and chat format made comparisons to the slicker and more expensive American talk shows inevitable, the program, and those who put it on the air, kept insisting that it wasn't just a Canadian Carson clone, it was a showcase of the kind of performers and personalities that made this country as pretty-good as it is. The problem was, despite the revolving door of distinctly Canadian guests who paraded in front of the *90 Minutes'* cameras during its brief run, the program sure felt

In 1976, Gzowski left radio to develop what would become one of the CBC's most high-profile failures of the seventies: *90 Minutes Live*.

like bargain-basement Carson, which is to say a *Tonight Show* rip-off too poor to bag the big guests.

After two seasons in which Gzowski played the role of public whipping-boy for the program's failure, he quietly left *90 Minutes Live*. One year later, after a widely unwatched season with former *Take 30* host Paul Soles in Gzowski's chair, the show was finally gassed. To this day, Gzowski still speaks of the entire affair with palpable regret. There is one thing, however, that *90 Minutes Live*, for all its fundamental wrongheadedness, makes plain: whatever Peter Gzowski's appeal is, it belongs on radio.

Gzowski turned to the writing of non-fiction as a retrenchment measure, and after producing some well-reviewed work, he returned to CBC-Radio. There he acted as guest host for Don (*Hee Haw*) Harron on *Morningside*, and the late Barbara Frum on *As It Happens*, finally taking over the former in 1982 when Harron left.

Which takes us back to September 1995, shortly after Gzowski renewed his *Morningside* contract, and prolonged national collapse for another calendar year. Gloria Bishop, the show's executive producer, gathered staff to boost morale by describing her vision of what the show means to its listeners. Wrote Liam Lacey in the *Globe and Mail*, "She said that, although Canada was perhaps the most urbanized country in the world, it is also

sparsely populated overall and maintains a myth of itself as a village. *Morningside*'s job is to sustain that comforting impression."

If you've never understood Gzowski or his program's appeal, Bishop's pep talk may be all you really need to know about *Morningside*, for it makes at least two things perfectly clear: first, why the program means as much as it does for the loyal but limited number of Canadians who listen, and second, why the uninitiated are likely to remain so as long as the show insists its principle function is to soothe. If, as stated by its executive producer, the program's purpose is to offer comfort by appealing to a myth – a "village" myth in an "urbanized" society – certain conditions are necessary in order for the program to appeal: the listener must first of all have a need to believe, even against evidence to the contrary, in the myth of Canada as a village, a need which also implies a concurrent desire to deny any aspects of national experience that don't fit that myth. Moreover, the listener must also find the myth comforting, which in turn implies a demographic with a strict set of values: somewhat older and conservative, somewhat nostalgic and sentimental, even somewhat frightened. By its own admission, for the program to work, *Morningside* depends upon the listener's desire to escape from the urbanized Canada into a comforting if mythical one – the virtual village. Gzowski himself has referred to the show as "a sort of village bulletin board for the nation."

This explains why *Morningside* is a daily parade of officially approved Canadiana – music, pundits, politicians, gardeners, poets, farmers, and professors whose idea of Canada might already have gone the way of Yukon gold by the time Expo '67 opened.

Gzowski's *Morningside* is the audio equivalent of Robert Bateman's wildlife paintings, W. O. Mitchell's prose or Kevin Sullivan's *Road to Avonlea* TV series: an appealing invocation of a mythical Canada, (predominantly rural, simple, moral), whose absence in real life merely boosts its mythical currency. It is, in other words, a willful act of denial – a comfort zone.

This accounts for the ripple of panic which courses through the inhabitants of Gzowski's village every time it looks as if he might actually take his leave. Since the national village erected by *Morningside* is small, fragile and mythical, and since it exists to offer people succor from the threat of change, there is a sense that it could not endure any change itself; that the elder's departure would surely spell the end of the village itself.

Then again, the most impressive thing about cultural myths is that since they are born from the need to believe in something, they have a proven knack for making truth irrelevant. Need dictates its own truth. For example, the assumption that Gzowski and *Morningside* exert some adhesive influence over the direction of the country. If only 15 percent of the country's listening, who is holding everybody else's country together? Or, like some ignorant, leprous rabble who lurk outside the village walls, does the other 85 percent not matter since it's not listening?

Gzowski has remained at *Morningside* since 1982, continuing to interview in his comfortably rumpled style while annually generating doubt about his continued employment and appearing tired and disgruntled to forgiving reporters. Whether or not one believes that whither goes Gzowski, so goeth the nation, this much is certain: when he finally stops threatening

Gzowski's *Morningside* is the audio equivalent of Robert Bateman's wildlife paintings, W. O. Mitchell's prose or Kevin Sullivan's *Road to Avonlea* TV series: an appealing invocation of a mythical Canada.

and really does make his exit, an idea of Canada, if not the real thing, will probably go with him. The fact is, if the elder leaves, only 15 percent of the country might feel that their village is on the brink of oblivion. The other 85 won't even notice, and for a perfectly understandable reason: because they've never been invited inside.

Postscript:

In August 1996, Peter Gzowski once again suggested publicly that he'd had it with holding the country together. This time, however, he actually seemed to mean it. The 1996-97 season of *Morningside* would be his last. "I've said it almost every year and I've always meant it," he told the *Globe and Mail*'s Christopher Harris. "I would hate to be the person who had to bet about whether I changed my mind about anything." Predictably, the Gzowski-as-national-Bondfast talk arrived quickly. "It's going to be a real loss when Peter leaves that slot," said bureaucrat/broadcaster Knowlton Nash. "It sounds excessive to say this but Peter Gzowski is in a sense Mr. CBC, and in a sense he's Mr.Canada." Extreme, yes, but fitting. For with his departure, Gzowski surely takes on the same status as the country that might have collapsed without him: like *Morningside*'s Canada he melts into myth.

Raising Kain: Peter and Karen on *90 Minutes Live* →

"No one could be that sensitive and actually mean it, could they?"

– CRAIG MACINNIS ON DAN HILL'S MONSTER HIT, IN THE *TORONTO STAR*, 1987

Honesty's Too Much
Dan Hill's Hit From Hell

It can't be easy being Dan Hill. Not just because of that famous, world-class sensitivity – although that's gotta be tough – but because of the legacy of that sensitivity. Or specifically, the legacy wrought by the biggest hit song in the performer's career, one which has become virtually synonymous with moist-eyed, cheek-on-the-pillow masculine caring, "Sometimes When We Touch."

That song, which appeared on the Toronto-born singer-songwriter's third album, *Longer Fuse,* in 1977, altered nothing less than the terms of the then-23-year-old Hill's existence: until then, he lived quietly in the home of his American-born parents (father Daniel, African-American by birth, is a former chairperson of the Ontario Human Rights Commission), playing guitar, writing songs and enjoying the encouraging but modest success his fledgling career had snagged so far. His first album, 1975's *Dan Hill,* had yielded both a hit ("You Make Me Want To Be") and a Juno award for most promising male singer; his second, *Hold On,* while not as successful, hadn't done badly for a sophomore effort either. Then came *Longer Fuse* and the song that changed Dan Hill's life.

A nakedly emotional expression of romantic longing sung by a high-voiced man who seems to verge on sobs, "Sometimes When We Touch" nevertheless hit the international pop charts with less a whimper than a bang: over a million copies of the song sold worldwide, the album itself selling 200,000 copies in Canada and 500,000 in the U.S. The song won Hill multiple Junos for best composer and best male singer and *Longer Fuse* won best-selling album. In subsequent years, "Sometimes When We Touch" went on to become one of the most frequently covered Canadian-penned easy-listening ballads of the period between Paul Anka's "My Way" and Bryan Adams's "Everything I Do (I Do It For You)," and inspired renditions by Cleo Laine, Oscar Peterson, Ginette Reno, Marty Robbins, Tina Turner and Tammy Wynette. Not only that, "Sometimes When We Touch" entered the pantheon of contemporary easy-listening classics: in the western world, you'd be hard-pressed to find an elevator that doesn't play it. The song was, with everything the term implies, a monster hit for Dan Hill. But as everybody knows, the scariest monsters are the kind that won't go away. They just keep coming back, lurching out of the darkness, clinging with the fierce, unstoppable tenacity of the undead. For Dan Hill, "Sometimes When We Touch" turned out to be just such a monster.

Two facts account for this otherwise purely supernatural mutation of an over-sensitive pop ballad into a lurid, flesh-consuming beast: first, the fact that, for every person who loved the song passionately and intensely, there seemed to be someone else who detested it with equal conviction; and second, that Dan Hill couldn't seem to follow it up if his

Hill on Ice: Dan (in rugby shirt)
guests on a Toller Cranston figure skating special →

life depended on it. As he said of the song's success in 1987: "It hurt me a lot, really. It hurt because I simply did not have a hit to follow it up. I can blame that on my songs, I can blame it on my record company or whatever. But the facts are I just didn't have a follow-up hit. The song opened the door, but I just couldn't get through." Which left Dan Hill in the most unenviable position of being stuck in the threshold of his own success, a one-hit wonder with a hit as many people gagged on as cried over.

Not that the monster didn't have an upside: it paid for the singer's east end Toronto home and got him out of his parents' basement, and the royalties from the myriad covers, versions and perpetual easy-listening rotation meant that Hill had made enough from the song to bankroll a career: the success of "Sometimes When We Touch" was such that he could keep singing and writing songs for a living as long as he wanted. The question, when you consider that money took you about as far up as the upside went before it tilted sharply downward, was how long did he want to? By the early eighties, contempt for the song was so widespread that even the title had become a sort of generally accepted shorthand for insufferably treacly pop sensitivity, and the night was rare in a campus pub when some drunken bunch of collegiate yobs didn't break into a contemptuously rowdy verse or two of the song. Dan became Down Hill and Dan Hell, his sales plummeting almost as fast as his credibility. Then writer's block struck, the last thing the sensitive creative ego needs. And all because he'd dared to be as honest and open in his songwriting as he was in his heart. (That'll teach him.) Ten years after the hit broke, Hill told the *Toronto Sun*: "I was like the punching bag, and I think I walked around in a daze for a couple of years."

Eventually, the burden of the song was such that Hill felt he was buried alive and completely beneath it, which is why he decided to pack up his six-string in the mid-eighties and head to L.A. to work as a songwriter. Because curiously, for all the relentless derision the monster hit gener-

Maple Sap **The Worst Canadian Singles of All Time**

1. "From New York to L.A." Patsy Gallant (1976) This song is offensive on so many levels, it's difficult to know where to start. Here's what happened: Gallant took the melody from Gilles Vigneault's nationalist ode to Quebec, "Mon Pays," and recast it with an absurd set of lyrics documenting her entirely fictional rise to stardom south of the border. Add to the mix a grating, self-loving vocal performance and trashy disco production, and you have the worst Canadian single ever. An affront to Quebec nationalists, an affront to disco music itself. But primarily, an affront to our ears.

2. Any song by Loverboy You pick one. We can't decide. "The Kid Is Hot Tonite" (1980)? Maybe "Working For The Weekend" (1981)? Or how about "Hot Girls In Love" (1983)? Then again, there's "Lovin' Every Minute Of It" (1985). They're all frightening examples of just how derivative Canadian stud rock became in the eighties. Simply too much tight leather and irony-free testosterone for our taste.

3. "Rock 'n' Roll Song" Valdy (1972) A pathetic whine from a boring folkie. Valdy complains about some hoser who dared to request a "rock 'n' roll" song at one of his gigs. Rather than get so offended, the sensitive Valdy should have just lightened up and cranked out some Guess Who covers.

4. "Music Box Dancer" Frank Mills (1979) This instrumental hit is so happy-sounding and eager to please, it makes "Up With People" sound like Kurt Cobain. Unfit even for dental waiting-room listening, "Music Box Dancer" is Pure Evil.

5. "Seasons In The Sun" Terry Jacks (1973) Jacks, along with then-wife Susan, formed the Canuck AM radio juggernaut known as The Poppy Family in the late sixties. They recorded some captivatingly weird singles like "Which Way You Goin' Billy" (1969), "That's Where I Went Wrong" (1970) and "Where Evil Grows" (1971). Terry even had a moderate-size solo hit in 1972 with the environmentally friendly "Concrete Sea." But something went dramatically wrong, and Jacks decided to tackle a melodramatic travesty with a pedigree that should have given him cause to reflect: "Seasons In The Sun" had been written by Jacques Brel, translated into English by Rod McKuen, and covered by the Kingston Trio. Jacks's version went through the roof, providing him with his first (and last) international hit. "Seasons In The Sun" was impossible to avoid in 1973, although we desperately tried to. The song's massive success is basically inexplicable, except as one of those numerous lapses in taste the seventies produced: sure, as the song said, "It's hard to die"; but it was even harder to listen to this tripe.

6. "Standing In The Dark" Platinum Blonde (1984) The ultimate eighties hybrid: they dyed their hair like the Police, they made flashy videos like Duran Duran and they sucked like A Flock of Seagulls.

ated in Canada, it drew nothing near the hostility in Europe or the U.S. In Los Angeles, Hill was not only welcomed, he was actually wanted, and before long began successfully penning chartbound songs for people like George Benson, Jeffrey Osborne, Teddy Pendergrass and later, Celine Dion. His confidence back and his self-respect restored, Hill again felt confident he could shake off the clinging fiend that was "Sometimes When We Touch." More than 70 new songs packed into his suitcase, he resumed working on his own albums in Toronto, a vastly happier Dan Hill. Looking back on the L.A. resurrection, Hill said: "I think it saved me from totally crashing in terms of confidence. If I'd stayed in Toronto, I think I

would have just pumped out more and more albums, and just doubted myself more and more. Going to L.A. saved me."

Still, these days, the monster has not gone away entirely. On the contrary, it seems to make a messy appearance every time the singer sits down to an interview. With the certainty of winter in Winnipeg, the monster from the past invariably intrudes on the present. By now, of course, Hill must know it's coming; must hear its dragging footsteps and irregular wheezing lurking behind every journalist's question, braced for the moment when the beast springs from the quesioner's mouth. And when it does, he's ready for it, scaring the beast back from whence it came with a healthy blast of

disarming self-deprecation: "Let's face it," he said to the monster when it sprung from the mouth of a *Globe and Mail* interviewer in 1987, "I'm sick of the song, and I expect everybody else would be."

Sense and Sensitivity The Essential Dan Hill

If you're a Dan Hill fan, chances are you already own his "Sensitive Guy" trilogy: *Dan Hill* (1975), *Hold On* (1976) and *Longer Fuse* (1977). These early albums represent Hill distilled: the essence of his earnestness. With ballads like "You Make Me Want To Be," "You Say You're Free" and the unavoidable "Sometimes When We Touch," Hill quickly established himself as an emotive force to be reckoned with: a guy who deserved to be in the upper echelon of seventies sensitive guys, right up there with Alan Alda and Phil Donahue.

---

7. "Superman's Song" Crash Test Dummies (1991) The Dummies' breakthrough hit is an interminable piece of pop-culture pseudo-profundity about comic-book heroes. A typically verbose piece of drivel from lead singer/ guy with annoyingly deep voice/ostentatious English-lit major Brad Roberts. Give us Bryan Adams any day.

8. "The Americans" Gordon Sinclair (1974) Yes, professional contrarian/ curmudgeon Gordon Sinclair actually recorded a single at one point, and we have to be grateful that it was a spoken-word recording. Had Sinclair chosen to warble a tune, no doubt it would rank higher on our list. Sinclair recorded an editorial he had written for Toronto radio station CFRB on how those poor Americans weren't given enough credit for being good guys on the world stage. (Funny how little things like Vietnam sort of hurt their reputation in that area.) In fact, there were two versions of "The Americans": Detroit broadcaster Byron MacGregor took Sinclair's words, added a bit of patriotic music in the background and came up with a smash hit in (of all places) the U.S.A.

9. "(You're) Havin' My Baby" Paul Anka (1974) The song that made Anka the number-one enemy of the National Organization For Women, "(You're) Havin' My Baby" has significance beyond its painfully obvious troglodyte views on sexual politics. We believe that the song was the linchpin in an intricate, covert plot by former fifties idols Anka, Frankie Valli and Neil Sedaka to wreak sonic havoc in the seventies: just revenge, they felt, on all the people who had rejected them when the Beatles came along.

10. "Sometimes When We Touch" Dan Hill (1977) True, this song is an extremely easy target. It turned Hill into the whipping boy of pop critics around the world, and even popped up as the saccharine theme to one of the worst movies of the seventies, the equally saccharine *Moment By Moment* with Lily Tomlin and John Travolta. Twenty years on, the song's reputation hasn't improved. The honesty is still too much.

11. "Tears Are Not Enough" Northern Lights for Africa (1985) Sure, the cause was absolutely noble: famine relief in Ethiopia. And true, it wasn't as offensive as USA for Africa's immodest ditty, "We Are The World." But in musical terms, this has to rank as a major disappointment. Consider the bizarre conflagration of all-star Canuck talent in the room that day: Neil Young, Joni Mitchell, Bryan Adams, Burton Cummings, Geddy Lee. Hell, even Tommy Hunter was there. Think of the possibilities! Unfortunately, the composers (music by David Foster, lyrics by Bryan Adams and Jim Vallance) chose to travel down the middle of the road, and missed a great opportunity to come up with a song people could actually listen to a decade later.

Obsession Hockey Days and Nights in Canada

At first glance, it's slightly jarring to see hockey analysis coming from an egghead media guru like Marshall McLuhan. You just don't expect a Rocket Richard wrist shot to be within his frame of cultural reference. But let's not forget, Marshall McLuhan was a *Canuck* egghead media guru. Surely, in all of his years exploring the message of the medium, he caught a few periods of *Hockey Night in Canada*.

Naturally, Rocket Richard's symbiotic relationship with hockey fans would interest McLuhan: the game has never produced a more potent pop icon. When the fiery Richard was suspended from the Stanley Cup Playoffs in 1955, Montreal fans rioted in the streets. Today, the Rocket's red glare has lost some of its intensity, but he still inspires passion. (Yes, even after his ultra-cheesy Grecian Formula ads in the seventies gave us the immortal line, "Hey Richard, two minutes for looking so good!") In 1996, a permanent exhibit called "Univers Maurice Richard" opened, appropriately enough, in Montreal's Maurice Richard Arena. Featuring high-tech interactive games, it's basically an electronic manifestation of the symbiosis between Rocket and his fans. No doubt, McLuhan would have been intrigued by it.

Of course, Rocket Richard isn't the only pop superstar hockey has spawned. (He is, however, the only player to inspire a riot, an interactive tourist attraction and a Grecian Formula commercial.) The game has produced countless Canadian pop moments and catchphrases. For the record, here's but a sampling:

← Maurice "Rocket" Richard

Foster Hewitt with the guys

Foster Hewitt at microphone

Hockey Broadcasters

Canadians have never had much success producing soap operas. Maybe that's because there has been one ongoing national drama hogging all our attention for more than 60 years: *Hockey Night in Canada*. At the height of its popularity in the fifties, *HNIC* even made a star out of a guy who shilled for the show's sponsor, Imperial Oil. In live commercials during the game, actor Murray Westgate would sign off with the tag line, "Always look to Imperial for the best!" He was so convincingly friendly in his cap and uniform that several viewers believed he actually owned an Imperial Oil gas station. Long after the spots ended, Westgate was typecast in this sort of genial role. Such was the awesome cultural influence of *Hockey Night in Canada* and its behind-the-mike legends.

Foster Hewitt

Born: Toronto, 1902.

Died: Scarborough, 1985.

Trademarks: From his vantage point in the "gondola" at Maple Leaf Gardens, fans grew familiar with Hewitt's famous lines, "He shoots, he scores!" and "Hello Canada and hockey fans in the United States and Newfoundland."

Broadcast History: Hewitt is generally acknowledged as the first person in the world to do a radio broadcast of a hockey game. (Although some sources say it was the long-forgotten Norman Albert.) Hewitt's first broadcast was on March 22, 1923, at the old Mutual Street Arena in Toronto. Naturally, the equipment wasn't exactly state-of-the-art. In those early days Hewitt spoke into a telephone, and for a short time even broadcast from a puny glass booth rinkside. He quickly abandoned that vantage point after the windows became so foggy he couldn't see the action. During the Depression, Hewitt became the best-known voice in the country: at the height of his radio popularity on *Hockey Night in Canada*, he was receiving 90,000 fan letters a season. Hewitt made the move to the new medium of television in 1952, and by 1967 he was sharing Maple Leaf play-by-play duties with his son, Bill. He made his final NHL broadcast in 1978.

Broadcast Style: Hewitt's high-pitched, nasal voice became particularly high-pitched and nasal whenever an exciting play was made. On air he had no discernible sense of humour. (By all accounts he wasn't exactly a laugh riot away from the mike, either.) The reserved Hewitt felt he should never become the focus of the broadcast: the game should always be paramount.

Ability to Pronounce French-Canadian Names: Almost non-existent. Particular problems with Yvan Cournoyer's name, which Hewitt would often mangle beyond recognition.

Instant Replay: "I just described it the way I thought I should and, when a score was made, I said, 'He shoots, he scores!' and that stuck."

Colour Comment: Near the end of his broadcasting career, Hewitt was selected by CTV sports honcho Johnny (*Sports Hot Seat*) Esaw to do the play-by-play for the 1972 Canada–Soviet Union "Summit On Ice." (Former player Brian Conacher did colour commentary.) Fittingly enough, Hewitt got to make the epochal call on Paul Henderson's winning goal in Game Eight of that series. Hewitt often referred to the '72 series as his career highlight, even though the hard-to-pronounce Yvan Cournoyer was on the Canadian team. (Those Russian names were no picnic, either.)

Danny Gallivan

Born: Sydney, Nova Scotia, 1917.

Died: Montreal, 1993.

Trademarks: Described Montreal defenceman Serge Savard's pivoting move as a "Savardian spinnerama." A hard shot was a "cannonading drive." Players would "negotiate contact with the puck." Goalies would make "scintillating" saves in a "larcenous fashion."

Broadcast History: In 1950, the regular Montreal Canadiens broadcaster, Doug Smith, became sick. A nervous Gallivan was called in at the last minute to do the play-by-play for a Detroit-Montreal game. In 1952, Gallivan was called back to do the Habs gig full-time. He retired in 1984, leaving broadcast partner Dick Irvin to fend for himself.

Broadcast Style: Wonderfully hyperbolical and dramatic. Renowned for his lilting tone and creative approach to hockey vocabulary. Bristled at any suggestion that he favoured *les Canadiens*. So what if he did? They won 16 Stanley Cups in the 32 years he was their announcer.

Ability to Pronounce French-Canadian Names: Pretty good. But then again, you could argue that it was a basic job requirement for a broadcaster doing Montreal Canadiens games.

Instant Replay: "I was out for a walk in Los Angeles, and there were these signs. Everything was 'rama' – Cinerama, Bowlerama. So Savard's move became the spinnerama."

Colour Comment: Gallivan taught high school Latin before he entered broadcasting, thereby paving the way for his linguistic meanderings in later life.

Don Cherry

Born: Kingston, Ontario, 1934.

Trademarks: Thumbs-up gesture (single or double). Omnipresent English bull terrier "Blue." Sartorial trademarks abound, including three-and-a-half-inch starched white collars, impossibly loud plaid jackets and a variety of ties featuring either hockey-team logos or cartoon characters. Nickname "Grapes" derived from Cherry. Catchphrases: "Beauty;" "not too shabby."

Broadcast History: After a long minor-hockey career yielded extremely modest financial rewards and only one game in the NHL, "Grapes" found a new lease on life as a coach with the Boston Bruins from 1974-1979. Cherry even won the Coach of the Year award in 1976, but ultimately found himself with the hapless Colorado Rockies in 1979-1980. His outspokenness cost him that job in the spring of 1980. That's when Ralph Mellanby, then the executive producer of *Hockey Night in Canada,*

came calling. Mellanby, of course, realized that Cherry's characteristic bluntness (the ability to call a Swede a Swede) would make great television. The rest, as they say, is vintage Grapes. His four-and-a-half-minute intermission segment, "Coach's Corner" (with Ron MacLean as his foil, the sober voice of reason), has become a national institution, often enjoying higher ratings than the game itself. Cherry has marketed his brand of down 'n dirty Canuck boosterism wisely with countless endorsements, a chain of bars called Don Cherry's Grapevine and his annual "Rock 'em Sock 'em" hockey-highlight videos.

Broadcast Style: Beauty! Not afraid to go into the corners and mix it up, Cherry is an unabashed supporter of the tough Canadian players ("grinders") he loves so much. (Cherry has an almost pathological fixation on former seventies Boston Bruins John Wensink and Stan Jonathan.) He passionately believes that fighting belongs in hockey and holds pure disdain for "pinkos" in society and players from socialist Sweden, particularly cheap-shot artist Ulf Samuelsson. On occasion, his analysis stretches beyond the hockey arena and enters the political arena. During the Gulf War, Cherry went on a flag-waving tirade against those "wimps and creeps" who opposed Canada's participation. (If any other sports commentator appropriated the public airwaves to flog his/her political views, it would surely mean instant professional self-immolation. But the massively popular Cherry can get away with it.) He's a uniquely Canadian creation, combining the beer-loving hoser charm of the McKenzie Brothers, the right-wing curmudgeon quality of

Gordon Sinclair and the genuine, hundred percent–proof hyper-nationalism of Stompin' Tom. Actually, the similarities between Grapes and the creator of "Bud the Spud" are telling: both Cherry and Connors have strong working-class constituencies, and a certain hip cachet with the university-age population. Both men are uncompromising, which elicits extreme reactions: you either love them or hate them, and neither Cherry nor Connors seem to care which one it is.

Ability to Pronounce French-Canadian Names: On a level with Foster Hewitt, perhaps even worse. Of course, Cherry's pronunciation of French-Canadian names is on an advanced Berlitz level compared to his muddy attempts at Swedish, Finnish, Czech or Russian monikers.

Instant Replay #1: "I'm trying to keep this country together. I'm the fucking glue that holds it together."

Instant Replay #2: "Jaromir Jagr is everything that's wrong with the NHL."

Colour Comment: As a certified Canadian pop-culture icon, Cherry is starting to attract academic interest. In 1995, University of Guelph professor Ric Knowles wrote a research paper called "Post 'Grapes,' Nuts and Flakes: Coach's Corner as Post-Colonial Performance." Knowles repeated the oft-heard claims that Cherry promotes "dangerous traits such as misogyny, homophobia and xenophobia, all in the name of Canadian patriotism." Knowles even had the gall to criticize Cherry's grammar! The cultural meaning of "Grapes" was also explored in a 1994 Sociology of Sport course at Hamilton's McMaster University. Perhaps one day a Canadian post-secondary institution will offer a full four-year degree in Don Cherry Studies. Sign us up!

Grecian formula

Supported by heavy television advertising

COMBE INC.
GRECIAN FORMULA
30 second TV
"Three Years"

MAURICE OC: When it comes to feeling young, a lot of it's up here.

ANNCR VO: Three years ago, Maurice Richard said goodbye grey hair, hello Grecian Formula 16.

MAURICE OC: It was so easy. Remember.

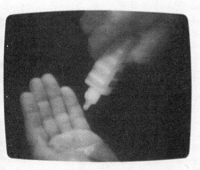

ANNCR VO: Grecian's as easy to use as water. Works for any colour hair.

MAURICE VO: The change was so gradual ...

and looks so natural ...

no one even noticed.

MAURICE OC: Today, I still leave just a touch of grey ... the wife likes it.

COACH OC: Hey, Richard! Two minutes for looking so good!

ANNCR VO: Look as young as _you_ feel with Grecian Formula 16. Liquid or creme.

- **Gradually changes grey hair to natural looking colour**

- **Used by over 2 million men**

Art Hindle and George Armstrong in *Face Off*

Big-Screen Hockey Face Off

More than a quarter of a century after it was released, *Face Off* (1971) stands alone as the most exquisitely awful Canadian movie ever made (ponder *that* for a moment): sublime in its ineptitude, dated beyond belief, a Canuck cheesefest *par excellence.*

The world of pro-hockey serves as the background for the tragic tale of Billy Duke, rendered earnestly by a young Art (*E.N.G.*) Hindle. Billy is one helluva hockey player, a top draft pick in his rookie season with the Toronto Maple Leafs. His downward spiral begins when he starts a steamy love affair with a peacenik pop-rock singer named Sherri Lee Nelson (played by a tie-dyed Trudy Young in her post–*Razzle Dazzle*

period). Sherri Lee is the lead singer of a groovy group called The Final Chorus. As the movie's press release points out, her songs are giving her "an international reputation with the 'now' generation." Cool! (In reality, the band's material sounds like stuff The Poppy Family would have rejected for being too mainstream.)

Initially, the relationship goes well. Walking around Toronto in one of those "falling in love" montage sequences, Sherri Lee purchases some love beads and gives them to Billy. The grateful but confused hoser jokes, "I don't know how I'll explain them to the coach." Later in the sequence, we experience a frightening seventies flashback, when we see the

What really lifts *Face Off* into cheesy hyper-space is the presence of real-life hockey players struggling to act as themselves.

happy couple bouncing up and down on a waterbed. Sadly, the affair spells trouble for both parties. They're from two different worlds: he's a strait-laced small-town bruiser, she's a sensitive, trippy flower-child.

Being a hippie, Sherri Lee abhors hockey violence and the "establishment" Leaf management. Disconsolate, she hits the bong pretty hard with her counter-culture pals. Being a clean-living hockey

Puckish Thoughts Books About Hockey

Books about hockey are the backbone of the Canadian publishing industry. Don't believe us? Check out the new releases in your local bookstore just before Christmas, and you'll find reams of prose about our national sport. On the high end, there are expensive coffee-table books packed with vintage photos of old-time hockey legends: these contain countless shots of Gordie Howe elbowing toothless players. (Ah, those were the days.) On the low end, there are semi-literate autobiographies by players like Dave "Tiger" Williams. In between these two extremes you'll find statistical guides, hockey joke books and even thick memoirs by obscure referees. Hockey-crazy Canucks have an insatiable appetite for this stuff. In an effort to separate the wheat from the chaff, here's our list of five of the coolest hockey books ever written.

1. Net Worth: Exploding the Myths of Pro Hockey by David Cruise and Alison Griffiths (1991) Perhaps the best piece of sports journalism ever to come out of this country. With meticulous detail, Cruise and Griffiths document the shameful history of management-labour relations in the NHL. In 1995, this was turned into a CBC-TV movie starring Al (*King of Kensington*) Waxman as Jack Adams, the Detroit Red Wings owner who destroyed Ted Lindsay's plans to start a players' union.

2. The Game by Ken Dryden (1983) The most insightful player ever to don goalie pads, Dryden always seemed to be looking at the big picture. In post-game interviews, his analysis was usually more cogent than anyone else's, including the broadcast crew's. *The Game* is his take on life with the Montreal Canadiens. Although Dryden's writing is a tad over-earnest, there will never be a more thoughtful "inside the NHL" book written. This is light-years away from the standard jock autobiography.

3. Slapshots: The Best and Worst of 100 Years of Hockey by Stephen Cole (1993) The funniest hockey book ever written, *Slapshots* answers all of the questions about hockey you never even thought to ask, like "What was goalie Gump Worsley's favourite recipe?" (Answer: "Gump's Pineapple Squares.") A truly bizarre compendium of utterly useless hockey info.

4. Gross Misconduct: The Life of Spinner Spencer by Martin O'Malley (1988) The tragic life story of Brian "Spinner" Spencer, a marginal player who made it to the NHL briefly before his life imploded. *Gross Misconduct* offers a helpful reminder that not all father-son hockey relationships are based on the positive Walter and Wayne Gretzky model.

5. Riding On the Roar of the Crowd: A Hockey Anthology compiled by David Gowdney (1989) An excellent compilation, with contributions from a truly diverse range of hockey scribblers. Everyone from Hugh (*Two Solitudes*) MacLennan to former Philadelphia coach Fred Shero is included here, as well as a hilarious "poem" consisting of a sample of Foster Hewitt's stream-of-consciousness commentary.

player, Billy can only vent his frustration by beating the living hell out of every hockey player in sight. In addition to Hindle and Young, the cast features a couple of classic Canuck stalwarts: a post-*Wojeck*/pre–*Animal House* John Vernon shows up as Leaf coach Fred Wares, and Austin (*This Is The Law*) Willis plays Graydon Hunter, the "socially amiable but single-minded" owner of the Leafs. But what really lifts *Face Off* into cheesy hyper-space is the presence of real-life hockey players struggling to act as themselves. The film features the big-screen debuts of former Leaf captain George "Chief" Armstrong, and ex–Boston Bruin bad boy Derek Sanderson. To describe their perfor-

mances as wooden would be unfair to the lumber industry. Populating the cast with real hockey stars provides the viewer with countless surreal moments to cherish: at a Maple Leaf New Year's Eve party, we see Young, the former *Razzle Dazzle* pal of Howard the Turtle, dancing with a well-lubricated Paul Henderson, the guy who would go on to score the most important goal in Canadian hockey history about a year later. Also not to be missed is the sight of rugged Leaf rearguard Bob Baun reading *Love Story* while waiting for a team flight to take off. Add in a cameo by eccentric ex–Leaf owner Harold Ballard as the team doctor and a more-than-occasional boom mike dropping into the

shot, and you have a profoundly bizarre cinematic experience: a hoser *Romeo and Juliet* with Maple Leaf Gardens substituting for Verona.

Postscript: It's worthwhile noting that Scott Young (Neil's father) cowrote the script for *Face Off*. He had already penned the quintessential Canadian hockey trilogy for young readers: *Scrubs on Skates* (1952), *Boy On Defence* (1953) and *A Boy at the Leafs' Camp* (1963). Young certainly knew the hockey world inside out, and no doubt there's a connection between Sherri Lee's hippie character and the behaviour of his musician son.

"Got him, got him, need him!" A Brief History of Hockey Cards

1910-1913 The first hockey cards ever are issued by Canadian cigarette companies. This enables consumers to enjoy photos of their favourite National Hockey Association players while sampling that smooth nicotine flavour.

1920s A few candy companies start to distribute hockey cards. Cigarette companies continue to do so.

1930s For the first time, hockey cards are issued with chewing gum. Dentists rejoice. Two Canadian gum companies print cards for a brief period: the long-forgotten World Wide Gum Co. and the legendary O-Pee-Chee. During this decade, the St. Lawrence Starch Company also releases its initial series of Bee Hive hockey photos.

1950s The Canadian company Parkhurst enters the card sweepstakes and dominates the scene until 1964. (The 1951-1952 Parkhurst Gordie Howe card is generally acknowledged as the most valuable hockey card, worth over $2,000 today.) The American company Topps begins printing hockey cards as well.

1968 O-Pee-Chee re-enters the hockey-card market. The late sixties and early seventies represent a peak period for hockey-card popularity. In certain schoolyards across Canada, the frenetic, ruthless trading activity makes the Wall Street stock market look absolutely mild by comparison. Hockey cards are also used for a practical purpose during this period: to stick into the spoke of a bicycle wheel to make annoying "clicking" noise while riding high-handlebar/banana-seat bikes.

1970s In addition to NHL cards, O-Pee-Chee releases World Hockey Association cards. This means lots of photos of players with huge sideburns in loud, colourful uniforms. (No one got rich from this series: the 1977-1978 Paul Shmyr WHA card is now worth a measly buck.) The short-lived but extremely funky Esso "Power Players" are also released during the seventies.

1990-1992 After a relatively quiet period in the eighties, the hockey-card market goes absolutely insane. American companies Upper Deck, Score and Pro Set flood the market. The bubblegum association with hockey cards wanes. At hockey-card conventions, it's not uncommon to see kids spend hundreds of dollars purchasing complete sets. Card collecting during this period seems to have more to do with financial investment than a love of the game. Old fuddy-duddy seventies card collectors wonder, "Whatever happened to buying a pack at a time? Where's the gum? There's supposed to be gum!"

1995 By mid-decade, the mania for collecting hockey cards levels off. Squeezed out of the market by a glut of high-powered American competitors, the Canadian company O-Pee-Chee stops issuing hockey cards.

Puck Rock Songs About Hockey

1. Theme from Hockey Night in Canada (1967) Canada's unofficial national anthem. The *Hockey Night in Canada* theme is so entrenched in our culture, it's hard to believe it's only been around since 1967. That's when the program's powers-that-be asked a young jingle composer named Dolores Claman to come up with a new signature tune: they wanted a rousing opener in the style of the American adventure-show themes that were so popular in the mid-sixties (e.g., *Mission: Impossible*). Claman offered them two made-to-order melodies. Obviously, *HNIC* chose the right one: her theme has kicked off the Saturday-night ritual ever since. Note: Claman was riding high in 1967. Earlier in the year she had cowritten the Ontario theme song for Expo '67, "A Place To Stand." If you grew up in that province, you'll remember its immortal "Ontari-ari-ari-o" refrain.

2. "Rock 'em Sock 'em Techno" Don Cherry with BKS (1993) Cherry is (as far as we know) the only hockey commentator to do the lead vocal track on a rave-friendly techno song. Grapes hooked up with Toronto techno gods BKS (featuring Chris Sheppard) to do the tune, which is an absolutely surreal combination of pro-Canadian hockey boosterism with hard-core synthesized computer rhythms. Still, Cherry gets full marks for effort: he thoroughly embraces the trippy rave universe and gamely utters incantations like "Probert, Probert, what a man: we see him, it's slam-bam. Let's go! Let's go!"

3. "Fifty-Mission Cap" The Tragically Hip (1992) Canada's band of the nineties tackles the bizarre tragedy of Bill Barilko, the Maple Leaf defenceman who scored the Stanley Cup–winning goal in the spring of 1951, only to disappear on a fishing trip that summer. In true Canadian fashion, a hockey card plays a central role in the song. Lead singer Gord Downie is in blistering vocal form here.

4. "Gretzky Rocks" The Pursuit of Happiness (1995) Avid hockey fan/lead singer Moe Berg constructs a simple but effective ode to the Great One, with particular emphasis on the Edmonton Oiler years. Note: This wasn't the first time Gretzky had inspired an artist: in the eighties he had his portrait done by Andy Warhol.

5. "Hockey" Jane Siberry (1989) Siberry cre-

Bruins: Phil Esposito   Canadiens: Peter Mahovlich   Rangers: Eddie Giacomin

ates an impressionistic primer on the role of hockey in the Canadian consciousness. Although she doesn't immediately strike us as a kindred spirit of Don Cherry, this is a wonderfully nostalgic piece that includes references to the 1955 Rocket Richard riot and the ancient art of using galoshes as goalposts.

6. "All Along the Watchtower" Jim Schoenfeld (1975) Born in Galt, Ontario, Jim Schoenfeld played for the Buffalo Sabres during the seventies: he was an above-average defenceman with above-average sideburns. A bit of a fashion plate in the staid NHL, Schoenfeld mistakenly believed that he possessed at least a modicum of musical talent. How else can we explain the existence of his album *Schony*? In a classic case of musical hubris, the immodest, tone-deaf Schoenfeld assaults several Beatles songs and the Sinatra standard "It Was A Very Good Year." But the absolute stunner on the album is his version of "All Along the Watchtower." By caterwauling a Bob Dylan song that had been a hit for Jimi Hendrix, Schoenfeld manages to desecrate two musical legends at once. Call the Zamboni, the ice needs cleaning!

7. "The Hockey Song" Stompin' Tom Connors (1973) Canada's Poet Laureate/pop mythmaker does his best Foster Hewitt, describing the visceral pleasures of the "good old hockey game." Naturally, the name of the star player in the tune is Bobby, and not Sergei or Jaromir. "The Hockey Song" has recently replaced Gary Glitter's "Rock and Roll Part 2" as the clapalong tune of choice at hockey rinks across Canada and (gasp!) the U.S. Note: In what is perhaps the greatest all-time intersection of Canadian icons, Stompin'

Canada's unofficial national anthem, the *Hockey Night in Canada* theme is so entrenched in our culture, it's hard to believe it's only been around since 1967.

Tom hoisted the Stanley Cup above his head at a Parliament Hill concert on Canada Day, 1993.

8. "Big League" Tom Cochrane (1988) A typical Cochrane combination of rock bombast and catchy melody, "Big League" documents the generic story of a kid struggling to make it to the NHL. Never rises above the level of cliché.

9. "The Ballad of Wendel Clark, Parts I and II" The Rheostatics (1987) How Canadian is this band? Well, in 1996 they released an album of music inspired by the Group of Seven. Here they pay homage to rugged winger Wendel Clark: the quintessential hard-working Canuck player and the pride of Kelvington, Saskatchewan. It's a mediocre song, but we're sure that Don Cherry approved of the subject matter.

10. "Honky the Christmas Goose" Johnny Bower (1965) He was the backup goalie the last time the Leafs won the Cup (in Canada's Centennial Year). For that reason, Toronto hockey fans should forgive him for this charity Christmas single which is as bad as its title would indicate.

11. "Pandemonium" Tommy Hunter (1972) An ode to Paul Henderson's last-minute winning goal in Game Eight of the "Summit on Ice." Canada's "country gentleman" performed the song on his show a few weeks after Henderson's marker had prompted an outbreak of national insanity.

12. *Puck Rock* Various Artists (1994) Out of Vancouver, a delightful punk/heavy-metal compilation of hockey-related tunes. Selected tracks: "Gump Worsley's Lament" – Huevos Rancheros; "What's Wrong With Lumme" – Glenn Ford and the Piers; "Our Stanley Cup" – The Smugglers; "Overtime" – D.O.A.; "I'm Gonna Play Hockey" – Hanson Brothers; "Drinkin' Whiskey Playin' Hockey" – Tankhog; "Hockey Sucks" – Sweaters.

13. "The Hockey Song" Jughead (1992) Not to be confused with Stompin' Tom's ditty, Jughead's tune is a strange but accurate reading of our national mania for the sport. Tells the story of a Canadian travelling around the world who can think about only one thing: you guessed it, hockey. In alphabetical order, the song's chorus lists the myriad forms of our national obsession, including: air hockey, ball hockey, kitchen hockey and table hockey.

14. "Signin' With The NHL" Bruno Gerussi (1978) The Beachcomber/Celebrity Cook/Shakespearean actor was a true Canadian icon, so it only made sense for him to lay down this rather offbeat track about our national sport.

15. "Clear The Track, Here Comes Shack" The Secrets (1966) A musical tribute to hockey's court jester Eddie Shack. With lyrics by former *Hockey Night in Canada* personality Brian McFarlane, "Clear The Track" hit number one on the Toronto CHUM radio chart. Note: The Secrets became frustrated at being known only for this hockey novelty song. They changed their name to "The Quiet Jungle" and were never heard from again.

"Here's a shot! Henderson made a wild stab for it and fell. Here's another shot, right in front. They score! Henderson has scored for Canada!"

– FOSTER HEWITT, LUZHNIKI ARENA, MOSCOW,
THURSDAY, SEPTEMBER 28, 1972, AS PAUL HENDERSON SCORED THE WINNING GOAL
IN THE DECIDING GAME OF THE CANADA–SOVIET UNION HOCKEY SERIES

Nyet Nyet Soviet Paul Henderson's Big Score

On July 20, 1969, ten million Canadians watched on TV as Neil Armstrong became the first man to walk on the moon. On September 28, 1972, TWELVE AND A HALF million Canadians tuned in to see Paul Henderson jam a last-minute rebound past Vladislav Tretiak. You've gotta love it: more hosers were interested in watching Hockey Night in Moscow than Armstrong's lunar leap for mankind.

But then again, it makes sense. Hockey and television are Canuck obsessions: mix the two of them together, throw in the red menace and a whopper of a national identity crisis, and you've got a potent ratings cocktail. Certainly, the '72 "Summit On Ice" was the most compelling soap opera ever screened in Canadian homes. For 27 days that September, we were glued to our sets, facing the abyss – well, at least the distinct possibility that Canada was no longer the world's supreme hockey power. And if we weren't the best hockey players on the planet, then who the hell were we?

Fortunately, we didn't have to answer that question. When a relatively obscure winger from the Toronto Maple Leafs scored with a mere 34 seconds remaining, our national implosion was put on hold (for a while, anyway). Of course, in a tele-visual instant, Paul Henderson's life changed forever. He was transformed into a pop icon: the national saviour who

could skate. The mythology had us believe that he combined the best qualities of Gordie Howe, Stompin' Tom Connors and the Fathers of Confederation. In reality, Henderson was just a better-than-average player who happened to bang one in while twelve and a half million people were watching in schools, homes and workplaces across the country.

After the conquering hero returned to Canada, he had to hire a secretary to answer the deluge of fan mail. Henderson's endorsement opportunities went through the roof, and the federal Liberals – in the middle of a wobbly election campaign – pleaded with him to make a few appearances on their behalf. (The non-partisan hero politely declined.)

The rest of Henderson's hockey career was, to understate the case, anticlimactic. Within a few years of saving the country, our saviour was out of the NHL, playing in the hockey hotbed of Birmingham, Alabama.

Today, a quarter century after the series, the Soviet Union doesn't exist, there are scads of Russians earning hard currency in the NHL and the term "Team Canada" now refers to a bunch of dorky-looking provincial premiers going overseas with the PM to try to attract international investors.

Times have changed, but Paul Henderson will never escape his indelible pop moment: it's in a state of perpetual replay. As he said in 1992, the twentieth

anniversary of that seminal Canadian TV event, "Even today, no matter where I go, people want to thank me for scoring the Goal."

- -

Game Eight Scoring Summary
Team Canada 6, Soviet Union 5

First Period

1. Soviet Union: Yakushev (Maltsev, Liapkin) 3:34
2. Team Canada: P. Esposito (Park) 6:45
3. Soviet Union: Lutchenko (Kharlamov) 13:10
4. Team Canada: Park (Ratelle, D.Hull) 16:59
Penalties: White (holding) 2:25, P. Mahovlich (holding) 3:01, Petrov (hooking) 3:44, Parise (minor, interference, 10-minute misconduct, game misconduct) 4:10, Tsygankov (interference) 6:28, Ellis (interference) 9:27, Petrov (interference) 9:46, Cournoyer (interference) 12:51

Second Period

5. Soviet Union: Shadrin 0:21
6. Team Canada: White (Gilbert, Ratelle) 10:32
7. Soviet Union: Yakushev 11:43
8. Soviet Union: Vasiliev 16:44
Penalties: Stapleton (cross-checking) 14:58, Kuzkin (elbowing) 18:06

Third Period

9. Team Canada: P. Esposito (P. Mahovlich) 2:27
10. Team Canada: Cournoyer (P.Esposito, Park) 12:56
11. Team Canada: Henderson (P. Esposito) 19:26
Penalties: Gilbert (major, fighting) 3:41, Mishakov (major, fighting) 3:41, Vasiliev (tripping) 4:27, D. Hull (high-sticking) 15:24, Petrov (elbowing) 15:24.

Shots On Goal:

Team Canada	14	8	14	- **36**
Soviet Union	12	10	5	- **27**

Henderson after scoring goal →

The 'EH' List Canada's Hollywood

Viewed purely as a domestic enterprise, the history of Canadian movies is a heartbreaker: a story of hopes crushed by foreign interest and indifferent governance, of talent dashed on the rocky shoals of power and greed. If, on the other hand, one expands one's perspective so that the history of Canadian movies includes the history of Canadians *in* movies, the story grows considerably more upbeat.

Not only have Canadians been involved in Hollywood virtually since movies first got engaged to business, the roles they have tended to assume have been both substantial and revealing. When one studies the list of Canadians who have had successful careers in American movies or TV, certain patterns or categories begin to cohere: lots of strong supporting or character actors, several versatile but impersonal directors, a few key technical and animation innovators, and an astonishing number of Canadians specializing in the impersonation of either bland authority figures or shamelessly hammy villains. Rarely the star, but always performing impeccably from the sidelines: as things go for Canada in international diplomacy, so it apparently goes for the movies. Ever the bridesmaid, and always around when we're needed. If the world were a sitcom, Canada would play the neighbour who pops in through the kitchen door for the show's real stars to bounce schtick off before politely withdrawing again. It may seem like a thankless role, but the real stars know better: it's characters like Canada that make them shine that much brighter.

Geneviève Bujold

This list of noteworthy Hollywood Canadians is divided into the following categories: movie-industry pioneers – those Canucks who made a significant on- or off-screen contribution during film's infancy – are here called "Voyageurs"; actors who've specialized in playing innocuous ship captains, chiefs of staff, etc., are labelled "Bland Authority Figures"; actors who have made careers of being reliable sideline players we call "Support Staff"; that enduring class of villainous Canadian ham we call "Northern Nasties," a class not, incidentally, to be confused with the group of characters, as pure and nice as a downy snowfall, we call "Ice Cream Canucks." And finally, we call that genre of dependably unexciting, Canadian-born directors "Unteurs," since their bland, businesslike efficiency represents the polar opposite of the "director-as-artist" auteur theory.

Obviously the list is neither completely comprehensive nor categorically absolute: some Bland Authority Figures are also strong Support Staffers and occasional Northern Nasties. Donald Sutherland, for instance, has been all three at one time or another. While the prolific and enduring Allan Dwan qualifies as a Voyageur, he's also the original Canadian Unteur, capable of assembling an efficient, but rarely earth-shaking, movie out of just about any dramatic raw material thrown his way.

Finally, we have not included people who have been discussed elsewhere in the book. Thus, while Bill Shatner, Leslie Nielsen and Lorne Greene are all Bland Authority Figures *par excellence*, their peculiar talents and specialties have been amply dealt with on other pages and require no reiteration here. This also accounts for the otherwise conspicuous absence of a discussion of Canadians in Hollywood comedy.

Now, without further ado, The "Eh" List:

Bujold, Geneviève: (Born 1942, Montreal, Quebec.) Fine-featured, dark-eyed and petite, Genevieve Bujold is one of those rare women actors who can seem both fragile and indomitable simultaneously, a quality which accounts for no small part of her indisputable allure. While vacationing in Europe as a student, she was spotted by the world-renowned French director Alain Resnais and he cast her opposite Yves Montand in *La guerre est finie* in 1966. She has made movies in three significantly distinct movie industries: Europe: *King of Hearts* (1966), *The Thief of Paris* (1967), *The Trojan Women* (1972), Canada: *Act of the Heart* (1970), *Kamouraska* (1973), *Dead Ringers* (1988) and the U.S.: *Earthquake* (1974), *Obsession* (1976), *Coma* (1978), *Tightrope* (1984), *Choose Me* (1984). An actor of keen instinct and palpable intelligence, stardom has nevertheless eluded her, which generally seems to be the lot of many of Canada's finer female exports. (See Kidder, Nelligan and Shaver, for example.) Still, once seen she's impossible to forget, which might explain why, as recently as 1995, she was being sought to play a Starfleet commander in the series *Star Trek: Voyager*, a role which subsequently went to Kate Mulgrew after Bujold reportedly balked at the production schedule. Had she accepted the mission, however, it would have marked a significant day in Mondo Canuck history, as Bujold would have been the second Starfleet commander after Bill Shatner to hail from Montreal. Support Staff.

Burr, Raymond: (Born 1917, New Westminster, British Columbia. Died 1993.) While best known as one of TV history's most enduring Bland Authority Figures because of his lead role in the long-running *Perry Mason* series (1957–1966), the hulking, foghorn-voiced Burr built his career on a series of seriously nasty movie turns, often lurking menacingly in the shadowy urban crannies of *film noir*: *Desperate* (1947), *Raw Deal* (1948), *The Pitfall* (1948), *Abandoned* (1949), *His Kind of Woman* (1951). It was he who was the terrifying killer who sneaks up behind wheelchair-bound voyeur James Stewart in Hitchcock's 1954 *Rear Window*, and it was he who played the nasty D.A. who vindictively nails Montgomery Clift in 1951's *A Place in the Sun*. While Mason made him living-room friendly, Burr was easily the scariest Canadian ever to haunt Hollywood movies. Bland Authority Figure, Northern Nasty, Support Staff.

Carson, Jack: (Born 1910, Carmen, Manitoba. Died 1963.) "The Canadian-born Carson," reads Jack Carson's entry in *Leonard Maltin's Movie Encyclopedia*, "had few equals in the portrayal of obstreperous, obnoxious, often dull-witted lunkheads." Couldn't have put it better ourselves. Possibly the ultimate Canadian character actor, the large and loud Carson specialized in sheer outsize obnoxiousness: over the course of a quarter-century career, he managed to annoy some of the brightest stars in the business, including Jimmy Stewart, James Cagney, Joan Crawford, Judy Garland and Paul Newman. Yet through it all, there was always something endearing about Carson's high-decibel wheedling, something needy, desperate and ultimately pathetic. As Canadians, it is therefore clearly our duty to be proud of him. Support Staff, Northern Nasty.

Chong, Tommy: (Born 1938, Edmonton, Alberta.) The most drugged-out comedy team in movie history was formed in Vancouver, when Edmonton native Tommy Chong, a former R&B guitar player, met Los Angelino Richard "Cheech" Marin in the late 1960s. After recording a number of hit albums revolving around various forms of pharmaceutical slapstick, they successfully hauled their bong to the big screen for a series of movies – *Up in Smoke* (1978), *Cheech & Chong's Next Movie* (1980), *Cheech & Chong's Nice Dreams* (1981), etc. – in which just saying yes made comedy possible: dope was to Cheech and Chong what vermouth was to Dean Martin. How to tell the difference between the Canadian and the American in this duo? Easy: the Canadian was the passive and stupid one who always had the munchies. Support Staff.

Cronyn, Hume: (Born 1911, London, Ontario.) Diminutive, versatile and intelligent character actor whose movie career began in Hitchcock's *Shadow of a Doubt*

The most drugged-out comedy team in movie history was formed in Vancouver, when Edmonton native Tommy Chong, a former R&B guitar player, met Los Angelino Richard "Cheech" Marin in the late 1960s.

(1943). Whether playing eccentric, nasty, cowardly or crotchety, he rarely walked away from a scene without leaving a burn mark. A noted playwright (*Foxfire*) and screenwriter (Hitchcock's *Rope* in 1948 and 1949's *Under Capricorn*) as well as actor, Cronyn never strayed far from the stage. Northern Nasty, Support Staff.

Czerny, Henry: (Born 1959, Toronto.) After years on the Toronto theatre scene, this classically handsome actor with the cobalt glare was cast by John N. Smith as the child-molesting priest Father Lavin, in the acclaimed CBC-NFB miniseries *The Boys of St. Vincent* (1993). Notwithstanding Czerny's chillingly convincing performance in that film, the program's critical kudos on both sides of the border put him in instant demand in Hollywood and at home. While his appearances in Canadian movies have ranged from gelid husbands (1995's *When Night is Falling*), to discombobulated yuppies (1995's *The Michelle Apartments*), his American appearances have demonstrated less variety: opposite Harrison Ford in 1994's *Clear and Present Danger* and Tom Cruise in 1996's *Mission: Impossible*, Czerny has appeared as a calculating, self-serving prick of the first order. In the long-standing tradition of casting intense Canadians as evil incar-

nate (see Huston, Plummer, Sutherland, Vernon et al.), Czerny appears to be a toweringly creepy addition. Northern Nasty, Support Staff.

Day, Richard: (Born 1896, Victoria, British Columbia. Died 1972.) One of Hollywood's most competent, influential and celebrated set designers, whose knack for studio-standard "realism" made him a favourite of top-flight directors including Erich Von Stroheim (who gave the Canadian his first set-decorating job on 1919's *Blind Husbands*), William Wyler (1936's *Dodsworth*), Fritz Lang (1941's *Man Hunt*), John Ford (1941's *How Green Was My Valley*) and Elia Kazan (1951's *A Streetcar Named Desire* and 1954's *On the Waterfront*). Possibly the ultimate behind-the-scenes Canuck, Day was to a movie's director what someone like Jack Carson was to a movie's star: a key supporting player. Support Staff.

Dressler, Marie: (Born 1869, Cobourg, Ontario. Died 1934.) After debuting opposite Chaplin in 1914's *Tillie's Punctured Romance*, this big-screen star went on to become one of the most popular performers of early talkies. An Oscar winner for her appearance opposite Wallace Beery in *Min and Bill* (1930), Dressler was an adept, scene-stealing sideliner, as her most famous moment in the movies testifies. Her wordless reaction in 1933's *Dinner At Eight*, after platinum bimbo-bombshell Jean Harlow announces, "I was reading a book the other day...," is arguably the funniest double take in the history of the movies. Voyageur, Support Staff.

Durbin, Deanna: (Born 1921, Winnipeg, Manitoba.) The most popular Canadian-born movie star after Mary Pickford was another paragon of purity, but for a subsequent generation: in

Deanna Durbin →

Deanna
Durbin

dozens of musicals and semi-musicals, the sweet-singing, teenage Durbin played the wholesome but perky ingenue whose irrepressible charm got her out of any scrapes she might unwittingly have backed into. When her popularity failed to keep up with her age, she walked away from the screen entirely in 1948, granting no interviews or public appearances since. Ice Cream Canuck.

Dwan, Allan: (Born 1885, Toronto, Ontario. Died 1981.) Dwan, who directed more than 400 movies in a career that spanned a half century, first went to Hollywood in 1911. Representing the Chicago-based American Film Company, Dwan had been asked to look into what had been delaying one of the company's productions out west. Upon arrival, he found out. "I suggest you disband the company," Dwan wired back. "You have no director." His bosses wired back: "You direct." Thus began one of the most prolific and wide-ranging directorial careers in movie history. Famous for his cagey but practical problem-solving techniques, it was Dwan who is credited as the first to devise the moving dolly shot and, while working with D. W. Griffith on *Intolerance* (1916), the crane shot. A producer and writer as well as director, Dwan's omnivorous talents allowed him to work efficiently and effectively in just about any narrative form: documentary (1927's *West Point*), family adventure (1937's *Heidi*), westerns (1939's *Frontier Marshall*), costume adventure (1939's *The Three Musketeers*), comedies (1945's *Brewster's Millions*) and war movies (1949's *The Sands of Iwo Jima*). In other words, not only the original Canadian- born Unteur, the ultimate one as well. Unteur, Voyageur.

In Hollywood since the mid-1960s, Furie has demonstrated a Jewison-like knack for making minor work with major stars.

Ford, Glenn: (Born 1916, Quebec City.) In California from the age of eight, this likable but restrained railroad executive's son based an enduring career on a combination of rugged good looks, a relaxed onscreen demeanour and a wide-ranging, cowpoke-to-comedy versatility. The first significant talkie-era male star to draw first breath in Canada, Ford's most memorable appearances include: *Gilda* (1946), *A Stolen Life* (1946), *The Man From the Alamo* (1953), *The Big Heat* (1953), *The Blackboard Jungle* (1955). Never quite a star of the first rank, but as solid a second-biller as Canada ever produced. Ice Cream Canuck, Bland Authority Figure, Northern Nasty.

Fox, Michael J.: (Born 1961, Edmonton, Alberta.) A precociously talented army brat raised in Vancouver, Fox first gained stardom as Alex P. Keaton, the teen-yuppie Republican in the enormously popular Reagan-era sitcom *Family Ties*. Indeed, it may be to his detriment that he ranks as one of the definitive icons of that all-or-nothing era. After making an effortless switch to big-screen stardom in 1985's *Back to the Future*, Fox's popularity both soared (1987's *Secret of My Success*, 1989's *Back to the Future II*) and skidded (1991's *The Hard Way*, 1993's *Life With Mikey*). The combined commercial failure of such earnestly noncomedic efforts as *Light of Day* (1987) and *Casualties of War* (1989), along with the dismal performances of such later comedies as *For Love or Money* (1993), and *Greedy* (1994), would suggest

that Fox's appeal might be as anchored to the eighties as Deanna Durbin was to the late Depression. Ice Cream Canuck.

Furie, Sidney J.: (Born 1933, Toronto, Ontario.) A TV director from age 21, Furie's feature career began with low-budget movies made in Canada before he left for England in 1960. There, his work was praised for its stylishness and scorned for its superficiality, a response which more or less defines the entire trajectory of Furie's wide-ranging but unspectacular career. In Hollywood since the mid-1960s, Furie has demonstrated a Jewison-like knack for making minor work with major stars. Though he has directed such marquee magnets as Michael Caine in *The Ipcress File* (1965), Marlon Brando in *The Appaloosa* (1966), Frank Sinatra in *The Naked Runner* (1967), and Robert Redford in *Little Fauss and Big Halsy* (1970), few of these collaborations rank prominently in posterity. Unteur.

Hill, Arthur: (Born 1922, Melfort, Saskatchewan.) Intelligent, able, perennially silver-haired actor who brought an unstressed but firm authority to a range of lawyers, doctors, politicians, scientists and military officers. Always good but never intrusive, Hill was sometimes easy to confuse with other career authoritarians like Hal Holbrook or fellow silver-haired Canuck, Leslie Nielsen. As comfortably efficient on TV (*Owen Marshall, Counselor-at-Law* (1971-1974) as he was in movies (1971's *The Andromeda Strain*, 1976's *Futureworld*), Hill, like fellow Bland Authority Figures Bill Shatner and Lorne Greene, was every bit as convincing pitching instant coffee in TV ads as he was interrogating witnesses. Bland Authority Figure, Ice Cream Canuck, Support Staff.

Hiller, Arthur: (Born 1923, Edmonton, Alberta.) After working for CBC-TV, Hiller moved to New York in time for the so-called "Golden Era," during which, like Norman Jewison, he directed both live and episodic TV drama. In Hollywood since the late 1950s, Hiller's movie career is as wide-ranging in subject as it is undistinguished in expression. It is thus revealing that his two best films – 1964's *The Americanization of Emily* and 1971's *The Hospital* – were based on the best scripts he was ever offered. His commercial zenith was the blockbusting hippie-era hugfest *Love Story* (1970), followed by 1976's disaster-comedy *Silver Streak*. As the president of the Academy of Motion Picture Arts and Sciences since 1993, he has lately become conspicuous as the man with the electroshock Einstein haircut who opens the annual Oscar nomination ceremony. Ice Cream Canuck, Unteur.

Huston, Walter: (Born 1884, Toronto, Ontario. Died 1950.) Versatile, intense and intelligent character actor, father of director-actor John Huston. After a long stage apprenticeship, the big-voiced Huston switched to movies at the dawn of talkies. As capable of compelling lead performances (1933's *Gabriel Over the White House*, 1936's *Dodsworth*) as he was indelible supporting turns (1942's *Yankee Doodle Dandy*, 1946's *Duel in the Sun*), he was also a bad guy's bad guy: his turn as the cackling, unflossed codger in his son's *Treasure of the Sierra Madre* (1948) is an unforgettable exercise in greedy feral energy. Possibly the ultimate Canadian-born supporting presence – strong yet sidelined – as son John certainly knew when he cast Walter as the dying ship's captain who appears only long enough to deliver the Maltese Falcon to Bogart's Sam Spade. Northern Nasty, Support Staff.

Kidder, Margot: (Born 1948, Yellowknife, Northwest Territories.) Husky-voiced, distinctive and effortlessly sensual, Kidder has had a career which seems almost a paradigm for the experience of Canadian women performers in Hollywood. Like Genevieve Bujold, Kate Nelligan and Helen Shaver, Kidder started off in Tinseltown with lead potential – culminating with four turns as Lois Lane opposite Christopher Reeve's Superman – before being relegated to the periphery. While her post-Lois roles have often been in disappointing vehicles – 1989's *Mob Story*, 1990's *White Room* – she is rarely less than striking. In 1996, Kidder made headlines briefly after being found, wandering and disoriented, by Los Angeles police. Support Staff.

Kotcheff, Ted: (Born 1931, Toronto, Ontario.) Like Norman Jewison and Sidney Furie, Kotcheff's career kicked in when he left Canada to pursue the more encouraging opportunities offered in England during the 1950s. After much TV work and a couple of passable features – 1965's *Life at the Top*, 1971's *Outback* – he turned heads back in Canada with his funny, salty and energetic adaptation of his buddy Mordecai Richler's *The Apprenticeship of Duddy Kravitz* in 1974. (In a graceful example of backhanded hometown praise, former *Maclean's* critic

> Massey, arguably the movies' ultimate patriarch, always looked down on those around him, sometimes with divine concern, sometimes with terrifying wrath.

John Hofsess called it "the best Canadian film the United States has ever produced.") Since then, Kotcheff's career has proven nothing if not free-ranging, encompassing everything from westerns and comedies to – his biggest box-office score so far – right-wing paramilitary fantasies: not only was it Kotcheff who brought the character of John Rambo to the screen in 1982's *First Blood*, he made the very first of the Reagan era's rousing back-to-Vietnam wet dreams, *Uncommon Valor*, a year later. More recent credits include *Weekend at Bernie's* (1989). Kotcheff's assessment in Ephraim Katz's *The Film Encyclopedia* – "assured technical skill if no particular distinction" – could well stand as the motto for all Canadian Unteurs in Hollywood. Unteur.

Massey, Raymond: (Born 1896, Toronto, Ontario. Died 1983.) Archetypal Canadian supporting character actor: commanding but never overwhelming, and able, like Donald Sutherland later, to shift deftly from paternalistic calm to terrifying fanaticism between roles. Indeed, it was this inescapable quality of paternalism which more or less defined Massey's career. Over the course of a career which encompassed two turns as Abraham Lincoln (1940's *Abe Lincoln in Illinois*, 1962's *How the West Was Won*), one as fanatical abolitionist John Brown (1940's *Sante Fe Trail*), and a brilliant but underrated performance as James Dean's icily stern father in 1955's *East of Eden*, Massey, arguably the movies' ultimate patriarch, always looked down on those around him, sometimes with divine concern, sometimes with terrifying wrath. By the early 1960s, he had fulfilled his Canuck destiny by becoming one of the era's best-loved Bland Authority Figures on

TV: the firm but kindly Dr. Gillespie on the *Dr. Kildare* television show (1961-1966). Northern Nasty, Support Staff, Bland Authority Figure.

Morse, Barry: (Born 1918, London, England.) As Lt. Philip Gerard in the top-rated American series *The Fugitive* (1963-1967), Barry Morse played one of the most doggedly determined cops in TV history. Week after week, he pursued the unjustly suspected wife-killer Richard Kimble (David Janssen) with a tenacity which, if you thought about such things, gave away the actor's Canadian citizenship: though he was playing an American, Morse's Gerard was like some kind of Energizer Mountie. Moreover, as Gerard was at once fearsome and sympathetic – just a cop doing his job – the character was both a righteous authority figure and a bad guy: a triple-threat Canuck if ever there was, even if the actor who played him was born in England. Sadly, never again did Morse really have a large- or small-screen role quite as ripe as Lt. Gerard: while he was never less than good – if occasionally high-toned and hammy – he was rarely so in much that mattered. Also, like Christopher Plummer's, the chameleonic Morse's accent could shift from British to American to generic mid-Atlantic depending on the dramatic climate. Bland Authority Figure, Support Staff, Northern Nasty.

Nelligan, Kate: (Born 1951, London, Ontario.) Trained at London's Central School of Speech and Drama, this impeccably professional, stage-trained actress had, in the early 1980s, a brief shot at above-the-title Hollywood stardom. Yet, as admirable as her work was in such Nelligan vehicles as 1981's *Eye of the Needle* – opposite Donald Sutherland's

> **Instrumental in establishing the Hollywood star system as we now know it, Pickford was one of the first movie stars to exert complete control over her projects, image and career.**

terrifying Nazi spy – 1983's *Without A Trace* and 1985's *Eleni*, audiences never warmed to her clinically precise but emotionally remote characterizations. Since, she has moved to the periphery and blossomed in a series of memorable supporting and secondary roles: 1989's *Love and Hate* (a CBC-TV miniseries aired in Canada and the U.S.), 1991's *Frankie and Johnny*, 1994's *Wolf*, 1995's *Margaret's Museum*, 1996's *Up Close and Personal*. Like a true Canadian, she seems to shine brightest from a slight distance. Support Staff.

Petrie, Daniel J.: (Born 1920, Glace Bay, Nova Scotia.) In describing the oeuvre of Daniel J. Petrie, whose career began as a Broadway actor following a wartime stint in the Canadian army, it is impossible not to resort to terms like "tasteful," "professional," "well-intentioned," "inoffensive" and "just plain dull." Like fellow Unteurs Furie, Hiller, Kotcheff and Jewison, Petrie seems capable of working in just about any genre without making a dent in any of them. That is why his best film, the often-harrowing cop drama *Fort Apache, The Bronx* (1981) therefore seems *suspiciously* good, as if by accident. Other films include *The Neptune Factor* (1973), *Lifeguard* (1976) and *The Betsy* (1978). In 1984, he paid homage to his country by making a tasteful, professional, well-inten-

tioned and just plain dull movie on Canadian soil. Called *The Bay Boy*, it featured Kiefer Sutherland, in his movie debut, in a role inspired by Petrie's own childhood. Would that it had been about growing up as Donald Sutherland and Shirley Douglas's son. Unteur.

Pickford, Mary: (Born 1893, Toronto, Ontario. Died 1979.) The biggest star ever to pass through U.S.-Canadian customs – if not the biggest movie star *period* – was also the original Ice Cream Canuck: in her post-adolescent, ringletted heyday, Pickford parlayed a precociously fearless innocence into the most popular screen persona of the silent era. For years one of the world's top box-office draws, she was as fiercely tenacious a businesswoman off-screen as she was a guileless waif on. Instrumental in establishing the Hollywood star system as we now know it, Pickford was one of the first movie stars to exert complete control over her projects, image and career. With Douglas Fairbanks and Charlie Chaplin she altered the course of studio history by forming United Artists Corporation, the very first star-controlled production company, in 1919. Two years earlier, she had negotiated a staggering $350,000-per-picture contract with First National. If, by 1996, Jim Carrey was commanding over $20 million per picture, he had Mary Pickford, also amusingly known as "America's Sweetheart," to thank. Ice Cream Canuck.

Pidgeon, Walter: (Born 1897, East Saint John, New Brunswick. Died 1984.) As solid a supporter as the Dominion ever shipped southward, Pidgeon performed impeccably from the sidelines of dozens of movies. Possessed of a rich voice and an almost scholarly demeanour, he furnished unflappable support in a myriad of

Christopher Plummer as Sir John A. MacDonald

Mack Sennett

secondary roles ranging from newspaper publishers to submarine commanders. Perhaps best known as Greer Garson's somewhat dispassionate love interest in *Mrs. Miniver* (1942), his most resonant moment in Canadian terms is easily his turn as the blandly megalomaniacal scientist in 1956's *Forbidden Planet*, if only because he plays a guy who wakes up one day to find that fellow hoser Leslie Nielsen has landed on his planet. Bland Authority Figure, Northern Nasty, Support Staff.

Plummer, Christopher: (Born 1927, Toronto, Ontario.) Patrician and precise, Plummer is the kind of classically trained actor who always seems to be visibly slumming it in the movies. Indeed, his most famous off-screen utterance was a withering dismissal of the most popular movie he has ever appeared in, 1965's blockbuster musical *The Sound of Music*. For Plummer, the great-grandson of Canadian prime minister Sir John Abbott, it was "the sound of mucus." It is hard to tell if his apparent contempt of the medium is what's kept him from good roles – "I've never had a great part in a movie," he admitted in 1982. "I've never really made an impact in a film" – or if the lack of good roles is what accounts for his disdain. Still, for someone who so clearly lives for art, he's certainly appeared in a lot of shite: *Lock Up Your Daughters* (1969), *Aces High* (1976), *Starcrash* (1979), *Vampires in Venice* (1987), *Liar's Edge* (1992). Best Mondo moments: as the overly tanned, medallion-wearing psycho-killer stalking Elliott Gould in 1978's *The Silent Partner*, and as the Klingon commander out to toast Captain Kirk in 1991's *Star Trek VI: The Undiscovered Country*. Needless to say,

> **During the silent era, Sennett was the undisputed czar of screen comedy, an actor, director, writer, impresario and self-made mogul who successfully married blistering hilarity with assembly-line production.**

the spectacle of Plummer chin-to-chin with Bill Shatner is nothing short of the intergalactic ham-off of the next millennium. Support Staff, Bland Authority Figure, Northern Nasty.

Reeves, Keanu: (Born 1965, Beirut, Lebanon.) Reeves lived in Australia and New York before moving to Toronto later in his childhood, so his claim on Canuckhood is, admittedly, tenuous. Still, since his formative training and professional years correspond with that time spent on the shores of Lake Ontario, far be it from us to make the guy give back his flannel. Besides, as one of the most perplexing stars of his generation – has any male beauty since Tony Curtis seemed so refreshingly unconcerned about appearing out of his depth? – the almond-eyed, slightly zoned-out actor is like Chris Plummer in reverse: instead of slumming in movies while pining for the footlights, Reeves takes on high-toned movie roles (1988's *Dangerous Liaisons*, 1991's *My Own Private Idaho*, 1992's *Bram Stoker's Dracula*, 1993's *Much Ado About Nothing*), when maybe he should stick to schlock like *Speed* (1994). Let's face it: who else would – as Reeves did in 1995 – put off a multimillion-dollar movie career in order to play Hamlet in Winnipeg? One doubts even Mr.

Plummer loves Shakespeare quite that much. Ice Cream Canuck.

Rubinek, Saul: (Born 1948, Wolfrathausen, Germany.) Born in a German refugee camp and raised in Toronto, the curly-haired, compulsively squirming Rubinek is currently one of the best Canadian-bred supporting actors working. Indeed, watching him, one regrets he wasn't around when the movie was made of Mordecai Richler's *The Apprenticeship of Duddy Kravitz*. Best at playing fast-talking, seedy cowards – 1984's *Against All Odds*, 1987's *Wall Street*, 1992's *Unforgiven* and 1995's *Nixon* – Rubinek has, unsurprisingly, earned the attention of some of Hollywood's more daring directors, including Oliver Stone, Clint Eastwood and Brian De Palma. Curiously, his work in Canada (like Donald Sutherland's) tends to be far less edgy, as performances in Canadian movies like *The Outside Chance of Maximilian Glick* (1988) and *The Quarrel* (1991) attest. Sometimes it takes an American to see how dirty a Canadian can be. Northern Nasty, Support Staff.

Sennett, Mack: (Born 1880, Danville, Quebec. Died 1960.) If popular comedy currently belongs to Canada, the first Canuck to stake the claim was Mack Sennett. During the silent era, he was the undisputed czar of screen comedy, an actor, director, writer, impresario and self-made mogul who successfully married blistering hilarity with assembly-line production. Originally an actor, he picked up his directing skills by closely observing no less a pro than D. W. Griffith, for whom he worked as a performer, writer and eventually a director himself at Manhattan's legendary Biograph studios. Leaving Griffith and Biograph in 1912, Sennett established Keystone Pictures

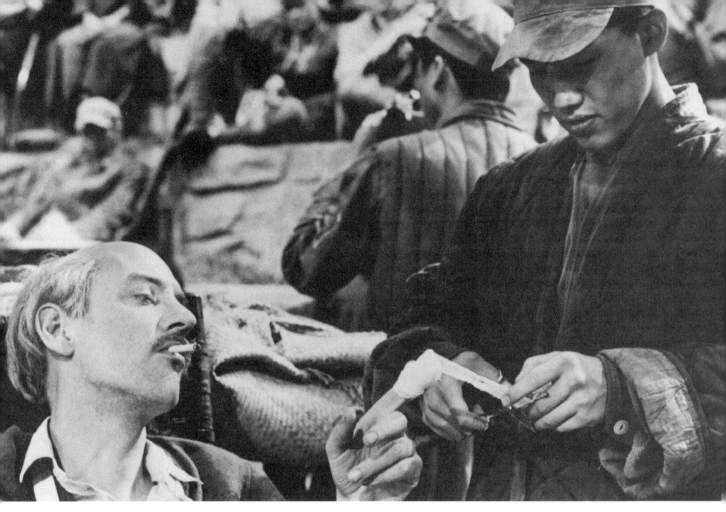

Donald Sutherland as Bethume

with himself as head. It was there, initially as a director and later as producer, that Sennett refined the kinetic American slapstick tradition to a form of genuine popular art: no one had Sennett's comic vision or timing, which was only made more apparent by countless inferior imitations. Over the decades in which he was screen comedy's king, he either discovered or significantly abetted the following careers: Charlie Chaplin, Roscoe "Fatty" Arbuckle, Chester Conklin, Harry Langdon and Gloria Swanson. He is arguably the chief architect of American silent comedy, and it should surprise no one reading this book to learn that he was a Canadian. *Voyageur.*

Shaver, Helen: (Born 1951, St. Thomas, Ontario.) With the exception of her sharply observed turn as a woman awakening to her Sapphic inclinations in 1985's *Desert Hearts*, this compelling, sultry-voiced performer has largely been wasted in wife-and-girlfriend bimbo limbo on-screen: her main function in 1986's *The Color of Money* was to certify aging Paul Newman's ageless beauty; as her role in the awesomely dreadful *Bethune: The Making of a Hero* (1990), it was to certify Donald Sutherland's messianic righteousness. Which is way too bad: as long as she's being paid primarily to make her male costars look good, one senses Shaver is only demonstrating a fraction of what she can do. Indeed, one *knows* it: *Desert Hearts*, with practically no guys around at all, is proof. *Support Staff.*

Shearer, Norma: (Born 1900, Montreal, Quebec. Died 1983.) Legend has it that Irving Thalberg, the "boy wonder" producer who inspired F. Scott Fitzgerald's *The Last Tycoon*, first spotted Norma Shearer, whom he would marry in 1927, in a bit part in a movie called *The Stealers* (1920). Impressed as well as smitten, Thalberg took three years to track Shearer down, by which time he was working for former Saint John, New Brunswick, resident Louis B. Mayer at the mighty MGM studios. Under Thalberg's guidance, the moderately talented, moderately attractive Shearer, who had come to New York with her family after her father's business in Canada collapsed, nevertheless became one of the studio's top stars, and remained so until Thalberg's untimely death at 37 in 1936. Proof of Thalberg's strategic role in Shearer's ascent can be found in the fact that, in his absence, she turned down lead roles in both *Mrs. Miniver* and *Gone With the Wind.* By 1942, she had married a significantly younger ski instructor and permanently retired. Her Quebec-born

Alan Thicke

brother Douglas (1899-1971) headed MGM's sound department for more than four decades, earning no less than a dozen Oscars for the studio. Voyageur.

Silverheels, Jay: (Born 1919, Six Nations Reserve, Ontario. Died 1980.) Born – believe it or not – Harold J. Smith, Silverheels was the handsome and athletically gifted son of a Mohawk chief. He joined the movies as the craze for westerns was in full swing, which meant a lot of work on horseback dressed in some Hollywood designer's idea of full tribal regalia: *Broken Arrow* (1950), *The Battle at Apache Pass* (1952), *Saskatchewan* (1954). But it was TV, in the role of loyal sidekick Tonto to The Lone Ranger, that made Silverheels an Eisenhower-era popcult icon. While his unequivocal subservience to "kemo sabe" induces cringing in more enlightened times, the fact is he was the most visible and best-loved Native in popular culture during his era. Support Staff.

Smith, John N.: (Born 1943, Montreal, Quebec). Former NFB documentary director who made a successful shift to Hollywood production with the implausible but enormously popular 1995 hit *Dangerous Minds*. After shifting from drama to reality-based docudrama at the NFB (1986's *Sitting in Limbo*, 1987's *Train of Dreams*, 1989's *Welcome To Canada*), Smith made *The Boys of St. Vincent* in 1993, a harrowing but gripping account of systemic child abuse at a Catholic boys' school. Aired to a chorus of acclaim on both sides of the border, *Boys* paved the way for Smith's entry to Hollywood production. An earnest and committed liberal who makes films to make points, he may be the only filmmaker currently in the North American commercial mainstream who represents

> **Due to the fortuitous combination of his scarecrow physique and cultivatedly eccentric manner, Sutherland can't help seeing the contented outsider no matter where he appears.**

the NFB tradition of socially engaged movie practice. Ice Cream Canuck.

Sutherland, Donald: (Born 1934, Saint John, New Brunswick.) Tall, gaunt and endowed with a voice as rich and deep as Hudson Bay, Donald Sutherland is one of Canada's most satisfying Hollywood exports primarily because he's one of the unlikeliest. Due to the fortuitous combination of his scarecrow physique and cultivatedly eccentric manner, Sutherland can't help seeing the contented outsider no matter where he appears, which makes him possibly the most sheerly Canadian of Canadians performing in movies today. Not surprising, considering his gothically feral appearance, he began in a number of geek-and-psycho roles before scoring counter-cultural success as the glibly anti-authoritarian Hawkeye Pierce in Robert Altman's *M*A*S*H* (1970), a movie which made him an A-list star through most of the 1970s. As undeniably brilliant a performer as he is a dubiously inconsistent judge of scripts – it is typical of Sutherland to career from a breathtaking cameo in *JFK* one year (1991) to a humiliating turn in *Buffy the Vampire Slayer* (1992) the next – Sutherland has always seemed as fiercely unpredictable and independent off-screen as on. In other words, if being Canadian means

not fitting in, no one has misfitted quite so glamorously. Bland Authority Figure, Northern Nasty, Support Staff.

Sutherland, Kiefer: (Born 1966, London, England.) The son of actor Donald Sutherland and actor-activist Shirley Douglas, this eerie ringer for his father – replete with that *voice* – became an unlikely teen heart-throb in a series of youth-oriented eighties vehicles: *The Lost Boys* (1987), *Young Guns* (1988), *Flatliners* (1990). While a vastly less substantial performer than his father, the younger Sutherland nevertheless has on-screen presence to burn, and has apparently inherited dad's rather eccentric approach to project selection: one year he may be on hunky display in a teen-mag pin-up version of *The Three Musketeers* (1993), another as a psycho-kidnapper terrorizing Sally Field in *Eye For An Eye* (1996). Ultimately, like his father, he may prove too unconventional an actor to settle comfortably into romantic or heroic leads, but one gets the impression that, like Donald, he might thrive on the periphery. Northern Nasty, Support Staff.

Thicke, Alan: (Born 1947, Kirkland Lake, Ontario.) Actor, writer, composer, comedian, musician, talk-show host, program developer: as a key but often uncredited force in just about every conceivable aspect of mainstream American TV production, Alan Thicke may be the ultimate generalist currently working in the medium of television – the Forrest Gump of Hollywood Canadians. After a brief and unhappy stint at the CBC as a writer-performer, Thicke moved to Hollywood where he began penning specials for such light-entertainment superstars as Barry Manilow, Tony Orlando and Olivia Newton-John. Unbelievably, at the same time as he was

Mary Pickford

filling Barry Manilow's mouth, he was also contributing salty schtick to the stand-up arsenals of Sam Kinison, Richard Pryor and Robin Williams.

A musician since childhood, Thicke also proved himself an adept composer of catchy theme tunes, tinkling out the themes for *Wheel of Fortune*, *The Facts of Life* and *Diff'rent Strokes*. By the end of the 1970s, he had brought two of the boldest comedy experiments in U.S. TV history to air: *Fernwood 2-Night* (1977-1978) and its successor, *America 2-Night* (1978). In the eighties he entered his talk-show period: first in the afternoon on CTV, and later on the ill-fated late-night entry *Thicke of the Night*. Then came several years as the insufferably lovable father figure on the sitcom *Growing Pains* (1985–1991). In the mid-nineties, he appeared in another sitcom,

> **Alan Thicke may be the ultimate generalist currently working in the medium of television – the Forrest Gump of Hollywood Canadians.**

Hope & Gloria. Unsubstantiated rumours also place him on the grassy knoll in Dallas on November 22, 1963. Ice Cream Canuck.

Vernon, John: (Born 1932, Montreal, Quebec.) Not surprisingly, it began with that unmistakable voice: after winning a scholarship to the Royal Academy of Dramatic Arts in London, England, the blue-eyed, rough-complexioned Vernon was asked to provide the voice of Big Brother in the 1956 movie version of *1984*. Returning to Canada, he divided his time between classical theatre and dramatic TV, the most noteworthy latter

effort being the mid-sixties CBC series *Wojeck*, in which Vernon played a dogged, clench-jawed coroner a full 20 years before Jack Klugman started gnawing American network scenery as Quincy. But it is as a Hollywood villain that Vernon made his most lasting pop-cultural impression. In dozens of movies – and most notably 1967's *Point Blank*, 1969's *Tell Them Willie Boy is Here*, 1971's *Dirty Harry*, 1973's *Charley Varrick*, 1976's *The Outlaw Josey Wales* and 1978's *National Lampoon's Animal House* – Vernon has brought a chilling grace and intelligence to his bad-guy turns which has made him one of the most watchable purveyors of artificial evil in contemporary movies. Of all the Canucks who have been so very good at playing bad, Vernon is the undisputed baddest. Support Staff, Northern Nasty.

Sheer Hoser
Bob and Doug Take Off, Briefly

By 1981, the program, *SCTV*, was finally showing signs of hard-won success. Not only had the show finally been picked up for national broadcast by the CBC, who'd turned it down when it was shopped as a concept five years earlier, it had attained the great brass ring of Canadian broadcasting: an American network slot on NBC.

Could be that's why Rick Moranis wasn't too happy when his boss, Andrew Alexander, came in to tell the cast the bad news about the Canadian-content problem. In fact, he was pissed. He'd had the CanCon boom lowered over his head before, and it had left a nasty, lingering bump. Before taking up comedy, Moranis had been a Toronto top-40 deejay when the state-imposed Canadian content regulations went into effect. This, of course, meant that a certain percentage of his playlist had to be certifiably Canadian. Moranis saw it as an act of legislative interference, a manifestation of the worst kind of Canadian parochialism: an example of the government imposing national culture on the populace. And what really galled him was the underlying assumption behind the boss's suggestion that, despite the fact that most of *SCTV*'s writers and performers were Canadian – and therefore couldn't help but reflect a Canadian point of view in their work – it still just wasn't Canadian enough. (Besides, what could be more Canadian than satirizing American pop culture?)

← Bob McKenzie

Doug McKenzie →

The Great White North album cover

Still, *SCTV* executive producer Andrew Alexander was in something of a jam the day he came to talk to the crew – a jam which had in fact been created by the program's long-overdue good fortune. As it turned out, the Canadian version of the show was two minutes longer than the American version, because the CBC – bless its grey-flannel heart – had fewer commercials. Therefore, CBC had told Alexander to come up with two extra minutes for the Canadian edition of the show. And, the Corporation stressed, make that two extra *distinctly Canadian* minutes. That's what bugged Moranis; it stuck in *SCTV* head writer Dave Thomas's craw, as well. In 1981, Thomas recalled his initial response: "We're Canadian and we're doing a show. How Canadian do you want to get?" You want Canadian? Moranis thought. Really, distinctly, incontrovertibly Canadian? Well, you got it, bub. "So I said, 'Get us some back bacon, a grill, some cases of beer,'" Moranis told *Quest* magazine in 1982. "We'll give you Canadian. 'Good day, how's it goin'?"

And that's how Bob and Doug McKenzie, the Canadian uberhosers who were almost as big as the Beatles for a fleeting media moment, were born. The irony of this creation story was not lost on Dave Thomas. "When Rick and I portrayed the characters, we weren't trying to make any kind of political statement," Thomas noted with some understatement in 1985. "We were, if you'll recall, just trying to fill two minutes of Canadian content that was legislated by the Canadian government. I'm not sure if I believe that entertainment is an issue of nationalism, or that it should be protected like that, but Bob and Doug are sort of the freak results of that legislation."

Perhaps since they were the ones who had bitched with such artful sarcasm, it was left to Moranis and Thomas to cough up the last-minute CanCon. Which they did, and precisely according to Moranis's snarky guidelines: a flat with two folding chairs was hauled in, along with a barbecue laden with back bacon, a map of Canada for a backdrop and several cases of Canadian beer in stubby bottles. This was to be the set for the so-called McKenzie Brothers: two toque-bearing, parka-wearing, prototypically Canuck dimwits whose role was to fill those two distinctly Canadian minutes with some entirely unscripted banter about some distinctly Canadian topic, like how to get a mouse into a beer bottle for a free case, or why doughnut shops have fewer parking spots than tables. And, just in case the Canadian angle was too subtle, the boys opened the segment with a theme song that evoked the sound of drunken loons washed up on a Muskoka beach: "*Coo roo coo coo, coo coo coo coo! Coo roo coo coo, coo coo coo coo!*"

It was Moranis and Thomas's intention that the throwaway gag would be just that: thrown away once the point had been made about the sheer idiocy of the Canadian content regulation. Which is one of the reasons that the two comedians, both of whom were among the program's most accomplished writers, decided not to bother scripting the segment. What was the point? In one day,

THE COMPLETE
HOSER'S
HANDBOOK

"A book for us, eh? Beauty!"

The official guide to identifying the complete Hoser (or Hosette) that you prob'ly are even if you think you know the score (Habs: 6; Leafs: 0) and you been down the States a few times . . .

I f you have more than a couple cases of two-four waiting to go back to the In & Out Store . . .

I f you think Coke is something you mix with a mickey of rye, not something you put up your nose . . .

I f a hot turkey sandwich with chips 'n' gravy and a Half-Moon for dessert is a darn good supper . . .

T hen you'd better get in goal cause this book's a centre shot on you!

"Inside every Canadian hides a Hoser waiting to get out and switch on the hockey game."
Beauty Calabash, That Summer in Paris, Ont.

HUGH BREWSTER & JOHN FORBES

Hosermania spinoff

they taped 40 two-minute segments of the mock program called *The Great White North*. Of those, ten were selected for broadcast. Pulling off their toques and unzipping their parkas, Moranis and Thomas probably thought that would be the last they'd hear about Bob and Doug McKenzie. And good riddance, eh?

Then, after a few weeks, the letters started to come in. The show had always received mail, but the volume was growing, not just because of the program's expanded broadcasting domain: most of it was rapturous praise of the McKenzie Brothers. The second indication that the throwaway skit had bounced back big time came at a club in Regina, where Moranis and Thomas – who taped the show in Edmonton – were trying out the routine on a live audience. They were shocked to walk onstage and see no less than 200 toque-bearing heads, most of them loudly emitting the choicest of McKenzieisms: "Take off, eh!," "Hosehead!," "*Coo roo coo coo, coo coo coo coo...!*," "Zoom in!" To the infinite surprise of those who had started it, Hosermania was officially under way.

The next indication of the McKenzification of the masses was the first annual Back Bacon Festival, held again in Regina. (A city which therefore qualifies, for reasons perhaps too dark to be developed here, as Hosermania's Sarajevo.) "When we arrived," Moranis recalled, "there were 500 people dressed exactly like us and screaming at us."

For reasons the McKenzies' creators were far too dumbfounded to account for, Bob and Doug had officially mutated into one of those genuine TV-issue popcult phenomena: the kind usually generated by hit shows, and which move people to suddenly start acting, speaking and dressing like the prime-time supernova of the moment. It had happened with Davy Crockett, *Star Trek*, *Saturday Night Live* and Fonzie, and now it was happening with Bob and Doug. "We'd been told we were a phenomenon," Moranis told an interviewer at Hosermania's height, "but we didn't really believe it until we saw ourselves along with Brezhnev on *The National*. There was Knowlton Nash, talking about us." He added: "We'd like to have him on our show, but he's such a hoser. Brezhnev, that is, not Knowlton."

While Moranis (Bob) and Thomas (Doug) weren't sure why Bob and Doug had caught on like brushfire – "At the moment, we don't even know where they're from," Moranis admitted – they were astute enough popcult observers to know that it wouldn't last: as sure as Molson brewed beer and moose were ugly, something else would come along sooner than later. In early 1982, Moranis confessed, "I worry about Bob and Doug McKenzie. Something that hot has to cool off. I'd just like to sell some T-shirts before they do." Choosing one of three recording deals which had come in a single week, Moranis and Thomas went into a studio to record the McKenzie Brothers' one and only album, which appropriately contained a vocal cameo by hoser deity (and lead singer of Rush) Geddy Lee. The record, released in autumn 1981, went through the roof, vaulting to number one in Canada and selling more than 300,000 copies in less than a month. In November of that year, Hosermania reached peak popcult hysteria in Toronto, on the day that Moranis and Thomas agreed to participate in a Hoser Day parade, which made its boisterous way from suburban Scarborough all the way to the A&A – "Eh and Eh"? Get it? – record store in the heart of downtown Toronto.

The parade drew an estimated 5,000 people, the vast majority of whom were

----

Hoser Etymology

During the brief period of McKenzie mania in the early eighties, the word "hoser" became more popular than back bacon itself. It was used to describe that distinctly Canadian prototype parodied by Moranis and Thomas: the beer-swilling, toque-wearing, down-home type of guy. But what does the term actually mean? The answer can be found in the 1967 book, *A Dictionary of Canadianisms*, which defines the verb "hose." To wit: "Transferred use of a vulgarism referring to the male role in copulation. Slang. Take advantage of, treat unfairly. From the *Globe and Mail*, Dec. 15, 1964: 'I'm sick and tired of the way the Rangers got hosed by the officials in this league.'"

Since we're amateur etymologists, we're assuming that a "hoser" is someone who "hoses." As the dictionary points out, "Many persons today use this term in complete ignorance of its vulgar origin." So that's what it means. Now take off.

dressed in full B & D regalia: parkas, toques, earmuffs, flannel and mitts. (Keeps your beers warm, eh?) Cars were driven by suds-swilling yahoos coo-roo-coo-coo-ing it for their lives, and decorated with such wry masking-tape messages as "This is our float, eh?" One vehicle even had a canoe on top, stacked high with cases of beer and teetering toque-heads.

Then things started to take a turn for the weird. It got to the point where Thomas couldn't even go Christmas shopping with his wife without fans shrieking, "Take off, you hoser!" in his face, a development that kept him pretty well housebound for months. Other lives were beginning to be made miserable by the McKenzie phenomenon too. A friend of Thomas's complained that his wife, a teacher, had completely lost control of her class because every single kid was making like Bob and Doug. In Edmonton, it was arguably even scarier: there, a car rally was held in which schoolteachers were all dressed like Bob and Doug. Meanwhile, back in Regina, where the symptoms of mass hysteria known as the McKenzie Syndrome were first diagnosed, people were wearing toques and parkas to RoughRider football games in ninety-degree heat.

But strangely, the most peculiar expressions of Hosermania, not to mention the most widespread and intense, came not from Canada but the States, where the Bob and Doug phenomenon was even bigger. And uglier. For Thomas, easily the most unsettling moment in Bob and Doug's 15 minutes came at a record store in California where 800 kids had been drinking beer for several hours by the time Moranis and Thomas showed up at 11:00

Bob and Doug McKenzie: The original Dumb and Dumber

a.m.: "It was a real mob," Thomas told an interviewer in 1986. "It wasn't an audience. It was a mob. It was pretty scary. It was so loud that even with the microphones and giant speakers, Rick and I couldn't hear each other. We looked at each other and said, 'Is there any point to this?'"

Apparently there was. Instead of walking away from the act before it had a chance to cool, Moranis and Thomas decided to accept the inevitable offer to take the McKenzie Brothers to Hollywood. In 1982, the two announced that they'd be leaving *SCTV* to codirect and costar in a feature-length, big-budget movie about Bob and Doug to be called *Strange Brew*.

When the movie – which had something to do with Bob and Doug waging battle against a megalomaniacal brew-

It got to the point where Thomas couldn't even go Christmas shopping with his wife without fans shrieking, "Take off, you hoser!" in his face.

meister played by Max von Sydow – was released the following year, it unspooled to largely empty theatres for a couple of weeks before disappearing altogether. The mobs had pulled off their toques, finished their beers and moved on, and the malls were once again safe for Dave Thomas to go quietly Christmas shopping. Within a year or so, Moranis and Thomas were on separate, but not parallel, career tracks. While Moranis became an enduringly bankable Hollywood com-

edy star, Thomas's post-hoser profile was much lower. Certainly the *Strange Brew* experience dampened what directorial ambitions either might have had: despite his indisputable clout, Moranis hasn't directed anything since, and Thomas's sole directorial effort, the John Travolta spy comedy *The Experts*, was deemed unreleasable.

Still, ephemeral as Hosermania was, its legacy bears consideration. For a brief time, not only did the intense beam of continental popcult obsession light on something both Canadian and absurdly so, but it made it cool to be a hoser. So what if it came and went faster than a beer on a hot afternoon? For it was a beauty while it lasted, eh?

"Canadians are — I don't know how to say it — retiring, laid-back. We tend to shy away from dramatic confrontations and that's the essence of good theatre, good movies, good television."

— NORMAN JEWISON

Canadian Pinko Norman Jewison

Combing the three decades of press clippings generated by Norman Jewison, called "the most successful Canadian director in the history of the movies" by *Maclean's* magazine in 1988, one occasionally experiences jarring moments of dissonance, when the guy you're reading about simply doesn't gibe with the Norman Jewison who is such an entrenched senior member of the Canadian cultural establishment. For example, turn to a 1966 article in *The Hollywood Reporter* concerning Jewison's gentle Cold War comedy *The Russians Are Coming, The Russians Are Coming*, and you'll find the film-maker being bluntly referred to as "a Canadian pinko." Or take this quotation, which comes from Jewison's Los Angeles agent, Larry Auerbach: "We have terrible fights. He wants to do movies nobody wants to finance. Then there's the politics. I wish Norman would shut up about American politics — he's known as a Canadian here, an outsider. He's getting better, but all the anti-American statements he made in the 1960s really hurt him in this town."

Norman Jewison a pinko? An anti-American outsider with a case of verbal runoff about politics? Hold the phone – can this be the same Norman Jewison we in Canada know today, the avuncular figure who presides over the stately Canadian Film Centre in suburban Toronto, who has been profiled generously by just about every mainstream organ in the country and whose beaming, bearded face has been flashbulbed flanking his wife at tony black-tie events by the dozens? The man who makes such inoffensive entertainments as *Moonstruck*, *Other People's Money* and *Only You*? Are we sure we're talking about the same guy?

The fact is, we are. Moreover, it's in the apparent contradiction between the image of the politically outspoken Canuck pinko and the staid establishment fixture that the real Canadian essence of Norman Jewison may dwell. For the contradiction between the commitment to politics and the commitment to entertain — between mobilization and amusement, between anger and eagerness to please — and even the belief that the two can happily serve the same master, is a deeply liberal notion. The peculiar trajectory of Norman Jewison's career, from the man who was considered a Canadian threat in the 1960s, to the man who seems to spend as much time making public appearances as movies in the 1990s, must be understood in the context of Jewison's deep-seated liberalism.

It makes sense that Canada gives good liberal entertainment. By definition, liberalism implies such decent notions as tolerance, empathy, cooperation and negotiation, qualities which both flatter and suit a certain entrenched Canadian self-image: the world's peacekeeper, a leading producer of A-list newsreaders and globally renowned for icy politeness. The Libra of the first world. While one wonders at the extent to which this may be a flaw defensively dressed up as an asset, it has nevertheless evolved into a defining Canadian trait among a certain segment of influential Canuck, though few define it quite as richly as movie director Norman Jewison.

If artistic production is the antithesis of compromise or second-guessing, then Jewison is no artist.

Born in 1926 in Toronto, Jewison is a paradigm of paradoxical liberalism. He's the guy who wants to change the world without offending it, who wants to be nationally certified but internationally renowned, who calls himself Canadian but his stories universal, who fervently believes it possible to make controversial statements with corporate money and who feels that even bad news can and must be entertaining – the bitter-pill approach to pop entertainment. "When you're dealing with a heavy subject and it involves people's fears," he said in 1991, "you have to present it in a way that they don't feel you're delivering a message. So, if you have something to say, you have to slip it in, sort of sugarcoat it." (We'll note here that Jewison, when not making movies, produces a world-class maple syrup on his farm outside Toronto.)

As Jewison himself explains, his work is defined by compromise, by the anticipation and avoidance of conflict. If artistic production is the antithesis of compromise or second-guessing, then Jewison is no artist, as he also freely admits. In defending his decision to "sugarcoat" the ending of 1991's *Other People's Money*, the story of a greedy Wall Street bond trader (Danny DeVito), which Jewison altered when the original, downbeat ending tested badly, the director told an interviewer: "If I were a 'pure' artist, making movies only for me, maybe I would have told the studio and the audience to go screw themselves. But I guess I'm not a pure artist in that sense. I make movies for an audience and I do care what they feel. And don't forget, when you're making a movie, you're gambling with other people's money."

This explains why, when Jewison

It is a measure of both his reputation and his limitations that, while he was able to work with some of his era's biggest stars he was rarely the director to coax their best work.

would find himself competing for projects with less compromising sensibilites than his own, it was all too easy to imagine the better movies those alternatives might have produced. Jewison replaced Sam Peckinpah on 1965's *The Cincinnati Kid*; the slick blandness of the final result might have been avoided if he hadn't. Conversely, perhaps the best thing that happened to the troubled *Malcolm X* project in 1992 was that Jewison did not make it. (Admittedly, that Spike Lee made the film did not necessarily improve matters.)

After being trained as an actor and director at the BBC (1950-1952) and a stint at the CBC (1952-1958), Jewison arrived on the American entertainment scene, to work for CBS, in 1958. It turned out to be an opportune moment for someone of his talent and temperament. Demonstrating that venerable Canadian knack for polished mainstream versatility, he quickly became known as an efficient director of variety entertainment, helming celebrated programs for Judy Garland, Frank Sinatra, Harry Belafonte, Danny Kaye and others, before obtaining his first studio movie contract in 1962.

After proving himself commercially viable with a series of light comedies (1963's *Forty Pounds of Trouble* and *The Thrill of It All*, and 1964's *Send Me No*

Flowers), Jewison moved as efficiently through genres as through vogues and stars, never committing or imposing himself on any, but working competently and profitably in almost everything he took on. It is a measure of both his reputation and his limitations that, while he was able to work with some of his era's biggest stars – Steve McQueen, Al Pacino, Faye Dunaway, Jane Fonda, Sylvester Stallone, James Caan, Burt Reynolds, Bruce Willis – he was rarely the director to coax their best work.

It's tempting to attribute Jewison's period of greatest clout and notoriety – the mid-sixties to early seventies – as much to timing as anything else. It was the period when Jewison's own liberal sensibilities happened to mesh with the popular *zeitgeist*, when, in other words, it was possible for a message movie to make a buck. *The Russians Are Coming, The Russians Are Coming* (1966), for example, was a delicately barbed send-up of small-town anti-Communist paranoia: a warmer, fuzzier *Dr. Strangelove*.

A passionate supporter of civil rights, a friend to both Martin Luther King and Bobby Kennedy, with whom Jewison was to dine the night the senator was killed, Jewison directed one of the quintessential sixties exercises in rousing liberal sentiment, *In The Heat of the Night*, in 1967. It was possibly his peak moment: not only was the movie an easygoing piece of anti-racist entertainment, it won a passel of Oscars, including 1967's Best Picture, and certified Jewison's Tinseltown muscle. After *In the Heat of the Night,* Jewison was able to work with just about anyone he liked, and with the right to final cut, which is only contractually extended to those directors whom Hollywood is convinced have their fingers firmly on the public pulse.

Perhaps if Jewison was a less committed liberal, or even a more artistically driven one, he might have weathered the political turbulence of the years after *In the Heat of the Night*, and his movies – like those of kindred liberals Sidney *(Dog Day Afternoon)* Lumet and Arthur *(Bonnie and Clyde)* Penn – might have been charged by the raging sociopolitical turmoil. Instead, following the deaths of King and Kennedy, and the election of Richard Nixon to the White House, Jewison packed up his family and fled America in disgust for Europe, where ironically, both the scope of his interest and the impersonality of his films intensified, moving, in his own generalist fashion, between musicals (1971's *Fiddler On the Roof*, 1973's *Jesus Christ Superstar*), science fiction (1975's *Rollerball*), political satire (1979's *And Justice for All*), urban naturalist drama (1978's *F.I.S.T.*) and back to romantic comedy (1982's *Best Friends*).

Since the early eighties, Jewison has seemed equally as determined to position himself as a benefactor and elder statesman to his native country's struggling cinema as he has to make movies; it's arguable that he's fared better with the former task than the latter. In 1988, the Canadian Film Centre, a posh and elite training facility for promising Canuck movie-making talent, opened in Toronto under Jewison's influential imprimatur. It's revealing that the place is as often called "The Norman Jewison School" or "The Jewison Centre" as it is its proper name. (In his bid to nurture talent within the national industry he supports but doesn't work for, he has also allowed many young Canadian directors to act as observers on his films.)

On the screen, meanwhile, Jewison's work continued to waver in and out of focus: 1984's *A Soldier's Story* gathered considerable momentum from the fortuituous mix of performances, script and the by-now-clear evidence that, even after all these years, race is the issue to which Jewison responds most acutely. *Agnes of God* (1985), a meditation on spirituality, featuring seismic dramatic collisions between Jane Fonda and Anne Bancroft, is Jewison at his well-intentioned worst. *Moonstruck*, made in 1987, is cute, and 1990's *In Country*, a hopeless and redundant attempt to deal with post-Vietnam trauma. Neither 1991's *Other People's Money* nor 1994's *Only You* seemed of much interest to either public or critics, but by then, in Canada at least, Jewison had so successfully established himself as a figurehead of the national cinema – most ironic when one considers that he's never made a movie exclusively with Canadian money – that his movie-making had become a kind of adjunct to his national celebrity. Needless to say, America needn't worry about Norman Jewison anymore.

For all his influence, power and success, Jewison remains proof that you can take the Canadian out of Canada, but not Canada out of the Canadian: despite the international critical applause generated by *Fiddler on the Roof* (1971), it was the largely negative hometown response that Jewison fixated on in interviews: "I just felt like a child who had been slapped," he said in 1973. It's also telling that, back on home turf, nothing can make the otherwise unflappable director fulminate quite so sputteringly as the suggestion that he can't really be considered a Canadian director until he makes a Canadian movie on Canadian soil with Canadian money. "Money has no person-ality," is one terse response to this persistent query, and this, from 1988, is another: "The world is not interested in hearing about your heroes. They want you to entertain them, move them."

Recommended Viewing:

In the Heat of the Night (1967) Considering that few films date so ungracefully as issue films, it speaks well of Jewison's skill that *In the Heat of the Night* has aged so well. For instance, it still beats the stovepipe slacks off *Guess Who's Coming to Dinner*.

Jesus Christ Superstar (1973) Okay, we realize this is a stretch but, self-important post-hippie kitschfest that it is, *J.C. Superstar* is a full-metal howler of a movie to watch. In adapting Andrew Lloyd Webber and Tim Rice's shallow but seminal rock opera, Jewison makes the fatal error of buying into the material's deluded self-importance. Best scene? A tough question, but we'd pick either the Israeli Army artillery that chases Judas (Carl Anderson) across the desert, or the finale, in which the entire cast participates in a Vegas-style showstopper in the middle of the desert. Like, wow.

Risky Viewing:

Rollerball (1975) Jewison's single foray into science fiction is a painfully earnest and unwisely dull indictment of media violence which is neither violent enough to entertain nor coherent enough to convince. The subject is a sport, a kind of heavy-metal combination of hockey, roller derby and gladiatorial combat, which a brainlessly desensitized public gobbles up like there's no tomorrow – which, if the movie's operative thesis is to be believed, there isn't. Wearing an assortment of crotch-gripping futuristic polyester jumpsuits, James Caan plays the Gretzky of Rollerball: he's a lone principled wolf surrounded by sensation-peddling corporate sharks. The only thing that might relieve the self-important verbosity of the script would be some really megaviolent game scenes, but even these are rendered sluggish by the director's conscientious refusal to have any fun. Consequently, neither do we.

California Dreamin': Jewison's Plunge →

> "Sometimes it happens that a film director makes most or all of his films during an era in which his particular virtues are not highly esteemed; but later, when fashions change, when the public grows bored or exhausted with a certain approach, or a certain kind of story, they rediscover, with great delight, the works of someone they previously ignored or underrated."
>
> – CLAUDE JUTRA

Fade to Black
Claude Jutra's Mon Oncle Antoine

It's as if, speaking to critic John Hofsess on the very day of the Montreal premiere of 1973's gothic romance, *Kamouraska*, Jutra already knew he was doomed to the state of cultural oblivion which would eventually consume him. Jutra was, for a fraction of a Warholian moment, the best-known, most highly praised and most popular movie-maker in the country, and yet he was somehow convinced the blanket of oblivion might drop over him at any time. He was right, of course. Eventually, it did.

Truthfully, it probably had less to do with prescience than pragmatism that Jutra seemed so convinced of his own artistic neglect. After all, at the time of *Kamouraska*'s opening, Jutra was already long past the point of romantic delusion in the career department: he'd simply been working as a French-speaking film-maker in Canada for too long.

Born in 1930, Claude Jutra was the upper-middle-class product of three generations of Montreal physicians. Despite high and inevitable expectations that he too might pick up the family stethoscope, he knew from a very early age that what he wanted to do was something practically no one in Canada, and certainly no one in Quebec, was doing: he wanted to make movies. One wonders if the fact that Jutra's parents bought him camera equipment when he was 16 had anything to do with his conceding to attend medical school a couple of years later – a polite trade-off between understanding bourgeois. At any rate, the education in medicine seems, in retrospect, a mere exercise in familial obligation. As Jutra once told critic Martin Knelman: "The two great gifts our family made to Quebec society were first that my father decided to practise medicine and second that I decided not to." Jutra continued to indulge his passion for film-making while attending medical school.

In 1948, at age 18, Jutra caught the attention of the National Film Board with an award-winning short film called *Perpetual Motion*. The NFB sent no less an institutional luminary than animator Norman McLaren to the young medical student's home (the two would later collaborate on the pixillated *A Chairy Tale* in 1957), and Jutra was offered a job at Canada's official, state-run studio. Chopped liver this was not: at the time, the Board was still headquartered in Ottawa, and one was far more likely to find ex-pat U.K. types there than

French-Canadians, let alone precociously gifted French-Canadians who were not yet 20. "Anything French was a non-entity," Jutra told Knelman about those NFB years. "Those were the years of total colonization."

The fifties was a decade of ascent for Claude Jutra. In addition to attending theatre school in Montreal and working at the NFB in Ottawa, he hosted a French-language TV show about movies, wrote the first original teleplay produced in Montreal and came to work among the core of the Board's formidable, if Anglo, documentary dream team: Stanley Jackson, Colin Low and Tom Daly. After making *A Chairy Tale* with mentor McLaren, Jutra travelled to France where he met idol Jean Cocteau, directed a short film (based on a Cocteau story)

Jacques Gagnon (Benoit) and Claude Jutra (Fernand) in *Mon Oncle Antoine*

produced by French New Wave *wunderkind* François Truffaut and eventually travelled to Africa with the pioneering ethnographic documentarist Jean Rouch.

By the time he returned to Canada in 1961, the signs of continued ascendancy seemed firmly in place. The Board had shifted headquarters from Ottawa to Montreal, and under the leadership of future CBC head (and future Juno Award namesake) Pierre Juneau, the tides of Franco-Canadian nationalism were flooding even the grey institutional corridors of the NFB. Here Jutra found himself working alongside such seminal Quiet Revolution–era film-makers as Gilles Groulx, Gilles Carle, Pierre Perrault and future collaborator Michel Brault.

For Jutra, who was interested in making a full-length film, the appearance of

Claude Jutra suddenly found himself playing a role no French-Canadian — no, make that *Canadian*, period — ever had before: he was the most famous movie-maker his country had produced.

promise proved illusory: the NFB was profoundly indifferent toward feature production. Realizing he'd never get a dramatic feature made there, he managed the remarkable feat of privately financing and producing *A Tout Prendre*, the brashly confident and nakedly autobiographical first feature directed, written by and starring Claude Jutra. (Among other things, this is the film in which Jutra seems to

foretell his own demise, when the character he plays imagines walking off the end of a dock to a watery oblivion. Predictably, that scene would be shown endlessly on the occasion of the film-maker's death.) *A Tout Prendre*'s achievement was as enormous as its scale was small: a winner of a number of international awards, it effectively marked the first splash of the coming wave of Quebec cinema of the 1960s. The ripples were felt as far away as Hamilton, Ontario, where future critic and film-maker John Hofsess saw it at McMaster University in 1963: "It was a life-changing film," Hofsess wrote in 1975, "that made me aware for the first time that there was, or could be, and someday would be, a Canadian film industry, and that Jutra would head the ranks of our best directors."

Claude Jutra, director of *Mon Oncle Antoine*

Although *A Tout Prendre* landed with a splash, it would take six years and several celebrated shorts before Jutra would produce the movie a great many people around the world consider to be the very best this country has ever produced. (Two international critics' polls conducted by the Toronto International Film Festival in 1984 and 1993 selected it as Canada's best movie ever made.) *Mon Oncle Antoine* was the product of denial and accident.

Approaching Jutra with an idea for a movie, the writer Clement Perron was crushed when the director told him he didn't think the idea was any good. To humour the crestfallen scribe, Jutra invited Perron for a drink, which the latter took as an occasion to complain at length about what a miserable life he'd led. Raised in the lunar asbestos-mining region of Abitibi, a place whose labour strikes eventually paved the way for the nationalist activism of the 1960s, Perron told Jutra about the way the English mining-company president would contemptuously toss Christmas presents into the muddy streets once a year, how the local priest would tipple from the communal wine stock and how Perron's dipsomaniacal uncle worked as both the operator of the village's general store and the local undertaker. He recalled the night he and his drunken relative took a fateful Christmas Eve trip through the snow to pick up the body of a teenage farmboy, and how they lost the body when it fell from the back of the plastered old man's sleigh. That's when Jutra interrupted Perron's self-pitying autobiographical discourse, and suggested the writer turn that into a script.

The film that Claude Jutra mined from

The imminent future of Quebec hangs over the drama of *Mon Oncle Antoine* like a gathering cloud.

the raw ore of Perron's biography was shot largely in 1969 on a budget of $450,000. It was filmed in the simultaneously barren and beautiful Abitibi region of Quebec by Jutra's old friend Michel Brault, whose cinematographic efforts on *Mon Oncle Antoine* remain among the most starkly beautiful images of any film ever made in Canada: Brault's subtle use of colour, lighting and frames within shots contribute enormously to the unstressed melancholy of the film, which remains a potently convincing example of movie storytelling as the art of showing over telling.

As the young Benoit, the Perron character, Jutra cast the unknown Jacques Gagnon, a teenager he'd discovered when he picked up the kid hitchhiking. To play the terminally weak Antoine, Jutra cast veteran Jean Duceppe. And as the fascinatingly unfathomable Fernand, the store clerk who hums to himself all-knowingly while plotting the seduction of his boss's willing wife, the director cast himself.

Without once stressing the connection between the events of the drama and the current situation in Quebec (this was a year before the cataclysmic October Crisis), the imminent future of Quebec hangs over the drama of *Mon Oncle Antoine* like a gathering cloud. The name of the reviled Premier Maurice Duplessis can be spotted above a tavern urinal, and the movie's best line is delivered as a disgruntled worker empties the last drops of a quart of beer into his glass: "There's another one the English won't get."

When the film, which was financed by

the National Film Board exclusively, was completed in 1970, it met the fate of many institutional achievements: it sat on a shelf for nearly a year. Still, rumours of the basement masterwork persisted, and eventually *Mon Oncle Antoine* was sprung upon the public at various festivals and special screenings in 1971. Momentum began to build. Unusually for a French-language film, the movie tended to be more lavishly praised by English- than French-speaking critics who, in the fervour of the era's militancy, seemed to miss the subtlety of Jutra's depiction of incipient nationalism entirely, and accused the film-maker of apoliticism. The film also managed to generate more business and interest in English Canada than any Quebecois movie had to that point. American critics seemed to respond as positively to the movie as their Anglo-Canadian counterparts – the movie had a successful run in New York – and Claude Jutra suddenly found himself playing a role no French-Canadian – no, make that *Canadian*, period – ever had before: he was the most famous movie-maker his country had produced.

Not that Jutra's glory days mattered, when all was said and done. His much-anticipated adaptation of Anne Hebert's *Kamouraska* was not only severely truncated for what would turn out to be a tepidly unprofitable commercial release, the historical romance was cited by a number of hostile francophone critics as yet further proof that Jutra was a mere pictorial escapist at a time when more overtly political films were presumably what the province needed.

But soon this would be moot, as tax-shelter funding legislation kicked in and the government-dependent industry, which had shifted orientation overnight

A Selective Guide to Canada's Coolest French-Language Movies

from culture to commerce, lost all interest in supporting French-language film-making. By the mid-seventies, Canada's most celebrated movie-maker was directing episodes of the CBC journalistic anthology series *For the Record*, in Toronto, a place which he described as "a foreign country. A very *friendly* foreign country, but still a foreign country."

In the next decade, Jutra would complete four more disappointing critically savaged features – 1975's *Pour le Meilleur et Pour la Pire*, 1980's *Surfacing*, 1981's *By Design* and 1984's *La Dame en Couleurs* – before entering his final phase of national notoriety by disappearing suddenly from his Montreal home in November 1986. This was when the country learned that Claude Jutra had succumbed to Alzheimer's disease, the cruel, incurable condition which bulk-erases huge blocks of memory from its sufferers. In the six months of speculation before Jutra's body washed up on the icy shores of the St. Lawrence River in April 1987, Claude Jutra was back in the news again, but this time only in a supporting role to the disease which drove him eventually to suicide: the then relatively unknown disease was frankly more newsworthy than the film-maker it had fatally struck. While there was some talk of Jutra's cultural contribution in the national media attention, it was largely lost among the more sensational din of pseudo-scientific speculation. Once again, but now for the last time, Claude Jutra had been the victim of the failure of memory.

Le Chat Dans le Sac (1964) What a time capsule. Made at the National Film Board at the time the Quiet Revolution in Quebec was permeating just about every level of cultural and political life in the province, Gilles Groulx's story of the final days of a dying relationship between an Anglo-Jewish theatre student (Barbara Ulrich) and a moody intellectual Quebecois nationalist (Claude Godbout) deftly paints the cultural divide in Canada as an affair doomed from the start. Rife with jump cuts and voice-overs, shot in shimmering black and white and burnished with the music of John Coltrane, the movie is more than just a vivid evocation of a rich historical moment, it reminds you there's a connection between romance and politics where the issue of "separation" is concerned.

Mon Oncle Antoine (1970) A genuinely deserving Canadian classic, but suffice it to say that everything you've heard or read about it is true, and it hasn't so much as gained a wrinkle in the quarter century since it was made.

Les Ordres (1974) Four years after Pierre Trudeau invoked the draconian War Measures Act at the height of 1970's October Crisis – a decision which gave police and military the authority to detain, without explanation or charges, anyone in custody they considered suspicious – director-cinematographer Michel Brault, who shot Jutra's *Mon Oncle Antoine*, made this harrowing, citizen's-eye account of what it's like to wake up one morning in a police state. Still hard-hitting and controversial, due to Brault's angry conviction that what Trudeau imposed on the citizens of Quebec was no less evil than the FLQ itself.

Les Bons Debarras (1980) After *Mon Oncle Antoine*, this is easily the finest example of the regional mini-genre you could call the Quebec Rural Gothic. Set largely in the woods near a small remote town, the late Francis Mankiewicz's movie, based on Réjean Ducharme's script, concerns an intensely overdependent mother-daughter relationship (Marie Tifo and the amazing child-actor Charlotte Laurier), which gradually mutates into something scary indeed. Like Jutra, Mankiewicz uses the forbidding beauty of the Quebec landscape as a character in the drama, as though the trees themselves were gradually closing in on the characters' fates.

Jesus of Montreal (1989) With his typical blend of despair, grace and humour, Denys Arcand, the country's premier social satirist, uses the production of a controversial, revisionist passion play on Mount Royal as a tragic indictment of a world completely corrupted by the remorseless values of commerce. The story of an enigmatic actor (Lothaire Bluteau) whose dramatic rendering of Christ makes him a reluctant celebrity and corporate-vulture magnet, on one level the movie is really just a variation on that hoary old moral hypothesis about what might happen if Christ materialized today. It's no small part of Arcand's gift that it feels as though the question is being asked for the very first time. The answer, needless to say, will not please spiritual optimists, but that's why God created Americans.

Léolo (1992) In the five intervening years between the release of the much-hyped *Un Zoo La Nuit/Night Zoo* and the release of this, commercial-director-turned-feature-film-maker Jean-Claude Lauzon seemed to venture a long way indeed. Where the first movie felt like a dated feature-length francophone episode of *Miami Vice*, the autobiographical phantasmagoria of *Léolo* appears to be built to last. The surrealistically charged story of a young boy whose poetic inspiration swells in direct proportion with the genetic dysfunctionality of his working-class family, Lauzon's second movie is a mesmerizing, visually rich examination of madness from the inside out.

Le Confessional (1995) This, the debut feature from Robert Lepage, Canada's reigning theatrical boy genius, merely confirmed what many had suspected already: the guy is just way too talented not to be an alien who fell from space, miscalculated and landed north of the border instead of south. Like so many Quebecois movies about dark family intrigue, Lepage's loosely autobiographical story of two brothers (Lothaire Bluteau and Patrick Goyette) attempting to solve a deeply buried paternity mystery is provocatively played out against the shooting of Alfred Hitchcock's *I Confess* in Quebec City in 1952. As graceful as it is economic at floating between parallel storylines and time periods, Lepage's film manages to rivet your attention even if you've long figured out the so-called mystery. The riddle, however, is sufficiently captivating that the answer doesn't matter.

The Friendly Giant
Canada's Boom in Kidkult

In the world of children's entertainment, Canada is something approaching its own Hollywood: it enjoys world renown and near-global market saturation. It is looked up to and envied, and it has been far more often challenged than surpassed.

Moreover, this is the way it's been for years. Way back in the early sixties, the CBC's *Friendly Giant* show was one of the most widely exported, not to mention respected, Canadian television productions in history, while other staple CBC kid productions like *Chez Hélène* and *Mr. Dressup* fared almost as well. From there, things only grew to even more Friendly dimensions: by the mid-1980s, the business of selling and producing children's recordings was, between the international successes of Raffi, Sharon, Lois and Bram, Fred Penner, Eric Nagler and others, a virtual Canuck monopoly.

Today, Canadians are still leading the pack with TV production for kids. By 1996, Canada was holding the position of the second-largest creator and exporter of children's television in the world, second only to – take a wild guess here, folks – the United States. In total, such Canadian-produced programs as *Lamb Chop's Play Along*, *Babar*, *Big Comfy Couch*, the various *Degrassi* series, *Dudley the Dragon* and the computer-animated *Reboot* were being seen in approximately 140 countries outside our own. Now, considering the relative size of the Canadian television industry compared to that of the U.S., there's something rather curious about the fact that we do such a bang-up job of babysitting the world's kids, isn't there?

The Friendly Giant   **Razzle Dazzle**   **Mr. Dressup**

So what gives? One might go along with the "kinder gentler Canuck" theory that Canadian kids' shows don't talk down to kids but directly to them, in their own language, à la Friendly or Mr. Dressup. Where so many American programs aimed at kids treat them as glucose-addled consumers with the intelligence and attention span of june bugs, Canadian shows treat them as intelligent people in their own right.

As tempting as it is to embrace this flattering view, there are a couple of things it doesn't account for: first, the fact that two of the most prominent programs which best seem to exemplify this kinder, gentler, smarter approach to children's programming, *Friendly* and *Dressup*, were in both cases developed, created and hosted by Americans (Bob Homme and Ernie Coombs, respectively) who'd honed their craft in the U.S. before coming to Canada; and second, it would be somewhat outrageously self-serving to assume that all widely exported Canadian kids' shows are exercises in low-key, good-for-you programming. Like any self-respecting media-producing capitalist nation, we sell a lot of junk for kids too. (Remember *The Littlest Hobo* or the deliriously hyper-caffeinated *Hilarious House of Frightenstein*?)

More likely, this knack for speaking to children through drama, music and entertainment seems like yet another manifestation of the country's status as cultural outsider, the permanent sidekick to the world's greatest superpower, the scrawny, adolescent Robin to someone else's well-muscled Batman — the same thing, in other words, which accounts for so much of Canada's peculiar pop-cultural

strengths, from parodic comedy and journalism, to character acting and middle-of-the-road music. On one level, kids, like Canadians, are marginalized, and we know well how to appeal to fellow second-class citizens. On another, it takes a certain knack for stepping outside oneself to speak effectively to children, to project oneself beyond grown-up concerns and attitudes to effectively imagine the interests and priorities of their world. That takes a real knack for situational schizophrenia, a Canadian knack if ever there was one.

Here then are Canada's proudest moments in kiddiekult, the children's shows that resound in many grown-up minds.

Polka Dot Door

Produced: 1970–1993

Concept: Two superkeen and friendly grown-ups – usually of the male and female variety – spend half an hour playing with toys, books and stuff they find lying around their brightly coloured playhouse. Throughout, they gamely converse with a number of stuffed toys and dolls with whom only they seem able to communicate: "What's that you said, Marigold? You want to sit on the pink chair? Well, all right..." Every once in a while, the series' true star – an enigmatic, genetically indeterminate, seven-foot-tall biped who says only the word "Polkaroo"– drops by to play a trick on the adults, only to leave suddenly without saying goodbye. Strangely, they're always happy to see him when he comes back to screw with their minds again.

Defining Quote: "You mean Polkaroo was here and I missed him? Awwww..."

The Friendly Giant

Produced: 1958–1985

Concept: A very friendly giant (host Bob Homme) invites kids into his castle for 15 minutes of music, reading and breezy, unscripted conversation between Friendly and two friends who never seemed to go home: an ever-so-slightly sarcastic giraffe named Jerome, and a harp-playing rooster in a bag named Rusty. Both creatures were voiced by Rod Coneybeare.

Defining Quotes: "Here we are inside and here's a little chair for one of you, and a bigger chair for two more to curl up in, and for someone who likes to rock, a rocking chair in the middle. Now look up, look waaaay up, and I'll call Rusty." Theme song, "Early One Morning." At the end of each episode, the cow jumped over the moon.

Mr. Dressup

Produced: 1967–1996

Concept: Always ready to create fun from scratch just by reaching into his "tickle trunk," Mr. Dressup (Ernie Coombs) never failed to show his two closest buddies, a boy named Casey and a mute dog named Finnegan, a maximum good time with minimal means. Actually, Finnegan wasn't exactly mute, for he would often whisper things to Casey which the rather precious puppet would then relay back to Mr. Dressup. It is no small measure of the latter's bottomless decency that he never once demanded the dog just speak up and talk to him directly.

Defining Moment: That magic time when Mr. Dressup would open up the tickle trunk and pull out a new costume.

Razzle Dazzle

Produced: 1961–1967

Concept: An early, pre-Sesame Street example of slam-bang variety-show principles applied to kid's programming, this fast-paced blend of sketches, jokes, quizzes and contests featured the future Mr. Suzanne Somers, Alan Hamel, as host, and young Michele Finney, followed by younger Trudy Young, as co-hosts. Also featuring a sardonic, rather tranced-out-looking turtle named Howard, *Razzle Dazzle* was a genuine, home-grown kid-kult phenomenon: its fan club, which received daily secret messages only club members had the necessary equipment to decode, once exceeded 100,000 Canadian kids. "Things like this just aren't supposed to happen at the CBC," a corporation official admitted at the time.

Defining Quote: "Hold Everything!… Here's the show for Kids and Turtles!"

Reboot

Produced: 1994 to present

Concept: Set entirely within a computer, this pioneering, all-computer-animated program is about a dreadlocked cyberhunk named Bob who, with the wisecracking help of spunky cyberbabe Dot Matrix and her little brother, Enzo, fearlessly guards the computer world of Mainframe from all manner of virus, short-circuit and would-be electronic megalomaniac. The killer gimmick: every time the unseen "User" plays a game on the computer in which the show is set,

the entire environment becomes the game, and the characters become players in it. McLuhan would have loved it.

Defining Quote: "Reboot!"

Tales of the Riverbank, a.k.a. Once Upon A Hamster

Produced: 1959–1985; 1995–present

Concept: A virtual rodent microcosm of life's rich pageant lived by the riverbank with Hammy, a cheerful and enterprising hamster, who just happened to be played by a real honest-to-pete hamster. Which was, of course, the program's defining gimmick: all the animals were, in fact, animals whose voices were added by actors speaking in very high, squeaky voices. Small wonder the program was such an enduring hit with children and pharmaceutically stimulated adults alike.

Defining Moment: Hammy and guinea-pig pal GP decide to go for a boat ride on the river, with intriguing and mirthful results.

The Kids of Degrassi Street/Degrassi Junior High/Degrassi High

Produced: 1980-1990

Concept: Life in a working-class school in Toronto's multi-ethnic East End, told scrupulously from the kids' point of view. These three series, collectively aimed at an audience aged 10-15 and featuring several actors who grew up in public by playing the same character over the course of a decade, were one of Canada's most successful programming exports of the eighties: broadcast in more than 40 countries, watched regularly by approximately 10 million people weekly in Canada, Great Britain and the U.S. alone. The secret? The producers' unwavering commitment to bullshit-free teen cred: not only were all

cast members originally non-professionals drawn from the neighbourhood where the series was shot, no script went before the cameras without a rigorous accuracy check by the kid themselves. The result? One of the few series in the history of television to treat kids less like target demographics or stereotypes than plain old honest-to-god screwed-up people.

The subjects? Abortion, AIDS, substance abuse, sexual orientation and harassment, getting laid, smoking and generally surviving adolescence.

Defining Scene:

Glenn: "I'm moving in with this guy."

Snake: "Yeah, so what?"

Glenn: "Well, he's gay."

Snake: "Why would you want to move in with one of those guys?"

Glenn: "Because I'm gay."

Chez Hélène

Produced: 1959–1973

Concept: At Hélène's place, a brightly befrocked mouse named Susie and a slightly superannuated teenager named Louise (preschool heartthrob Madeline Kronby) engage in pedagogically scrupulous conversations, games and songs designed to raise a nation of fully bilingual preschoolers. The aim of this English show, inspired by a theory of teaching languages to children, was to gently coax Anglo kids to learn and speak French. Everybody speaks both languages except poor Hélène (Hélène Baillargeon) who, being a unilingual francophone, seems to need everything explained to her two or three times before it sinks in. Needless to say, the toll taken on unformed Anglo-Canadian imaginations probably did as much for the cause of separatism as René Lévesque.

Defining Quote: "Oh, Su-zee !"

New Disorder Kids in the Hall

When *Kids in the Hall*, the Toronto-based, Lorne Michaels–produced sketch show that had been seen in the U.S. and Canada for five years finally went off the air for good in January 1995, the sound of head-scratching could still be heard at the funeral: just what was that anyway? Even the final program's last image – Kids Dave Foley, Bruce McCulloch, Kevin McDonald, Mark McKinney and Scott Thompson being dumped and buried in a mass grave – seemed engineered to promote this legacy of confusion. Funny? Tasteless? Horrific? Stupid? *All* of the above?

← Kids in the Hall, 1988 (back row, left to right:
Kevin McDonald, Scott Thompson, Bruce McCulloch,
Dave Foley. In chair: Mark McKinney)

Loved, disdained and puzzled over with equal intensity, *Kids in the Hall* might have left behind only one certainty about which there was unequivocal agreement: no matter what you thought of it, whether it struck you as funny, infuriating, obtuse or offensive, there had never been anything in the history of Canadian comedy quite like it. Which, considering the sheer free-wheeling richness of the national comic tradition – from Wayne and Shuster to Martin Short – is no small certainty to bear: it's like everyone agreeing that there's never been another hockey player quite like that one, or that this landscape painting is absolutely distinct in the history of Canadian landscape painting. To be noticed as a unique experiment in Canadian comedy, *Kids in the Hall* really had to stick out.

Of course, it helped that Lorne Michaels was holding the stick. One night in the mid-eighties, during his constant scan for new Canadian comedy talent, the former comedian and current *Saturday Night Live* executive producer caught the Kids' act at the Rivoli, the downtown Toronto bistro at which the comedy troupe was the unofficial house act. (The group name, incidentally, comes from Jack Benny's term for the hordes of comics who used to wait in the hall outside his office, hoping to sell jokes to him.) Consisting of two ex-members of a Calgary improv troupe, McCulloch and McKinney, and three Torontonians – Foley, McDonald and Thompson – the Kids practised a form of high-concept, mind-bending sketch comedy which Michaels would later liken to "the Monty Python of the eighties." Like that of the Pythons, the Kids' comedy was as cerebral as it was surreal: it hit the solar

The comedy of Kids in the Hall may belong somewhat closer to Doug Coupland than Doug McKenzie in the great Canadian cultural archives.

plexus only after rebounding off your brain. A particularly popular Rivoli-era sketch, which Michaels most likely saw, was typical of the Kids' conceptual approach: a group of guys sit around a campfire, tearfully guzzling brews while mourning a dead friend. Gradually, the realization hits us: these guys aren't just the dead man's best friends, *they killed him.* Struck immediately by their daring and originality – sex and gender anxiety being an almost obsessive object of the Kids' comic scrutiny – Michaels took the group under his wing. "I think they're the next wave," Michaels told the *Globe and Mail* in 1990. "Like all things that are new and interesting, it takes looking at to adjust your eye to it, to realize it's not going to be what you're used to."

Under the umbrella of his Broadway Video organization, Michaels managed to get Home Box Office (HBO) in the U.S. to draw up a development deal for a Kids' special, which in turn convinced the otherwise innovation-shy CBC to hop in, as well. Thereafter, everything clicked: the special was sufficiently successful to convince HBO and CBC to coproduce a series, and by 1989, the made-in-Toronto *Kids in the Hall* show was on the air weekly across North America. In 1992, the show was scooped from HBO by CBS, where its Friday-night ratings occasionally even outdrew NBC's *Late Night With*

David Letterman: this corresponded with positively effusive displays of approval in such prominent publications as *Newsweek, The New York Times, GQ, The Village Voice* and *Rolling Stone.*

So how is it, that three years later, the Kids were no longer and their legacy is one of confusion? Part of the reason undoubtedly has to do with the group's ambivalent position vis-à-vis the so-called "Canadian comic tradition," a tradition the Kids themselves never seemed to put much stock in: "It's a popular question," McCulloch once deadpanned to a reporter who'd asked the dread "C.C.T." question. "While I guess I admire the people from *Saturday Night Live* and Second City, I don't really feel that much affinity with them. I probably feel closer to The Tragically Hip."

For the fact was, while there were certain aspects of the group which seemed unmistakably Canadian – like the Kids' hoser-deluxe, WASPier-than-thou names, for instance – there were others that were pretty well unprecedented in popular home-grown comedy. While the backbone of our "tradition" has always been sketch comedy, it has equally always been sketch comedy directed at some readily identifiable target outside itself, like politics (*Royal Canadian Air Farce*) or pop culture (*SCTV*). The Kids' approach to sketch, on the other hand, was so purely conceptual as to verge on solipsistic: while Rick Moranis might do an uncanny David Brinkley or Woody Allen, McCulloch's specialty were people like "Cabbagehead," a cigar-smoking sleazeball with a large legume for a scalp. One of Scott Thompson's most popular characters, the ridiculously effete "philosopher

Brain Candy, 1996

queen," Buddy Cole, was, while less purely gonzo than Cabbagehead, another completely self-contained comic creation. Indeed, Mark McKinney's "Headcrusher," the deranged urban nut-case who rages incessantly to himself while pretending to pop people's heads between his thumb and forefinger, might aptly symbolize the entire comic universe of the Kids: insular, twisted and utterly unaccountable to reason. Getting the Kids' comedy therefore didn't depend on one's familiarity with the pop-culture object satirized: it depended entirely on one's ability to find the Kids' wavelength and hang on for dear life. It did not come to you: you went to it. And if you couldn't ride the wavelength, tough – the Kids surfed on anyway.

Dave Foley once spoke proudly of the program's utter disregard for anything outside its own obsessive sphere of inspiration: "Some of the greatest events of the past several decades have taken place recently and we're proud to say they have had absolutely no bearing on the show," he said in the globally unsettled year of 1991. "Like, we don't do a lot of Gorbachev material." A couple of years later, McCulloch offered this unsurprising insight into the Kids' comedic methodology: "We're not very big on theory," said the man who created Cabbagehead. "We just do it. Most of our ideas begin like, 'There's this guy...'"

When pondering the Kids' apparently wilful rejection of the parodic strain in Canadian comedy, the issue of age – or specifically, the relationship between what you find funny and when you were born – becomes unavoidable. The Kids tended to split response along genera-

> **That so many people didn't get what the Kids were doing simply confirms the troupe's validity as something legitimately innovative and subversive.**

tional lines. While their show was massively popular on college campuses, older people, even those merely old enough to have been raised on *SCTV* or *SNL*, were far less likely to find the show funny than those whose sense of humour had been forged even a few years later.

In this sense, the comedy of Kids in the Hall may belong somewhat closer to Doug Coupland than Doug McKenzie in the great Canadian cultural archives. The first genuinely popular Canadian expression of post-boomer, Gen-X comedy, it exhibited precisely the same insouciant disdain for the issue-driven comedy of previous generations that Coupland's equally self-insulated characters reserved for the boomer world. Even the Kids' relentless gender-bending and office bashing seems, in retrospect, closer in attitude to Coupland than to anything else in Canadian comedy. And, in the same way that Coupland's languidly solipsistic fiction short-circuited any sense of its national or regional affiliation, so the Kids' comedy seemed to come from a place defined less by things like borders and birthright than by matters of age and sensibility.

That so many people didn't get what the Kids were doing simply confirms the troupe's validity as something legitimately innovative and subversive. Just as the task of erecting something like a "Canadian

comedy tradition" was within our grasp, the Kids in the Hall came along and knocked the foundation out from beneath the very assumptions that made that tradition possible. Which in the long run is both good and necessary. Frankly, if there's one Canadian comic tradition that we might be well advised to endorse, it's the kind that believes comic traditions are so much freeze-dried moose dung in the first place.

Since folding the show, the Kids haven't disappeared, but, in the post-*SCTV* manner, they haven't (with the exception of *NewsRadio*'s Dave Foley) exactly flourished, either: Thompson (*The Larry Sanders Show*) and McKinney (*Saturday Night Live*) were both visible in American programs less than a year after *Kids* shut down, and McCulloch released an album with the deliciously Canadian title of *Shame Based Man*. In spring 1996, the first Kids' movie – a pharmaceutical farce called *Brain Candy* – was released to lukewarm public and critical response, leaving it highly unlikely the boys would bother to regroup for another. No matter, by that time, they'd already made their point loud and clear. Which is: there *is* no point.

"To hear 'Early Morning Rain' done with flugelhorns kind of makes me feel good.
I actually heard that in an elevator once and it was good. I was proud."

– GORDON LIGHTFOOT

Blood on the Tracks Gordon Lightfoot

Of Canadian pop music careers, few have demonstrated such stubborn, off-the-mat tenacity as Gordon Lightfoot's. If this hadn't already been apparent, it became abundantly clear by the late 1980s when, in an extremely controversial cost-cutting measure, former prime minister Brian Mulroney's Conservative government effectively dismantled the national railway system. Suddenly, the steel spine which had acted as Canada's most enduring symbol of national unity (ask Pierre Berton) was broken, leaving concerned Canadians scrambling for other metaphors – CBC-Radio? Hockey? How about highways ? – which might provide mythic succour for a splintered sense of national self. For many, the deregulation of the state-sponsored passenger-railway system was nothing less than the severance of the national lifeline: without it, the body of the country was paralyzed, and utterly unable to coordinate the spasmodic jerks of its individual parts. Chaos loomed, the centre (wherever the hell it was) simply could not hold.

But Gordon Lightfoot would hold, and if you'd been following the veteran folksinger's 25-year career, that fact was every bit as remarkable as the fact that one of the country's most efficient metaphors for national experience had just been legislated into history. Fact was, Gordon Lightfoot had not only outlasted a drinking problem and protracted periods of writer's block, he'd outdistanced the institution which he'd built part of a career singing about. The Canadian railway system – at least the one mythologized by Lightfoot and Berton – might be gone, but the Orillia, Ontario–born performer was still around to sing about it. Surely that counted for something, even if only metaphorwise.

Yet, typical of Lightfoot, he made no attempts to storm the controversy and sing for a stay of the railway's execution. When asked about the cuts, he'd decline comment: "I'm not qualified to be a politician," he said to the *Toronto Star* in 1992. This despite the fact that, of any Canadian music performer, he was the one most likely to draw attention to the imminent blow to national identity represented by the issue of railway deregulation: not only was one of his first hits called "Steel Rail Blues," his generation-old concert show-stopper was a six-minute romantic ode to how the history of Canada is the history of its railways.

Called "The Canadian Railroad Trilogy," the song was originally commissioned by the CBC for a 1967 Centennial TV special called *100 Years Young*, and it became as closely identified with Lightfoot as "Big Yellow Taxi" was to Joni Mitchell, "Suzanne" to Leonard Cohen or "Takin' Care of Business" to BTO. To find another singer whose career was so imbued with boxcars and big spaces, you practically had to go back to Woody Guthrie. Still, Lightfoot, whose career began in the wake of the late-fifties', early-sixties' folk movement often called "protest singing," refused to use the song for purposes of protesting the government's plans for the railway. (As it turned out, the more than comfortably well-off singer apparently agreed

Like Leonard Cohen, Joni Mitchell and a number of his stool-perched contemporaries, Lightfoot became known as a supplier of songs well before being recognized as a performer in his own right.

Lightfoot and admirers in the mid-sixties

with the government's suggestion that the public maintenance of the service was simply too costly.) In fact, the only time he agreed to perform the song in the context of the deregulation issue was, perhaps appropriately, over the airwaves of the same public broadcaster who'd originally commissioned it. The last time Gordon Lightfoot was heard singing "Canadian Railroad Trilogy" on the CBC was on *Front Page Challenge,* just a few friendly feet from that other smithy of national railway mythology, Pierre Berton. Which compels us to stress that Lightfoot has outlasted both the railway and Canada's longest-running state-sponsored game show.

At the peak of his early popularity during the mid-1960s, the lean, handsome, honey-toned baritone was riding the crest of a musical wave that hap-

pened to wash a lot of Canadians up on the shores of continental notoriety. While the more generationally specific cacophonies of rock music were by that time coming to represent the very idea of youth culture, the brief folk revival which preceded it had nevertheless opened a market for singer-songwriters who could appeal to an audience too hip for Sinatra but scared by the Stones. (Today they'd be listening to Hootie and the Blowfish.) Canada, with its wide rural population, regional acoustic-music traditions, far-flung bar circuit and long history of musical broadcasting, proved a particularly industrious supplier of soft, smart and sensitive music. Like Leonard Cohen, Joni Mitchell and a number of his stool-perched contemporaries, Lightfoot became known as a supplier of songs well before being recognized as a per-

former in his own right. Folk duo Ian and Sylvia were the first to cover his songs "For Lovin' Me" and "Early Morning Rain," and in 1965, Peter, Paul and Mary, who would introduce a young Lightfoot at that year's Newport Jazz Festival, had a stateside hit with "For Lovin' Me."

What's most interesting about the ensuing rush to record Lightfoot's songs is not just the sheer number of covers, but the fact that they hurdle so many bounds of pop musical genre. Apart from folk interpretations, Lightfoot's early songs were recorded, and often as hits, for people like Marty Robbins, the Johnny Mann Singers, Chad and Jeremy, Judy Collins, Elvis Presley, Barbra Streisand, Harry Belafonte, Bob Dylan and George Hamilton IV. In the early nineties, a Los Angeles punk outfit called Clawhammer

Lighfoot then   Lightfoot now

even recorded Lightfoot's "Sundown." The cross-genre appeal of his songcraft would serve Lightfoot well in the future, particularly when the folk circuit had largely weeded over by the early 1970s.

Difficult as it is to imagine now, when Lightfoot's musical output has slowed to a virtual trickle and his public appearances rarely spill beyond the ritual, not quite annual, week-long appearances at Toronto's Massey Hall, Gordon Lightfoot was one of Canada's hottest and most prolific music exports from the mid-sixties to mid-seventies. He and his songs were everywhere: touring, on TV and radio, sprinkled liberally among the repertoires of the unlikeliest performers. And yet, unlike, say, Mitchell or Cohen, whose careers were built on similar foundations during the same era, Lightfoot hasn't maintained nearly the same degree of enduring extra-Canadian interest and credibility as the others.

While Lightfoot's fans are nothing if not avid – as the Massey concerts, a sold-out rite of spring in Toronto since 1967, make plain – it's also clear that they come not to taste the fresh fruits of artistic vitality, but to enjoy the past preserved in sweet musical aspic. It's equally clear that Lightfoot, unlike Cohen, Mitchell, Neil Young or Bruce Cockburn, is perfectly happy to hold fast those remaining fans by giving them exactly what they want.

Which may be one of the reasons Lightfoot's career seems to have stuck in a steady but unexciting holding pattern for so long: much time has passed since the risk-taking impulse in seducing new fans was overtaken by the more pragmatic priority of holding on to those you have. Still, while the singer is notorious for the

control he exerts over his image and career (one story has him angrily buying up and destroying – in his basement, with an axe – dozens of copies of an unauthorized compilation album he was unhappy with), there may be more to Lightfoot's latter-day stasis than mere fiscal conservatism.

Consider his background: unlike his contemporary, Stompin' Tom Connors, a Maritimer whose artistic impulses are clearly rooted in the celebration of the working-class Canadians he grew up sharing smokes and beer with, Lightfoot is a solid product of the smalltown Ontario middle class: growing up in Orillia, he was a boy soprano and later a teenage member of a barbershop quartet. Unlike Cohen, the urban poet-romantic who came to music only after establishing a literary career, Lightfoot turned to recording his own music after a solidly commercial apprenticeship recording jingles and working as a session singer. (He even did a stint as a singer-dancer on CBC-TV's *Country Hoedown*). Of his folk-era Canadian contemporaries, he is thus the one whose inspiration has often seemed as professional as it is personal, which might also account for his loyal but limited following today: there is neither the fury of politics nor the fire of poetry in his work, just good, solid, made-in-Ontario songcraft.

While Lightfoot sings lovingly of Canada, his hoserism falls far short of Stompin' Tom's love-it-or-leave-it variety. While he sings of heterosexual love, his songs feature none of the multitextured, self-deprecating irony of Cohen's. Not surprisingly, though, this emphasis on form over feeling has occasionally left the singer with nothing to sing about: he has experienced epic bouts of inspirational

drought, and in 1985 even threatened to hang up his guitar and retire for good to his home in Toronto's tony Rosedale neighbourhood. It's a good thing he didn't (and it's real hard to imagine that such a fan-sensitive pro ever would), for that would have meant being outflanked both by *Front Page Challenge* and the national railway itself. Apparently, Gordon Lightfoot has embraced and learned to love what for some Canadians is the next best thing to artistic inspiration or even immortality: he's an institution – his very own railway that is forged in Gord's gold.

Recommended Listening:

Ironic, isn't it, that shortly after his 1976 nautical-disaster dirge, "The Wreck of the Edmund Fitzgerald," Gordon Lightfoot sank without a trace from the charts. Even Canadian M.O.R mogul David Foster couldn't help matters, although he valiantly tried by coproducing and cowriting the 1986 Lightfoot stiff "Anything For Love" (Now *that's* cold: after all, Foster even managed to help Natalie Cole win a truckload of Grammies duetting with her dead father!) Still, it would be downright un-Canadian (not to mention extremely short-sighted) to deny Lightfoot his proper place in the hoser musical pantheon.

Along with The Guess Who and Anne Murray, Lightfoot was our most visible musical ambassador in the sixties and early seventies. That fertile period for Lightfoot is neatly reinterpreted on *Gord's Gold* (1975). This compilation contains re-recorded versions of the train songs ("Canadian Railroad Trilogy," "Steel Rail Blues"), the rain songs ("Rainy Day People," "Early Morning Rain"), the macho strutter "For Lovin' Me" and the still-breathtaking "If You Could Read My Mind." If you're a Lightfoot purist, you'll find the original versions on albums like *The Way I Feel* (1967), *Did She Mention My Name?* (1968) and *Sit Down Young Stranger* (1970). For Gordie in his Captain Canada role, check out the 1971 composition "Nous Vivons Ensemble/We've Got To Stay Together," written shortly after the War Measures Act was invoked.

PopCanLit Canada's Pulp Mill

Compared to other areas of mass-cultural activity, noteworthy Canadian forays into the realm of popular fiction have been, while fascinating, relatively rare. At least there are concrete reasons. The Canadian publishing industry is a small one which caters to a limited and therefore, by definition, "specialty" market. Moreover, not even the total sales of a smash Canuck bestseller would amount to more than a drop in a Stephen King–size bucket, which means that even the most "popular" Canadian-only authors aren't really popular in mass market terms at all.

It's also worth noting that this restricted industry scale appears to have had an impact on the kinds of books selected, valued and promoted by Canadian publishing. Seeing themselves as the purveyors of the institutionally cherished notion of "CanLit," Canadian publishers have often concentrated on books which are "distinctly Canadian" in terms of content; this means lots of critically praised novels about coming of age on the prairies or, more recently, coming of age as a first-generation child of immigrants in one of the country's major urban centres. CanLit has meant a thriving publishing tradition of poetry and books of Canadian history, countless books on Canadian institutions, industrial titans and politicians, and scad upon scad of volumes containing the personal memoirs of the nationally well-known. Needless to say, it has also meant a shitload of books about hockey.

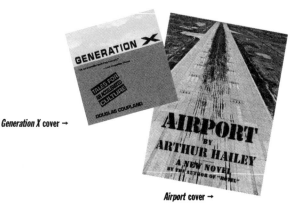

Generation X cover →

Airport cover →

Not that we deplore CanLit or would presume to wish even one of these books out of existence – although it's debatable whether the national health is served by yet another edition of fan letters to Peter Gzowski – just that our concern lies with those forms of Canadian cultural expression which, for whatever reason, have transcended the realm of specialty interest in Canada.

In short, what fits most snugly into the category of Canadian pulp are those books specifically designed with the bagging of big audiences in mind: books for bucks. Interestingly, in the process of aiming as broadly as possible, most of Canada's more successful pulp puts itself in opposition to CanLit in a revealing way. While Canadian literature is virtually defined by books set in Canada, most PopCanLit isn't: Arthur Hailey's *Airport* wasn't Pearson or Dorval; William Gibson's future replaces nations with corporate states; and the primary backdrop for Douglas Coupland's emblematic members of *Generation X* happens to be the American Southwest. All of which is an attempt to justify why you're holding a book that spends more time talking about Harlequin romances and Arthur Hailey than about Margaret Atwood or Robertson Davies. And while this is intended as no slight on Atwood's or the late Davies's writerly capabilities, the fact is, their work just isn't pulpy enough. Which is a criticism most writers could live with.

Here then is a selective guide to some of Canada's most conspicuously popular literary phenomena:

Douglas Coupland

Canadian authors have contributed two key catchphrases to contemporary pop-cultural discourse: William Gibson's "cyberspace" and Douglas Coupland's now-unavoidable "Generation X." The title of this Vancouver-born former art student's first novel, published in 1991 when he was 29, is a phrase that was pounced upon by the media with an omnivorous frenzy one would expect more appropriately reserved for the discovery of extraterrestrial life. Then again, perhaps a form of extraterrestrial life is exactly what Coupland's book – an easy-reading, sound-bite-size account of three incurably ironic twentysomething characters adrift on the seas of post-electronic *ennui* – helped boomers discover.

Prior to Coupland's galvanizing novel, which might well have been read by more people curious about the new generation than people actually of that generation, boomer-dominated culture seemed to regard even the potential existence of a malcontented junior demographic with a combination of denigration, denial and dismissal. Coupland gave it a name and a label and, ergo, a marketability it had lacked before. Thus, the boomer media establishment finally had a reason to acknowledge the so-called Generation X: if it can be packaged, it can be sold, and if it can be sold, it must exist.

Interestingly, Coupland's vision of generational *ennui* is deeply rooted in the Canadian obsession with the meaning of mass media: it's not just pop culture but one's attitude to it, that defines Coupland's Generation X. This places the book on the same shelf as products by all those other Canadian thinkers, writers and film-makers who view the world through a TV screen darkly.

William Gibson

This Virginia-born former hippie, resident in Canada since the late sixties, coined the term "cyberspace" in a science fiction novel called *Neuromancer* in 1984, and has found himself swatting off labels like "visionary," "genius" and "prophet" ever since. Although he was born in the States, Gibson's vision of a corporate-controlled world in which technology has superseded humanity was not only perfectly poised as the literary harbinger of the wired era, it also makes him the logical pulp-fiction heir to Marshall McLuhan.

Insofar as so much Canadian popular culture is based on the consequences of living in a media-saturated world, Gibson's sensibility is definitely Canuck. Incidentally, he claims as two of his most-admired authors J. G. Ballard and William S. Burroughs, also faves of David Cronenberg, whose 1983 movie *Videodrome* is a positively Gibsonesque science fiction thriller about the invasion of the body by corporate technology.

Arthur Hailey

Undoubtedly Canada's preeminent pulp storyteller: 150 million books sold in 38 languages, 11 movie adaptations of his books, a smashingly successful background in commercial TV drama, and, arguably, the father of that most period-specific of 1970s kitsch-cult phenomena, the disaster movie. (It was Hailey's mega-bestseller *Airport* upon which the 1970 movie of the same name was based, and *Airport* which kick-started the whole disaster-movie cycle.)

A British-born (in 1920) Canadian citizen, Hailey established himself as a crack engineer of fast-paced "Golden Era" TV drama: his 1956 teleplay *Flight Into*

Danger was one of the most successful of its day, inspiring three prime-time TV productions. Hailey shifted his attention to novel-writing in the late 1950s.

While his books will never cost Michael Ondaatje any sleep – of his work Hailey has said, "I hope it's workmanlike" – he does have a knack for orchestrating intrigue on an epic scale. Demonstrating a journalist's obsession with facts and detail, the typical Hailey formula is to establish an appropriately large and powerful industrial setting – an airport, an automotive corporation, a major network-news operation – then let a cast of antagonistic two-dimensional characters loose in it: an approach as close to designing a board game as writing a novel. It is the precise observation of the machinations of these settings which gives Hailey's books whatever disposable charge they have.

Harlequin

Staggeringly successful, Canadian-established publisher of romance fiction: the McDonald's of mass-market mush, the Coca-Cola of clinch and swoon. Founded by Canadian publishing executive Richard Bonnycastle in 1949, Harlequin was originally a multigeneric publisher of various kinds of commercial pulp – westerns, mysteries, cookbooks, and so on – until Bonnycastle's wife, Mary, noticed something interesting. The Mills and Boon line of British romance books (which Harlequin started distributing in 1957) were doing so extraordinarily well among female readers that Mary Bonnycastle suggested to her husband that Harlequin concentrate on publishing romance fiction exclusively. Which is exactly what the company began doing by 1964.

As canny a commercial publisher as any in pulp history, Harlequin changed the way niche-specific books were made available to targeted consumers. First of all, the company made sure that its strictly formulaic books were visible in places women frequently were: drugstores, supermarkets, department stores. Also, it offered its books at competitively cheap prices, which made it even easier to drop a Harlequin or two in with the groceries. Harlequin was the first publisher to use TV to promote books, an especially smart move considering how much Harlequin readers tended to watch, not to mention how much they *like*, TV, particularly daytime soaps, the Harlequin fictional universe.

Today, the Harlequin empire's domain is breathtaking: a book sold every six seconds to over 50 million women annually; three billion books shipped worldwide to 100 international markets. According to the company's own estimate, if one were to read all the Harlequin books sold over the past decade, at a rate of a book every two hours, it would take a quarter of a million years to finish, which is even longer than *Front Page Challenge* ran on the CBC.

Leslie McFarlane (a.k.a. Franklin W. Dixon)

Like Arthur Hailey, Leslie McFarlane (1903-1977) was nothing short of a pulp machine. The Carleton Place, Ontario, native pounded out four novels, 100 novellas, 200 short stories, 75 television scripts – including several for Lorne Greene's *Bonanza* – 50 movie scripts and countless magazine articles. Yet his most widely read work (50 million books sold) wasn't even associated with McFarlane until he published his autobiography a few years before his death.

The book was called *The Ghost of the Hardy Boys*, and it revealed, after 50 years, that the author of the immensely successful juvenile series about the two sleuthing offspring of an American detective was in fact written by a Canadian. It seems that back in the late twenties, after McFarlane had established himself as a successful pulp freelancer, he was approached by the American publisher Edward Stratemeyer. Stratemeyer had been impressed by McFarlane's anonymous work for him on a series called *Dave Fearless*, and asked the young writer if he'd take on the first three books in a new series, *The Hardy Boys*.

McFarlane agreed to write the books under the following conditions: Stratemeyer would present McFarlane with the plots, which the writer would expand upon and polish, but not change. McFarlane would keep his own authorship of the series a secret, and the pseudonymous "Franklin W. Dixon" would be used. But here's the one McFarlane must have been kicking himself a full half century over: the writer was to receive no royalties from book sales above and beyond the final once-only fee Stratemeyer offered of $125 per book. Possibly because he was hungry, possibly because he was young, or maybe just because he was an all-too-eager-to-please Canadian, McFarlane agreed to the terms and wrote 21 volumes in the series over the course of 20 years.

We shall hoist the maple leaf over McFarlane's memory by noting that there seems something almost poignantly Canadian about the fact that one of the century's most beloved and widely read authors of fiction for young people was actually an Ottawa Valley lad who let somebody else take all the credit and all the cash. Then again, $125 dollars did go quite a way back then.

Franklin W. Dixon's *The Secret of the Old Mill* →

THE HARDY BOYS

THE SECRET OF THE OLD MILL

> "Canada is a land of multiple borderlines, psychic, social and geographic. Canadians live at the interface where opposites clash. We have, therefore, no recognizable identity, and are suspicious of those who think they have."
>
> – MARSHALL MCLUHAN

The Circuitry of Sainthood
Marshall McLuhan's Northern Visions

Fascinating but dimly illuminating anecdotes abound about Marshall McLuhan, the pioneering pop-media theorist and the most famous Canadian in the world during the 1960s. The fact that, for example, he rarely sat through more than 20 minutes of a movie at a time, and that he practically never watched television, the very medium at the centre of his incantatory sermonizing on post-electronic civilization. The fact that he was a devoutly committed Catholic convert, and that he once tried to patent a formula for removing the odour of urine from underwear. The fact that he wore clip-on ties, slept fitfully and insisted in face of ample empirical evidence to the contrary that the miniskirt was simply not sexy.

Poring over the ever-mounting volumes of material on Herbert Marshall McLuhan, who died New Year's Eve, 1980, at the age of 69, one comes across bizarre but inarguably arresting personal snapshots of a man whose epic feats of intellectual perplexity are, if anything, even more vociferously debated today than they were when McLuhan was one of the hottest tickets on the talk shows of the coolest medium. Was he, as Tom Wolfe once famously wrote, "the most important thinker since Newton, Darwin, Freud, Einstein, and Pavlov, studs of the intelligentsia," or a faddish charlatan slyly cashing in on a particular moment by sending up an impenetrable smokescreen of flummoxing, pseudo-theoretical electrobabble – the pop-intellectual Riddler to the world media's stymied Batman? Were such epoch-seizing aphorisms as "the global village" and "the medium is the message," as Norman Mailer sug-

gested, among "the most useful remarks uttered in the 20th century"? Or, as a couple of generations of McLuhan detractors have now insisted, do such media-magnet phrases ultimately reveal a sucking theoretical vacuum shrink-wrapped in the slick sloganeering of the postwar world's savviest self-promoter?

While it's not our place to answer such questions – our interest here is in McLuhan as a Canadian pop-cultural superstar at a time when only Lorne (Pa Cartwright) Greene had anything approaching the good professor's international brand-name visibility – we raise them because they certify the enduring masscult validity of the man as a figure who, like it or not, irrevocably shifted the perception of perception itself, which is to say, the way we interpret and inhabit our world. Before McLuhan, electronic media was about its manifest content. After McLuhan, electronic media was

about environment, the new world order wired by multidirectional circuitry to the collective central nervous system of post-electronic civilization, concepts now elementary to our discussion of mediated existence, and without which (and maybe this is the caveat), people like Moses Znaimer and Ted Turner would be unimaginable. If he was right – and the question, "What if he is right?," as Wolfe noted, was what kept people listening even beyond understanding – then we may only be beginning to come to terms with the sheer daunting scope of his prescience: perhaps we must add da Vinci to Wolfe's menu of stud intelligentsia.

And if McLuhan wasn't right? Well frankly, who cares? For the fact is, no North American intellectual of his era held the world's ear quite as intensely and obsessively as this incessantly talkative, grammatically impeccable, six-foot-two professor of English litera-

Marshall McLuhan: Medium Massage

Plugging *Understanding Media*

ture from Toronto, and none mainlined the peculiar *zeitgeist* of the era with such voracious, surgical precision. *Wired* magazine, the glossy American cybermag, proclaimed him "electronic culture's immortal saint" as recently as 1996 and, in his introduction to the 1994 re-publication of the Gospel According to Saint Marshall, otherwise known as *Understanding Media: The Extensions of Man*, the American liberal intellectual Lewis Lapham confirmed the reason to keep tuning in McLuhan in terms so starkly prosaic only the professor himself might have a hard time understanding it: "Understanding Media," Lapham wrote, "describes the world I see and know." Or, as William Kuhns said: "We are living in a time he would have understood." Maybe so, but would we understand him?

For our purposes, of course, there is simply the inescapable fact that Lapham's so-called "sage of the north" was a Canadian, raised in Winnipeg and catapulted to counter-culture-era celebrity from Toronto. The real question is, could he have been produced by any country but Canada?

Herbert Marshall McLuhan was born in Edmonton, Alberta, in 1911, but was raised in Winnipeg and spent his academic career at the University of Toronto. (His father sold insurance and his mother, most interestingly, was a professional travelling elocutionist.) These latter two places compel attention in terms of McLuhan's eventual calling as messianic interpreter of the mediated world. Winnipeg, as an isolated urban prairie community with fearsomely unhospitable winters, has proven one of English Canada's more productive incu-

A classic Canadian spectator-savant, McLuhan's genius was to see things in terms of structure, connections and relations.

bators of media-conscious media practice: a conspicuous number of the country's more prominent journalists and broadcasters started there; Neil Young, Monty Hall and comedian David Steinberg grew up there; and during the 1980s, the city's cinematic co-op, the Winnipeg Film Group, produced two of the country's most accomplished deadpan ironists – John Paizs (*Crime Wave*) and Guy Maddin (*Tales from the Gimli Hospital, Careful*). Maddin, for one, cites the wickedness of Winnipeg winters as a likely reason why the city has proven so fertile for postmodern practice: since it was so cold so often, people learned to entertain themselves inside. For Maddin, that meant countless hours of movies and TV; for McLuhan, a youth spent largely behind books.

In Toronto, where McLuhan taught in U of T's English literature department and opened the McLuhan Centre for Culture and Technology in 1968, the future patron saint of media theory found himself in Canada's largest, and eventually most overmediated, urban centre. Situated almost precisely at the centre of the continent, strafed by broadcasting signals from the United States, and the busiest media-production centre in the country, Toronto may well be the capital of Anglo-Canadian, post-electronic schizophrenia: while inarguably the imperial centre of English Canada, it's also the Great Nowhere of national

experience. No Canadian city has played Elsewhere as effectively or as often as Toronto (though lately, Vancouver has been giving T.O. a run for its money in this department), and the American movie industry recognizes it as one of the busiest moviegoing burgs in the world. If the most salient characteristic of the English-Canadian identity is its lack of identity, Toronto is the place where that lack feeds and thrives. Perhaps this is why the city has produced some of the country's most adept generalists, chameleons, observers and shape-shifters: Harold Innis, Jim Carrey, David Cronenberg, Moses Znaimer, Robert Fulford, Wayne and Shuster, Norman Jewison, Ivan Reitman, Atom Egoyan, the Kids in the Hall, *SCTV* – all did hard developmental time in Hogtown, the same place from which McLuhan would scramble the world's receivers with the publication of *Understanding Media* in 1964.

Himself a formidably adept cross-referencing generalist (understanding him was once likened by colleague T. W. Cooper to "tracking a kangaroo"), McLuhan's approach to interpreting media was simultaneously so inspiring, perplexing, expansive and infuriating because it was so omniverous: by all accounts, there wasn't anything, from corporate image-building to topless bars, about which he did not have some kind of arresting, penetrating and thoroughly unprecedented observation. A classic Canadian spectator-savant, McLuhan's genius was to see things in terms of structure, connections and relations. Not what things were, but how they became something experientally distinct in the way they connected. Thus, the observations that lay at the core of his

Discussing media theory with comedy team Rowan and Martin

pioneering postmodernism: the notion that civilization itself shifts according to the dominant paradigms of communication and expression of the age – that is, we don't create systems of communication, they create us – and that the movement from print to visual culture integrated our experience of media so intimately with our physiology that electronic media are virtually an extension of our physical experience of the world. This was the idea from which David Cronenberg drew such lurid inspiration in 1983's deliriously McLuhanesque horror satire *Videodrome*. In the movie, flesh melded with media in the most ickily literal manner imaginable, and featured a strangely familiar messianic guru named Brian O'Blivion, who existed only as a televisual image prone to spouting such ear-catching perplexities as, "The television is the retina of the mind's eye."

At the height of his late-sixties notoriety, McLuhan was one truly ubiquitous Canuck: a regular guest on talk shows, a visible buddy of Pierre Elliott Trudeau's, the subject of a *Newsweek* cover and a *Playboy* interview, volubly admired by Wolfe and Mailer, a pricey speaker at corporate think-tanks, the punchline for at least one *New Yorker* cartoon. Not surprisingly, this notoriety sowed the seeds for the enduring anti-McLuhan backlash, and nowhere more deeply than in Canada itself. Characteristically dubious of border-crossing celebrity in the first place, Canadians seemed doubly threatened by the notion of a celebrity intellectual sprung from their midst: a pop guru from the U of T campus was apparently more than many Canadian critics could bear. Universities have long functioned as havens for Anglo-Canadian

Consider This: '60s Britain = Music and fashion. '60s America = Music and politics. '60s France = Culture and politics. '60s Canada = Media theorists?

intellectual protectionism, and the notion of a pop incursion on the campus was apparently nothing short of transgressive. First there was the fact of "pop" itself, the very idea of which many intellectuals felt it was the duty of the universities to act as walled fortresses against. Then there was the notion of celebrity, which in many minds couldn't, and shouldn't, be reconciled with the notion of academic credibility. Finally, there was McLuhan's inspired and inspirational generalism, which must have caused considerable shudders amongst those for whom departmental specialization was as much a matter of professional survival as intellectual inclination. Suddenly, along comes this guy who hangs out with hip writers and world leaders, who is sung about by rock bands and appears in Woody Allen movies, who's rudely offering cogent readings of, well, everything. And who refuses to give up his tweedy

berth at U of T and move to New York or L.A. or someplace where celebrities are supposed to live.

That's why, as an epitaph, you couldn't come up with a more Canadian-sounding one than this, offered by Edward T. Hall after McLuhan's passing: "He was a great man. Much too great to be famous." Such an assessment would hardly have surprised McLuhan, as his omniverous willingness to offer interpretations of, as Michael Bliss suggested, "anything in literature, history, the whole universe, past, present and future" also included the way things worked in Canada. Concerning his own fame, McLuhan said, "A superstar today is just another word for a sitting duck."

Another Fine Messer
The Down-Home Tradition That Will Not Die

This is the telling tale of two of Canada's most popular and enduring traditions: Maritime jubilee and country TV shows. The former tradition, which reached its zenith of popularity with CBC-TV's Halifax-based *Don Messer's Jubilee*, features a genial "family" of regulars performing traditional Maritime folk tunes, jigs, reels and fiddle music. *Singalong Jubilee*, another down-home Halifax musical showcase, was easily the form's most popular entry after Messer's hugely controversial cancellation in 1969, and *Rita & Friends*, currently one of the CBC's few bona fide in-house hits, is compelling proof of the endurance of this TV musical legacy.

The country show, while appealing to a similar audience sensibility, is nevertheless different from the jubilee tradition. While, like the Maritime music program, it dates back to the infancy of Canadian broadcasting, its musical interests are less geographically precise. As showcases for country-and-western music, these shows – best exemplified by the perennially popular *Tommy Hunter Show* on CBC – were more continental than regional in musical interest. As "country music" can refer to everything from bluegrass and Texas swing to new country and Grand Ole Opry, these programs tended to roam a more open range than the eastern shows.

What the traditions shared was twofold. First, both attracted avid and loyal fans who stuck by them year after year, and who probably crossed over by the thousands: if you watched *Singalong Jubilee*, chances were you dug *Tommy Hunter*, too, and if you couldn't live without *Don Messer's Jubilee*, you likely didn't miss *Country Hoedown* either. The other thing these programs shared is that just about every single one of them was cancelled while it was still popular: *Don Messer's Jubilee* was nothing short of a top-10 hit when CBC canned it in 1969, and *The Tommy Hunter Show* was also pulling in large and loyal audiences when it was unplugged in 1992.

This pattern of the premature cancellation of Canada's indisputably popular folksy Maritime and country shows points to one of the more revealing contradictions in Canadian TV culture: the fact that, while Canada's viewing public has traditionally had a large rural, conservative and working-class base, most of Canada's broadcasting executives have been well-heeled, urban hipster wannabes. They work in Toronto with their eyes on L.A., and they twist their ponytails in a knot every time they switch from Jay Leno to Rita MacNeil. (Or from Johnny Carson to Don Messer. Or from David Letterman to Tommy Hunter.) So, impervious to utter lack of public demand, they cancel the dread fiddle-and-twang to try to perpetrate a little home-grown urban hip, which invariably goes down with viewers like the *Edmund Fitzgerald*. Anyone remember *90 Minutes Live*? *Good Rockin' Tonight*? How about *Friday Night! With Ralph Benmergui*?

What usually happens then, following the humiliation of having tried and failed at hip again, illustrates another way in which the country and Maritime jubilee shows are similar: they will not die. Like the step-dancing version of *Night of the*

Don Messer protest on Parliament Hill, 1969 →

Taping *Don Messer's Jubilee*

Living Dead, they come back to life. Perhaps not with the identical name or cast of personalities, but definitely with the same musical orientation and audience in mind. In the same way then that the sinking of Ralph begat Rita, the hoedown often replaces the horror, and the fiddle follows the failure. Thus, while the executives come and go – many simply disappearing after too many failures have attached themselves like barnacles to their c.v.'s – the fiddle-and-twang tradition goes on, an enduring testament to the strength and depth of Canada's roots in the country.

Part One Don of the Dead: The Messer Affair

As challenging as it's always been to divine the logic behind CBC programming decisions, the cancellation of *Don Messer's Jubilee* in 1969 ranks as possibly the most purely baffling move in the Mother Corp.'s history. Nearly three decades after Don Messer fiddled his final jig on the national airwaves, the reason for why the show was terminated still perplexes as much as ever: just what in god's name did they think they were doing? After all, despite the fact that the weekly half-hour musical series, a showcase of Maritime roots music taped in Halifax, was scorned by critics and derided by hipsters, it was nothing short of a no-brainer ratings blockbuster. Simple and cheap to produce, fixed in content and format, regional to the max and beloved by hundreds of thousands, *Don Messer's Jubilee* was quite simply one of the most successful programs in the CBC's history, even drawing more viewers than the mighty *Hockey Night in Canada* for three of its ten seasons.

Over the course of its run, the pro-

gram made bona fide national stars out of its sincere, talented and decidedly untelegenic regulars: Don Tremaine, the genial ex-Mountie who acted as host; Charlie Chamberlain, the lumberjack-turned-singer with a penchant for rakishly tilted headgear; Marg Osburne, the beloved singer whom the CBC's own publicity department once described as an "unabashedly plump woman"; and, of course, Messer himself, the quiet, diminutive bandleader who'd been fiddling professionally since he was seven years old.

Even stranger about the CBC's decision to yank the show was that by 1969, despite its age and unchanging format, *Jubilee* was hardly in a state of decline. On the contrary, square as it might have seemed to downtown types, *Jubilee* was still ranked in the top ten most watched Canadian programs, a ranking from which it hadn't budged in a decade. Typically, the public corporation didn't offer anything but the vaguest of explanations for the decision to pull the plug on Messer, and what it did offer merely stoked the fires of public outrage (something about seeking, according to a 1973 obituary on Messer, a "younger look"). Even more insensitively, the Corporation seemed perfectly willing to bend the truth publicly when it claimed "diminishing size and nature of the program's audience" was the reason for the show's cancellation. One might think, in the absence of any logical explanation, and given the illogical (and condescending) explanations that *were* offered, the CBC would at the very least have been prepared for the outcry the Messer cancellation would set off. Yet in this, as in every other aspect of the Messer affair, the

Corporation seemed utterly unprepared.

No event in Canadian popular culture, with the exception of Paul Henderson's series-clinching 1972 goal against the Russian hockey team, triggered such intense public response as the cancellation of *Jubilee*. In Ottawa, a contingent of traditional fiddlers and old-time step dancers converged on Parliament Hill for a musical protest, drawing no less than 300 placard waving supporters. One of the event's organizers, a three-time North American fiddling champion named Graham Townsend, saw the cancellation of the program as nothing less than a state-imposed civil rights violation: "The Negroes in the United States fight for their rights," he told a Canadian Press reporter. "We in Canada must fight for the Don Messer show. The young generation at the CBC wants to kill it."

Soon, the Messer affair was raging inside the House of Commons, as well. Indeed, it was raised by no less an *eminence grise* than the still-fiery former prime minister and Messer fan John Diefenbaker, who like Mr. Townsend also managed to contextualize the cancellation in terms of American racial politics, if in an even less politically sensitive manner: "Many people," Diefenbaker thundered, "are asking that this show be continued, and they are not particularly pleased with the fact that the Black Panthers and the like apparently have an inside track at the CBC." Thinking this a rather melodramatic analogy, Liberal MP Barney Danson rose to address Gerard Pelletier, Secretary of State: "Will the minister, " Danson wondered, "ask the CBC to fiddle while the member for Prince Albert burns?"

The mail flew into the CBC like

Country Hoedown cast

schoolyard snowballs. The Corporation, though steadfastly unmoved, was practically buried in confused and angry dispatches from jilted Messerites. Newspapers across the country were inundated with similar cries of anger and despair: "Personally," wrote one *Toronto Star* reader, "I think some of the tripe that is showing on TV is not fit for a man or beast and the *Don Messer Jubilee* (sic) is one of the few programs that my family and myself are able to tolerate. It is a stabilizer in a time of unrest." Wrote another *Star* reader: "Don Messer's out. Why? It is one of our best – really good music and clean entertainment. I suppose in its place we will get a revolting and obscene movie, or a band of long-haired folks, flopping around, singing dee dee dum etc., etc." Even the *Star*'s customarily rancorous Patrick Scott (the TV critic

once dubbed "Canada's rudest man") reserved a rare, if eerily Diefenbakerian, expression of lament for the premature burial of *Messer's Jubilee*: "The next time some 'soul brother' tells me how 'groovy' some new TV show is," wrote Scott in 1969, "I'll personally foot the bill to renew Don Messer."

Not that any of this saved the show, of course. After a decade at the top of the ratings, Don Messer was removed from the air, taking a small chunk of the Canadian public's heart along with him. He died in 1973.

Part Two You Can't Keep a Good Hoedown: The Revenge of the Roots

The Messer affair, while exceptionally intense, is not an isolated incident in the history of Canadian television broadcasting. In 1992, for example, more than two

decades after the CBC dropped *Don Messer's Jubilee*, the Corporation announced the end of another popular, long-running unhip musical show, and for reasons that evoked memories of 1969. After 27 seasons, the weekly country-music showcase *The Tommy Hunter Show* was extinguished because, as network program director Carol Reynolds enigmatically explained to Canadian Press reporter Bill Anderson, "There comes a time when every artist and every broadcaster says: 'Let's look for a change, or let's end it.'" While the ensuing hue and cry among viewers – who, in 1992, numbered 837,000 every minute the show was on the air – didn't match the intensity of the Messer aftermath, the scenario was otherwise eerily similar: a popular, established musical program with a largely rural and working-class

Tommy Hunter with The Rhythm Pals

audience had again been axed by Toronto-based programming executives with the scantest of explanations. But everybody thought they knew why, for the whole thing gave off the unmistakable stench of urban condescension. Like *Don Messer's Jubilee*, *The Tommy Hunter Show* just wasn't hip enough for the CBC, so it had to go. Indeed, the suspicion of pseudo-sophisto snobbism was borne out months later with the debut of *Friday Night! With Ralph Benmergui*, a stupendously inept, monumentally ill-conceived attempt at a hip, late-night musical-variety show. Ironically, *Friday Night!*'s mix of ersatz Burbank glitz and oh-so-lame schtick managed to reflect far worse on the Corporation than anything that had appeared on the combined 40 years of Don Messer or Tommy Hunter shows. Euthanized after one and a half

excruciating seasons, *Friday Night!*'s replacement turned out to be as revealing as it proved popular: *Rita & Friends*, a homespun musical-variety series hosted by yet another beloved but untelegenic Maritimer. Nearly 20 years after his passing, it seemed that Don Messer had claimed his revenge.

Just as the appearance of the enormously popular MacNeil program represented an allusive link with the regional musical tradition embodied by Don Messer, so did Tommy Hunter represent a link with the other dominant but equally derided form of Canadian musical-variety programming: the country-and-western show. When Hunter first appeared on the CBC, it was as a regular on one of the network's first "cornpone" productions, the hugely popular *Country Hoedown*, which he joined at age 19 in

1956. While the country shows like *Hoedown* and *Hunter* and the Maritime roots shows like *Jubilee* were distinct forms in certain regards – the former were usually based in Toronto, for example, and showcased less traditional musical forms than the latter – what they shared is ultimately more significant in this context than what they did not.

Besides, even historically, the two kinds of musical programs are inextricably linked. For example, when CBC sought a summer replacement for the popular *Hoedown* show in 1959, it turned to a young Halifax producer named Bill Langstroth, who fulfilled the network's regional concerns with *Don Messer's Jubilee*. Later, when the CBC sought a summer replacement for Messer, it turned to Langstroth again. This time the banjo-picking producer created another popular

Don Messer with Marg Osburne and Charlie Chamberlain

but sneered-at Maritime music showcase called *Singalong Jubilee* which, among other things, was the program that introduced Anne Murray to Canadians. (And incidentally, to Langstroth, whom she eventually married.) Likewise, when *Hoedown* wound down after nine seasons, the CBC turned to the program's most popular regular, Tommy Hunter, to pick up where the old show left off: by the time the CBC cancelled Hunter's show in 1992, the London, Ontario-born singer had thus been a featured performer on the network for nearly four consecutive decades. The other point where the history of Canada's country and regional music programs intersect is in the context of a program called *Countrytime*, this time a Nova Scotia–based *country* show which the CBC quickly rushed to air in 1970 in a desperate attempt to appease the national outcry over the premature disappearance of *Don Messer*.

But certainly the most significant way in which these musical-broadcasting traditions hew to each other has less to do with historical circumstance than with the long-running conflict of cultural values they reveal to be at work in a certain corner of Canadian popular culture. Their persistent popularity – currently confirmed by the success of *Rita & Friends* – reminds us of the extent to which rural and working-class tastes remain a cultural contender in Canada. This fact, in turn, underscores the gap between the sensibility of the Canadian network programming class – especially at the CBC – and the sensibility of the Canadians they program for, a gap that has never been more baldly apparent than in the context of these down-home music shows.

Without doubt, the programming class at the CBC has historically regarded the persistent popularity of these programs with something like acute embarrassment, as though someone in a plaid shirt had crashed a posh cocktail party and started step dancing all over the Persian carpet. Indeed, the seemingly instinctive snobbism leveled at these programs over the years by CBC officials has occasionally been nothing short of stunning. Back in 1961, for example, in a *Chatelaine* article, an unidentified CBC drama producer had this to say about the apparently unaccountable success of *Don Messer's Jubilee*: "It exudes a sick making sincerity – you know, all the homely virtues cooked up in one sweetly indigestible batch of fudge."

The specific culinary analogy notwithstanding, such a sentiment suggests another manner in which the regional and country music traditions have been forced to share the same destiny: in the casual and often cruel hostility among citified critics and programming executives they provoke. "Mass audience cornball hits," is how Patrick Scott flushed the genre in 1970, before calling *Countrytime* "another bad music show without a hint of comedy, conscious or otherwise, to redeem it." In 1957, *Toronto Telegram* entertainment columnist Alex Barris watched an episode or two of the hugely popular *Country Hoedown* program and sniffed: "People who like western music, it seems, are not impressed by fancy production or imaginative music arrangements." Nor, apparently, by the tastes of Canada's urban elite.

Rural Rhythms

Country Hoedown, 1956-1965, CBC
The show that turned the then-unknown Tommy Hunter into a bona fide Diefenbaker-era sex symbol.
Cast: host Gordie Tapp, Tommy Hunter, Tommy Common, The Hames Sisters, Lorraine Foreman, King Ganam ("The King of the Fiddle") and his band, Sons Of The West.

Don Messer's Jubilee, 1959-1969, CBC
Cornpone love in that attracted more than three million viewers per week in its heyday.
Cast: Don Messer and His Islanders, Charlie Chamberlain, Marg Osburne, host Don Tremaine, the Buchta Dancers.

Singalong Jubilee, 1961-1974, CBC
The first step in Anne Murray's march toward world domination.
Cast: singing host Bill Langstroth, Anne Murray, blind balladeer/guitarist Fred McKenna, Catherine McKinnon, singing trio The Dropouts, Ken Tobias, Gene MacLellan.

The Tommy Hunter Show, 1965-1992, CBC
Hunter described his own show as "a Canadian thumbprint... laid in granite." Others weren't quite so poetic. Entertainment writer Ed Gould once called it "Lawrence Welk in cowboy boots."
Cast: Tommy Hunter, fiddler Al Cherny, vocal instrumental trio The Rhythm Pals, the Allan Sisters, diminutive miniskirt wearer Debbie Lori Kaye.

Hee Haw, 1969-1993, CBS/Syndicated
True, this was an American show, but it was developed by a pair of ex-pat Canadians: Frank Peppiatt and John Aylesworth. This explains why *Hee Haw* had such a strong Canuck presence: Gordie "Cousin Clem" Tapp and Don "Charlie Farquharson" Harron were given carte blanche to indulge in their hick schtick. The absolutely moronic rapid-fire humour wedded with hurtin' tunes made *Hee Haw* seem like a rural version of *Rowan and Martin's Laugh-In*. Note: Before he moved to the States, John Aylesworth created the format for the CBC's long-running *Front Page Challenge*.

Countrytime, 1970-1974, CBC
The only national weekly show in Canadian history to originate from a high-school gym in Dartmouth, N.S.
Cast: host Don Tremaine, Vic Mullen and the Hickorys, Myrna Lorrie.

Goin' Down the Middle of the Road Canadian Easy Listening

Easy-listening music (a.k.a. adult contemporary music): the subliminal soundtrack to postsuburban existence, as perverse as strip malls, as offensive as ice cream, as unavoidable as billboard advertising. If this ubiquity isn't apparent at first, that's as it should be. It's supposed to be unobtrusive and vaguely comforting, to slide as snugly into your lifestyle and sensibilities as an immaculately preserved Buick Towne and Country slips into the Members Only spot at the golf club. Indeed, the primary appeal of easy listening seems to be the impression of keeping discord at bay: beyond the smoked windows, outside the climate-controlled environment.

If you hate it, if you're one of those who feels latent claustrophobia ratcheting up to homicidal psychosis by crowded elevators dripping synthetic strings from the ceiling, there is nothing easy about easy listening at all. It, in fact, is hard: hard to take, hard to listen to and hard as a loaf of stale Wonderbread as it bludgeons your consciousness with mind-numbing kindness. (Incidentally, it's our hope that this bleak assessment of easy listening's appeal and constituency doesn't seem unduly snide and condescending. However, for those who would ask where we get off with this unkind stuff about Canuck easy listening, we would answer, the first floor.)

Celine Dion →

Hagood Hardy   Percy Faith

If M.O.R. (Middle-of-the-Road music) is not your thing, and yet you are also a person who takes a certain degree of thoughtful pride from your Canadian citizenship, the following fact will offer little by way of succour: Canadians are easy-listening champs. Some vital statistics on the Big Easies:

Guy Lombardo

Violinist and leader of immensely popular, slow-tempoed dance band The Royal Canadians. In 1928, named as purveyor of "the sweetest music this side of Heaven" by the *Chicago Tribune*.

M.O.R.igins: Born London, Ontario, in 1902, died 1977. Formed band in 1917 along with two brothers – vocalist, saxophonist and flutist Carmen Lombardo, and drummer and trumpeter Lebert Lombardo – and pianist Freddie Kreitzer. Toured Southern Ontario extensively through early twenties before moving permanently to U.S. in 1923. From home base of Cleveland, Ohio, and later, Chicago, band steadily built popularity through personal and radio appearances.

Breakout Moment: In 1929, Lombardo's Royal Canadians take up residency at Roosevelt Grill in New York, from which they broadcast the first of their widely listened-to New Year's Eve specials. Continental fame followed hot on the heels of that first rendition of Lombardo theme song "Auld Lang Syne," eventually making The Royal Canadians one of the most popular M.O.R. outfits of its era. By the early seventies, Lombardo's group had sold in excess of 300 million recordings.

Wisdom: "Happy New Year!"

Percy Faith

Conductor, composer, arranger, pianist.

M.O.R.igins: Born Toronto, in 1908, died 1976. Began playing violin and piano as a child, worked as silent-film accompanist as teenager. At 18, Faith's hopes for career as concert pianist were dashed when he badly burned his hands putting out fire on younger sister's clothes. He turned to composing. Worked at CBC during the 1930s, and moved to the U.S. in 1940, where he became the highly popular arranger-composer for top-rated radio shows. Later specialized in string-laden pop themes from movie scores, like the 1959 monster hit "Theme From A Summer Place."

Breakout Moment: Faith had been enjoying steady but gradual success as a composer, recording artist and music-industry executive for years before "Theme From *A Summer Place*" broke out, but that was the song that made Faith an easy-listening household name.

Wisdom: "People said rock & roll was making delinquents out of youngsters. I used rock & roll triplets in the *Summer Place* theme and proved that youngsters will accept anything that sounds musical if it is presented properly."

Hagood Hardy

Composer, arranger, vibraphonist, pianist, percussionist, unsuccessful Liberal candidate.

M.O.R.igins: Born Angola, Indiana, in 1937. After moving as an infant to suburban Oakville, Ontario, he learned piano and vibraphone, first forming his own jazz band while a political science student at the University of Toronto. Moved to U.S. in 1961 and toured with Herbie Mann and George Shearing, before returning to Toronto later in decade. Developed career as composer for movies and TV – and especially commercial jin-gles – which he alternated with other recording and performances. In 1995, ran unsuccessfully against former Ontario premier Bob Rae in provincial election.

Breakout Moment: In 1972, Hardy is asked to score a sentimental Salada Tea commercial about grandparents greeting their visiting family, the expanded version of which becomes a huge international hit three years later. "The Homecoming" as the tune is called, moves 300,000 albums in North America and wins Hardy *Billboard*'s Instrumental Artist of the Year award for 1976. The song has assumed the status of bona fide M.O.R. classic: the elevator's equivalent of "Stairway to Heaven," the "Layla" of Loblaws.

Wisdom: "I've never worked a day in my life. I mean that."

Frank Mills

Poet, composer, pianist, archconservative.

M.O.R.igins: Born Verdun, Quebec, in 1942 to British parents, Mills could play piano by ear at age four. A McGill University drop-out, Mills joined the short-lived Sirocco Singers after a stint selling industrial gases, then became member of (almost as short-lived) The Bells. Went solo in early seventies, and struggled – even to point of obtaining a taxi licence – until the phenomenal success of "Music Box Dancer" in 1978. Once claimed songwriting "is like brushing my teeth." Went on to write the song "Most People Are Nice."

Wisdom: "I have no patience with separatists. They're like a bunch of wailing teenagers. Slap their face and sit them down, that's my attitude. Until you've grown up and become intelligent, don't bother. I feel that way about most minorities."

David Foster

Producer, composer, pianist, singer, award magnet, M.O.R. Midas.

M.O.R.igins: Born in Victoria, British Columbia, in 1949, Foster began piano at age five. Joined Victoria band The Strangers, then played with Ronnie Hawkins before joining briefly successful Vancouver pop outfit Skylark.

Moved to Los Angeles in 1972, where he worked as studio musician for A-list pop stars like Rod Stewart, Michael Jackson, Barbra Streisand and George Harrison. Mentored by Quincy Jones, Foster stepped out as producer in his own right with work on albums by Chicago, Alice Cooper, Hall & Oates, Barbra Streisand, Anne Murray, Gordon Lightfoot and Earth Wind and Fire. As producer of Celine Dion's English-language crossover smash *Unison*, Foster was instrumental in paving way for the multi-octave Quebec gamine's international success. Famous for insisting on full control in the studio, a demand which is rarely challenged by hit-seeking superstars. By mid-nineties, indisputably the world's most successful producer of full-bodied M.O.R. pop, having worked on Grammy-grabbers Natalie Cole's *Unforgettable* and Whitney Houston's *The Bodyguard* soundtrack.

Wisdom: "My first job, my only job, is to get hits."

Celine Dion

Willowy power-ballad singer with five-octave range.

M.O.R.igins: Born Charlemagne, near Montreal, in 1968. Dion, through the careful mentorship of her manager Rene Angélil, who she married in 1994, has become one of the biggest international pop stars of the current decade. In fact, very nearly as big as Dion childhood idols Barbra Streisand and Judy Garland.

Breakout Moment: After growing up as one of Quebec's most popular pop stars, Dion (with the advice of Angélil) made the commercially crucial but culturally risky decision (considering the state of linguistic sensitivity in Quebec at the time) to release an album in English in 1990. Produced by David Foster and called *Unison*, it was a smash, and paved the way for Dion's thus-far unimpeded ascent up the international pop charts. Her 1996 single "Because You Love Me" became a worldwide number one. Dion continues to record in French: her 1995 album *D'eux* sold over two million copies in France.

Wisdom: "I have never checked into a room myself. I don't even know how to order room service."

David Foster

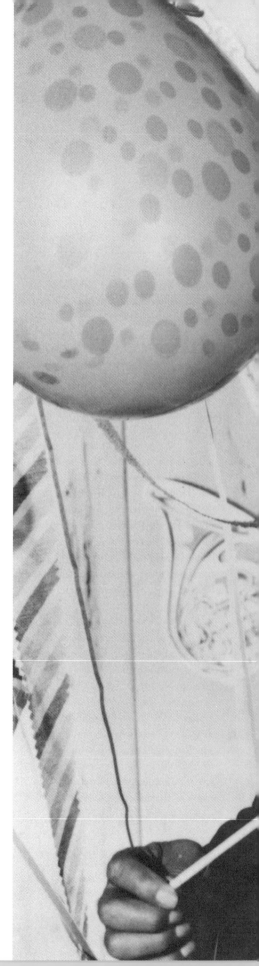

Guy Lombardo →

A Great Broad Anne Murray

One of the reasons you have to love Anne Murray is that she loved what Lester Bangs wrote about her. The now-deceased American rock critic's 1973 review of Murray's M.O.R. radio smash "Danny's Song," and its baldly libidinous irreverence – not exactly a breakaway trend in Canadian entertainment criticism – turned more than a few toques back in the Dominion. How dare this big-city, drug-addled, punk-loving rock critic wax sexually about Our Annie, the former phys. ed. teacher from Springhill, Nova Scotia, (pop. 4,700), whose image is so wholesome she's described in terms usually reserved for national anthems and carbonated soft drinks: "A deep, rich, true voice, with a natural sense of pitch and timing," writes *The Oxford Companion to Popular Music*. "One of the purest and most versatile voices," adds the *The Faber Companion to 20th-Century Popular Music*. "Pure," "true," "natural."

Like a certain persistent myth of Canada, Anne Murray is emblematic of simple, wholesome, unsoiled virtue. She is the driven snow that blankets our nation like a cloak of downy innocence, that protects us from the libidinous nastiness emanating from across the border. That's why so many Canadians were more than a little pissed at Lester Bangs (a most un-Canadian name) when he dared to imagine what he might whisper in her "well-formed Canadian ear." How dare he? After all, as Larry LeBlanc wrote in *Maclean's* in 1974, "If you close your eyes and think of a naked Anne Murray, parts of her always come up airbrushed."

Still, one influential Canadian who wasn't pissed at Bangs was the surgeon's daughter from Springhill herself. Then again, this is a woman whose highest form of praise for another woman is that she's "a great broad." As she told Leblanc over 20 years ago: "I thought (Bangs's review) was great. I got a big charge out of that... He seems to be a fan, and if that's the way he feels about me, great. It certainly turned a few heads around." Which introduces one of the key paradoxes of the Murray persona: while doing little to challenge the myth of scrubbed, small-town, average-girl milkiness which has clung to her since the first soaring of "Snowbird," she's never exactly promoted it, either: "The image thing has always been a problem," Murray said in a 1980 interview. "You know, Anne Murray, the girl next door. Who cares?"

One of the defining factors of Anne Murray's celebrity is the juxtaposition of her I-don't-give-a-shit attitude with safe-as-buttermilk music. Even back in the late sixties, on the CBC-TV show *Singalong Jubilee*, the seminal East Coast music program hosted and produced by Murray's future husband Bill Langstroth, the fresh-faced gamine with the drop-dead contralto would often appear barefoot, a gesture of plucky, self-assured serenity which nicely complemented the calm unflappability of her singing style. Affable, talented and born to the game: the Great One of easy listening, the Trudeau of treacle. Naturally, she challenges the charge of effortlessness. According to Murray, the only thing that's easy about what she does is liking it. She told the *Globe and Mail* in 1985: "You know, I'm working just as hard to sound relaxed as other singers are to sound strained."

Thanks to the musical-variety tradition of broadcasting in Canada, a tradition still chugging in the CBC's mid-nineties

One of the defining factors of Anne Murray's celebrity is the juxtaposition of her I-don't-give-a-shit attitude with safe-as- buttermilk music.

Our Anne: With Mike Douglas and Jim Nabors

With Gene MacLellan

Cringing

hit *Rita & Friends*, Anne Murray had already captured the attention of many Canadians by the time she caught the continent's with "Snowbird" in 1970. Following an initial slump during which she gnawed on fears of being a one-hit wonder, she took flight again, quickly soaring to heights no Canadian female pop singer ever had: a mainstay on both pop and country charts through most of the seventies and much of the eighties, 30 hit singles in 21 years, so many awards she opened a museum in Springhill to hold them, serial appearances on American TV and variety shows and one of the most dedicated followings of any recording artist of her era. (Make that notoriously dedicated: it was Murray's nightmarish experience with a Saskatchewan farmer, the "fan" who once grabbed her hands during a concert and wouldn't let go, that introduced the very concept of celebrity stalking to most people.)

Murray's long-evident appeal to lesbians has never ceased to be a source of wryly insensitive media amusement. Here's Leblanc back in '74: "Even though Anne remains decidedly heterosexual she has the flinty good looks, the athletic figure, broad shoulders and boyish hairstyle that naturally make her a darling of the butch set." Flinty good looks? The *Chicago Tribune* put it rather less poetically: "There's always going to be this lingering whiff of phys. ed. classes about the woman."

As the preeminent Canadian pop sensation of the 1970s, Murray was of course at the forefront of what would be the most successful moment for music-making Canucks before the chart-topping mid-nineties successes of Alanis Morissette, Celine Dion, Shania Twain and Bryan Adams. If you weren't hearing Murray's ear-catching contralto on top-40

or country stations round about 1974, it was just as likely to be Gordon Lightfoot, Joni Mitchell, Neil Young, The Guess Who or Bachman-Turner Overdrive. And that's only to mention acts who managed more than a single chartbuster. It was the prime of the Trudeau era, when it was possible to hear the sky's-the-limit promise of 1967, which probably explains why few citizens could complain about our preeminent cultural export: a country could do a lot worse than be represented by Anne Murray.

Trouble was, apart from the white-bread music and mail-order fashion sense, Anne Murray didn't play Anne Murray that well. Once, in the process of promoting a 1985 CBC special which took her to London, she had this to say about having to sing Culture Club's "Karma Chameleon" on camera: "It just about killed me," she confessed. And why? "Because it's such a piece of shit." (Now there's incentive to tune in.) Of guest band Bananarama, who appeared on the same special, Anne said: "They're three broads from London."

In 1993, when *Toronto Star*'s Judy Steed asked Murray what she remembered about her first impressions of future husband Bill Langstroth, she said: "He was an asshole. He was so outrageously overwhelmingly outgoing, he was outrageous." Add to this bullshit-free conversational style Murray's absolutely non-negotiable control over business and media matters – Steed, a veteran investigative journalist, remarked of her meeting with Murray that "never in all my years in journalism have I been so carefully controlled" – and you have a person who may be more like the country than we like to admit: covered by a blanket of soft, pure whiteness, but hard and unyielding as rock underneath.

As one of our most successful travellers of middle-of-the-road culture, Murray belongs in a tradition that spans from Guy Lombardo to Celine Dion. As a perennial pop-country crossover star, she anticipated k. d. lang and Shania Twain. As someone who came up through the East Coast music-television tradition, she's part of a Maritime musical continuum that includes Don Messer, Rita MacNeil and the Rankin Family. As a career-focused control freak, she's a kindred spirit to Bryan Adams and Gordon Lightfoot. And, as a profane conversationalist, she's the pop-musical answer to Gordon Sinclair. Only, as Lester Bangs once noted, a heckuva lot hotter.

Recommended Annie:

As we approach the millennium, Anne Murray's once vice-like grip of the Canadian radio airwaves has evolved into something resembling a weak handshake. Her last streak of unbroken chart success came in the late seventies and early eighties, with turgid, plodding songs that by now have turned into wedding-reception standards: "You Needed Me" (1978), "I Just Fall in Love Again" (1979) and "Could I Have This Dance?" (1980). ("You Needed Me" was reportedly Ronald and Nancy Reagan's favourite song, but we won't hold that against Annie). Still, Murray's voice is an undeniably powerful instrument: she ranks right up there with Burton Cummings, Celine Dion and k. d. lang in terms of Canuck pyrotechnic prowess. Surprisingly, it's her earlier material that's aging the best. Back when Murray was the fresh-faced poster girl for CanCon, she selected her songwriters wisely and produced some inoffensive down-home pop. Recommended: "Just Bidin' My Time" (1969, written by her *Singalong Jubilee* colleague, Gene "Snowbird" MacLellan), "Sing High, Sing Low" (1970, written by Brent Titcomb), "It Takes Time" (1971, written by Shirley Eikhard), "Cotton Jenny" (1971, written by Gordon Lightfoot).

Big News The Real Canadian Star System

When it comes to having a TV-news star system, Canada is not alone in its profound love of the electronic era's professional class of news messengers. The British have long demonstrated undue affection for reporters and newsreaders, and no country in the world pays its top newspeople as much as the American networks. Still, where British and American news stars must be seen in the larger context of those countries' seemingly endless rosters of TV celebrities, the Canadian TV-news star is a slightly different animal. While a U.S. anchor like Dan Rather is just one of *thousands* of American small-screen celestial entities, the top Canuck newsreaders stand alone at the top of our TV heap.

On television, the journalist represents one of the very few forms of Canadian celebrity – outside of sports stars – whom other Canadians will turn in *just to watch*. In Canada, there are no talk-show hosts or sitcom stars who compare with the popularity of David Letterman or Jerry Seinfeld, no drama series that packs in the couch potatoes like *ER*, no soap operas that generate a thriving TV-celebrity subculture like those in other countries.

Journalism is therefore one of the few areas of domestic TV production where Canadians can and must hold their own. The result is that everybody – both in and outside the profession – takes the business of TV news reporting dead seriously. This explains why, without doubt, the biggest stars in Canadian TV are people like CTV's Lloyd Robertson and CBC's Peter Mansbridge. While Canucks feel absolutely no compunction about lapping up countless hours of U.S. talk shows, sitcoms or dramas, we have a definite preference and insatiable appetite for home-grown news.

To acquire a sense of the star power generated by the practice of TV newsgathering in this country, we beg your consideration

of three Canadian case studies: instances when the news itself made news.

Case One The *Seven Days* Affair

By the time the Canadian Broadcasting Corporation finally pulled the plug, in 1966, on the massively popular, but terminally controversial, current affairs program *This Hour Has Seven Days* after two seasons, the spectacle of pro–*Seven Days* pickets in front of the CBC building on Jarvis Street in Toronto had become a familiar sight. From the beginning, the program had demonstrated two qualities which never ceased to send tremors along the broadcasting institution's closed corridors of power: it was cocky and – even worse – viewers loved it.

First aired in October 1964, the innovative program, which mixed satirical music and investigative film reports with confrontational and fearlessly probing interviews, had become nothing short of a Canadian phenomenon, at its peak reaching an audience of 3.25 million viewers, or almost one-fifth of the entire country. In just about any other broadcasting context but the CBC, those numbers alone would have forgiven any misgivings brass might have had, but not there. "The CBC isn't ready for this kind of journalism," Bud Walker, a CBC executive observed. "We want our producers to be creative, but not too creative." The fact was, the CBC regarded *Seven Days* – and particularly producer Douglas

Star anchors: Lloyd Robertson   Knowlton Nash   Peter Mansbridge

Leiterman and producer-host Patrick Watson – with the mounting fear and disdain the Corporation reserved only for its object of greatest fear: loose cannons on the corporate deck. Loose cannons with high ratings yet.

Of course, the same qualities that made the show such a hit made the CBC quake: its irreverence, its audacity, its innovative and patently nonobjective approach to TV journalism. If *Seven Days* didn't like a particular interview subject, it was as clear as the machine-gun-shaped microphone stuck in the interviewee's face. It was afraid of no one – cabinet minister, Nazi or Pope alike – and occasionally seemed even messianic in its zeal to rout out high-level duplicity and judicial botch-ups. A *Seven Days* interview held such potential for disaster, Prime Minister Lester Pearson eventually ordered his cabinet members not to appear on the show. One of the program's most famous moments was also one of its most revealing: following an interview with Isabel Lebourdais, a writer who had been investigating charges of judicial miscarriage in the case of Steven Truscott, a teenager dubiously convicted of rape and murder in adult court, co-host Laurier Lapierre started crying. A couple of years later, largely as a result of the doubts sparked by the *Seven Days* interview, the Truscott case was reopened.

Beset by constant scrapping between the program's staff and CBC brass over the issue of journalistic independence, *Seven Days* became something else that never fails to chill the Corporation's soul: a hot news story in itself, and worse, a news story in which journalists couldn't help siding with their besieged colleagues *against* the CBC. In 1966,

after parliamentary intervention and despite immense public and press uproar, *This Hour Has Seven Days* was finally taken off the air by CBC senior management. Within months, most of the tapes containing the program were erased for reuse by the CBC.

Case Two The Mansbridge Affair

In 1987, Knowlton Nash heard the heart-stopping news: Peter Mansbridge had been offered a million bucks (Cdn.) a year to leave the CBC and co-host the CBS morning show in the States. Worse, Mansbridge, the CBC's top political correspondent, was apparently actually taking the offer under consideration. Nash, a veteran newsman and bureaucrat who had also happened to anchor the CBC's high-profile nightly news flagship *The National* since 1978, sprang into defensive action. Over the years, Nash had seen a number of CBC colleagues lured either from the country or the network on the promise of filthy lucre – Morley Safer and Lloyd Robertson both started with the CBC – and he had decided that, doggone it, it wasn't going to happen again. No way. Not this time. Not only was keeping Mansbridge on the comparatively modest CBC payroll a matter of national pride, it would help to preserve the integrity of that most hallowed of national institutions, CBC news.

Mansbridge, the balding newsreader who'd been discovered while announcing flight arrivals and departures at the Churchill, Manitoba, airport could not be allowed to slip from the Mother Corp.'s grasp. That's why Nash, who favoured glasses shaped like twin TV screens, was prepared to make the ultimate sacrifice to keep Mansbridge anchored on the

If Mansbridge agreed to stay, Nash would vacate the coveted swivel chair of *The National* to make way for the former airport employee.

Canadian public airwaves. Meeting with Mansbridge over pita-bread sandwiches late one night in November 1987, Nash made Mansbridge an offer no irrational nationalist could possibly refuse: if Mansbridge agreed to stay, Nash would vacate the coveted swivel chair of *The National* to make way for the former airport employee. The younger man accepted – thereby becoming the highest-paid anchor in CBC history.

"This was the most difficult decision of my professional life," said Mansbridge in a white-knuckle press release. "But what it came down to was that, to me, money isn't everything but Canada is." Across the nation – well, at least in journalistic circles across the nation – once the tears of joy and relief were wiped away, Nash was hailed as the saviour of the country's proud journalistic tradition, the man who'd given up the nation's most prominent reading-aloud job in order to keep the country together. Who had, by so selflessly turning away from the teleprompter, done nothing less than "altered the course of Canadian broadcasting history," according to *Starweek* magazine. (Incidentally, a few years later, after he'd settled into the high-paying job quite nicely thank you, it seemed that Mansbridge had allowed the flag he once wrapped himself in to slip a little: "Look. I love the country, we all do, but I think we all got carried away by the

Barbara Frum

This Hour Has Seven Days

flag business. I don't wear a maple leaf on my underwear," he revealed, though this time not in a press release.)

Case Three The Frum Affair

On the March 26, 1992 edition of the national evening news program *The National*, Peter Mansbridge stared out from the TV screens of the nation not even a million bucks could make him leave, and soberly announced that the veteran CBC interviewer Barbara Frum, host of *The National*'s sister program *The Journal*, had died of leukemia.

If the news of the 54-year-old radio and TV veteran's terminal illness came as a surprise to many viewers, the fact it was announced on *The National* probably did not. For even if one actually believed, as Mansbridge said that evening, "for a vast majority of Canadians, Barbara Frum *was* the CBC," it only made sense that her passing would be prominently observed by the national public broadcaster's flagship news program. To some, however, what was surprising was the epic scope of that observation. Not only was the passing of Frum the lead item on that night's news, and so by implication the most important event *in the world* that day, the item itself was a whopping nine minutes long – almost half of *The National*'s total length. Minutes later, after squeezing all the remaining newsworthy events of the day into what little time remained, *The National* was followed by *The Journal*, the current affairs program Frum had hosted since 1982. That night's entire program was given over to what Barbara Frum had meant to her profession, her friends, the CBC and the country itself. All in all, the hour-long *National/Journal* package had spent approximately *50 min-*

utes reporting on the death of a CBC journalist. To put this in perspective, bear in mind that the equally respected and famous veteran American TV journalist Harry Reasoner had passed away not long before Frum, yet the response in the American media, while respectful, was nothing compared to the national state of mourning in Canada caused by the death of Barbara Frum.

Moreover, *The National* and *The Journal* were hardly alone in their elaborate public mourning of the deceased interviewer: CBC-Radio's *Morningside* program devoted almost an hour to remembering host Peter Gzowski's longtime friend Frum, and *As It Happens*, the current affairs radio show Frum had built a national reputation as host of, played extensive excerpts from Frum's years as an irresistibly scrappy host-interviewer. When Frum's memorial service took place in Toronto's Massey Hall a few days later, the event was televised in its entirety by the CBC's cable news network, Newsworld.

Outside the Corporation, the response was similarly extensive and intense: countless miles of column inches were devoted to Frum in the nation's newspapers, with certain words and phrases recurring so frequently they took on an almost incantatory power: "an institution," "part of the family," "a national treasure," "a link in our nationhood," "a legend."

If some thought the state of prolonged national mourning by the national media a little much, not only were their objections easily drowned out by the spectacular cacophony of public grief, they were missing the point. For the fact that the media response to Frum's passing might have been over the top – and, let's

face it, it was – is beside the point. More important is that it did happen, and, perhaps, could only have happened in that particular way in this particular country, one of the few places on earth where the passing of a TV journalist could be easily believed to be the most important event to transpire in the course of human or natural events on that day.

After timing the length of the coverage of Frum's death on CBC television, *Financial Post* columnist Gordon Sinclair, Jr. wrote: "*The National*'s genuflecting to one of its own made me wonder if Mother Teresa, Pierre Trudeau and Wayne Gretzky were to die on the same day whether their loss would have managed nine minutes on *The National*." The answer is obvious. Of course they wouldn't: none of them are TV journalists.

Anchors Away

Without question, one of the more peculiar, but consistently successful, Canadian export commodities is the newsreader: that serenely unflappable breed of attractive broadcasting professional who looks into a camera and reads the news of the day as it scrolls by on the teleprompter stationed a few feet from their unbloodshot eyes. For reasons that may have as much to do with neutrally accented blandness as anything else, not only are Canadians good at this, they're positively in demand. In recent years, in fact, a disproportionate number of the talking newsheads in the U.S. have been Canucks: Peter Jennings, Robert MacNeil, Terrilyn Joe, Thalia Assuras, Kevin Newman, Linden Soles, John (formerly "J.D.") Roberts, Keith Morrison, Arthur Kent. So high is Canada's reputation as a breeding ground for newsreaders, American network talking-headhunters apparently always have one eye pointed northward for more. Why? Because Canada gives good talking head.

News anchor Peter Jennings

Leslie Nielsen Dumbs Down
The Case for a Canadian Hero

In *Death of a Salesman*, 1958

In the past decade, the government of Canada has been replacing certain lower-denomination banknotes with coins: in 1987 the one-dollar bill gave way to a coin, then in 1996, the two-dollar bill — one of the few remaining things that set us apart from the heathen Yank — was also pulled from circulation in favour of a thick, two-toned disc heavy enough to create speculation it was designed to keep taxpayers from blowing across the border in high winter winds. No matter. The point is this: each time paper currency gives way to metal, there's a vigorous discussion in official circles as to which national symbol will grace the new coin. Problem is, by the mid-eighties, when the one-dollar bill was about to be retired, the Canadian mint had pretty well run the gamut of emblematic, not to mention interesting, distinctly Canadian icons: beavers, elk, maple leaves, Canada geese — all used up. Mounties, respected prime ministers, even schooners — all previously enlisted in the cause of adorning the national cash.

This probably explains the whiff of desperation given off by the choice of appropriate national symbols for the one- and two-dollar coins especially: a waterfowl unflatteringly called a loon in the first case, and a singularly nasty northern mammal, the polar bear, in the latter.

The time has come to stop the madness before it gets out of hand; before, that is, we find ourselves reaching into our pockets and thumbing embossed reproductions of watersnakes, mosquitoes, carp and raccoons, or start spilling change with cameos of Brian Mulroney and Joe Clark across the Seven-Eleven counter. Here's our solution: forget the conventional national symbols — the flora, fauna and esteemed members of state — and, taking a cue from those fabulously successful American Elvis stamps, replace them with towering figures from Canadian popular culture. People with high public recognition and integrity to burn. People like Leslie Nielsen.

That's right, Leslie Nielsen. The notion only sounds ridiculous until you find yourself confronted with the daunting evidence to the contrary. The fact is, Leslie Nielsen may be one of the most significant avatars of distinctive Canadianness to be found in the known universe: a man so unmistakably and incontrovertibly Canuck in his talent, persona and philosophy, he deserves his own coin, if not an immense likeness of himself blasted directly onto the side of a mountain in Northern Alberta. Consider the proof.

Leslie Nielsen is the son of a Mountie.

Born in Regina, Saskatchewan, in 1926, Nielsen is the youngest of three sons born to Danish immigrant Ingvard Nielsen. An officer of the Royal Canadian Mounted Police, Nielsen senior raised his family at various remote police outposts — including one only 200 miles from the Arctic Circle — before retiring to set up his own private-eye business in Edmonton. Later in life, son Leslie would close the familial loop by appearing as a Mountie in a poorly received 1979 CBC dramatization of the life of Louis Riel, and in 1996, in an episode of the CTV series *Due South*.

As Frank Drebin, *The Naked Gun* hero

Lorne Greene taught Leslie Nielsen to talk.

After an unsuccessful attempt in 1945 at storming the movie business in Los Angeles, Nielsen took an all-night deejay gig in Calgary. From there he went on to Lorne Greene's Academy of Radio Arts, which eventually led to a scholarship with a theatre company in New York. Thanks to the Voice of Doom's mentorship, the professional dam broke, and Nielsen's career was officially under way.

Leslie Nielsen was almost Marshal Dillon.

It's true. The long-running role of *Gunsmoke*'s Marshal Dillon was offered to Nielsen, who turned it down, before it went to James Arness, which leaves the Canadian imagination reeling over what-might-have-been popcultwise. Just think: had he slapped on Dillon's badge, Nielsen and *Bonanza*'s Ottawa-born Pa Cartwright, Lorne Greene, would have been the tallest-riding cowboy heroes in American TV.

Leslie Nielsen was almost Lorne Greene's son.

A few years after turning down *Gunsmoke*, Nielsen turned down an offer to play one of Lorne Greene's motherless sons in the forthcoming American network series *Bonanza*. Imagine: first the Ponderosa, then the world.

The Nielsen family contribution to Canadian parliamentary democracy.

Nielsen's older brother, Erik, famous for his abrasive, deadpan wit, was a longtime Conservative MP from the Yukon. Under the leadership of Dudley Dooright–lookalike, former prime minister Brian Mulroney, Erik was appointed Tory House leader and then deputy prime minister.

Leslie Nielsen built his career playing bland supporting types.

After his leading-man movie debut in 1956's *Forbidden Planet*, Nielsen quickly retreated to the narrative sidelines and his true, not to mention truly Canadian, calling: as a blandly efficient, dependably unexciting supporting character actor in dozens of movies (*The Vagabond King, The Opposite Sex, Tammy and the Bachelor*) and hundreds of TV shows (*Bracken's World, The Bold Ones, The New Breed, The Protectors, Peyton Place*). In doing this, he joined the ranks of other enduring Hollywood Canadians who found a comfy corner most often in the back seat: Walter Huston, Jack Carson, Hume Cronyn, Raymond Burr, John Vernon and Raymond Massey among others.

Career maintenance playing bland authority figures.

If there's a particular dramatic specialty, apart from the essaying of bland supporting types, for which Canadians have displayed a suspicious knack, it's the impersonation of bland authority figures. People in control who never break a sweat, never cross the line to megalomania, whose perfectly managed hair speaks volumes of their claim to authoritative legitimacy: John Vernon as the mayor in *Dirty Harry*, Arthur Hill as *Owen Marshall, Counsellor-at-Law*, William Shatner at the bridge of the Starship Enterprise, Raymond Burr as Perry Mason, and, needless to say, Lorne Greene as Pa Cartwright. In his career, Nielsen has played countless drably in-charge types: doctors, lawyers, officers, studio heads, politicians. Nielsen's definitive authoritative role was his appearance as the captain of the soon-to-be-upended ocean liner in the 1972 disaster-movie high-water mark *The Poseidon Adventure*.

He's the missing link between Lorne Greene and Jim Carrey.

In 1980, when Leslie Nielsen agreed to make fun of his blandly authoritative persona by playing a doctor fond of slapping hysterical airline passengers in the hugely successful disaster-movie spoof *Airplane!*, he probably had no idea he was altering the course of history. Okay, maybe not history, but you get the gist. Not only did the stab at self-parody reinvigorate a moribund career – Nielsen has since become the bankably professional deadpan boob in movies like *The Naked Gun* series, *Dracula: Dead and Loving It* and *Spy Hard* – he effectively established a link between two noble Canadian popcult traditions: the Bland Authority Figure and the Postmodern Popcult Parodist. In other words, by vaulting from straight to spoof, by making plain the cultural connection between playing the boss and playing the fool, he traversed a pathway linking Pa Cartwright to Ace Ventura. A Canadian popcult pioneer.

Leslie Nielsen knows his place.

The keys to personal and professional self-attainment according to Leslie Nielsen: "If I couldn't be an actor, I would only consider being an astronaut, a sea otter or a gynecologist."

"My life is a kind of vacation, I have nothing to prove to anybody or goals beyond just enjoying my friends."

"My axiom is never ask a question."

"I have no driving ambition or goals. I play golf, I travel a good deal, I loaf."

We now rest our case and leave final judgement to you, fellow citizens of the Dominion: for a man who's so selflessly given so much to so many, and who's done so in such supremely Canadian fashion, what's a measly little coin?

The Great Outdoors
A Wilderness Worth Watching

Atom Egoyan's 1987 movie *Family Viewing* contains one of the slyest send-ups of a Canadian TV-viewing quirk found anywhere. In the background of this dramatically freeze-dried and formally rigorous satire about nuclear-family meltdown in the electronic age, one hears the constant drone of TV nature shows. ("And so the mother iguana, aware that the predator is approaching the nest, prepares to defend her eggs...") As in many Canadian homes, the TV is always on somewhere in Egoyan's movie, and it seems always to be tuned in to the gory Darwinian spectacle of one citizen of the wild kingdom devouring another. Egoyan's is an unstressed irony, hardly a howler, but a penetrating insight nevertheless: here you have a movie about alienated urbanites so radically disenfranchised from their own feelings and desires they can barely converse, yet they're obsessed with the electronic simulation of the natural world. It's as though nothing can be trusted, believed or even felt – including the natural itself – unless it's validated by TV, which delivers nature with conflict, a climax and lots of commercials.

Playful canoe high jinks
on *The Forest Rangers* →

In terms of their possible role in Canadian culture, *Family Viewing*'s take on nature shows is a sharp one. It's one of the great paradoxes of our national life that we Canadians probably spend as much time indoors watching our vast and majestic wilderness as we do outdoors living it. It's not surprising that the nature-oriented Discovery Channel is popular with Canucks. Why go outside when you can watch baby seals and pine trees in climate-controlled comfort? Even the great Canadian pastime of "cottaging" (travelling through dense weekend traffic to a distant and crowded place that feels like the suburbs with speedboats) reflects this distinctly Canadian eco-ambiguity. While we go to cottages ostensibly to unwind close to nature's bosom, we drag along TVs, VCRs, cell phones, CD players and laptops. For many Canadians, roughing it in the bush really means doing without pay-per-view.

Could be we're talking about the logical result of our peculiar cultural schizophrenia, for Canada is a country of firmly rooted couch potatoes spread sparsely across an immense, uninhabitable and unforgiving wilderness. As *Saturday Night Live*'s Lorne Michaels observed about his fellow countrypersons' statistically staggering capacity for TV-generated junk, it's precisely because of bad weather and big spaces that we stay inside, huddled around the old electronic fireplace: it's just so much easier to tune in *Baywatch* than dig your car – which probably won't start anyway – out from under three feet of snow. On the one hand, this fact has been a key influence on Canada's particular popcult propensities: it's hard to imagine our brand of postmodern comedy, for example, without all that TV. On the other, it has bred

one of the country's most interesting indigenous cultural phenomena – the great Canadian outdoors show, or nature you don't have to leave home to watch.

Canadian forests, lakes and little furry things have been packaged in three televisual forms: the adventure show, the nature documentary and the fishin' show. Here's the lowdown on all of them.

The Great Outdoor Adventure Show

One of the heartiest and most successful of the Canadian-bred nature-program types, the Great Outdoor Adventure Show has proven something of a specialty for the good old nation-binding CBC. While locales, eras and characters may change, the basic elements of the Great Outdoor Adventure Show more or less remained intact over the nearly 30 years of the form's glory years, spanning from the debut of *The Forest Rangers* in 1963 to the 1990 cancellation of the Energizer bunny of the group, *The Beachcombers*. These programs, collectively seen in hundreds of countries, bear particular attention because, for thousands of kids in places like Saudi Arabia, Zambia and Finland, they *were* Canada.

To identify a card-carrying constituent of the Great Outdoor Adventure Show, the program must have these elements:

1. A group of kids, siblings or buddies who act as self-appointed eco-cadets in some photogenically far-flung corner of the Canadian mild frontier.
2. Reasonable, tolerant and nonviolent authority figures who may be single parents, RCMP officers, nature professionals or all three.

3. Chases involving all manner of wilderness vehicle: helicopters, twin-engine planes, jeeps, horses and, where geography permits, speedboats.
4. A wise, and occasionally wisecracking, Native character whose presence reaffirms the comforting myth of Canada as a country not beset by race problems.
5. Family values: in their responsible Canadian way, these programs, invariably described by their creators as "family shows," promote only the best in liberal middle-class values – conservation, nonviolence, teamwork, tolerance and an ability to deftly operate a canoe at an alarmingly early age.
6. Animals: preferably a highly motivated and intelligent canine who can run for help in an emergency.

The Forest Rangers, 1963-1965, CBC

Concept: A group of plucky but conscientious kids act as eco-cadets from an abandoned but curiously radio-equipped Hudson Bay fort near a Northern Ontario town called Indian River. They have the RCMP (as embodied by Gordon Pinsent) on their side, as well as a hunky Metis character (played by a blond Ukrainian in a wig named Michael Zenon) called Joe Two Rivers. Also featured the most indelible theme music this side of *Hockey Night in Canada.*

Typical Plot: The Rangers capture two Soviet spies up to no good close to the DEW line, one of whom is seized in the jaws of Joe Two Rivers's bear trap.

Cast Members: Pete – Rex Hagon; Chub - Ralph Endersby; Kathy – Susan Conway; Ranger Keeley – Graydon

The Beaver: 20-minute incisor workout

Adventures in Rainbow Country

Its Only Natural
Hinterland Who's Who

In terms of TV depictions of the Great Canadian outdoors, none have seared their way into the national consciousness quite like *Hinterland Who's Who*, the surprisingly long-running series of one-minute public-service announcements from the Canadian Wildlife Service.

In 1963, CWS head Winston Mair came up with the then-novel idea of using television to raise public awareness of hoser wildlife. The CWS joined forces with the NFB and devised the formula for the series.

Each one-minute spot opened with the *Hinterland Who's Who* logo and a distinctive phrase of music – a doleful flute melody that, for most Canadians over 30, is as recognizable as the theme to *Hockey Night in Canada*.

Then, in footage shot by naturalists, we'd see our best-known critters just chillin' on their own turf. Each member of Canada's nature all-star team got their own spot: the loon, the beaver, the Canada goose, even the canvas-back duck.

In *Hinterland*'s early years, each minute-long epic was narrated off-camera by John Livingston, a guy who redefined the term "leisurely pace." His languid, mellow tones practically lulled the viewer to sleep as he shared pearls of wisdom like "with all the wood-cutting the beaver has to do, it's fortunate that his incisor teeth never stop growing."

Truly, *Hinterland Who's Who* could make a minute seem like an hour. So how have these mind-numbingly boring spots stayed on the air for more than 30 years? Simple, *Hinterland* has sold nature to us in a modest, distinctly Canadian way: no flashy effects, no snappy background music under Livingston's narration, and (god forbid) no rapid-fire editing to liven up the pace. If you wanted raging battles between animals, you had to watch *Wild Kingdom*. *Hinterland* was the classic Canadian soft-sell: nature without any televisual jolts.

Gould; Mike – Peter Tully; Sgt. Brian Scott – Gordon Pinsent.

How It Improved Lives: "It has action without violence – and there's a great difference between them, you know."– Fred Rainsberry, supervisor, CBC children's programs.

Sign of Success: The series was sold to over 50 countries. Its tongue-twisting Norwegian title was *Skogwokterlubben*.

Adventures in Rainbow Country, 1970-1971, CBC

Concept: A moppet-haired teenage boy with an inexplicable mid-Atlantic accent foils poachers, thieves and messy campers in Northern Ontario.

Typical Plot: Playing a priest instead of his customary Mountie, Gordon Pinsent goes shooting the rapids but finds himself in peril, requiring our 14-year-old hero to rescue him from the raging torrent.

Cast Members: Billy – Stephen Cottier; Pete – Buckley Petanawabo; Billy's mother – Lois (Mrs. Moneypenny) Maxwell; Billy's sister, Hannah – Susan Conway; Dennis Mogobgub, bush pilot – Wally Koster; Roger Lemieux, nature photographer–Albert Millaire; Dougal MacGregor, tugboat skipper – Alan Mills.

How It Improved Lives: "(Our hero) leads the life of the True North Strong and Free in that he goes fishing for brook trout, puts down his sister and accepts his Indian buddy as damned nearly an equal." – Leslie Millin, the *Globe and Mail.*

Sign of Success: During its one season on the air, *Rainbow Country* regularly drew more than four million viewers per episode, making it the CBC's highest-rated weekly show ever. Amazingly, the CBC cancelled it for budgetary reasons.

The Beachcombers, 1972-1990, CBC

Concept: Lovably irascible scow operator Nick Adonidas (Bruno Gerussi) tools up and down the Pacific Coast in the *Persephone* in search of stray logs and adventure. Also hangs out with pals at Molly's Reach coffee shop, and frequently battles with his rival, Relic. One of the longest-running and most popular Canadian programs ever.

Typical Plot: This time playing neither Mountie nor priest, Gordon Pinsent appears as a Maritime swordfisherman with claims to mystical powers, which he plans to use to take possession of a prize log.

Cast Members: Relic – Robert Clothier; Jesse Jim – Pat John; Molly – Rae Brown; Hughie – Bob Park; Dana Battle – Janet-Laine Green; John Constable, Mountie - Jackson Davies.

How It Improved Lives: "It may not be the greatest show in the world, but at least we're doing nothing wrong."– Jackson Davies, *Beachcombers* cast member.

Sign of Success: René Simard guested as himself in a 1979 episode. Also, Gerussi's Zorba-like antics inspired a Vancouver rock band to call themselves "Bruno Gerussi's Medallion."

Danger Bay, 1984-1989, CBC

Concept: Grant Roberts (Donnelly Rhodes) is the single father of two precocious and environmentally aware teenage kids, as well as being a marine veterinarian at the Vancouver Aquarium. Together they track down and nonviolently apprehend people less aqua-sensitive than themselves.

Typical Plot: With the game assistance of his kids, Grant tracks down and nonviolently apprehends some poachers of sea otters. Not to be confused with the

Bruno Gerussi of *The Beachcombers*

episode where Grant and the kids track down and nonviolently apprehend some horse rustlers.

Cast Members: Jonah – Chris Crabb; Nicole – Ocean Hellman; Joyce Carter, seaplane pilot – Deborah Wakeham; J. L. Duvall – Susan Walden.

How It Improved Lives: "We had to have a good reason. The character whom Grant Roberts hit in the show was a CIA operative who was threatening the life of Grant's son and was about to blow the brains out of a seal. It seemed one of those situations that justified a punch in the jaw."– Paul Saltzman, *Danger Bay*'s executive producer, explaining why his hero finally had to hit someone after 79 episodes of keeping his fists to himself.

Sign of Success: Yet another Canuck outdoors show that was sold to over 50 countries.

The Great Outdoor Documentary

Since nature conventionally refuses to conform to three-act TV plotlines, it is the job of the Great Outdoor Documentary to take the raw documentary evidence of the natural and find a TV-friendly plot to sculpt it into. Survival from predators is perhaps the most durable nature-doc plot of them all, with reproduction and the rearing of young being almost as hearty perennials. Voice-over is essential for two reasons: first, it's an effective way of imposing a sense of nail-biting drama over shots of prairie dogs scampering down holes; and second, it's an equally effective way of projecting human value systems on the natural world – good versus evil, maternal nurturing versus masculine aggression (you get the idea).

The Nature of Things, 1960-present, CBC

Concept: Long-running show dealing with nature and technology. Hosted by veteran biologist David Suzuki since 1979, it's the brainiac of nature shows: its environmental agenda is never concealed, nor is its intelligence. Suzuki is *Wild Kingdom*'s Marlin Perkins with a Ph.D. Topics have included "Crying Wolf" and "Where the Heron Finds its Home."

This Land, 1970-1986, CBC

Concept: Derived from a series called *This Land of Ours*, this show was designed to bring the vast Canadian wilderness to thousands of city-dwellers. Hosted in its later years by John and Janet Foster, an impossibly healthy, nature-loving couple who used various modes of Canuck transportation – canoe, snowshoes, fishing boat, dogsled – to get to their remote, mosquito-infested destinations. *This Land* explored flannel-shirt subjects like cottaging, parks, caribou and canoeing… lots of canoeing. The Fosters also hosted *Wild Canada* and *To The Wild Country*.

Lorne Greene's New Wilderness, 1982-1987, CTV

Concept: Canada's eco-friendly "Voice of Doom" added pithy commentary to rather innocuous footage of various critters. This was his second kick at the nature-show can, following closely on the furry heels of *Lorne Greene's Last of the Wild* (1974-1979).

KEG Productions

A Toronto company headed by Ralph Ellis, the Wayne Gretzky of outdoorsy programming. KEG has sold countless nature documentaries around the world, including *Man of the Wilderness* (1989), *A Passion for Canoes* (1991) and *Profiles of Nature* (1984-1994). In 1988, KEG even produced *Wild Guess*, a wildlife game show for kids.

The Great Gone Fishin' Show

Structurally speaking, the Great Gone Fishin' Show prototype was set by *The Red Fisher Show*, which ran from 1968 to 1990. This was the formula: the genial Red would welcome us into Scuttlebutt Lodge, "the tall-tale capital of the world." In reality, it was a Toronto studio festooned with such unmistakable totems of outdoorsy masculinity as mounted game, log walls, rocking chairs and a roaring fireplace. He then introduced us to his guest for the episode, a buddy with whom the host went fishing. For the following 22 or so minutes, we watch films of the host and his buddy bagging a few big ones. Although the show's title occasionally changed (it was known briefly as *Our Great Outdoors* and *Outdoor Adventures*), the formula didn't: the show remained intact over several decades and countless imitators.

Current entries in the Great Gone Fishin' genre include *Canadian Sportfishing* (1984-present), *Fish'n Canada* (1984-present) and *Going Fishing* (1993-present). While all of these shows give solid advice on important issues like where to find worms, none of them possess the hypnotically cheesy qualities of *The Red Fisher Show*: the cheap production values and Red's kitschy banter about "the ones that got away."

Naturally, these fishing shows have inspired parodies. On *SCTV*, "The Fishin Musician" segment was hosted by Gil Fisher (John Candy), a fishing enthusiast who regularly went gill-shredding with rock stars. In one memorable episode, Gil went fishing with "white punks on dope" Fee Waybill and the Tubes.

A more recent Red Fisher parody is *The Red Green Show* (1990-present), hosted by the relentlessly grinning Steve Smith. This inexplicably popular show manages to make the McKenzie Brothers seem like Nichols and May. If depleted fishing resources don't kill off the Great Gone Fishin' Show tradition, Red Green might.

Apopalypse Now
The Nineties Sound Explosion

No doubt about it: the eighties were a grim time to be a Canadian pop music nationalist. Everywhere you looked, Canadian bands were caught in some nightmarish musical-cloning act. It was like an experiment gone slightly wrong, the musical response to the pod used by Dr. Seth Brundle in Cronenberg's 1986 film, *The Fly*: each time a band would emerge from the cloning chamber, all you could notice was the distance between what they were and what they wished to be. Platinum Blonde was the Bi-Way version of the Police, Luba a pocket-size version of Stevie Nicks, Bryan Adams was low-cal Springsteen, Loverboy the hoser's Van Halen, Corey Hart the preteen Sting, The Spoons a faded Xerox of Depeche Mode. Suddenly, after the chart triumphs of the post-CanCon seventies, which saw an unprecedented number of Canadian acts pass through the pop spotlight, the industry (like the era's politics) grew increasingly conservative. The aping of established mainstream formula became the priority, and the first bands to be signed were those that could pass for someone else. It was the musical answer to those tax-shelter movies in which Canadian cities were cast for their knack at seeming to be both somewhere and nowhere at the same time: indistinctiveness wasn't just the point, it was the selling point.

Ten years later, as predicted by uber-producer Daniel Lanois, the Canadian music industry isn't just thriving, it's humming on several different levels. Not only are our big mainstream acts bigger and more globally mainstream than they've ever been before – Bryan Adams, Celine Dion and Shania Twain are three of the world's top-sellers in their fields – the fringes are on fire too: by 1996 there were no fewer than 200 labels across Canada, ensuring that the fertile fields of up-and-coming musical activity would constantly be tilled for sprouting talent. But it is the territory

The conditions for this bumper crop of pop Canadiana are intimately connected with the circumstances which also led to the "grunge" or "alternative" explosions in the States.

between mainstream and fringe – pretty much a wasteland during the eighties – which really reflects the new vibrancy and confidence of Canadian music in most interesting and promising ways. This is

the realm of music which is popular on its own terms, which has built national or modest international followings without concession to mainstream calculation. Indeed, there are really only three things that bind otherwise disparate acts like Sarah McLachlan, Sloan, The Tragically Hip, Loreena McKennitt, 54-40, Crash Test Dummies, Hayden, Odds, Bass Is Base, Ashley MacIsaac, Blue Rodeo, Cowboy Junkies, treble charger and Barenaked Ladies together: they're distinctive on their own terms. They've built large and loyal followings on their own

Barenaked Ladies

terms. They live and work in Canada.

The conditions for this bumper crop of pop Canadiana – which pioneering independent-label founder Bernie Finkelstein, of True North Records, has likened to "a huge creative renaissance" – are intimately connected with the circumstances which also led to the "grunge" or "alternative" explosions in the States. Taking a page from the punk-rock rule book, frustrated by the conservatism and commercialism of the major labels, bands everywhere became determined to do it their way: building a fan base close to home; record-

ing, releasing and selling their own independent cassettes and CDs; making their own cheap videos; exploiting the national promotional opportunities made possible by the launching of MuchMusic in 1984; and, of course, gigging unto death. Among the more obvious benefits of this approach is the preservation of distinctive creative identities: since the do-it-yourself approach provides opportunities for exploration and exposure independent of the mainstream, mainstream criteria exert little or no influence on what many of these artists do. The result has been nothing short of one of the

richest periods in Canadian pop music history. Here is a selective guide to the jewels of its renaissance.

Barenaked Ladies

This band of belligerently sububuran Scarberians (the local term for residents of the sprawling Toronto suburb of Scarborough) may be utterly mainstream in their goofball antics and preteen appeal, but their route to success was strictly indie. After selling a whopping 85,000 copies of their cheaply produced five-song Barenaked Ladies cassette, they landed a

Dream Warriors

lucrative recording deal with Sire Records, and within the course of a year catapulted from tiny club dates to headlining a smashingly successful national tour. While securing this avid national following, the Ladies have also consolidated considerable critical and popular interest in the U.S. and Britain. Consisting of five irrepressibly goofy guys – Steven Page, Ed Robertson, Tyler Stewart, Jim Creeggan and Andy Creeggan (replaced by Kevin Hearn) – who bounce frantically around the stage while pounding out acoustic odes to such mall-cult staples as Kraft Dinner and McDonald's cashiers, the Ladies are definitely an acquired taste. To some, their eager, unplugged, puppy-dog unpretentiousness is an irresistible alternative to rock pomposity; to others, they seem like a band desperate to land their own Saturday-morning cartoon.

Self-Analysis: "I wish I understood why some people get so angry at us. And I don't mean critics but just people. There's no need to be mad about it – just don't like it. People are allowed *not* to like it." – Steven Page, 1994.

Recommended: *Gordon* (1992), *Maybe You Should Drive* (1994).

Crash Test Dummies

Like Barenaked Ladies, this enormously popular Winnipeg band, consisting of former university classmates, purveys a kind of quirky but smart easy-listening pop which seems to be something of a Canadian growth industry: light alternative. Due largely to overeducated frontperson Brad Roberts's sleepy buffalo baritone and tendency toward arch-lyrical irony, the Crash Test Dummies' unmistakable sound either turns your head or makes you bolt for the door. Avidly loved in

After establishing herself as the undisputed heir to the towering vocal legacy of Patsy Cline, lang branched out from country to other forms of pop balladry.

countries as far-flung as New Zealand and Germany, the Crash Test Dummies caught a catapult to fame much like that which flung the Barenaked Ladies into our collective face: within two years they graduated from campus coffeehouses – where they also circulated a self-produced five-song EP cassette – to appearances on *Saturday Night Live* and the David Letterman show. Apart from their enormously successful albums, the CTD's have also landed songs on the soundtrack releases for such subliterate entertainments as *The Flintstones* and *Dumb and Dumber*.

Self-Analysis: "When you have an academic training, you learn to think critically. I have a very methodical approach to writing. Things don't just pour out of me, due to some inspirational muse. I usually write a bunch of crap and then edit it." – Brad Roberts, 1995.

Recommended: *God Shuffled His Feet* (1993).

Dream Warriors

If this bracingly innovative hip-hop outfit from Toronto's Jane-Finch corridor had done nothing more than take a sample of the theme song from the archetypically cheesy Canadian game show *Definition* to the top of the British charts – which they did in 1991 on "My Definition Of A Boombastic Jazz Style" – they'd warrant our hushed respect here. But the fact is, they've done so much more. Founding

Dream Warriors King Lou (Louie Robinson) and Capital Q (Frank Allert) have faithfully carried the Canuck hip-hop banner through some pretty lean years for the genre north of the border. Along with Devon, Maestro Fresh Wes and Snow, the West Indian-born Warriors have been one of the few rap acts to achieve mainstream success in this country. Moreover, they've brought a sensibility and style to hip-hop which, because of its cultural and musical roots in the polyglot urban reality of Jane-Finch, is utterly distinct from either its British or American counterparts.

Self-Analysis: "The lyrics are our instrument, and we know how to blow our instruments." – King Lou, 1991.

Recommended: *And Now the Legacy Begins* (1991).

54-40

Named after an unkept campaign promise ("54-40 or fight!") made by eleventh American president James Polk to annex most of Canada, 54-40 was founded in the postpunk aftermath of the early 1980s. This hard-working, hard-thinking, hard-rocking Vancouver foursome has been steadily building a body of musical work which ranks as one of the most substantial and impressive ever produced in Canadian pop. Indeed, if there's a Canadian rock tradition this band proudly represents, it's the tradition of sheer sonic tenacity which ultimately fortified the brick-by-brick careers of bands like Rush and The Tragically Hip. Fronted by the quietly magnetic lyricist and lead singer Neil Osborne, the band is capable of turning on a dime from the evocative folk melodies of "I Go Blind" (1990) to the industrial arena-rock riffage of "Nice to

k.d. lang

Luv You" (1992) – and then back again. While major success has so far eluded the band – though it sure came close with 1992's platinum-selling *Dear Dear* – 54-40's signature brand of post-psychedelic poetic hard rock could probably never maintain more than a momentary foothold in the mainstream anyway. Thankfully, one senses they have other less pragmatic reasons for making music.

Self-Analysis: "We have no angle."
– Brad Merritt, 54-40 bassist.

Recommended: *Show Me* (1987), *Dear Dear* (1992), *Smilin' Buddha Cabaret* (1994), *Trusted By Millions* (1996).

k.d. lang

The security of k.d. lang's current position in the musical mainstream is as impressive as it is unlikely. After all, this is a woman whose career began fronting a band (The Reclines) that traded in a most uncommercial combination of raw punk energy and immaculate country-and-western classicism, and who has never shied from publicly sharing some of her less-than-mainstream inclinations, including the fact that she's a vegetarian lesbian. But instead of being sentenced to permanent fringe status for her lifestyle or candor, she has made an ascent up the ladder of international pop notoriety which was as graceful as it was swift.

A decade after her high-kicking cow-punk phase, lang was unquestionably one of the most respected female pop vocalists in the business. When lang recorded *Shadowland* in 1988, her producer was not only the legendary Owen Bradley (mentor to lang's idol Patsy Cline), she was joined in the studio by no less a chorus of country luminaries than Kitty Wells, Brenda Lee and Loretta Lynn. It's that voice, of course: pure, clean, soaring, expansive, like a wind in the Alberta Rockies. Versatile too: after establishing herself as the undisputed heir to the towering vocal legacy of Patsy Cline, the Consort, Alberta-born lang branched out from country to other forms of pop balladry. With a set of pipes like that, combined with a popular constituency that grows with every new musical direction she takes, lang looks likely to be around for a long time.

Self-Analysis: "I'm always on the verge of something. And that's just where I like to be. It's once you get over the edge that you have all the trouble." – k.d. lang, 1992.

Recommended: *A Truly Western Experience* (1984), *Shadowland* (1988), *Absolute Torch and Twang* (1989), *Ingénue* (1992), *All You Can Eat* (1995).

Daniel Lanois

Along with Bruce Fairbairn (Aerosmith, Bon Jovi) and David Foster (Barbra Streisand, Chicago), the Hull, Quebec–born Daniel Lanois materialized during the 1980s as one of Canada's preeminent studio maestros. After starting the decade modestly by producing bands like Martha and the Muffins and The Parachute Club, Lanois finished it off by making fast friends with sonic visionary Brian Eno and contributing his distinctive auteurist audio touch to blockbusting efforts by U2, Peter Gabriel, Bob Dylan and Robbie Robertson. Called "the most important record producer to emerge in the Eighties" by *Rolling Stone*, Lanois specializes in bringing a song's emotional core to the surface of the listening experience: texture and mood are the defining priorities of Lanois's musical universe, not hits, hooks or hum-along choruses. While this quality is baldly apparent on most albums he has produced for others – any album he touches inevitably becomes at least partly "a Daniel Lanois album" – it is nowhere more so than on the producer's two solo albums, 1989's *Acadie* and 1993's *For the Beauty of Wynona*. Understated, elusive and gorgeous, they are Lanois distilled to his global-village roots.

Self-Analysis: "I sing these sounds to musicians in the studio and they look at me blankly and say, 'Yeah, but what notes do you want?' But I don't care about notes. I care about sounds that create a mood, a texture." – Daniel Lanois, 1989.

Recommended (as producer): *The Unforgetable Fire* (U2, 1984), *So* (Peter Gabriel, 1986), *The Joshua Tree* (U2, 1987), *Robbie Robertson* (1987), *No Mercy* (Bob Dylan, 1989), *Achtung Baby* (U2, 1991).

Recommended (as performer): *Acadie* (1989), *For the Beauty of Wynona* (1993).

Sarah McLachlan

Extraordinarily gifted and intelligent singer-songwriter who is often lumped with the mildly loopy likes of Loreena McKennitt, Jane Siberry and Tori Amos, but who deserves credit for her absolute distinctiveness. Even after dozens of listenings, her immaculately rendered, sinuously erotic, multitextured albums – 1988's *Touch*, 1991's *Solace*, 1993's *Fumbling Towards Ecstasy* – offer up previously undetected pleasures. Discovered performing in her native Halifax by Vancouver musician Mark Jowett in 1985, when McLachlan was 17, the multi-instrumentalist McLachlan was coaxed to come to Vancouver to sign with Jowett's independent label Nettwerk Records. (She wanted to go, but her darned parents insisted she finish high school first.) Arriving eventually on the left coast, she recorded her first album, *Touch*, in 1988. Released by Nettwerk, it sold 50,000 copies in Canada, and was picked up for distribution by Arista in the U.S. From there, the singer's reputation blossomed in perfect tandem with her artistry: *Solace* was twice as successful as *Touch*, and *Fumbling Towards Ecstasy* sold 1.5 million copies on its way to a Grammy nomination. By 1996, McLachlan had colonized cyberspace as well: in one 24-hour period shortly after it went on-line, McLachlan's home page on the World Wide Web drew no less than 20,000 eager point-and-clickers, and her page on the Nettwerk Web site draws 4,000 visitors per week.

Self-Analysis: "I find people in general sexually attractive. But then I find trees sexually attractive too."
– Sarah McLachlan, 1994.

Recommended: *Touch* (1988), *Solace* (1991), *Fumbling Towards Ecstasy* (1993).

Alanis Morissette

The achievement of Alanis Morissette, the Ottawa-born singer-songwriter whose mighty single-machine of a third album, *Jagged Little Pill*, was the pop music phenomenon of 1995–1996, only grows more staggering when you consider the height of the odds stacked against her. As a former kids'-show star (of the perpetually syndicated *You Can't Do That On Television*) and big-haired teenage dance diva, she exploded on the American pop scene dragging a potential legacy of embarrassment with her.

Barely in her twenties, Morissette was one of the first artists signed to Madonna's Maverick label, which counted as a double-negative whammy: anyone that young *must* be synthetic according to cynical industrythink, and no friend of the erstwhile material girl was likely to find fast favour in a pop press which had, by the early 1990s, made Madonna-bashing something of a professional ritual. Moreover, Morissette arrived on the scene as a young female, and in a business which, in both critical and creative terms, is still steeped in the boys-rule mythology of rock & roll. And, like many female pop stars – Madonna included – Morissette's success is closely tied to the contribution of a male producer (Glen Ballard), which only left another flank open to fire at: without Ballard, Morissette-bashers sniffed, the kid's a doughnut hole without the doughnut. Her songs redolent with big rage, bad words and bashing guitars,

Morissette was also accused of producing faux alt-rock for suburban teenyboppers. Finally, in what was surely the most infuriating development in the entire Morissette-bashlash, her fans could care less what anybody said. They loved Alanis and loved her big: *Jagged Little Pill* racked up a breathtaking 14 million in sales by mid-1996, and was still heading north as Morissette's largely sold-out tour of North America and Great Britain managed to keep the heat up beneath the year-old release.

In February 1996, Morissette took home four Grammies, including the mother of them all: Album of the Year. Not surprisingly, she has nowhere been met with more vituperative skepticism than good old, offspring-eating Canada, which hadn't produced the likes of her mutant out-of-nowhere pop success since fellow Ottawan – and prominent media-punching bag – Paul Anka

stormed the charts in the late fifties. None of which ultimately matters except this: however it came together, *Jagged Little Pill* is that rare pop album which is both perfect on its own terms and perfectly clicks with the moment into which it was released. True, some observers of Canuck popcult might liken her to the Bryan Adams of post-Nirvana alternative rock: a calculated student of the mainstream whose primary creative impetus is the feeding of the largest mass-musical appetite of the moment – the same talent demonstrated by Canadian M.O.R. maestros from Lombardo and Anka, to Dion and Twain. But really, who cares as long as the music doesn't suck? Laden with smashing hooks, soaring melodies and swaggering choruses, *Jagged Little Pill* is almost compulsively listenable, and the sheer force of personality which emerges from the album marks one of the most distinctive female pop voices to cock the world's ear since, well, Madonna.

Self-Analysis: "Maybe this year was a year for women to have been more public, and yes, what's happened to me has propelled me into a position where I have to be more verbal about my feminism. But I have had female artists, who I won't mention, come up to me and say, 'Yeeah, we're takin over!' And I shake my head and say 'No we're not. We're joining.'" – Alanis Morissette, 1996.

Recommended: *Jagged Little Pill* (1995).

Jane Siberry

For all the rampant commercial cloning which went on in Canadian music during the 1980s, certain distinctive sounds could be heard beneath the benumbing din of predigested pop: 54-40, k.d. lang, The Tragically Hip and Jane Siberry. One

of the least likely of Canada's international cult stars, the Toronto-born- and-based Siberry has, over the course of seven albums in 15 years, nevertheless built up a following as avid as it is widespread. The vocally gifted former student of microbiology's songwriting specialty is the minute observation of momentary magic: she sings whimsically but evocatively of such quotidian phenomena as hockey, dogs and waitressing, but she beholds them with a sense of wry, poetic wonder, kind of like an observant child crossed with … a student of microbiology. As utterly mystifying to some listeners as she is revelatory to others, Siberry has never succumbed to compromise, even if it has meant trading mainstream success for artistic independence. Then again, maybe the chronically obtuse Siberry – who once actually said, "I'm interested in how to translate polymorphous ideas into the flat medium of a pop song" – wouldn't know how to find her way to the mainstream with a search party and a road map.

Self-Analysis: "In the States, they see my work as Canadian because of all the snow we get up here." – Jane Siberry, 1988.

Recommended: *No Borders Here* (1984), *The Speckless Sky* (1985), *The Walking* (1987), *Bound By The Beauty* (1989), *Maria* (1995).

Sloan

Because it's the music business, and because the band in question was a barely known young Canadian indie outfit from Halifax, the signing of Sloan in 1992 by Geffen Records (Nirvana's label) was met with as much suspicion as it was excitement. Nirvana's *Nevermind* had started doing platinum somersaults,

Sloan

the major labels were on a regional
indie signing spree and the Sloan deal
seemed to say more about the size of
the nets being cast than the quality of
the quarry sought. Or at least until you
heard "Underwhelmed." The first single
from the Geffen LP *Smeared*, the song is
nothing short of a classic of bored, middle-class male malaise: where Nirvana's
"Smells Like Teen Spirit" veers with sonic
schizophrenia between lullaby and cater-
waul, "Underwhelmed" is far too
disengaged for such naked extremes: cau-
tiously but cunningly, it rocks somewhere
in between, gradually building on an
irresistibly snaky riff to a lyrical conclu-
sion somewhat closer in phlegmatic tone
to the Replacements' Paul Westerberg
than the late Kurt Cobain: "I missed the
point," the band repeats several times in
flawless, deadpan, jangle-pop harmony, "I

**Sloan has been quietly developing
a reputation as one of the country's best bands ever: smart,
tuneful, unaffected, funny and
(hopefully) built to last.**

missed the *pooooiiiiint!*" At last. A home-
grown anthem for the nation's young,
intelligent and unimpressed: the pop music
expression of Doug Coupland's
post-boomer ennui, The Kids in the Hall's
high-concept, anti-content comedy and
Atom Egoyan's cinema of chronic emotional cross-purposes.

A leaderless democracy consisting of four
singing and songwriting Haligonians – Jay
Ferguson, Chris Murphy, Patrick Pentland
and Andrew Scott – Sloan never quite
lived up to the commercial promise of the

Geffen signing, but that hasn't prevented
the group from quietly bearing out the
promise of that first single's masterstroke.
Now three albums old – 1992's *Smeared*,
1994's *Twice Removed* and 1996's *One
Chord to Another* – and no longer with
Geffen, Sloan has been quietly develop-
ing a reputation as one of the country's
best bands ever: smart, tuneful, unaf-
fected, funny and (hopefully) built to
last. In 1996, *Twice Removed*, cited as "the
Rosetta Stone of a subculture," topped
Chart magazine's poll of "the 50 Best
Canadian Albums of All Time," beating
out such otherwise obvious contenders as
Neil Young, The Tragically Hip, The
Band, Joni Mitchell, Rush and The
Guess Who. "Underwhelmed," in turn,
finished second in the list of best 50
Canadian singles. It's almost impressive.
Long may Sloan moan.

Hayden

Self-Analysis: "The first time we played with Geffen, we played an instore in Detroit and there was a million people there, and I was like, 'We're going to be huge! Boys, get ready to be *huge*! If this is the reaction we're getting in the States...!' It was probably ten paces from the border." – Chris Murphy, 1996.

Recommended: *Smeared* (1992), *Twice Removed* (1994), *One Chord to Another* (1996).

The Tragically Hip

Possibly the definitive Canadian rock act of the current decade, this group of Kingston, Ontario high-school buddies – each of whom was taught phys. ed. by guitarist Paul Langlois's dad – combine hard-edged rhythm-and-blues stylings with the most unmistakably Canadian

The Tragically Hip combine hard-edged rhythm-and-blues stylings with the most unmistakably Canadian sensibility of any band since the maple-leaf heyday of The Guess Who.

sensibility of any band since the maple-leaf heyday of The Guess Who. Among singer-lyricist Gord Downie's geographically precise topics are such site-specific snippets of arcane Canadiana as missing hockey players, Tom Thomson and miscarriages of Canadian justice.

After doing years of nightly hard-time on the Southern Ontario bar circuit, the band began to acquire a fervent following for their hot-ticket live act, in which

mesmerising lead singer Downie sings, according to *Globe and Mail* critic Alan Niester, "as if rats are nibbling at his toes."

By the time their third album came out in 1991, the band was a ticket scalper's dream. Like Rush before them, The Tragically Hip are one of the very few Canadian acts capable of filling up concert halls across the country no matter what the circumstances: they've done it without airplay or hype, and they've done it without any American profile whatsoever. Appropriately, their overdue American coming out was arranged by no less a hoser luminary than fellow part-time Kingstonian Dan Aykroyd, who personally convinced Lorne Michaels to let the Hip play on *Saturday Night Live* in 1995. Michaels agreed, provided Aykroyd would introduce the boys

The Evolution of Canadian Pop

Alanis Morissette, The Tragically Hip, Bryan Adams, Shania Twain, k.d. lang, Crash Test Dummies, Sloan. Yes, we're in the middle of a full-fledged pop renaissance in this country, with dozens of Canadian performers regularly attaining critical and/or commercial success at home and abroad. But it wasn't always this way. Herewith, a capsule history of Canuck pop:

Pre-1967 Four Strong Winds That Blow Lonely

It's not that there weren't any Canadian pop stars before 1967, it's just that none of them lived here. While well-scrubbed Canuck hitmeisters like Paul Anka, Percy Faith, The Crew Cuts, The Diamonds

and The Four Lads all had sizeable North American hits in the late fifties and early sixties, each was made in the States with an American record company. In the early sixties, our airwaves and record stores were flooded with new music from Britain and the U.S., and it was practically impossible for Canadian groups to compete with the exploding Motown or Liverpool scenes.

There was almost no recording-industry infrastructure in Canada, which meant that the Canuck act that actually managed a home-grown national hit was as rare as February sunshine. Nevertheless, many rock acts enjoyed enough local popularity to thrive on a regional basis:

The Esquires in Ottawa; J.B. and the Playboys in Montreal; The Collectors in Vancouver; Mandala, The Lords of London and The Shays were local mainstays in Toronto.

By the mid-sixties, the coffeehouse folk scene was thriving in several Canadian cities. It was during this period that Canadian record companies – mostly subsidiaries of American companies – made their first sincere attempts to sign and develop home-grown talent. The importance of the folk scene in this regard was crucial: not only did it finally provide a context in which record companies were actually shopping for new Canadian talent, it, more than anything else,

Blood, Sweat and Tears   Ian & Sylvia

personally on the air. Aykroyd ended up hosting. Call it a conspiracy of Canadiana.

Self-Analysis: "This is our casserole. Come get some casserole. Some people will say, 'Great casserole!,' and other people will say, 'I hated that fucking casserole.'" – Gord Downie, 1992.

Recommended: *Road Apples* (1991), *Fully Completely* (1992), *Day for Night* (1994), *Trouble At The Henhouse* (1996).

Shania Twain

The best-selling female country vocalist since Patsy Cline, Shania Twain didn't quite roar out of nowhere in 1995 with her multi-platinum second album *The Woman in Me* (produced by husband Robert John "Mutt" Lange), but pretty close. Twain hails from the Northern Ontario industrial town of Timmins.

Her first album, which stressed the singer's bush roots by picturing her covered in furs, stiffed when released in 1993. Luckily, that was the same year the petite, shapely and charming Twain – then 28 – met Lange, the platinum-touch producer of The Cars, AC/DC, Bryan Adams and Michael Bolton. After meeting and falling in love in Nashville, Lange and Twain soon began collaborating on songs, which they eventually took into the studio. Bringing a hard-pop sheen to Twain's country compositions – like the future smashes "Whose Bed Have Your Boots Been Under" and "Any Man of Mine" – Lange created what would prove a monster crossover hit out of Twain's sophomore effort. Meanwhile, the formerly fur-covered girl from Timmins was given a

voyeur-friendly image makeover. No less a notorious babemaker than photographer-director John Derek (Bo's beau) was enlisted to enhance Twain's considerable sex appeal, and the resulting photos and music video proved to be the final spark which fired the rocket: if you happened to be looking that way in 1995 or '96, that was Shania Twain you saw streaking across the Nashville skyline.

Self-Analysis: "I don't think I'm sensational at anything. I'm good at what I do. I don't have a great voice. I mean, I'm no Mariah Carey. But I think I'm always improving. And I'm lucky, which helps."

Recommended: *The Woman In Me* (1995).

---

determined the predominant folk leanings of several soon-to-be Canadian music institutions. For example, Toronto's hippie haven, Yorkville, was the most influential music hangout of the period. Clubs like The Riverboat, The Penny Farthing and The Mousehole provided early performance opportunities for folkies like Bruce Cockburn, Gordon Lightfoot, Joni Mitchell and Neil Young. Similarly, Leonard Cohen would build his following and reputation in coffeehouses.

Period Playlist:

Singles: "Sh-Boom" – The Crew Cuts (1954), "Diana" – Paul Anka (1957), "Little Darlin'" – The Diamonds (1957), "Lonely Boy" – Paul Anka (1959), "Theme From A Summer Place" – Percy Faith (1959), "Clap Your Hands" – The

Beau-Marks (1960), "Fortune Teller" – Bobby Curtola (1962), "Four Strong Winds" – Ian and Sylvia (1963), "You Were On My Mind" – Ian and Sylvia (1964), "Shakin' All Over" – Chad Allan and the Expressions (1964), "I'm Not Sayin'" – Gordon Lightfoot (1965).

Albums: *Music From Hollywood* – Percy Faith (1953), *Paul Anka* – Paul Anka (1958), *Paul Anka Swings For Young Lovers* – Paul Anka (1960), *Ian and Sylvia* – Ian and Sylvia (1962), *Four Strong Winds* – Ian and Sylvia (1963), *Lightfoot* – Gordon Lightfoot (1965).

1967-1969 A Will But No Way: The Maple Leaves

In the two years following the Canadian cultural watershed of 1967, an incredible concentration of musical talent nurtured

by the various local club and folk scenes exploded nationally and internationally. The following Canadian-bred acts recorded maiden efforts between 1967 and 1969: The Band, Joni Mitchell, Neil Young, Leonard Cohen, The Guess Who and Anne Murray. Their success on home turf notwithstanding, many of these artists still felt that the only direction which held the promise of a lifetime career was south. Moreover, Canadian musicians like Denny Doherty (The Mamas and the Papas), Zal Yanovsky (The Lovin' Spoonful) and David Clayton-Thomas (Blood, Sweat and Tears) had already scurried stateside to join massively popular American supergroups. By the end of the sixties, although (thanks largely to a phenomenal recording year in 1969) nirvana had been

The Stampeders   The Poppy Family   Five-Man Electrical Band   April Wine

glimpsed and the promise of a golden age in Canadian pop twinkled on the horizon, that migration problem remained: how could that horizon be reached if there were few Canadian artists left in this country to chase it?

Period Playlist

Singles: "Suzanne" – Leonard Cohen (1967), "Ca-na-da" – Bobby Gimby and the Young Canada Singers (1967), "Canadian Railroad Trilogy" – Gordon Lightfoot (1967), "The Weight" – The Band (1968), "What About Me" – Anne Murray (1968), "Sugar Mountain" – Neil Young (1968), "Spinning Wheel" – Blood, Sweat and Tears (1969), "Laughing/Undun" – The Guess Who (1969), "These Eyes" – The Guess Who (1969), "Which Way You Goin' Billy" – The Poppy Family (1969).

Albums: *Songs of Leonard Cohen* – Leonard Cohen (1967), *The Way I Feel* – Gordon Lightfoot (1967), *Music From Big Pink* – The Band (1968), *Joni Mitchell* – Joni Mitchell (1968), *The Band* – The Band (1969), *Songs From A Room* – Leonard Cohen (1969), *Wheatfield Soul* –

The Guess Who (1969), *Canned Wheat* – The Guess Who (1969), *Clouds* – Joni Mitchell (1969), *Everybody Knows This Is Nowhere* – Neil Young (1969).

1970-1975 Original Hits, Original Stars: The Golden Age of CanCon

On January 18, 1971, despite vigorous opposition from the Canadian radio industry, the Canadian Content Regulations were officially implemented by the Canadian Radio-television and Telecommunications Commission (CRTC), effectively introducing what ranks as one of the single most important pieces of legislation in the history of Canadian popular culture. "CanCon," as it came to be known, required all domestic AM radio stations to play at least 30 percent Canadian content between the hours of 6:00 a.m. and midnight. That's a lot of airtime which suddenly needed to be filled with the sound of Canadian music.

Despite opposition to CanCon, which persists even today (Bryan Adams, for example, calls it an outmoded system that promotes mediocrity), the fact remains that initially the system was like a shot of pure adrenaline to a national recording industry that had otherwise barely registered a pulse. For example, although the careers of Anne Murray and The Guess Who predated the CanCon requirements, their careers were vaulted into another dimension entirely by the legislation.

Consider the chain reaction the regulations set off almost overnight: instantly, more Canadian songs were heard on radio, more stars stayed in Canada, more people went to see bands they'd *heard* on radio, more recording studios were built to meet the radio demand, and, of supreme importance, there were more Canadian hits at

home and abroad than ever before.

It was the golden age of Canuck pop, a time when one couldn't turn on top-40 radio without hearing some chartbusting Canadian act. Moreover, it was not only the era of such tenacious chart-climbers as BTO, The Stampeders, Edward Bear, Lighthouse, Five-Man Electrical Band, Ian Thomas and April Wine, but also countless one-hit wonders like Crowbar, A Foot in Coldwater and The DeFranco Family. Needless to say, with Canadian material like this to draw on, K-Tel compilation albums, issued from the company's Winnipeg headquarters, were as popular as hockey pucks.

Sure, there was a fair amount of dreck (Terry Jacks, Paul Anka's musical midlife crisis), but the first half of the seventies was a great time to be an impressionable young Canadian radio addict: CanCon made it easy to believe that, as far as pop music was concerned, Canucks took care of business every bit as fiercely as anybody else in the world.

Period Playlist

Singles: "American Woman/No Sugar Tonight" – The Guess Who (1970), "If You Could Read My Mind" – Gordon Lightfoot (1970), "As The Years Go By" – Mashmakan (1970), "Oh What A Feeling" – Crowbar (1971), "One Fine Morning" – Lighthouse (1971), "Where Evil Grows" – The Poppy Family (1971), "You Could Have Been A Lady" – April Wine (1972), "Make Me Do Anything You Want" – A Foot in Coldwater (1972), "Heart of Gold" – Neil Young (1972), "I'm A Stranger Here" – Five-Man Electrical Band (1973), "Takin' Care of Business" – Bachman-Turner Overdrive (1974), "You Ain't Seen Nothin' Yet" –

← Patsy Gallant

Crowbar

Bachman-Turner Overdrive (1974).

Albums: *American Woman* – The Guess Who (1970), *Stage Fright* – The Band (1970), *Ladies of the Canyon* – Joni Mitchell (1970), *After the Gold Rush* – Neil Young (1970), *Blue* – Joni Mitchell (1971), *Live At The Paramount* – The Guess Who (1972), *Bachman-Turner Overdrive 2* – Bachman-Turner Overdrive (1973), *Sundown* – Gordon Lightfoot (1973), *Court and Spark* – Joni Mitchell (1974), *Salt, Sun and Time* – Bruce Cockburn (1974), *Tonight's The Night* – Neil Young (1975).

1976-1979 After The Gold Rush

Despite a continuing onslaught of recording activity in the late seventies, the bloom was definitely off the CanCon rose. Perhaps it was simply evidence of the inevitable strain on volume imposed

Despite opposition to CanCon, which persists even today, the fact remains that initially the system was like a shot of pure adrenaline to a national recording industry that had otherwise barely registered a pulse.

by 30 percent–content regulations in a country with a relatively small population, or maybe just the cosmic destiny of the loopy seventies, but the cheese definitely started to outweigh the cream in Canadian music by 1976. The Guess Who had finally imploded after a series of shameful singles like "Glamour Boy" (1973) and "Clap For The Wolfman" (1974), and Burton Cummings, once the

country's finest rock vocalist, had started the power-lounge-ballad phase of his solo career. BTO, the enormously successful Guess Who spin-off band that also became its principle chart rival, also faded during this period. And let's face it, their late-seventies hoser-rock progeny – groups like Trooper and Prism – were just no match for the Winnipeg paunch-rock maestros. Yes, look back and wince, for it was also a time when folk-puppy Dan Hill and disco diva Patsy Gallant would sail to a secure berth at the top of national playlists.

Not that it was all uniformly indistinguishable dreck. On the contrary, it was dreck with range, scope and variety. In fact, two of the quintessential musical genres of the era – disco and punk – briefly reared their heads in Canada. In the hotly competitive dance-floor sweep-

The Diodes

stakes, Canadians produced a few best-selling, but otherwise acutely embarassing, records: a disco remake of Doris Day's "Que Sera Sera" by The Raes (1977), and – our personal favourite – Claudja Barry's "Boogie Woogie Dancin' Shoes" (1978), so far as we can ascertain, the only tribute to footwear in the disco genre's history.

While vibrant punk scenes flourished briefly in a few cities across the country, a combination of factors ensured that they remained largely isolated and local phenomena: due to punk's limited mainstream appeal, none of the major labels would sign punk acts, and radio was still in the highly lucrative business of promoting musical odes to disco footwear. Toronto's punk scene, which grew largely out of the local art-college and bar circuit, was defined by acts like The Diodes,

Demics, The Poles, Teenage Head and The Viletones. Meanwhile, the country's other major punk explosion was happening in Vancouver, with bands like D.O.A. and The Young Canadians attracting large and loyal spike-headed followings. The problem was, without the lifelines provided by airplay, promotion and touring, the scenes were too localized and fragile to last. Despite the legacy of a few choice tracks, the first wave of Canadian punk essentially died of neglect.

Period Playlist

Singles: "Stand Tall" – Burton Cummings (1976), "From New York to L.A." – Patsy Gallant (1976), "The Wreck of the Edmund Fitzgerald" – Gordon Lightfoot (1976), "Fly At Night" – Chilliwack (1977), "Sometimes When You Touch" – Dan Hill (1977), "Spaceship Superstar" –

Prism (1977), "Disco Sucks" – D.O.A. (1978), "Tired Of Waking Up Tired" – The Diodes (1978), "Hot Child In The City" – Nick Gilder (1978), "Raise A Little Hell" – Trooper (1978), "I Just Fall In Love Again" – Anne Murray (1979).

Albums: *The Whole World's Goin' Crazy* – April Wine (1976), *3:47 EST* – Klaatu, *2112* – Rush (1976), *Longer Fuse* – Dan Hill (1977), *Knock 'Em Dead Kid* – Trooper (1977), *High Class In Borrowed Shoes* – Max Webster (1977), *Brother To Brother* – Gino Vanelli (1978), *Comes A Time* – Neil Young (1978), *Armageddon* – Prism (1979), *Rust Never Sleeps* – Neil Young (1979).

1980-1989 Fashion Victims

Musically speaking, this period is possibly the driest, flattest and most uninspiring stretch on the entire trans-Canadian pop

Platinum Blonde   Loverboy   Rough Trade

highway. In a reflection of the era's lust for the fast buck, Canadian pop during the eighties was dominated by acts whose primary motivation was the calculated replication of what was already successful. Acts like Bryan Adams, Loverboy – a hoser cockrock outfit that actually released an album with the phallocentric title *Keep It Up* (1983) – Alannah Myles, Luba, Glass Tiger, Honeymoon Suite, Platinum Blonde and Corey Hart meticulously followed the American arena-rock rulebook of the day. Others followed the British technopop route to momentary visibility: The Spoons, Strange Advance, Men Without Hats, Images In Vogue. And the fashion! The fashion! Hair gel was available in vastly greater proportion than talent and good sense, and everybody dressed as if they'd just raided a spandex sale at Le Chateau.

Even the otherwise immutable Neil Young seemed absolutely adrift for much of the decade, moving indiscriminately between ill-advised electronic experimentation, the blues and – roll over, ShaNaNa! – even fifties retro rock. In 1984, much to the horror of resin-stained fans globally, Young even endorsed Ronald Reagan. Then, in 1985, the ultimate indignity: Young was told he was singing off-key by blow-dried yuppie-pup producer David Foster during the taping of the all-star Canuck benefit for Ethiopia, "Tears Are Not Enough." "That's my *sound*, man," Neil replied shortly before boarding a plane back to Southern California. Mercifully, by the end of the decade, Young had apparently recovered both his senses and his sense of direction.

Artistically, the decade's rare original moments tended to be provided by female vocalists: the tongue-in-chic erotic

Hair gel was available in vastly greater proportion than talent and good sense, and everybody dressed as if they'd just raided a spandex sale at Le Chateau.

ravings of Rough Trade's Carole Pope, the refreshingly crisp pop of Martha and the Muffins and the endearingly loopy stream-of-consciousness folk-pop of Toronto divas Jane Siberry and Mary Margaret O'Hara. The eighties also coughed up remarkable debuts from three stunningly gifted vocalists: k.d. lang's *A Truly Western Experience* (1984), Margo Timmins and Cowboy Junkies' *The Trinity Session* (1988) and Sarah McLachlan's *Touch* (1988).

Without question, the most important development in the Canadian pop industry during this period was the launching of Moses Znaimer's MuchMusic ("The Nation's Music Station") in 1984. Although populated by on-air personalities who seemed to know slightly less about music than shopping, the fact is, MuchMusic did more to promote and develop a national pop-star system than any development in Canadian music since CanCon. As a way of introducing new bands to a national audience in an expansive country where touring is risky, costly and exhausting, video quickly became an invaluable advertising tool for both established and up-and-coming acts. Certainly, MuchMusic has played a central role in the nineties Canuck pop renaissance.

Period Playlist
Singles: "Too Bad" – Doug and the Slugs (1980), "Echo Beach" – Martha and the

Muffins (1980), "My Girl (Gone, Gone, Gone)" – Chilliwack (1981), "Working For The Weekend" – Loverboy (1981), "High School Confidential" – Rough Trade (1981), "Eyes Of A Stranger" – Payola$ (1982), "Teenage Beer Drinking Party" – Teenage Head (1982), "Nova Heart" – The Spoons (1982), "Cuts Like A Knife" – Bryan Adams (1983), "The Safety Dance" – Men Without Hats (1983), "Rise Up" – Parachute Club (1983), "Run To You" – Bryan Adams (1984), "Sunglasses At Night" – Corey Hart (1984), "Tears Are Not Enough" – Northern Lights For Africa (1985), "Don't Forget Me (When I'm Gone) – Glass Tiger (1986), "Try" – Blue Rodeo (1987), "I'm An Adult Now" – The Pursuit of Happiness (1987), "First We Take Manhattan" – Leonard Cohen (1988), "Bye Bye Mon Cowboy" – Mitsou (1988), "Black Velvet" – Alannah Myles (1989), "Rockin' In The Free World" – Neil Young (1989).

Albums: *Metro Music* – Martha and the Muffins (1980), *Get Lucky* – Loverboy (1981), *Avoid Freud* – Rough Trade (1981), *No Stranger To Danger* – Payola$ (1982), *Rhythm of Youth* – Men Without Hats (1983), *Reckless* – Bryan Adams (1984), *No Borders Here* – Jane Siberry (1984), *A Truly Western Experience* – k.d. lang (1984), *Boy In The Box* – Corey Hart (1985), *The Thin Red Line* – Glass Tiger (1986), *The Tragically Hip* – The Tragically Hip (1987), *Shadowland* – k.d. lang (1988), *The Trinity Session* – Cowboy Junkies (1988), *I'm Your Man* – Leonard Cohen (1988), *Miss America* – Mary Margaret O'Hara (1988), *Touch* – Sarah McLachlan (1989), *Freedom* – Neil Young (1989).

"I'm gonna make some supper. Hope you like Kraft Dinner!"

– BETTY (JAYNE EASTWOOD) IN *GOIN' DOWN THE ROAD*, 1970

Porky's Canada Pigs Out

Certain aspects of Canadian cultural activity bear the stamp of this nation's rough, windswept, wilderness origins: ice hockey, wildlife prints, Farley Mowat, cottage-going, curling, toques. To this list we propose adding cuisine. How else to account for the enduring Canadian fondness for heavy, bland and non-nutritious fare than by noting that decades after there was any compelling reason to do so, Canadians still seem to eat purely for ballast: to bulk up to keep from being blown away. Indeed, it must be considered a providential accident of history that no less a pioneer of high-calorie, comfort-and-convenience cuisine than James Lewis Kraft, founding father of processed cheese and namesake of the unstoppable Kraft Dinner, was born in 1875 in Stevensville, Ontario. Moreover, a Canuck invented that handy, fattening favourite – the chocolate bar. Yes, in 1910, Arthur Ganong, a St. Stephen, New Brunswick, mogul with a sweet tooth, decided he'd had enough of messing up his pockets with sticky, individual chocolates. Within months, the world's first bars of chocolate (conveniently wrapped in tin foil) were rolling off Ganong's factory's line.

Possibly it betrays some of English Canada's high-cholesterol colonial heritage (British cuisine = fish and chips) that unfettered, fattening bulk food – like doughnuts and tuna-noodle casseroles – continue to hold such culinary influence in the nation's kitchens, but this doesn't account for the distinct but similarly high-density fare favoured by French Canada. Lest one forget, poutine is a cholesterol-boosting combination of french fries, gravy and *cheese*. And how's this for an unholy nutritional alliance: tortière, or, as it's often called in English, *meat pie*. Meanwhile, the Canadian passion for both convenience and conflation – i.e., the Kraft TV–commercial tradition of cramming as many heavy foods as possible into a single recipe – apparently knows no linguistic or cultural borders. In

While it is a cinch to track down a decent pad thai in Halifax, Toronto or Vancouver, we defy you to find a decent butter tart in Bangkok.

both French and English Canada, the casserole is king. Which brings us back to climate as the only excuse. It is not alarming then to learn that Canadian cuisine is not a terribly happening export product. While it is a cinch to track down a decent pad thai in Halifax, Toronto or Vancouver, we defy you to find a decent butter tart in Bangkok.

A couple of other pertinent Canadian culinary notes. While food has figured prominently and popularly in many international cinemas, Canada has yet to

produce anything like a *Tom Jones*, an *Eat Drink Man Woman*, a *Babette's Feast*, a *Scent of Green Papaya* or even – though this may be a blessing – a *9½ Weeks*. No heart-warming, cottage-set ensemble dramas based around the mouth-watering preparation of a burgers-and-macaroni-salad feast, no pulse-raising episodes involving the erotic application of beans and wienies. Instead: the drunken gluttony of the insensitive title character of *Mon Oncle Antoine*; the afterbirth eaten by monster-mom Samantha Eggar in *The Brood*; the bag of chips munched by a weeping and innocent state prisoner in *Les Ordres*; the candy bars scarfed by manfly Jeff Goldblum in *The Fly*; the character who eats his dead father's innards (with a spoon!) in *The Dead Father*; the hideously dripping ice-cream cone lapped at by the monstrous grandfather in *Léolo*. Mmmmm. Perhaps this is further proof that, while national weight statistics prove that Canadians like to eat, they eat less for the fun than the fill of it. It's a means to an end. A big, fat, Canadian rear end.

Curiously, in the same way that many Canadians would rather watch nature shows on TV than go outside and experience it, we also have a peculiar tradition of cooking shows that seem not to mesh with our otherwise purely functional approach to food. Then again, maybe it's another expression of that tradition of disembodied, mind-versus-matter alienation in Canadian cultural life. As with sex and nature, food preparation is something we'd just as soon watch as do. So go to the kitchen, grab the all-dressed chips and dip, and join us for a truly heavy trip through the highlights of Canadian culinary culture.

Cooking Shows

Benoit, Madame: Born Jehane Benoit in 1904 (d. 1987), she was the Julia Child of Canada, only more lovable and folksy. For decades her user-friendly recipes appeared in English- and French-Canadian magazines and newspapers, and she was a gently appealing fixture on both the CBC and Radio-Canada public networks. The author of 25 cookbooks, including the seminal *Encyclopedia of Canadian Cuisine*, which, when published in 1963, was the first comprehensive Canadian cookbook ever published. She became an advocate of microwave cooking, a position which raised no small number of eyebrows in more traditional culinary circles. Undeterred, she continued to champion the new technology, even doing commer-

cial endorsements for microwave manufacturers and publishing two volumes of her *Encyclopedia of Microwave Cooking*. In her early championing of this method, Madame Benoit was unconsciously recognizing something basic about the Canadian approach to food preparation and consumption: we like it ample and we like it fast, which is also why we like to zap.

Celebrity Cooks (CBC, 1975-1979): Low-budget, unrehearsed live-to-tape cooking show hosted by *The Beachcombers'* Bruno Gerussi. The alleged allure stemmed from the concept of famous people dropping by Bruno's studio kitchen to prepare their famous recipe, but its real appeal was the opposite. As the show was such a stingy affair, its definition of "famous" often seemed a lot closer to "available": Al Hamel, George Kirby, Marty Allen, Farley Mowat, Judy LaMarsh, Dinah Christie, Barbara Hamilton, Pierre Berton. (True, David Letterman appeared once to prepare spinach noodles for Bruno, but long before the future late-night star was *really* famous.) Moreover, since the show was unrehearsed and too cheaply made to allow for retakes, *everything* that happened wound up on the air: guests regularly cut, stabbed and seared themselves, and many of the exposure-starved celebrities seemed never to have entered a kitchen before finding themselves in Bruno's. Combine this with the well-documented fact that Bruno and guests helped themselves to large goblets of real wine while shooting the show, and you'll understand why *Celebrity Cooks* deserves not only a special place in the history of Canadian cooking shows, but in Canadian history, period.

Ad for *The Galloping Gourmet*

The Galloping Gourmet (CBC, 1968-1973): One of Canada's most popular cooking shows ever followed a decidedly unusual route to the national airwaves. It's inimitable host, the charmingly chatty, nearly six-and-a-half-foot-tall sensualist Graham Kerr, was a Brit who originally produced a cooking show in New Zealand for broadcast in Australia. Okay so far? Well, that show was such a hit Kerr was invited to Canada to produce another show for North American syndication, which he did. It too was a hit and more: a veritable blockbuster by cooking-show standards, seen from Halifax and Los Angeles, to Singapore and Manila. And frankly, it was Kerr who made it such a smash, for he was unlike anyone who had sliced raw zucchini on-camera before. Erudite, witty and boldly sensual in his appreciation of food, Kerr became a magnet for an audience largely comprising women who had

probably never seen a man cook, let alone a man who could, midway through slicing a juicy leg of lamb, look you straight in the eye and say, "There are only two things left for a man to do… And carving is one of them." Then there was the ritual, not-to-be-missed ending of the show, which was, both figuratively and literally, *The Galloping Gourmet's* "climax." Sitting down to tuck into the delicacy he'd just prepared, taking a long, slow sip of wine, Kerr would slowly raise a forkful to his mouth, insert the morsel and… well, you wouldn't think the look on his face was possible on a man still wearing pants.

Tasty Treats

Bacon: Canada's favourite meat, the definitive national variation of which is back bacon, the substance being constantly fried to crispy oblivion on a Coleman stove by *SCTV*'s Bob and Doug McKenzie. Basically, salty strips of fried, greasy pig meat, most often eaten with cholesterol-dense eggs and slabs of buttery toast, but also enjoyed on burgers, club sandwiches and – just to keep those greens from getting too healthy – chopped up on salads.

Beer: Uncontestably, Canada's most popular drink, the original soda pop of alcoholic beverages and the inspiration for countless commercials featuring inebriated twentysomethings. A gassy and filling brew made from malt and hops, we like to drink it in multiple-bottle bulk, which renders the beer-fuelled social experience a singular one: male beer drinkers belch regularly in each other's

faces when they converse, and must get up to teeter over a urinal at least once every 20 minutes. ("You don't buy it, you just rent it!") The hoser elixir of life, and therefore ubiquitous in such key hoser-texts as *Goin' Down the Road*, McKenzie Brothers skits and any home-grown drama in which characters cross a tavern threshold. On the corporate level, the beer business is, not surprisingly, one of Canada's biggest; it's impossible to attend a major sporting or entertainment event without staring a Molson or Labatt's logo in the face. Also known as "brews," "brewskis" or "browns."

Doughnuts: Variations: "donut, do-nut, dough-nut." Based on the shockingly disproportionate number of drive-in doughnut joints in Canada compared to the rest of the planet, this deep-fried doughy circle, usually dipped or glazed in some equally unhealthy sticky-sweet icing, is Canada's runaway-favourite snack food. Utterly lacking in nutritional value and intensely fattening, and best washed down with coffee saturated with sugar and cream, the doughnut is the unsung symbol of slothful Canadian suburban experience. It finally received its overdue pop-cultural certification in *Wayne's World*, when Mike Myers, as archetypal metalloid hosehead Wayne Campbell, made a point of stopping regularly at Stan Mikita's Donuts for a daily fix of deep-fried fat, an obvious homage to that great Canadian institution, Tim Horton's Donuts. Variation: the Beaver Tail, basically a flattened doughnut fried and rolled in sugar. Quebec snack-food variation: Vachon cakes.

Maple Syrup: Canada became the maple syrup capital of the planet because it boasted a ridiculous abundance of two of the substance's most basic ingredients: maple trees and winter. Sweet, rich and distinctively aromatic, the viscous brown liquid was first described by European settlers in the 1600s, though the Native practice of sapping maple trees for syrup in early spring was already centuries old. Primarily accustomed to honey as a sweetener, these early tasters of maple syrup and sugar were amazed at what their tongues were telling them: this stuff was special. And so it remains. As both a natural product and a souvenir-shop staple, maple syrup is one of Canada's proudest symbols of self: sugar-bush visits are practically an annual grade-school ritual in those parts of the country where maple forests thrive – primarily the Maritimes, Quebec and Ontario – and no self-respecting tourist to Canada can possibly leave the country without some of the substance. It's proof you were there. Indeed, like Niagara Falls, maple syrup may be more frequently consumed by visitors to Canada than by its citizens. The product of an environmentally dependent industry which can never match supply with demand, the stuff is as expensive as it is impractical. Ultimately, there just aren't a lot of uses for maple syrup, the richly unmistakable flavour of which tends to dominate everything it's mixed with or poured over. Still, this does nothing to diminish its status as proudly sticky Canadian icon, even if Canadians really do prefer their brewed brown liquids cold and gassy.

Derivation: maple sugar, maple fudge.

Doughnut-eating contest, Toronto, 1969

Wheatfield of Dreams
How Canada Fertilized Reagan's America

From the grim eighties, you'd really have to travel to find another decade when mainstream pop culture worked so heartily in the service of the status quo. To the forties, in fact, but at least then there was a war to justify tarting up propaganda as entertainment. By Reagan's decade, no excuse was necessary. With odious gusto, pop culture – by then well-established as a multinational corporate cash cow – embraced and endorsed the reigning conservative ideology anyway. Less surprising is the fact that a truly hair-raising number of the era's most blinding beacons of brainless denial were cooked up not by cynical boomers with Leave-It-To-Beaver fixations, nor by admen-cum-White-House speechwriters, but by Canadians. As if Brian Mulroney wasn't enough to answer for.

Rambo

First created by Kitchener, Ontario, native David Morrell in a novel, the character of survivalist psycho-vet John Rambo, particularly as impersonated by Sylvester Stallone in a trio of increasingly muscle-headed odes to bare-chested jingoism, is arguably the decade's most potent pop-cultural icon. It was Rambo who single-handedly rewrote Vietnam with a happier ending – "Can we win this time, sir?" – and it was Rambo who rendered right-wing fanaticism as a pulp romance of Nietzschean proportions. But that's not all. When the character was first brought to the screen in 1982's *First Blood*, it was Canadian director Ted (*The Apprenticeship of Duddy Kravitz*) Kotcheff who did the deed. Moreover, the first Rambo movie was shot in scenic British Columbia. And if that wasn't suf-

ficient cause for national shame, a year after *First Blood*'s success, Kotcheff directed what would be the first of the decade's many macho-revisionist Vietnam fantasies, *Uncommon Valor*. Boasting virtually the same back-to-Nam plot – but dumbed-down even more – 1985's *Rambo: First Blood, Part 2* would become one of the decade's defining blockbusters. Incidentally, the script for said blockbuster was cowritten by Sylvester Stallone and Kapuskasing, Ontario's James Cameron.

The Terminator

A mirthless killer cyborg programmed for unstoppable mayhem – thus a perfect emblem of the American global economic and political imperative – Arnold Schwarzenegger's definitive character was created by James Cameron a year before

the Canadian writer-director was enlisted to help Sly Stallone beef up and dumb down the character of John Rambo. In his 1984 incarnation, the Terminator was a scarily satirical emissary of imperial brute force, sent from the future to kill the mother of an unborn anti-government rebel. By 1991's *Terminator 2: Judgment Day* (also written and directed by Cameron), the character had undergone a radical make-over just in time for the Gulf War. Having developed a conscience of sorts, he maimed rather than murdered people, and even became a father figure to the kid he'd initially been sent to kill. It was around this time that George Bush, another gun-toting father figure, referred to Schwarzenegger, recently married into the Kennedy family, as "Conan the Republican." [Note: The then-eyepopping, now-ubiquitous morphing effects of

Michael J. Fox in *Family Ties*

Sylvester Stallone as Rambo

T2 were made possible by a Toronto software company called Alias.]

Michael J. Fox

This diminutive Edmontonian with impeccable timing was an industrious and effortlessly likeable embodiment of the Reaganite *zeitgeist* in popular entertainment. In the decade-spanning sitcom *Family Ties* (1982-1989), his role as the right-wing yuppie scion of aging hippies rendered the new conservatism as dimple-cute and aw-shucks harmless, while Fox's blockbusting appearance in 1985's *Back to the Future* enlisted him in the same time-travelling enterprise which was an ubiquitous part of the era's escapist entertainment. Like Rambo's return to Vietnam, the Terminator's arrival from the future or the baseball ghosts in *Field of Dreams*, *Back to the Future* saw time-surfing as a convenient way of changing the past so it might be more flattering to the present.

Ghostbusters

Not only was Czech-born, Hamilton-raised Ivan Reitman, *Ghostbusters'* producer and director, a key figure in the Canadianisation of comedy during the eighties (it was he who both produced the lowbrow blockbuster *Animal House* and acted as the catalyst that brought a lot of *SNL* and *SCTV* alumni to the big screen), this movie is one of the denial decade's key spectacles: an f/x-fuelled, big-budget comedy about a group of doofus parapsychologists who crack wise and win out in the face of supernatural apocalypse, the movie was a pop parable of Yankee teflonism perfect for a don't-worry-be-happy climate. As long as you could ridicule what scared you, the

Arnold Schwarzenegger's definitive character was created by James Cameron a year before the Canadian writer-director was enlisted to help Sly Stallone beef up and dumb down the character of John Rambo.

movie reassuringly suggested, you could blow it to ectoplasmic slime-bits! Small wonder *Ghostbusters* went on to become – until the similarly underintellectualized *Home Alone* came along – the most successful comedy in history, racking up a staggering $220,900,000 in North American box-office business alone. Also featuring Ottawa native Dan Aykroyd (who cowrote the script), Toronto-born ex-*SCTV*er Rick Moranis and Bill Murray, the star of what proved to be the most successful Canadian movie ever made – until the majestic *Porky's* came along – *Meatballs.* [Note: The latter was directed

by Ivan Reitman who, along with fellow Canuck James Cameron, also played a key role in the eighties superstardom of Arnold Schwarzenegger.]

Field of Dreams

Based on the novel *Shoeless Joe* by Canadian baseball enthusiast W. P. Kinsella, this neo-Rockwellian, magic-hour ode to trad family values comprises a virtual checklist of recurring Reaganite popcult concerns: it's about making up with a lost father, the same obsession that drives *Ordinary People*, *Back to the Future*, *E.T.* and *Indiana Jones and the Last Crusade;* it's about time-shifting in the interests of historical make-overs; and, most insufferably, it's about the mutation of the memory of the sixties into a kind of soft-focus theme park for history-impaired baby boomers.

Yankee Doodle Dandies →

The Reitman for the Job
Ivan the Vulgarian Storms Hollywood

Like an unreachable itch on a lion's flank, a certain small but livid complaint keeps asserting itself in profiles of otherwise hugely successful expatriate Canadians. You'll find it expressed in the numerous magazine articles about Paul Anka and Lorne Greene, for example, or more recently in stories about Jim Carrey or Alanis Morissette. And you'll certainly find it in stories about the man who may well be the single most influential figure in Canadian popular culture ever, film-maker/producer/writer – and uncanny *zeitgeist* barometer – Ivan Reitman.

In Reitman's case it's like this: after enduring years of denigration, condescension and dismissal at the hands of Canada's cultural establishment – sound familiar? – the Czech-born, Toronto-reared entertainment impresario finally punctured the global showbiz stratosphere in the late 1970s. That was the period when he not only produced *National Lampoon's Animal House*, a movie whose impact on screen comedy is still (perhaps too) vividly felt, he directed what became the most successful Canadian movie ever released to that point: the enormously successful *Animal House*-at-camp comedy, *Meatballs*. Within a half-dozen years, he had not only acted as the catalyst for the Canadian-driven, lowbrow takeover of Hollywood movie comedy, he'd directed what for years was the most successful movie comedy in history, the potently populist, supremely Reaganite spectacle *Ghostbusters* (1984). Still, in the same way

that Lorne Greene still felt that itch while lording over his rambling Hollywood estate, and Paul Anka felt it poolside in Las Vegas, Ivan Reitman could also feel that nasty irritation threatening to spoil his moment of most sublime extra-Canadian success.

It's that old hometown-resentment thing, the recurring sense among many overachieving Canucks that the more successful one becomes in American or global pop-culture terms, the more they gotta grind your meatballs back in the Dominion. Thus, in 1986, as *Ghostbusters* rested secure on its record, and Reitman on his fortune, and before the former McMaster University music student's sure grip on public demand would begin to show slippage with the megaflop romantic comedy *Legal Eagles* (1986), Ivan Reitman was still miffed at, of all things, the CBC. Talking to a *Saturday Night* reporter that year, he scratched furiously at a two-year-old wound inflicted by the

Mother Corp. It seems that after the phenomenal success of *Ghostbusters*, Reitman was characterized in a CBC news documentary as rather less an artist than a businessman: a laudable distinction in the U.S., a sign of spiritual bankruptcy in Canada. Two years later, and beyond all evident reason, Reitman was still steaming at the slight: "They don't have to like me," he told *Saturday Night*. "All kinds of people don't and all kinds of people do. But there was a condescension towards me – and my audience – that really bugged me."

Reitman was characterized in a CBC news documentary as rather less an artist than a businessman: a laudable distinction in the U.S., a sign of spiritual bankruptcy in Canada.

Poolside Canuck: Ivan Reitman

Yet, if Ivan Reitman had really stormed Hollywood intending to win the favour of fellow Canadians, he, of all people, should have known better. Born in 1946 to prosperous Holocaust survivors who smuggled their firstborn son out of communist Czechoslovakia beneath the nailed floorboards of a tugboat, Reitman's is an almost classic story of up-from-below immigrant pluck, populist variations on which would become both his signature and his fortune. One of his earliest memories after his arrival in Toronto in 1952 involves his first taste of bubblegum, an event that triggered a lifelong infatuation with North American junk culture. By the time he enrolled at McMaster's just-opened music school in Hamilton in 1965, Reitman had already proven himself a poor student, an avid fan of bad fifties comedy ("probably America's worst comedy years," he has said) and an irrepressible entertainer.

Bored by school, he founded a campus musical and dramatic society which included among its members such future collaborators and *SCTV* performers as Eugene Levy, Dave Thomas and Martin Short. And it was at McMaster that Reitman met chipper, long-haired magician Doug Henning, whose Broadway show he would successfully coproduce a

> **Bored by school, he founded a campus musical and dramatic society which included among its members such future collaborators and *SCTV* performers as Eugene Levy, Dave Thomas and Martin Short.**

decade later. By 1968, Reitman had made a student film called *Orientation* – a short comedy about a winning campus loser – which was sold for $20,000 and shown theatrically across the country.

Schwarzenegger in *Kindergarten Cop*

From here the Reitman story becomes a fluttering montage of names and events that read like a primer for the Canadian pop-culture future to come. Less than a year after graduating, he was at the centre of a national controversy when *Columbus of Sex*, a soft-core movie he'd produced, was seized by Hamilton's finest mere minutes into its second screening. At the highly publicized, year-long trial that followed, no less a luminary than Pierre Berton testified on behalf of the movie's dubious artistic merits. The publicity helped Reitman, who'd once referred to *Columbus* as "absolute horseshit," to snag a lucrative American distribution deal while still under probation for the obscenity charges. A couple of years later, he sold a similarly disreputable project – a splatter comedy starring Eugene Levy and Andrea Martin called *Cannibal Girls* – to veteran exploitation producer Samuel Z. Arkoff at the Cannes festival. In 1973, he landed a gig producing a variety/game-show parody called *Greed* at Moses Znaimer's newly established Citytv, and by 1977 he had produced two of David Cronenberg's earliest efforts, *Shivers* and *Rabid*. Proportionate to his mounting success and notoriety was the number of Canadian slings and arrows he had to duck: *Saturday Night*'s Robert Fulford haughtily savaged *Shivers* as a waste of public funds, and in 1977 a CBC-Radio reviewer refused to screen the Reitman-produced *Death Weekend* on the basis of the producer's reputation alone.

Undeterred, the boy from below the floorboards carried on. In 1974, he saw the touring *National Lampoon* comedy revue in Toronto, which featured a number of key future collaborators, including

Proportionate to his mounting success and notoriety was the number of Canadian slings and arrows he had to duck.

John Belushi, Bill Murray and Harold Ramis. He was sufficiently impressed to propose to *Lampoon*'s publisher, Matty Simmons, that they make a movie together, which led first to Reitman's own touring *National Lampoon* revue, and later to the $200-million-grossing *Animal House*. (It's comedy box-office record would only be broken by *Ghostbusters*.) This was followed by *Meatballs*, and then Reitman's inevitable move to Los Angeles.

Apart from *Ghostbusters*, which put him in the same ranking as Steven Spielberg, George Lucas and Canadian-born James Cameron in terms of Reagan-era influence and popularity, Reitman's other popcult coup of the eighties was the comedy make-over of another Hollywood outsider named Arnold Schwarzenegger (whose action superstardom had already been clinched by Cameron's *The Terminator*, released the same summer as *Ghostbusters*) with the immensely successful *Twins* and *Kindergarten Cop*. These were followed by the less successful Capra-corn comedy *Dave* and the stillborn pregnant-Terminator vehicle *Junior*.

Still, if Ivan Reitman's salad days are over – and it's certainly premature to say they are – he's already landed a secure position in contemporary Canadian pop-culture history. It was he more than anyone else who brought Canadian comedy to the movie mainstream, he who launched

the careers of David Cronenberg and Bill Murray, he who made *Ghostbusters*, and he – along with another Canadian, James Cameron – who made a Republican superstar out of an Austrian bodybuilder named Arnold Schwarzenegger. He is thus indisputably the most successful broker of comedy in movie history. Some would say that the price of such success has been his Canadianism, that by definition the kind of entertainment purveyed by Reitman is somehow anathematic to being a Canuck. One begs to differ, if only for one salient bit of evidence to the contrary: only a truly Canadian megasuccess could possibly harbour a two-year itch over something said by the CBC.

Recommended Viewing:

Meatballs (1979), Stripes (1981), Ghostbusters (1984) Reitman's best comedies work primarily because he gives Bill Murray free rein to indulge his smarm-ass tendencies. For camp/cult-friendly viewing, check out *Cannibal Girls* (1973) or the animated *Heavy Metal* (1981), which features an all-star roster of Canuck voices: John Candy, Eugene Levy, John "Dean Wormer" Vernon and August Schellenberg.

Risky Viewing:

Twins (1988), Kindergarten Cop (1990), Junior (1994) Reitman's worst comedies invariably involve Arnold Schwarzenegger, who is so inept at comedy even France doesn't revere him. Each one of these movies is based on a slim comic premise that offers a quick sight-gag and then goes absolutely nowhere: Arnie and Danny DeVito as twins, Arnie teaching kindergarten, Arnie pregnant. Incidentally, Reitman produced the execrable *Stop! or My Mom Will Shoot* (1992), an attempt to kickstart a comedy career for another muscle-bound action hero, Sylvester Stallone. Fortunately, it didn't take.

← Mountie Poster

Go Ahead, Make My Quota
The Royal Canadian Mounted Police

On July 8, 1874, the Canadian government dispatched 300 officers of the North West Mounted Police to a remote prairie location in present-day Southern Alberta. There had been reports that American whisky-traders were operating among the Blackfoot there, and the reports were taken seriously indeed by the recently instituted national police force. Just a month earlier, a number of Assiniboine had been massacred by whites at a traders' post in the Cypress Hills, and the government was determined to nip any further racist shenaniganism right in the bud. Canada could ill afford a costly Indian war, and it was one of the founding principles of the new police force that war with the Native population was to be prevented at all costs. There was simply too much money to be made on white settlement in the vast Canadian West to let racist violence screw things up.

After riding two full months, the NWMP arrived at their destination only to learn that the booze-traders had already hightailed it elsewhere. That's when the Blackfoot decided to determine whether the force's true intentions were to capture the Yankee traders or manage the Natives. Slyly, they told the NWMP of the whereabouts of some of the traders, and were most impressed indeed when the men in red promptly tracked down the Yankee villains and locked them up. Henceforth, relations between the Blackfoot and the North West Mounted Police were smooth as any between the representatives of white officialdom and Natives at the time of mass Western settlement. Welcome to the Canadian mild West.

The 1874 incident, which was hardly atypical of how the federal police force facilitated white settlement by undercutting potential Native hostility through negotiation and cooperation, explains much about the strangely unexciting trajectory of Canadian popular mythology over the next century.

First, it explains why the U.S. has a potent and infinitely pertinent Western mythology, while Canada, whose West was vastly larger and more threatening, does not: since the primary job of the NWMP, which became the Royal Canadian Mounted Police in 1920, was to prevent hostility before it happened, the potential for both outlawry and outlaw mythology, was effectively snipped before it could happen. Second, it explains why, while Canadians have allowed the ramrod-straight image of the red and blue cop as

bureaucratic enforcer (the same image exploited and perpetrated as late as 1996 by the CTV series *Due South*, which also aired in the States on CBS) to become one of its most internationally recognizable national symbols, cops have enjoyed nothing near the fictional interest in Canada that they've had in Britain, France or, most obviously, the United States. (Fact: before David Wellington's *I Love A Man in Uniform* was invited to Cannes in 1993, no other high-profile English-Canadian movie had taken a police officer as its subject. Furthermore, *Uniform* is about a fake: someone posing as a police officer.) It is one challenge to promote a national image of dutiful efficiency through the image of the mirthless Mountie, quite another to make compelling pulp out of it. Third, the 1874 incident underscores the precedence of

Studley Dooright: Paul Gross and David Marciano

management over struggle in popular, and most often official, Canadian mythology. Where American culture returns obsessively to the well of violence as source of both spectacle and regenerative spiritual baptism, Canadians defer to their ability to appease through the perfectly respectable but comparatively dull national virtues of compromise and negotiation: the world's peacekeepers, the global referees of fair play. Finally, the true story of the Mounties, the Blackfoot and the evil Yankee booze-traders helps us understand why the two most popular forms of tourist-shop kitsch across Canada were, until very recently, anyway, images of proud Mounties sharing shelf space with cute, puppy-eyed and thoroughly domesticated Indian dolls – Canadian history rendered as threatening as playthings in a roadside pitshop. Toys 'r us indeed.

The mythic function of the Mountie as symbol of effective management also accounts for the fact that, apart from the occasional TV series featuring Gordon Pinsent (*Due South, Forest Rangers*), Canadians haven't often been drawn to the Mounties for dramatic inspiration. Who wants to tell (let alone hear) a story about a police force dedicated to the prevention of violence? Thus, strangely enough, the popularizing and perpetation of Mountie mythology has largely been left to other countries. Americans have

made many more Mountie movies than Canadians have, and the inadvertent or intentional kitsch value of these is almost always rooted in the image of the Mountie's impossible purity or sense of duty. From Cecil B. DeMille's bloated 1940 *Northwest Mounted Police*, to the jaw-droppingly campy 1936 MGM musical *Rose Marie*, or from CBS television's 1955-1958 series *Sergeant Preston of the Yukon*, to the Brian Mulroney–jawed cartoon character Dudley Dooright, the image of the Mountie as perpetrated by American popular culture has never strayed that far from Canada's official image of the cop as dutiful, sexless bureaucrats with guns.

Curiously, the mythic legacy of the Mounties continues to be largely the domain of extraterritorial interests. When, in early 1995, the RCMP announced most humourlessly that it was going to clamp down on the unlicensed Mountie tourist-kitsch industry, which traded mostly in trinkets made in the Third World, it subsequently announced the exclusive licensing rights had been sold to no less a pioneering merchandising monolith than the California-based Walt Disney Company. Although some saw the rights sale as an outrageous besmirching of a proud national institution, the history of Mountie mythology suggests quite the oppo-

site: that the Disney-Mountie match might in fact be one made in merchandising heaven. Americans have always been more interested than Canadians in making pulp out of the RCMP, and who better to promote the earnest honourable role of Canada's national police force than the same company that turned conservative family entertainment into a billion-dollar global industry? Besides, by the mid-1990s, the RCMP could certainly use some high-powered image management: faced with growing skepticism of their methods and effectiveness, and widely ridiculed for botching security surrounding Prime Minister Jean Chrétien – who throttled a demonstrator in public in March 1996 and then blamed the incident on an inefficient RCMP – the force could do a lot worse than have on its side the company that made a mountain from a mouse.

They Always Play Our Man
American Mountie Schlock

(1936) Rose Marie
(1938) Heart of the North
(1940) Northwest Mounted Police
(1940) Man From Montreal
(1952) Wild North
(1953) Canadian Mounties vs. Atomic Invaders
(1954) Saskatchewan
(1954) Yukon Vengeance

Sonic Suburbia **The Rush Chronicles**

While complacency as a creative stimulus isn't widely credited, there is definitely a case to be made for the role of the cushy suburban adolescent lifestyle in the stimulation of certain kinds of Canadian expression. Canada is, after all, a wealthy country with countless suburbs, and suburban kids. In this country's pop culture, perhaps nothing, save beer commercials, states the case for suburban experience with more sheer sonic force than the impervious, generation-spanning success of the unkillable prog-rock power-trio Rush.

To comprehend, let alone appreciate, Rush, it helps if you did your growing up in the suburbs sometime during the late fifties, sixties or seventies. This is when both the sensibility of the band – which emerged from the sprawling suburbs surrounding Toronto the same year Pierre Trudeau was first elected prime minister – and its daunting number of diehard acolytes was forged. These were kids who spent an inordinate amount of time in rec rooms reading, watching television and listening to records: something to do until they worked up the nerve to buy hash oil.

As distinctly a creature of cushy Anglo-Canadian suburbia as Leonard Cohen is boho Montreal and Stompin' Tom is the working-class rural Maritimes, Rush has earned one of the most eccentrically successful positions in the global music market. The band has done that by understanding then capitalizing on an idea which, prior to their arrival, had been left curiously unexploited: positioning themselves outside of vogue and fashion, touring with the relentless tenacity of a Canadian winter, baldly fetishizing technical virtuosity and pop metaphysics, Rush connected with those kids who'd grown up with bikes, torn jeans, paperbacks and strip malls just like the boys in the band. When you consider the countless thousands of square suburban miles in North America, Europe and the U.K., it becomes quite

clear why Rush found itself the band of choice for millions upon millions of kids. As the band's drummer, lyricist and resident guru Neil Peart explained in 1984: "All of us grew up in suburban backgrounds. Modern angelstone split-level homes built in the late fifties or early sixties… We established ourselves in the suburban satellites of almost every city of North America." Which is a lot of satellite power – enough to keep one of the unlikeliest success stories in Canadian pop history bending the hedges of the world's suburbs for 30 years.

Like many Canadian bands, Rush can trace its beginnings to the locker-lined corridors of high school. Specifically, a high school in willowy Willowdale, near Toronto, Ontario, where both Geddy Lee (bassist, born Gary Lee Weinrib in

Toronto in 1953) and Alex Lifeson (guitarist, born Alex Zivojinovich in Fernie, British Columbia, in 1953) met and decided to do the only thing worth doing under the circumstances – they formed a band. Joined by original drummer John Rutsey, the band, which took its name from the schoolyard expression for a narcotic jolt, quickly established the pattern which would eventually render it one of the truly unstoppable forces in North American, let alone Canadian, rock: gig and gig and gig again.

Rush connected with those kids who'd grown up with bikes, torn jeans, paperbacks and strip malls just like the boys in the band.

Rush: Rec-Room Deities →

Alex Lifeson   Neil Peart   Geddy Lee

Strongly influenced by Led Zeppelin in its early days, Rush established a pattern of bullet-biting hard work for itself which was not only a natural outgrowth of the *nouveau riche* suburban work ethic, according to which 16-year-old kids who didn't have part-time jobs were losers, it built the foundation for the band's distinctive longevity. By performing constantly (at its late-seventies peak, Rush's touring schedule involved a staggering 200 shows per year), the group developed its famed technical virtuosity while at the same time establishing itself as a fan's band. Both traits would prove crucial to Rush's survival and distinction, because right from the getgo the band found itself ignored by radio and excoriated by critics. *The Village Voice*'s Robert Christgau once charged Rush with being "the most obnoxious band currently making a killing on the zonked teen circuit."

After meeting Jim Danniels, a 16-year-old high school dropout with a yen for management, the band kicked up its gig schedule and eventually recorded an album (in eight hours) for $9,000. Rush's debut was turned down by every single record label in the country. Danniels, however, was not to be deterred. He'd seen the lines of dour teenage boys which stretched in a tributary of torn denim from the doors of every church basement and high school auditorium where his clients played. He knew there was an audience who would pay to play that music in their very own rumpus rooms. That's why Danniels decided the band should start its own label. It's also why Rush is still around: the self-released album sold to the very kids Danniels knew it would, as quickly as cheap hash. Its brisk sales led to a plum offer from

For those who got it, it was musical nirvana; for those who didn't, it was unlistenably pretentious heavy metal for semiliterate hosers.

Chicago's Mercury Records – a $100,000 contract and fully funded American tour.

The groundwork for the phenomenon that we now know as Rush was thus laid, save for one key ingredient. Knowing that Rutsey was experiencing health as well as motivational problems (we'll assume 200 gigs a year might have had something to do with it), Danniels replaced the drummer with a man who would turn out to be as important to the development of Rush's sonic suburban onslaught as stompin' was to Tom Connors. His name was Neil Peart.

Born in Hamilton, Ontario, in 1952 and raised in nearby St. Catharines, Peart was a child of the same vast, indistinguishably meshing suburban spill extending a few hundred miles west of Toronto to the border city of Fort Erie, Ontario. The area is called the Golden Horseshoe, but, considering the world-beating proliferation of Tim Horton's shops it boasts, it might be more aptly named the Giant Doughnut. Thus, while Peart was growing up an entire Great Lake's–width away from Lee and Lifeson, he was suckled on many of the same musical and literary influences. And, in a funny way, the latter turned out to be every bit as important as the former in the forging of the band's definitive rock sound.

Like many literate suburban-mall rats, Peart was an articulate but unassuming

dreamer with a passion for the literature of science fiction and utopian fantasy. By the time he joined Rush, he had devoured the works of J. R. R. Tolkien and Frank Herbert, and later, the writings of the archconservative American individualist Ayn Rand.

Upon being enlisted by Danniels, Peart went to work forging his literary influences into the singular lyrical experience that is a Rush song: elaborate, near-epic stories set in some distant, technocratic future; arcane references to incidents and characters from the Rush reading list (typical mid-seventies song titles include "By-Tor & The Snow Dog," "Cygnus X-1" and "Cygnus X-1 Book II"), all brought to earsplitting

----

Boyz 'N the Burbs

In Canada, the voice of suburban experience is central not only to the rec room–incubated comedy of former mall-rats Mike Myers, Kids in the Hall and Jim Carrey, but in the music of performers like Rush, Barenaked Ladies and Max Webster (whose lead singer, Kim Mitchell, once had a hit song about that important suburban backyard feature, "Patio Lanterns"). Mike Myers and some members of Barenaked Ladies grew up in Toronto's ultimate satellite suburb, Scarborough (a.k.a. Scarberia): it shows in their work. Both Myers (with his suburban-hoser-character Wayne Campbell) and the Ladies (particularly on their first album, *Gordon*) are obsessed by the minute details of suburban life. They affectionately parody the bland, comfortable world in which they grew up: a universe of Kraft Dinners, Adidas gym bags, street hockey and doughnut shops. In both Canadian comedy and pop music, the suburban voice is shaped by the shared experience of countless hours of unsupervised TV viewing between school's end and the summoning for supper: it's a voice that's intelligent but rarely angry or political, and invariably informed by the various fantasy writers, TV shows and records that filled the hours between casseroles and butter tarts.

The Sound of the Suburbs: *2112* album cover   *Caress of Steel* album cover

sonic life by the increasingly ambitious, complex and technically immaculate musicianship of the trio, and garishly garnished by the hackle-raising stuck-pig wail of Geddy Lee. Needless to say, as a musical experience it was something of a crowd-splitter. For those who got it, it was musical nirvana; for those who didn't, it was unlistenably pretentious heavy metal for semiliterate hosers. The fact is, it was, and remains, both.

This persistent splitting of response would prove to be both boon and bane to the band. On the one hand, it served Rush's ethic of uncompromising independence: if so much of the critical and musical establishment couldn't stand them, it was proof they were sticking to their principles and sticking it to the status quo. Needless to say, this attitude also endeared them deeply to their equally disenfranchised suburban male audience. On the downside, it made Rush a virtual laughingstock for the band's first decade of visible success. The critical drubbing from 1974 to 1984 was as relentless as it was ruthless and, for people radically disenfranchised with the creeping pomposity of mainstream music, Rush's own anticorporate independence was read as outmoded funkless white-boy pomp-rock. Along with Pink Floyd, Journey, Styx and The Eagles, Rush was one of the bands you pointed to in the late seventies to explain what made punk rock necessary.

Yet, inevitable as such a dismissal is in the cruelly unforgiving realm of rock purism, only hindsight reveals how widely such attacks missed the point. For if it's independence, and not attitude, attire or, strangely, even music, that is the mark of musical integrity, Rush has it by

the megaton. Never has the band swayed from its influences and interests; never has it given in to prevailing perceptions of what's popular or commercial at the moment; and never has it placed any judgement of its worth above the feelings of its fans – those same people who were there with their fists in the air from the beginning, who made them possible, and who understood exactly where the band was coming from, because that's where Rush came from too, just a wheelie or two away from the strip mall.

However, considering the ubiquitousness of the suburban experience and the global popularity of the band, how Canadian can Rush really be? In a word or two pilfered from The Tragically Hip: fully, completely. In their blithe indifference to trend and fashion, for example, Rush occupies a seminal position in the grandly unpretentious tradition of Canadian hoser rock – The Guess Who, BTO, The Tragically Hip, 54-40, the whole uglier-than-thou sonic shebang. Also, in its refusal to sway course, let alone sink, in the squalls of adversity, the band embodies one of the most admirable strains of Canadian cultural life: the refusal to pack up and go away even though it's constantly criticized for not being "Canadian" enough. This is the same sheer Northern stubbornness that links the band with such unlikely but genuine fellow travellers as David Cronenberg and Moses Znaimer.

Finally, if there was ever any question of Rush's Canuck credentials, those doubts should be forever extinguished by this fact: when Bob and Doug McKenzie, the archetypal hoser siblings played by *SCTV*'s Dave Thomas and Rick Moranis, sought the most appropri-

ate musical icon to sing the chorus on their 1981 hit hosehead anthem "Take Off," they looked no farther than Geddy Lee, who was glad to oblige.

Note: Before we proceed to make recommendations, keep this in mind: like Stompin' Tom's, it is possible to love or hate the music of Rush, but it is far too distinctive and/or obnoxious to remain indifferent about. The problem is, if you're already a fan, you don't need to know this. And if you aren't, you probably never will be. At any rate, here goes.

- -

Recommended Listening:

Fly by Night (1975) Peart's first Rush album is the band's second, but that's why this is the best place to start. All the emerging themes, references, screeches and intricately orchestrated forms of cacophony begin here.

2112 (1976) The Ayn Rand–influenced sci-fi concept album, which many diehards still consider the pure, crystalline essence of Rush.

A Farewell to Kings (1977) An extension of the themes and musical approaches introduced in *2112*, and therefore another diehard favourite. If you don't like Rush, this is probably why.

Power Windows (1985) After seeming to tread water for an album or two (the band seemed torn between musical evolution and fan expectations), this one represents the emergence of a new Rush phase: distinct songs instead of epic suites, and the honing of Peart's lyrics from the so-chunky-you-can-eat-it-with-a-fork verbiage of the Rand phase. Predictably, many purists consider it something of a cop-out.

Chronicles (1990) A comprehensive, intelligent but ultimately perplexing collection of the band's best. Perplexing because, if you like Rush's music, you like it enough to own all this stuff already, and if you don't, *Chronicles* is more likely to remind you why than win you over.

"If there's any particular Canadian perspective, it's that we are a nation of observers."

– ANDREW ALEXANDER, CREATOR AND EXECUTIVE PRODUCER. *SCTV*

TV Nation **SCTV**

It's still possible to see *SCTV*, the TV parody show which existed in a number of incarnations from 1976 to 1984, in syndicated reruns in most parts of North America. Given the infinitely recyclable nature of the electronic universe, that fact is significantly less surprising than this one: not only can you still see the show, you can still be bowled over by it. It was, and remains, simply that good. One could even say it was the finest program of its kind ever to be produced in Canada, and possibly the finest comedy program ever produced in North America.

This claim is made in full awareness of the burden of proof it demands. But that's why one feels confident making it: the proof is right there on the screen. Just turn on the TV and roam around until you find a rerun of the program set exclusively in and around the only television station in the fictional small town of Melonville. When you do, maybe it'll be the program where John Candy, as the ludicrously self-inflated minor TV celebrity Johnny LaRue, slumps petulantly into a snowbank, sobbing over the injustice of not being permitted a crane shot for the cheap little Christmas special only he is convinced is *Citizen Kane*. Maybe it'll be the one in which Eugene Levy's Bobby Bittman, talentless showbiz-hack extraordinaire, is interrupted in the middle of a giant-phone-prop joke on *The Sammy Maudlin Show* by the unannounced Dave Thomas doing a deliciously snide Bob Hope. Or Martin Short as Jerry Lewis in a Bergmanesque *Scenes From an Idiot's Marriage*. Or...

← Five Neat Guys
(left to right: John Candy, Eugene Levy, Rick Moranis, Dave Thomas, Joe Flaherty)

SCTV: early days at Global

Sorry. Our enthusiasm is showing, isn't it? The problem is, once one's waters have been whipped up by *SCTV* memories, it's hard for the fan not to get sucked into a whirlpool of recollections – favourite characters, sketches, lines. To fall for *SCTV* was to fall into one of television's most intricate and elaborate satirical worlds. Where most of the hip comedy of its era was based on the discrete-sketch model of *Saturday Night Live*, *SCTV*'s major concern was with the adventurous mingling of character and concept, that is, throwing familiar (if bizarre) running characters into unfamiliar (and equally bizarre) situations. Taking the familiar *SCTV* staff, for example, and putting them in a parody of network-ratings wars based on *The Godfather*, or recasting the movie *2001* with Simon, Garfunkel and – for God's sake – Ernest Borgnine. Yet, while the show featured a rich roster of recurring characters – including the unethical, wheelchair-bound station owner, Guy Caballero (Flaherty); the braying station manager, Edith Prickly (Martin); the exuberantly talentless bimbo, Lola Heatherton (O'Hara); the professional talk-show suck-up, William B. (Candy); the torturously optimistic mega-nerd, Ed Grimley (Short); and the bitter career-long broadcasting failure, Bill Needle (Thomas) – *SCTV* was hardly your basic sitcom.

Rather than confining its characters to a particular set – or even dramatic universe – *SCTV*'s only limits were those of the televisual imagination. Understanding the basic nature of television "as flow" that TV-celebrity-mogul-prophet Moses Znaimer preaches about, *SCTV* created a world where programs and concepts intersected,

To fall for *SCTV* was to fall into one of television's most intricate and elaborate satirical worlds.

collided and cross-fertilized in a way some called surreal and others would later call postmodern. Whatever you call it, it was the first program to weave the experience of actually watching television into its very satiric fabric, which is to say *SCTV* understood our relationship to television more astutely than any program before or since. Therefore, the possibility that it might have happened in any other country but Canada is frankly inconceivable: we may have lousy weather, but we sure as hell know how to watch TV.

The story begins in 1973 when a 29-year-old transplanted Torontonian named Andrew Alexander walked into the original Second City improv theatre in Chicago. The son of a British aeronautical engineer living in Canada, Alexander's rather circuitous career had landed him a publicity job at Chicago's Ivanhoe Theatre, just around the corner from the legendary Second City founded in 1959.

Watching the show – Chicago's Second City had birthed the careers of everyone from Alan Alda to Alan Arkin – convinced Alexander that the concept of cheeky, sharp-toothed improv could fly back in his home of Toronto. He believed this despite the fact that there already was a Second City in Toronto: it had been opened by Chicago producer Bernie Sahlins the same year, but closed in only four months after failing to get a liquor licence. Undeterred, Alexander bought the rights to the name from Sahlins for one dollar plus royalties. Legend has it the deal was executed on a napkin.

Alexander then approached the owners of the Old Firehall theatre in Toronto, whose restaurant in the century-old building was in deep financial trouble. He talked them into hosting a Second City show, convincing some of the performers who'd been involved with the Sahlins venture to give it another shot. The first show was called "Hello Dali!," and featured nothing less than a sneak preview of a coming revolution in television comedy – Dan Aykroyd, Gilda Radner, Joe Flaherty, John Candy, Eugene Levy and Rosemary Radcliffe.

Unlike its Chicago cousin, which was fairly tightly structured and conventional in performance terms, Toronto's Second City was a lawless frontier town: performers were free to push limits as far as they could (Martin Short's sublimely original Ed Grimley character was born on a Second City stage), a factor which would be crucial to the explosion of Canuck comedy in the coming years. It would take two years before the Toronto Second City company would stop worrying whether they had a job the next night.

One of Alexander's concerns was the direct result of Second City's success: Dan Aykroyd and Gilda Radner had been plucked from the company by Lorne Michaels to work on a new Second City–inspired TV show to be called *Saturday Night Live*. As Alexander said in 1983: "I thought, 'Yikes, I can see what's going to happen. I'm going to lose the whole cast if I don't have something to offer them.'" With friend and partner Len Stuart, Alexander started peddling the idea for a Second City TV show in 1976. After the notion was rejected by both the CBC and CTV, Stuart and Alexander turned to the new, cash-strapped Ontario network

Andrea Martin as Edith Prickly

Global, which desperately needed Canadian programming to meet its broadcast-licence requirements. Global committed to 13 shows at absurdly low cost, and Alexander sat down with his stage performers to hammer out a concept. In just a few hours they decided to do what seems to come as naturally to Canadians as being polite: to spoof TV. The early cast of writer-performers Alexander recruited for the program included John Candy, Joe Flaherty, Catherine O'Hara, Eugene Levy, Andrea Martin, Harold Ramis and Dave Thomas. Despite the program's knockabout nomadic history, the central conceit remained intact – it would be set entirely in and around a TV station in the fictional middle–North American small town of Melonville. And it would be called *SCTV*.

In 1979, after three seasons and an ACTRA award as best Canadian TV variety show, Global cancelled the already-threadbare production on the amusing basis that it was too expensive. Luckily, Alexander found ITV, an Edmonton company that agreed to both finance and produce the show from its own studios: this meant higher production quality at reasonable rates. Meanwhile, the CBC agreed to run *SCTV* in 1980, and one year later, NBC, concerned about *Saturday Night Live*'s flagging viewership and hipster cred, jumped in the pool as well. *SCTV* became the first independently produced Canadian program ever to be picked up by an American network.

SCTV played to rave reviews and reasonable ratings for two years in NBC's late-Friday-night spot. But the network wanted more for its investment, and insisted the program be moved to prime time, even suggesting to Alexander that

Rather than confining its characters to a particular set — or even dramatic universe — *SCTV*'s only limits were those of the televisual imagination.

SCTV might run opposite the mighty ratings colossus *60 Minutes*. In a gesture of defiance which made him an entertainment-press hero for a moment or two, Alexander told NBC he'd rather have no network slot than one opposite Mike Wallace, and *SCTV* was up for grabs again. Alexander then took the program to pay TV in Canada and the U.S., where it was produced as a series of specials for a year. Without a regular slot, however, the program failed to recapture its audience. By 1984, *SCTV*, one of the finest, funniest and smartest comedy programs in TV history, was off the air.

The Melonville All-Stars
John Candy
Origins: born 1950, Toronto; died 1994.
SCTV Specialties: Large, overbearing neurotics; greedy, manipulative weasels.
Most Memorable Characters: lisping 3-D horror-show host, Dr. Tongue; low-key, mean-spirited Melonville mayor, Tommy Shanks; self-obsessed minor celebrity, Johnny LaRue; Orson Welles; Lutonian musician, Yosh Shmenge; co-host of *Farm Report*, Billy Sol Hurok; Luciano Pavarotti; Harry, "The guy with the snake on his face."
Postscript: Made a ton of movies in the decade between *SCTV* 's cancellation in 1984 and his premature passing at age 43, but very, very few of them tap more than

a spoonful from the reservoirs of intelligence and comic talent this man possessed. Sadly, Candy wasn't alone in making movies that wasted him: it would turn out to be a distressingly common refrain for the program's alumni. Most watchable are *The Silent Partner* (1978), *Stripes* (1981), *Splash* (1984), *Planes Trains and Automobiles* (1987), *JFK* (1991).
SCTV Quote: "Let's mambo!"

Joe Flaherty
Origins: born 1941, Pittsburgh, Pennsylvania.
SCTV Specialties: crazed authority figures; unconvincing liars; dumb people; oily pickup artists; people who yell a lot; cowering losers.
Most Memorable Characters: unconvincingly handicapped station owner, Guy Caballero; *Monster Chiller Horror Theatre* host, Count Floyd; dumb stud Rocco on *Days of the Week*; Jack Klugman as Quincy; Charlton Heston; Big Jim McBob, co-host of *Farm Report*.
Postscript: Unlike most fellow ex-Melonvillians, Flaherty has demonstrated little interest in building a substandard movie career, focusing his inarguably idiosyncratic talents on television shows like *Really Weird Tales* and *Maniac Mansion*.
SCTV Quote: "Okay, I don't know what it is, but whatever it is, it's gonna be reeeeeally scary, kids! B-r-r-r-r-r-r!"

Eugene Levy
Origins: born 1946, Hamilton, Ontario.
SCTV Specialties: facially contorted losers; vain, untalented and deeply insincere minor celebrities; image-impaired hucksters; very old people; anything involving expressive eyebrow manipulation.
Most Memorable Characters: frighten-

Curtain call: *(left to right:* Joe Flaherty, John Candy, Catherine O'Hara, Juul Haalmeyer, Andrea Martin, Eugene Levy, Martin Short)

ingly talentless talk-show maven, Bobby Bittman; post-senile oldster-at-large, Sid Dithers; sensitive hunchback-sidekick, Woody Tobias, Jr.; humourless, self-promoting anchorthingy, Earl Camembert; Lutonian musician, Stan Shmenge; teen-dance show host, Mel Slirrup; Ernest Borgnine; Neil Sedaka.

Postscript: After flirting with the big screen – the okay *Splash*, the rank-and-vile *Armed and Dangerous* – Levy has concentrated mostly on television and writing. He and Candy's oompah rocku-mentary *The Last Polka*, featuring the two of them as the Shmenge Brothers, was a post-*SCTV* highlight for both. Once spoke the God's-honest-truth when he said to an interviewer: "I think it's such a waste that all that creative talent we had hasn't been able to get a project together for the screen."

SCTV Quote: "How aaaaaaaaaah ya! But as a comedian, in all seriousness..."

Andrea Martin

Origins: born 1947, Portland, Maine.
SCTV Specialties: Jewish princesses; generously accented foreigners; women who get tossed around a lot; lesbians.
Most Memorable Characters: leopard-skinned take-charge type, Edith Prickly; neurotic, manicure-obsessed feminist, Libby Wolfson; uncontrollably twitching sex ther-apist, Dr. Cheryl Kinsey; Barbra Streisand; Liza Minnelli; Wicked Witch of the West.
Postscript: A movie career never took off after the dismal *Club Paradise* (1986), nor did a TV career after the abrupt can-cellation of the 1987 CBS sitcom *Roxie*.
SCTV Quote: Edith Prickly's laugh: a combined bray, cough and snort which defies any attempt at written representation.

It was the first program to weave the experience of actually watch-ing television into its very satiric fabric, which is to say *SCTV* understood our relationship to television more astutely than any program before or since.

Rick Moranis

Origins: born 1953, Toronto.
SCTV Specialties: nerds; nebbishes; dim bulbs; smooth-talking corporate professionals; Canadian stereotypes.
Most Memorable Characters: cheerful, video-obsessed tech-nerd, Gerry Todd; eighth-rate comedian, Skip Bittman; proto-hoser, Bob McKenzie; David Brinkley; Dick Cavett; Woody Allen.

TV Toss: Joe Flaherty and John Candy

Postscript: The biggest movie star of the *SCTV* graduating class, Moranis has been featured in *Ghostbusters* (1984), *Little Shop of Horrors* (1986), *Honey, I Shrunk the Kids* (1989), *Parenthood* (1990). In other words, by drawing upon one-tenth of his skills as a movie actor, he's probably earning a hundred times what he earned as a TV actor. His gain, our loss. In 1982, Moranis left *SCTV* to codirect the unsuccessful Bob and Doug McKenzie movie, *Strange Brew*, with Dave Thomas.

SCTV Quote: "Let's just bring up the old chroma a little bit here. There she goes…"

Catherine O'Hara

Origins: born 1954, Toronto.

SCTV Specialties: bimbo nymphomaniacs; intellectually underendowed teenagers; over-the-top femme fatales; loud and pushy older women.

Most Memorable Characters: megabimbo Lola Heatherton; Brooke Shields; Meryl Streep.

Postscript: Some okay turns in some okay movies: *After Hours* (1984), *Beetlejuice* (1988). But far more common are okay turns in terrible movies: *Heartburn* (1986), *Betsy's Wedding* (1990), *Home Alone* (1990). Another disappointing post-*SCTV* story.

SCTV Quote: "I wanna bear your children!"

Martin Short

Origins: born 1950, Hamilton, Ontario.

SCTV Specialties: superannuated showbiz bores; children; fiercely repressed optimists; people who get thrown around a lot.

Most Memorable Characters: cross-eyed albino nonentertainer, Jackie Rogers, Jr.; pathologically upbeat loser, Ed Grimley;

unpleasant middle-aged former child star, Rusty Van Reddick; Parkinson's-afflicted vaudeville veteran, Irving Cohen; self-admiring celebrity sycophant, Brock Linahan; Jerry Lewis; Pierre Elliott Trudeau; Katharine Hepburn; Lucille Ball.

Postscript: After Short's show-stopping mid-eighties TV turn – two seasons on *SCTV* followed by a single, stunning year on *Saturday Night Live* – it seemed as though this daring, deeply gifted performer might be the one among the *SCTV* crew to sustain a career which bore out, or at least maintained, the promise of his best sketch work. So it seemed. Short, like so many other Melonville grads, has instead had yet another spotty movie and TV career: *Three Amigos* (1986), *Cross My Heart* (1987), *Innerspace* (1987), *Three Fugitives* (1989) and *Captain Ron* (1992), the last perversely casting Short as straight man to that internationally renowned funnyperson Kurt Russell. (Kurt Russell?) In 1994, Short's eponymous prime-time sitcom was aborted after a few episodes.

SCTV Quote: I couldn't be more excited, I must say. This anticipation – it's making me mental!"

Dave Thomas

Origins: born 1948, St. Catharines, Ontario.

SCTV Specialties: really angry people who yell a lot; Scotsmen; veteran showbiz bores; bitter, underachieving media professionals; brainless Canadians.

Most Memorable Characters: cranky, terminally failing TV commentator, Bill Needle; nonintellectual toque-rack, Doug McKenzie; Mr. X – The Man With X-Ray Eyes; Bob Hope; Richard Harris; Walter Cronkite; Harvey K-Tel; Angus Crock.

> In other words, by drawing upon one-tenth of his skills as a movie actor, Moranis is probably earning a hundred times what he earned as a TV actor. His gain, our loss.

Postscript: Following the 1983 failure of *Strange Brew*, the Bob and Doug McKenzie movie vehicle cowritten and codirected by Thomas with Rick Moranis, Thomas's career got harder to track: he directed John Travolta in the largely unreleased *The Experts* a few years too early to cash in on the erstwhile Sweathog's renewed post–*Pulp Fiction* bankability. In 1990, his CBS show was cancelled after five weeks. Since 1993, Thomas has been featured as a beleaguered pharmacist in the American sitcom *Grace Under Fire*.

SCTV Quote: "Take off, eh?!"

Mr. Michaels Takes Manhattan
Saturday Night Goes Live

As a teenager growing up in the Toronto upper-middle-class neighbourhood of Forest Hill, Lorne Lipowitz cherished the chances he'd get to spend with his high school sweetheart Rosie's dad – the entertainer Frank Shuster. Lorne was obsessed with showbiz. His grandparents had run a small moviehouse near the University of Toronto where his mother worked the box office, and Lorne remembers that movies and movie stars were such conversational staples around the Lipowitz home that, as a kid, it was easy to believe these were real friends everybody was talking about: "Movies and movie stars were all we talked about around the dinner table," he told an interviewer many years later, when Lorne Lipowitz had long been established in showbiz himself as Lorne Michaels, creator and executive producer of *Saturday Night Live*. "I thought every normal family did that. I don't know how old I was when I finally realized my family didn't actually know Clark Gable."

Rosie's dad, on the other hand, while not quite Clark Gable, was the genuine showbiz article: Frank Shuster, one-half of Canada's most popular comedy duo ever, Wayne and Shuster. Needless to say, Lorne would've found Frank Shuster compelling company anyway, but the circumstances of their acquaintance simply made things that much more intense for the kid. First there was that impressionable age, before experience gets a chance to corrupt fantasy. Then there was the fact that Lorne was smitten with Frank Shuster's daughter Rosie, herself no slouch in the gag department: later in her career, she'd be one of *SNL*'s main writers. (She and Michaels would also be briefly married, clinching the Canadian-comedy lineage which links Wayne and Shuster and *SNL*.) Finally, there was the fact that, when Lorne was 14, his father died at the age of 48. As far as Lorne was concerned, a better mentor than Shuster couldn't have come along at a better time.

← Mike Myers as Wayne Campbell

Hart Pomerantz and Lorne Michaels

While Frank claimed that he never encouraged Lorne's showbiz ambitions – "I discourage the world from going into show business," he told *Maclean's* in 1993, "but anybody who wants it badly enough is going to do it anyway" – he did help the young man understand that there's more to comedy than just being funny. It's a discipline, he told Lorne. It has rules, traditions and a history, and to do it well you've got to be prepared to work hard. For Lorne, Frank broke down the mechanics of classic comedy, took it apart and showed him the nuts and bolts. Long after Michaels had become one of the biggest Canadian figures in comedy since Wayne and Shuster, he acknowledged his former father-in-law's influence: "He introduced me to the films of Preston Sturges. He could explain how Jack Benny played a pause. I think it's almost impossible to succeed in these fields without mentors."

Later in his own comedy career, after graduating from the University of Toronto, after working for CBC as one-half of the comedy team of Hart and Lorne, after writing for Woody Allen, Joan Rivers and Lily Tomlin, Michaels himself liked to mentor: he became a Frank Shuster to other people's Lorne Lipowitzes. After establishing himself as a writer – his stock rose particularly high after he won an Emmy for his writing on an acclaimed 1973 Lily Tomlin special – Michaels became almost militant in his commitment to seeking out young, fresh and new talent. He believed that comedy should be surprising to be funny, and the best way to find surprising comedy was by constantly reaching down and pulling the best and the brightest up from the bottom. Over the years, the practice

After establishing himself as a writer, Michaels became almost militant in his commitment to seeking out young, fresh and new talent.

would not only enhance Michaels's reputation as a comedic impresario, it would change the face of television – and later, but not for the better – movie comedy. Dan Aykroyd, John Belushi, Chevy Chase, Gilda Radner, Bill Murray, Mike Myers, Dana Carvey – all were introduced to the world by Lorne Michaels, and all were unknown at the time the introduction was made.

From the moment he had the clout to make demands of big networks, his demands invariably revolved around the issue of zip-locking freshness in comedy: how to keep it vital, contemporary, alive. Working in contexts ranging from the old-school gag factory of *Rowan and Martin's Laugh-In*, to the limit-pushing inspiration of Lily Tomlin, had taught Michaels a thing or two about TV comedy – what worked and what didn't, what was good and what wasn't, and most important, what he did and didn't want to do.

Michaels knew, for example, that there were certain basic ingredients to the kind of TV comedy he liked to watch. The talent had to be young and from outside the entertainment establishment. That's what gave them their edge and vitality, and that's what gave them the punkish fearlessness to sneer at anybody who deserved their sneers. He also wanted it live. By the early seventies, live television was well on its way to the medium's evolutionary dumpster. In the context of ever-cheaper and more versatile forms of recording, live

TV was regarded as outmoded, unnecessary and just too risky. For Michaels, the decline of live TV had taken some crucial things away from TV comedy: the thrill of spontaneity, the sense of danger, the fusion between performer and audience in a simultaneously experienced mass-media moment. Besides, doing comedy live was absolutely the best way of keeping it current, which, in turn, was a key factor in keeping it relevant and edgy. If you had these ingredients – young talent on live TV – Michaels felt you were well on the way to creating something special in the realm of TV comedy. That left only one thing missing. You had to have Canadians.

If this was part of Michaels's agenda when he first pitched the idea of *Saturday Night Live* to an understandably skeptical NBC (who thought the idea of a live program was devolutionary), he probably kept it to himself. After all, what he was proposing – a live, late-night comedy-sketch show aimed at an audience who probably wouldn't be home when it was on – was bold enough without this kicker: "Oh yeah, I also want it to be *loaded* with Canadians."

Yet, by the time Michaels was in a position to pitch the show to NBC, he had already noticed something about the relationship between Canada and comedy: not only were Canadians good at being funny, they were good at being a particular kind of funny. For example, they were first-rate mimics, and they were unparalleled at the art of parody, particularly pop-culture parody. It might even have been his former father-in-law who'd first brought this cultural peculiarity to Michaels's attention, as Wayne and Shuster was one of the very first prominent comedy acts in North America that

Live Myers

In the early nineties, the hottest comic actor in North America was Mike Myers. His comedy was basically a pop blender jammed with countless ironic references to obscure celebrities, heavy-metal music and cartoons like Scooby-Doo. Of course, his comic *pièce de résistance* was Wayne Campbell, the likeable hoser who hosted his own cable-access program with a techno-nerd named Garth. Soon the hoser was a certified *SNL* star, whose small-screen success led to big-screen treatment in both *Wayne's World* (1992) and *Wayne's World 2* (1993).

Since leaving *SNL* in 1994, Myers has kept a surprisingly low profile. Jim Carrey, another guy who spent some adolescent years in Scarborough, has replaced him as North America's most bankable comic actor.

Myers had a strong five-year run on *SNL* (1989-1994), and he fit perfectly into the show at a time when its emphasis had swung away from political satire, and focused almost entirely on movie and TV parodies. Some of his highlights:

Wayne Campbell: the suburban hoser who gave us early nineties catchphrases like "excellent," "party on," "schwing," "we're not worthy," "not!" and the immortal "and monkeys might fly out of my butt."

Dieter: the ambisexual German TV host of *Sprockets* who wore all-black and had a fixation on minor North American celebrities. Catchphrases: "Touch my monkey!"; "I'm as happy as a little girl."

Mick Jagger/Ron Wood: Myers did spot-on impressions of these two moss-gathering Stones, but the funniest was the entirely incomprehensible "Woody."

Angus: proud proponent of "All Things Scottish," the spiritual brother of the Dave Thomas *SCTV* character, Angus Crock.

Linda Richman: host of *Coffee Talk.* Based on Myers's mother-in-law, this character was often overcome with emotion, particularly when discussing the talents of Barbra Streisand. Catchphrases: "I'm farklempt!"; "It's like buttah"; "Talk amongst yourselves."

specialized in making fun of contemporary pop culture, in particular, movies and TV.

Michaels was convinced that this knack for media parody had its roots in the cultural conditions of Canada, a country where everybody watches TV that comes from somewhere else, and watches more TV because it's so flipping cold most of the time. Canada is a nation of chronic, ironic, detached observers, a list of attributes which, by the early 1970s, was in the process of shifting from the debit to the profit side of the cultural ledger. Michaels had already seen the incredible vitality of the recently formed Toronto Second City troupe – which included cast members Dan Aykroyd, Gilda Radner, John Candy, Andrea Martin, Joe Flaherty and Dave Thomas – and he'd noted the contribution the frostily ironic Canadian sensibility had made to the success of *National Lampoon* magazine, which contained a witheringly hilarious monthly column called "Canadian Corner."

Michaels sold NBC on the program, but not without a struggle: he wanted the network to commit to 20 shows, the network wanted 13. The compromise: 17 shows at $115,000 each, with six months to put the team and program together. It wasn't much time, but Michaels knew he could abbreviate the auditioning process. There were certain people he wouldn't have to audition because he knew they'd be perfect for the show. One of these was Dan Aykroyd, the Ottawa-born grandson of a French-speaking Mountie who'd impressed Michaels with his eerie talent for total character immersion while a member of Toronto's Second City. From Toronto he also recruited Gilda Radner,

By the end of its first season (1975-1976), *Saturday Night Live* was the definition of cool: the hippest thing to hit TV since *The Smothers Brothers Show*.

an American who'd gone to work for Second City after a gig with the enormously successful Toronto run of the pop musical *Godspell*. (Other *Godspell* alumni included Andrea Martin, Martin Short and Eugene Levy.) Rosie Shuster was hired on as a writer, and the musical department of *Saturday Night Live* was almost completely lorded over by Canucks: Paul Shaffer, later David Letterman's so-hip-it-hurts sidekick, was the show's first keyboardist, and *SNL*'s original music director was Michaels's former high school buddy, Howard Shore, later one of Hollywood's busiest and distinctive composers of original music for movies. (Shore's résumé includes *Silence of the Lambs* and David Cronenberg films *Dead Ringers* and *Crash.*)

Vindication of Michaels's hunches – about the comedians, about going live and even about using Canadians – took a while to come, but come it did. By the end of its first season (1975-1976), *Saturday Night Live* was the definition of cool: the hippest thing to hit TV since *The Smothers Brothers Show*, and the couch-spud experience of choice for the freshly mainstreamed, former underground publication *Rolling Stone* which couldn't seem to go to print in those days without containing something glowing about Lorne Michaels's late-night baby.

Among the new superstars the show

Young Dan Aykroyd in seventies CBC comedy *Coming Up Rosie*

Dan Aykroyd's Lives

Within the period of one month in 1996, three (count 'em!) dreadful Dan Aykroyd movies were released: *Getting Away With Murder*, *Celtic Pride* and *Sgt. Bilko*. Like so many other Aykroyd outings, these movies are forever consigned to the back-wall racks of video stores across North America. Along with most other *SNL/SCTV* alumni, Aykroyd now adheres to the career strategy of "quantity not quality." Almost 20 years after he left *Saturday Night Live*, it's frighteningly easy to forget just how good this Canuck once was: as a sketch player and mimic in the show's infancy, Aykroyd was in a league of his own. In one legendary skit, he appeared as the prototypical refrigerator repairman who forgot to wear his belt. That night, all of North America got to see a large portion of Aykroyd's ass as he bent over to take a look at the damaged appliance. Let's face it, the guy took chances. Herewith, some of Aykroyd's sublime *SNL* contributions:

Fred Garvin, Male Prostitute: not exactly the American Gigolo

Georg Festrunk: the "wild and crazy" guy, Czech brother to Steve Martin

Bass-O-Matic Salesman: TV pitchman with rapid-fire delivery screaming the praises of drinking liquid fish

E. Buzz Miller: overheated sleazoid looking for lust in all the right places

Richard Nixon: paranoid ex-president looking for support from John Belushi's Henry Kissinger

Irwin Mainway: morally reprehensible marketer of unsafe products, including "Bag o' Glass" for kids

Leonard Pinth-Garnell: snotty host of *Bad Playhouse*

Julia Child: TV cooking-show host who has on-air accident, just can't stop bleeding

Beldar Conehead: dour alien parental unit pretending to be from France

produced, like Gilda Radner, John Belushi and Bill Murray, one of the most popular was easily the ungainly-looking Aykroyd, whose chameleonic, utterly convincing impersonations of various hucksters, sleazeballs, presidents and aliens were unlike anything previously seen on network TV: precise, complete and verging on scary. Two decades later, long after *SNL*'s hipness factor had gone the way of Farrah Fawcett's flip, and after several dozen different cast members had failed to replicate the magic of the first seasons, Michaels was still in awe of what the kid from Ottawa had brought to the program: "Of all the people who did *Saturday Night Live* in the first five years, he was the one I always watched. I'd be standing just off camera, and he'd take my breath away."

In the spring of 1980, Michaels left *Saturday Night Live*. By that point, the show had been on the air for five seasons, and he was worn out from the relentless pace: getting a 90-minute show to air each week, battling with network executives and censors, constantly trying to appease a myriad of talented egos. He needed a break.

Michaels started his own company and made a foray into movie production. In 1984, he developed a prime-time comedy flop for NBC, *The New Show*. But it was the "old show" that stayed in his mind: none of the projects he was involved with gave him the creative satisfaction or high-

The Canadian Sketch-Comedy Family Tree

Wayne and Shuster
Rosie Shuster (Frank's daughter)

Lorne Michaels
(married Rosie Shuster)

Second City, Toronto/*SCTV*	*Saturday Night Live*	*Kids In The Hall*
	(created by Lorne Michaels)	(produced by Lorne Michaels)
Dan Aykroyd	Dan Aykroyd	Dave Foley
Martin Short	Martin Short	Scott Thompson
Mike Myers	Mike Myers	Bruce McCulloch
John Candy	Bruce McCulloch (writer)	Mark McKinney
Rick Moranis	Mark McKinney	Kevin McDonald
Catherine O'Hara	Howard Shore (musical director)	
Andrea Martin	Paul Shaffer	
Joe Flaherty	Phil Hartman	
Dave Thomas	Norm MacDonald	
Eugene Levy	Rosie Shuster (writer)	
Harold Ramis	Tony Rosato	
Tony Rosato	Robin Duke	
Robin Duke	Anne Beatts (writer)	
	Norm Hiscock (writer)	

Saturday Night Live stalwarts Dan Aykroyd (in the seventies) and Mike Myers (in the eighties) both received formative training in live comedy at Second City, Toronto. However, neither of them appeared on *SCTV*. Martin Short, of course, excelled on *SCTV* before making the move to *SNL* for one banner season in 1984-1985. Lesser lights Tony Rosato and Robin Duke made the move from *SCTV* to *SNL* in 1981 but with far less impact than their Canuck compatriots.

Two of the Kids In the Hall, Mark McKinney and Bruce McCulloch, had brief stints writing for *Saturday Night Live* in the mid-eighties, before returning to Toronto and the rest of the Kids. After *Kids in the Hall* concluded its run on CBC in 1995, McKinney and McCulloch renewed their relationship with *SNL*. McKinney became a cast member and McCulloch contributed some short films.

profile media visibility he'd had with *SNL*.

So the timing was right when the president of NBC Entertainment, Brandon Tartikoff, came calling in 1985. He wanted Michaels to return to *SNL*, ostensibly to reinvent the show for a new generation of viewers. Michaels accepted the invitation and, for better or worse, he's been the show's executive producer ever since.

Curiously, while some of Michaels's original principles have faltered – the show is no longer fresh or even slightly subversive – his commitment to Canadian comedy has not. Which, one supposes, is a mixed blessing, because it means that as Michaels's original program vision has slipped from his grasp, and as *Saturday Night Live* has devolved into a sort of formula-sodden finishing school for future stars of dismal comedies – Dana Carvey, Adam Sandler, David Spade, Chris Farley – there have always been some Canadians stuck aboard this stubbornly unsinking ship.

In 1985, when he was hired back to run the show after a five-year absence, he brought Mark McKinney and Bruce McCulloch – two Kids in the Hall from Toronto, to act as writers. And a few years after that, he hired the comic who would do more to deliver the Canadian experience to the world than anyone since Wayne Gretzky moved to L.A. – a kid from

Scarborough, Ontario, named Mike Myers.

Like Aykroyd, Myers was a media-saturated immersion-therapy specialist: he had that Canadian talent to sink so far into an impersonation, all traces of the impersonator disappeared. Heck, it appeared something of a distinguishing comedic trait, something Martin Short – who spent an awesome season on *SNL* the year before Michaels returned – demonstrated, as have Rick Moranis, Dave Thomas, Catherine O'Hara and Jim Carrey.

Myers, who had written an essay on his national hero, Lorne Michaels, when he was an eighth-grader in Scarborough, had been seen performing by the *SNL* boss at Toronto's Second City, and joined the show in 1989. That season, he introduced his most popular character, the most purely Canadian comic character to go stateside since Bob and Doug McKenzie: Wayne Campbell, middle-class hoser deluxe, the rock & roll rec-room rodent whose universe of interests is divided equally between such cerebral pursuits as hockey, air guitar and babes. It turned out to be the most popular recurring sketch the show had introduced in years.

Today, despite Michaels's understandable claims that critics of the program are merely overburdened by nostalgia, *Saturday Night Live* is barely a faint echo of what it once was: you can't be fresh, vital and cocky when you're also a generation-old TV institution specializing in the assembly-line production of minor movie stars for bad comedies. But, difficult as it may be for anyone who's watched the show in recent years, one mustn't let its chronic latter-day doldrums detract too much from *Saturday*

Today, despite Michaels's understandable claims that critics of the program are merely overburdened by nostalgia, *Saturday Night Live* is barely a faint echo of what it once was.

Night Live's real and estimable achievements: it was the nexus of a movement in comedy that provided a link between *National Lampoon*, Second City, *SCTV*, *Animal House* and *Kids in the Hall*, and is thus a crucial event in understanding the entire development of contemporary popular comedy. Moreover, it could not have done so without the key contribution of the Canadian comedic sensibility: the perfect attitude for comedy in the post-television age. It is for these things that we feel it necessary to applaud the achievements of Forest Hill's former Lorne Lipowitz, for without him we would not be able to draw a straight line which connects Frank Shuster and *Kids in the Hall*, and which passes through just about every other major moment in Canadian comedy in the process.

Like Aykroyd, Myers was a media-saturated immersion-therapy specialist: he had that Canadian talent to sink so far into an impersonation, all traces of the impersonator disappeared.

Space Oddity How William Shatner Learned to Stop Worrying and Love the Future

William Shatner never chose to leave the role that made him instantly recognizable, according to one estimate, to one-quarter of the earth's population. On the contrary, he has clung to the polyester-sheathed character of Captain James Tiberius Kirk, captain of the Federation Starship Enterprise, with the clenched tenaciousness of the terrier he physically resembles, and he has snapped viciously when anyone has attempted to sever his connection to the man at the dramatic centre of the biggest cult phenomenon in TV history. Indeed, he has striven mightily to ensure that the association stuck faster than tar on hardwood: "Captain Kirk behaved as William Shatner would," he once said, "or how the ideal William Shatner would behave in the face of danger, love, passion, or a social situation." To *People* magazine in 1982, he characterized his function in the *Star Trek* phenomenon thusly: "I am the fulcrum."

To fully understand Shatner's death-lock on the character of Captain Kirk, we must go back to the immediate aftermath of *Star Trek*'s cancellation by NBC in 1969. But first let us venture even further, to get a sense of how an upper-middle-class, Anglo-Jewish kid from Montreal might find himself commanding the bridge of the most famous spaceship in pop-culture history.

William Shatner was born in 1931, the only son of a prosperous uniform manufacturer. By age six, his pronounced dramatic inclinations were already on display in summer-camp productions, and by eight he was playing Tom Sawyer as part of the Montreal Children's Theatre. In high school, he balanced dramatic with athletic pursuits, where his coiled wrestler's body came in handy, and was

nicknamed "Toughy." Unable to convince his parents of the legitimacy of a theatrical calling, he enrolled as a student of commerce at Montreal's McGill University, where his passion for acting very nearly ruined his academic standing. Finally mustering the courage to tell his father James he had no intention of taking over the family clothing business, the young Kirk-to-be received his first five-year mission. James Shatner told William that if he hadn't made it as an actor in the next half decade, he'd have to join the uniform biz.

After graduating in 1952, Shatner took a job managing a summer-stock company, where it soon became evident that his dramatic skills far exceeded his managerial ones. After spending a lonely year in Ottawa as part of the Canadian

Repertory Theatre, he was invited to take on juvenile roles at the newly established Stratford Shakespearean Festival in southwestern Ontario. Legend has it that it was there that Shatner's singular, staccato line-delivery style was born. The understudy to lead Christopher Plummer – with whom Shatner would be reunited for a shameless ham-off nearly 40 years later in *Star Trek VI: The Undiscovered Country* – in the young Montrealer's first roman-numeraled gig, *Henry V*, Shatner was asked to take over when Plummer was ill with kidney stones. The problem was, Shatner hadn't learned his lines yet, and his stammering, self-conscious attempts to remember them were apparently received as a bold and unorthodox dramatic departure. As one laudatory biographer put it: "It was the birth of a

Canadians In Space

"That's one small step for hosers, one giant leap for hoser-kind."

In the "real" world, Canada hasn't exactly made high-profile contributions to space exploration. After you mention the Canadarm, Roberta Bondar and Marc Garneau, the list of interstellar Canuck icons becomes as woeful as a California Golden Seals power play. But in the world of pop culture, Canadians absolutely dominate space… the final frontier. Herewith, the evidence.

William Shatner: Captain James T. Kirk, U.S.S. Enterprise (Star Trek)

James Doohan: Montgomery "Scotty" Scott, Chief Engineer, U.S.S. Enterprise (*Star Trek*)

Barry Morse: Professor Victor Bergman, Moonbase Alpha (*Space: 1999*), High Priest Shalith (*The Starlost*)

John Colicos: Commander Kor, first-ever Klingon (*Star Trek*), Baltar (*Battlestar Galactica*), Governor of Omicron (*The Starlost*)

Lorne Greene: Commander Adama (*Battlestar Galactica*)

Christopher Plummer: General Chang, Klingon Chief of Staff (*Star Trek VI*)

Kim Cattrall: Lieutenant Valeris (*Star Trek VI*)

Douglas Rain: Voice of the computer "HAL" (*2001: A Space Odyssey*)

Leslie Nielsen: Commander John J. Adams (*Forbidden Planet*)

Helen Shaver: Betty (*Starship Invasions*)

John Candy: Barf (*Spaceballs*)

Rick Moranis: Dark Helmet (*Spaceballs*)

Dan Aykroyd: Beldar Conehead (*The Coneheads*)

Robin Ward: Garth (*The Starlost*)

dramatic style that would become the actor's trademark." And. So. It. *Would*!

After playing 100 roles in 60 plays, he participated in the Stratford company's 1956 visit to Broadway, which marked his first appearance before American audiences. Returning to Canada that year, he wrote and performed for the CBC, and was given the Tyrone Guthrie Award for most promising actor.

Dozens of stage and television opportunities followed, leading to high-profile Broadway roles and eventually a Theatre World Award. Yet for all the stage and occasional film work he landed (in 1961, the 30-year-old appeared opposite Spencer Tracy, whom Shatner inadvertently insulted by praising the veteran's memorization skills, in *Judgment at Nuremberg*), it was on the small tube that Shatner would make his deepest impression. Nowhere more so, incidentally, than on such horror-and-suspense anthologies as *Alfred Hitchcock Presents, One Step Beyond, Thriller*, and, most famously, as the panic-stricken airline passenger on the same now-legendary episode of *The*

Twilight Zone ("Nightmare at 20,000 Feet"), parodied in 1995 by Jim Carrey in *Ace Ventura: When Nature Calls.*

On the big screen, he appeared as a southern racist in schlockmeister Roger Corman's ill-fated attempt at social commentary, *The Intruder* (1961), and even found himself playing the lead in *The Incubus* (1966), a project which would have otherwise been entirely forgotten were it not for the fact that the entire thing was shot in Esperanto. That's right: Es. Per. An. *To*!

Though initially wary of episodic TV's typecasting tendency – he turned down *Dr. Kildare* before Richard Chamberlain took it – in 1965 he accepted the lead role as a crusading assistant D.A. in the doomed and forgotten *For the People.* What doomed it, incidentally, was the time slot: Sunday nights opposite the mighty Lorne Greene vehicle *Bonanza.* By this time, disenchanted and rendered nearly destitute by the failure of his own production company, Shatner was entertaining the notion of abandoning acting altogether, when he was offered a crack at

one more pilot. It was called *Star Trek*.

As Gene Roddenberry's James T. Kirk, William Shatner was the embodiment of Kennedy-era sensitive macho: articulate, reasonable and commanding, but always game to buss an intergalactic babe or bust a Klingon jaw. If it was the role of a lifetime for Shatner, that was not his decision to make. Fans, and the particular properties of the television medium, would make it for him. A low-ratings earner from the getgo, *Star Trek* nevertheless began to build its unprecedentedly rabid fan-base almost instantly. It was organized fan pressure that convinced NBC to leave the show on for a third season, and it was eventually fan pressure that made William Shatner realize that, if there was anything worth clinging on to (so to speak) for a lifetime, it was the role of Jim Kirk.

It first hit him in New Jersey in 1970. After 79 episodes, *Star Trek* had been cancelled, and the combination of an expensive divorce and a residual-free contract with Paramount, which owned the series and Kirk, soon left the actor every bit as broke as he'd been when Roddenberry first called. By 1970, he was doing summer stock for money, but not enough money that he didn't have to cut costs by driving from job to job in a pickup with a camper shell on the back. As Shatner recalls it, he was asleep in the camper, when a six-year-old boy knocked on the door. The kid had seen the strange sleeping apparatus and wanted to ask the inhabitant of the camper if it was a spaceship. Imagine his surprise when Captain James T. Kirk of the Starship Enterprise came to the door. It was then that Shatner began to realize the extent to which *Star Trek*, which would soon run in syndication across the States and 100 other countries, had taken on a life of its own.

Throughout the seventies, as the *Star Trek* cult was going nova, Shatner watched from the sidelines, maintaining solvency by appearing in a thankless series of movies (*Want a Ride, Little Girl?*, *Big Bad Mama*, etc.), TV-movies (*Horror at 37,000 Feet*, *Pioneer Woman*, etc.), short-lived series (*Barbary Coast*, etc.), game shows (*Celebrity Bowling*, *Don Adams' Screen Test*, etc.) and commercial endorsements for things like grocery chains ("At Loblaws more than the price is right!"). Small wonder that the former Captain Kirk was not pleased to hear that Paramount had decided not to go ahead with the *Star Trek* movie the studio had originally announced in the wake of the blockbusting success of *Star Wars*. "I feel it was an idiotic decision by the people at Paramount," he told a reporter in 1977, adding, "Its blockage stands as one of the greatest monuments to stupidity."

Within two years, Shatner would get his chance to don Kirk's form-hugging uniform again. Paramount had finally been talked into a *Star Trek* movie. And this time, having got him back in his grip, Shatner knew better than to let Kirk go: he appeared in all of the first six *Star Trek* movies, directed one himself and was even written into the film *Star Trek: Generations*, which was nominally designed to kick off the movie franchise of *Star Trek's* equally successful TV successor, *The Next Generation*. Despite the fact that in that movie Kirk seems unambiguously to expire, Shatner warned a reporter from the *Globe and Mail* not to play taps yet: "With *Star Trek*, anything can happen." And so it does: he has so far published two volumes of *Star Trek* memoirs, and released audio- and videocassette versions of the books, as well; and his science fiction TV series *TekWar*, based on a continuing series of self-penned novels, seems phonetically calculated to evoke *Trek* associations. Call him Kirk? Whatever. Just don't call him forgotten.

Captain Kirk

Cover of *The Transformed Man*

Shatner Sings

1968. It was the year that Joni Mitchell released her first album and The Band recorded *Music From Big Pink*. But for thousands of Trekkers (the non-nerd designation for "Trekkies"), the most significant Canadian musical event of the year was *The Transformed Man* – the album that marked the "singing" debut of Canadian actor William Shatner.

Shatner has always been a Renaissance man: stage thespian at Stratford, TV movie actor, novelist and, more recently, getting in on the ground floor of CD-ROM technology. But the decision to record an album is the biggest misstep in his career: in fact, it's a testament to Shatner's immense staying power that his career survived *The Transformed Man*.

The album contains a truly bizarre mix of elements, with these highlights: a reading from Cyrano de Bergerac to the tune of "Lucy In The Sky With Diamonds"; a version of Bob Dylan's "Mr. Tambourine Man," which culminates in Shatner repeatedly screaming the song's title; a recitation of Hamlet's "To Be or Not to Be" soliloquy with instrumental accompaniment; and Captain Kirk's own version of "It Was A Very Good Year." *The Transformed Man* is a potent combination of Shatner's overacting and third-rate acid-drenched instrumentals. In ads for the album, Shatner himself said, "The thrill I got from making this album was deeper and more satisfying than anything I have ever experienced. I was really in orbit. I hope you will be also." Beam us up.

Back on Earth: Shatner on *Beat the Clock* →

"If you look at the American shows, you see that every situation comedy is made by a machine —
the Norman Lear machine, the Mary Tyler Moore machine, or whatever. The trouble was, we didn't have a machine. I
decided that what we needed was someone to build a home-made ice cream machine, no matter how small."

– JOHN HIRSCH, FORMER CBC DRAMA HEAD, ON COMMISSIONING *KING OF KENSINGTON* (1976)

No Joke The Canadian Sitcom Paradox

Few questions are more perpetually head-scratching than that of Canadian sitcoms. Specifically, why Canadians can't seem to make them. Or to be precise, make them well. Stated categorically: Canadians have created some of the most appalling situation comedy in the history of television.

Not that we haven't tried to succeed at the genre. Indeed, at one point or another, just about every Canadian network has taken a crack at the format, and for a reason that is anything but mysterious: in the U.S., the sitcom is a prime-time mainstay which, if successful, can generate millions of dollars year upon year. Understandably intoxicated by such a possibility, Canadians, heeding the siren song of the market, keep on trying, their heads turned bravely away from the smoldering heap of home-cooked stinkers stretching horizonward behind them.

As Canadians attempted to create that obscure object of prime-time desire, two significant revelations have emerged; first, that the very attempt at producing domestic sitcoms has resulted in some of the most wincingly embarrassing moments in our cultural history. Indeed, if you remember watching any of these shows – many of them so horrifically unforgettable that they have scarred your memory permanently – the mere invocation of their names will probably make you flinch: *The Trouble With Tracy*, *Check It Out!*, *Mosquito Lake*, *Flappers*, *Not My Department*, *Dog House* ... And so on, and so on, ad nauseam. The second commanding fact that staggers from the cultural wreckage of the Canadian sitcom is that of the dozens produced over the decades, only one qualifies as something even remotely resembling a success (for reasons we explore later in the chapter), and even it seems increasingly like a rule-proving fluke: the 1975-1980 CBC series *King of Kensington*.

← The cast of *Dog House*

So what gives here? As anyone who has been turning these pages knows by now, comedy is practically a late-century Canadian birthright: it is our most successful and influential pop-cultural export, and something which seems to come as effortlessly to Canadians as skating in circles clutching wooden sticks. While one might suggest that Canadian comedic abilities tend to express themselves largely in non-sitcom forms, such as sketch comedy or impersonation, even this only goes as far as the border, for the fact is, Canadians have made enormous contributions to American situation comedy once they've left their home and native land. Indeed, were it not for the contributions of Canadian directors, writers and producers, programs like *M*A*S*H* (Burt Metcalfe, producer), *Seinfeld* (Marjorie Gross, writer), *Fernwood 2-Night* (Alan Thicke, producer), *Mad About You* (David Steinberg, director), *Family Ties* (Katie Ford, writer), *The Partridge Family* (Bernard Slade, producer) or *Roseanne* (Pat Bullard, writer) might not have been the popular and/or critical hits they were.

Clearly, what makes the difference in the case of the Canadian sitcom is not a matter of sensibility or talent but – so to speak – situation. Under the proper conditions (that is, in the United States), Canadians have not only managed to create situation comedy, they have managed to do it exceedingly well. The difference, therefore, must have something to do with the border itself, and the fact that, in terms of television production, when one crosses it one finds oneself in a vastly different industrial context than the one left behind: like walking from the 7-Eleven

The very attempt at producing domestic sitcoms has resulted in some of the most wincingly embarrassing moments in our cultural history.

into Bloomingdale's. The risk of failure in the production of situation comedy is so high, and the costs so steep, a huge industrial apparatus is necessary to absorb both the exorbitant costs and the constant potential for failure. In the U.S., of the thousands of series treatments received and considered by networks annually, only around a hundred are produced as pilot episodes. Of these, only 40 or so are given a green light to go on the air as a series, and of these, fully half will be cancelled before seeing the end of the first season. It is, in other words, the TV equivalent of the Darwinian spectacle of thousands of newly hatched baby tortoises attempting to make it across the beach to the surf before being plucked into oblivion by hungry gulls – it takes a lot of tortoises to keep the species going, and only the very best of them make it all the way to the waves.

In Canada, there simply aren't enough baby tortoises for the species to thrive. Lacking the resources, skills and seemingly bottomless talent pool of the American television market, Canadian producers work with far less raw material at far greater risk: there aren't thousands of treatments to sift through, and few networks can actually afford to produce *three* pilots, let alone a hundred. Which means that the chances for just plain impossible sitcom ideas – the kind that

wouldn't have made it past the treatment point in the U.S. – to actually be produced, aired and then *scheduled* are almost infinitely higher in Canada than the U.S.

We cannot neglect that other mad scramble for survival, the one that lures most of our best sitcom-writing and producing talent to the States in the first place. Perhaps in this, more than any other aspect of Canadian-comedy production, most of our finest talent is either already gone or inevitably to go, creating a nasty little hamstringer of a catch for Canadian sitcom production: Canadian writers leave the country because there isn't enough work and money to go around here, and one of the reasons there isn't enough work and money here is that most of our writers have naturally made the mad dash to warmer surf. When one considers that there are no economic indications that things will improve anytime soon, it's small wonder the sitcom situation in Canada is, so speak, no laughing matter.

However, since the perpetrators of this volume cherish and respect the notion of constructive criticism, allow us to share an idea. How about a low-budget series, cost-efficiently set *and* shot in one of the countless empty offices in Toronto's vast CBC Broadcasting Centre, about the byzantine bureaucratic processes that got such Canadian stinkers on the air in the first place. Now, *that* would be funny. Or would it?

Now, plug your nose and prepare for the following page. What follows is an exceedingly rough ride in our selective guide to the worst Canadian sitcoms of all time.

We Were Not Amused The Canadian Sitcom Hall of Shame

Toby (CBC, 1968-1969)

Concept: This first-ever CBC sitcom immediately established the depressing standard for Canadian ineptitude in the genre. A cheap knock-off of the popular U.S. teen series *Gidget*, *Toby* was our very own bland middle-class comedy about a precocious teenage girl with understanding parents and a smart-ass younger brother. To give it that distinctly Canadian feel, the 15-year-old Toby (played by Susan Petrie) had a crush on a Quebec exchange student, J. J. Roberge (Robert Duparc). Like most comedies from that era, it had absolutely no social relevance. Writer Bill Lynn admitted, "We're trying to get laughs. Sure kids spend time talking about Vietnam and drugs and sex – we just don't write about those times."

Critical Evaluation: The show's producer, Gloria White, candidly evaluated CBC's first entry in the sitcom sweepstakes as follows: "It would probably be rejected by U.S. television. But that's okay, we're in Canada. And at least it's a start." Well, sort of. Unbelievably putrid and derivative, *Toby* barely managed to stay on the air for one season.

The Trouble With Tracy (CTV, 1970-1971)

Concept: A positively prehistoric throwback to *I Love Lucy* and *Blondie*, *The Trouble With Tracy* featured Diane Nyland as the ditzy title character and Steve Weston as Doug Young, her perpetually befuddled adman husband. Each episode revolved around one of Tracy's hare-brained schemes to make money or help her husband's career. In one particu-larly unenlightened plotline, Tracy hires herself out as a maid just to spite the penny-pinching Doug. Although the show's gender politics seemed to emanate from the forties, the cast contained a representative of the burgeoning counter-culture by featuring Tracy's lazy "hippie" brother, played by Franz Russell. Perhaps the embarrassing quality of *The Trouble With Tracy* shouldn't have been too surprising: it was Canada's first five-day-a-week sitcom, which meant that each half-hour episode was cranked out in a mere eight hours.

Critical Evaluation: "The show's biggest weakness is the gross miscasting of Diane Nyland as the featured and scatterbrained Tracy" (*Toronto Star*).

Delilah (CBC, 1973-1974)

Concept: The CBC press release for *Delilah* explained the show's premise this way: "Can a young, attractive city girl find true happiness as a… yes, a lady barber, in a small Ontario town?" This sitcom explored the answer to that burning question for one miserable season. Terry Tweed played Della, the haircuttin' "city girl" surrounded by the requisite cast of resident zanies and local yokels. Barbara Hamilton, an ubiquitous presence in Canadian sitcom dreck, played Della's scheming Aunt Peggy. Make no mistake, *Delilah* wasn't exactly *Sunshine Sketches of a Little Town*. The first episode of the series revolved around a plumber arriving to fix a plugged drain. Seriously.

Critical Evaluation: Delilah unleashed some of the most vitriolic criticism in CBC's history: "The season's most dismal failure" (*Toronto Star*); "It is not enough simply to dismiss it as awful" (*Toronto Sun*); "The show's characters are thin and artificial, the concept merely a skeleton without any innate comedy, and the scripts – the worst part of all – are merely static collections of tiresome gags" (*Globe and Mail*).

Custard Pie (CBC, 1977-1978)

Concept: A series about a fictional comedy troupe whose four members live together in a dingy boarding-house-cum-dance-studio. In that hackneyed American-sitcom tradition, each plotline revolved around their struggles to pay the rent: one week they performed at a bowling alley, the next they appeared on a telethon. This mediocre seventies entry lasted one season. Note: The series was originally created as a vehicle for Dave Thomas, Catherine O'Hara, Andrea Martin and Saul Rubinek. However, this talented group of actors wisely decided to bail from the show after realizing they'd have minimal creative control. CBC's loss, *SCTV*'s gain.

Critical Evaluation: "One of those hyperthyroid shows about four young people who do silly things that are supposed to be funny, always at the highest pitch of hysteria" (*Globe and Mail*); "The desperate punchiness doesn't make anyone look good" (*Canadian* magazine).

Flappers (CBC, 1978-1981)

Concept: *The Great Gatsby* meets Wayne and Shuster. Embarrassingly broad comedy set in a Montreal cabaret in 1927. As in most Canadian sitcoms, the charac-

The cast of *Custard Pie* →

ters were reduced to one-dimensional traits: the flirtatious cigarette girl, the domineering chef, the fumbling waiter. In one episode, a nightclub singer named Bunny got the mumps. Non-hilarity ensued.

Critical Evaluation: "*Flappers* isn't at all funny. The humour is infantile and the situations predictable. During a recent press screening in a room of more than 50 people, there was hardly one laugh during the whole half hour" (*Ottawa Citizen*).

Snow Job (CTV, 1983-1984)

Concept: Utterly insipid sitcom about the sexy goings-on at a posh ski resort north of Montreal. Featuring a horny ski instructor and a buxom, brainless chambermaid, the mindless *Snow Job* managed to make *Three's Company* look like *The Importance of Being Earnest*. In one particularly poignant episode, the ski instructor tried to seduce a voluptuous redhead, only to discover that "she" was actually an old hockey team-mate who'd had a sex change.

Critical Evaluation: "*Snow Job* proves once and for all we can leer, nudge, wink and chortle just like the Americans – and for only a fraction of the bucks" (*Starweek Magazine*).

Check It Out! (CTV, 1985-1988)

Concept: Don (*Get Smart*) Adams manages a supermarket. Yes, that was actually the premise of this sitcom, and if you'd always harboured a suspicion that grocery stores were intrinsically unfunny places, *Check It Out!* confirmed it. In addition to the Yankee has-been Adams, the cast featured Dinah (*Party Game*) Christie as the love interest, the omnipresent Barbara Hamilton as the pushy supermarket owner and a gaggle of allegedly eccentric bagboys, stock clerks and security guards.

Critical Evaluation: "Slapstick farce desiged for an international market" (*Maclean's*).

Not My Department (CBC, 1987)

Concept: A feeble Canuck attempt to ape the successful British sitcom *Yes, Minister*. *Not My Department* focused on the profoundly unfunny antics of a group of Ottawa civil servants and bureaucrats in the so-called Department of Regional Incentive Targets. The luckless Shelley Peterson (wife of then-premier of Ontario David Peterson) played an assistant deputy minister named Margaret.

Critical Evaluation: "A major misfire… A weekly nightmare" (*Toronto Star*); "A bland hash" (*Ottawa Citizen*). *Not My Department* set a record for the lowest audience-enjoyment index ever recorded by the CBC. Production was halted after 12 episodes. Less than two years later, in a gesture of stunning hubris, the Mother Corp. attempted yet another Ottawa bureaucratic comedy: the equally shameful *In Opposition*.

In Opposition (CBC, 1989)

Concept: A lame CBC attempt to create a Parliament Hill version of *The Mary Tyler Moore Show*. Kathleen Laskey starred as Karen Collier, a rookie MP from the fictional riding of Moncton Macquedewawa. Living alone in Ottawa, Karen struggles to cope with her bumbling party leader, a gossipy secretary and self-important party hacks. In the wild and wacky world of the federal bureaucracy, what was a girl to do?

Critical Evaluation: "The first episode of *In Opposition* is as bad a show that has ever run on Canadian TV" (*Toronto Star*); "A political sitcom without politics – or laughs. A sour sweat hangs over *In Opposition* like a fog: it smells like fear" (*Ottawa Citizen*). Viewers tuned out in droves: the show was cancelled after six episodes.

Mosquito Lake (CBC, 1989-1991)

Concept: An exceptionally idiotic sitcom that explored the vicissitudes of that quintessentially Canadian pastime, cottaging. Manic comedian Mike MacDonald starred in this dud about a math teacher who dragged his reluctant family up to their bug-infested summer homestead. How bad was *Mosquito Lake*? Well, one entire episode revolved around the death of the cottage's fridge.

Critical Evaluation: "A barrage of moronic plots, clichéd characters and cheap sets. *Mosquito Lake* may be the least innovative CBC sitcom ever, and its uneven humour fully lives up to inglorious CBC traditions. It combines the worst of TV past and present: puerile adults and smart-aleck kids" (*Ottawa Citizen*); "It's not good at all. It's not even funny" (*Toronto Star*).

Dog House (YTV, 1990-1992)

Concept: A talking dog lives in suburbia with a middle-class family. Cheesy U.S. sitcoms about talking cars (*My Mother The Car*) and talking horses (*Mr. Ed*) were popular in the sixties, but Canada didn't get its own entry in the genre until this patently lame effort. Digby was a kind of canine Don Rickles: a rather jaded, unpleasant St. Bernard who traded wisecracks with an unspeakably bland mom – played by Shelley (*Not My Department*) Peterson – and her sitcom kids.

Critical Evaluation: "As an actor he's nonpareil" (Roger Schumacher, the trainer of Bodie, the dog who portrayed Digby).

King of Kensington's Al Waxman and Fiona Reid

The People's Champion King of Kensington

A likeable, if lightweight, program about Larry King, a working-class urban Jewish mensch – played by Al Waxman – whose irrepressible decency dictates that his nose must be stuck in everybody's business, *King of Kensington* (CBC, 1975-1980) stands alone as the sole domestically produced sitcom that Canadians actually seemed to want to watch.

Drawing between 1.5 and 1.8 million viewers weekly, the show turned Waxman and Fiona Reid – who played King's WASPy wife, Cathy – into certifiable Canuck stars: a remarkable achievement when you consider the high mortality rate of our home-grown sitcoms and the fact that mere months before the show's debut, Waxman was directing Xaviera

Hollander (a.k.a. "The Happy Hooker") in a dismal, low-budget feature called *My Pleasure Is My Business*.

Although *King of Kensington*'s popular breakthrough was a refreshing surprise, it didn't mean that Canada was suddenly producing sitcoms of transcendent quality. Indeed, if anything, the show was strictly formulaic, shamelessly indulging in stock characters, predigested morals and hackneyed situations. In one episode, King actually found himself delivering a stranger's baby at a snowbound restaurant on Christmas Eve. Yeesh.

The success of *King of Kensington* may be as much the result of timing as anything else – certainly King's gentle liberalism, a reflection of Trudeau-era

multicultural policy, stood in stark Canuck contrast to the cranky intolerance of ratings-titan Archie Bunker. Moreover, *King* was a conspicuously Canadian sitcom, and therefore unique: if you watched *All in the Family*, you sure weren't going to hear references to Toronto's Kensington Market or corny schtick about finance minister John Turner's resignation.

Still, the reasons behind *King of Kensington*'s long run are ultimately less compelling than the sad fact that its popularity has never been duplicated: 20 years later, it's the single blip on the flatline of Canuck sitcom failure.

> **"Can Canadians really believe, for instance, that a Lorne Greene or somebody – Hank Snow in the country field – feels as much about this country as somebody that stays here? I don't think so."**
>
> – STOMPIN' TOM CONNORS

Sturm und Twang **Stompin' Tom Connors**

In the late 1980s, at an undisclosed rural hideaway in remotest Southwestern Ontario, it occurred to Stompin' Tom Connors that he could resist the alarm call of national duty no more. Unitywise, the country was in shoddier shape than ever, and there wasn't anybody out there to hold it together the way Tom, and maybe only Tom, could – with a guitar, a song and a sturdy piece of plywood to stomp the bejeesus out of while singing stuff like: *The girls are out to bingo/And the boys are getting stink-o/And we'll think no more of Inco/On a Sudbury Saturday night!* Of course, no one else could campaign for national unity with quite the eccentric-troubadour flare of Stompin' Tom, but the fact remained that Connors had been in a state of self-imposed exile for a decade. In 1978, fed up with the frittering away of Canadian awards on what he called "border jumpers," Connors – like the hoser equivalent of Dirty Harry throwing away his badge – gave back all his Juno awards to the Canadian Academy of Recording Arts and Sciences and turned his back on a $100,000-a-year career.

A veteran of thousands of gigs, Connors was a wily student of tavern *realpolitik*: he knew a sure-fire way to win an audience over was to sing a song about where he was, and he wasn't afraid to wax hokey and ask folks to shake hands and say, "How's it goin'?" to neighbouring drinkers. He also made it policy that autographs were to be signed after every performance, and that everyone who wanted an autograph got one, no matter how long it kept the singer himself from throwing his size 12 boots on a nearby table and knocking back a few cool ones. And boy, you better believe it paid off. His distinct, if eccentric, brand of plain-speaking, hard-rhyming, East Coast blue-collar-cowboy nationalism had won him a fervent following in bars, lounges, concert halls and fair-grounds across the country, and all this in the virtual absence of airplay.

Radio, you see, had never known quite how to "format" Tom, which is understandable insofar as the guy is plainly unformattable: how many hard-core nationalist singing cowboys from New Brunswick can a playlist fit? None apparently, and that's no small part of the reason that Tom felt compelled to give back his pickup-full of Junos and hang up the plywood in protest. (His last live show before the self-imposed exile was in Alberta in 1976). There he was, working single-handedly to hold the country together with naught more than a rhyme, a stomp and a cold bottle of Blue, and he wasn't getting any respect. That's why one of the most singular figures in the history of Canadian popular culture – a man who combined the tireless grassroots itinerancy of Woody Guthrie with the belligerent knee-jerk nationalism of a hoser Merle Haggard – decided to stomp on out the door for a spell. And out he stayed, until he heard the call.

The exile – which caught much press attention but did little to trip those border jumpers – was only supposed to last a year but, once Connors retreated with his wife, Lena (whom he'd married in 1973 in a ceremony televised on CBC-TV's *Elwood Glover's Luncheon Date*), to the undisclosed rural retreat some claim is pretty near Guelph, Ontario, he found himself in no hurry to lay down the plywood and resume stompin' in any big hurry. After all, he had by that time already attained a genuinely remarkable degree of "distinctly Canadian" success:

Tom and Lena's wedding photo

Stompin'

"Canada is cordially invited . . ."
Stompin' Tom Gets Married on CBC-TV

Date: Friday, November 2, 1973
Time: 1:00 p.m. (EDT)
Bride: Lena Kathleen Joyce Welsh
Groom: Tom Connors
Where: Four Seasons Hotel, Toronto, Ontario
Show: *Elwood Glover's Luncheon Date*

The CBC press release from October 1973 promoted it this way: "Stompin' Tom isn't the first man to wed on national television, and he probably won't be the last. But, he is the first on Canadian television, and that makes this wedding very special. For the viewers at home no invitation is necessary. Just a simple setting of the dial and they can become a part of Canada's first nationally televised wedding."

To come to terms with this seismic Canuck pop-culture event, it's helpful to compare it to another TV wedding from the same era, the American wedding that the CBC press release is probably alluding to: in 1969, Tiny Tim got hitched to his substantially younger paramour, Miss Vicki, on Johnny Carson's *Tonight Show*.

Of course, this being Canada, the *Luncheon Date* wedding was vastly different. The host's daily lunchtime talk show was, in fact, the spiritual opposite of Carson's fast-paced Burbank schmoozefest. Even when the CBC started broadcasting in colour, the bland Glover always seemed to be in black and white. In fact, the host was so worried about the logistics of the event, he initially tried to dissuade the young couple from getting married on his show. But Stompin' Tom understood McLuhan's notion of the global village: the heart-on-sleeve patriot was extremely keen to have his extended family of Canadians attend his wedding over the public airwaves. Ultimately, the whole thing went off without a hitch, and in a 1975 memoir called, appropriately enough, *Elwood Glover's Luncheon Dates*, the host revealed that the Stompin' Tom/Lena matrimonial episode elicited the greatest viewer response in the show's history. Postscript: Stompin' Tom and Lena, happily married with one son, are approaching their 25th anniversary. Tiny Tim and Miss Vicki started divorce proceedings in 1972. Elwood Glover died in 1990.

hundreds upon hundreds of songs written, hundreds of thousands of albums sold, a TV series called *Stompin' Tom's Canada* and a couple of concert movies, and a touring schedule which would make even Rush wheeze.

There's no questioning the sincerity of Stompin' Tom's fundamentalist Canadian nationalism. As corny as it sounds, the country is his extended family. This is no opportunistic career-niche marketing: Stompin' Tom Connors is the honest-to-god real thing. Cut him and the sap runs. Prior to his return to the business in 1988, little was known about the past of the man who, according to some sources, had written a thousand songs while still in his teens but lost them on the road. (If you find them, incidentally, call us and we'll pass them on. Heh, heh.) Since the comeback, which has only broadened the singer's constituency to include a generation of fans who were still memorizing provincial capitals when he retired, much more of Tom's past has been permitted into the spotlight than before.

As he revealed in painstaking, frank detail (over 500 pages' worth) in a first volume of memoirs called *Before the Fame* (1995), Connors certainly knows of the working-class struggles of which he sings. Born in 1936 in Saint John, New Brunswick, to an unwed teenage mother who was eventually jailed for theft, Connors endured mental and physical abuse in an orphanage, followed by a cold, impersonal foster home, until the age of 13. That's when he ran away to get by any way he could: working on docks, thumbing rides, digging graves, taking advantage of the opportunity of the free nocturnal accommodation offered by jails. All the while, like the young Woody Guthrie, he studied,

wrote and then sang about the underclass folk he came across while wandering penniless from one end of this country to the other. As he told the *Toronto Star* in 1990: "I came into this damn business with patches on my pants. I know what it feels to be down below because I'm coming from nowhere, I'm coming from under park benches."

Connors began writing songs at age 11 but didn't make a full-time career out of singing until the now-legendary moment in 1964 he, at 28, wandered thirsty into the Maple Leaf Hotel in Timmins, Ontario, short the 40 cents for a glass of beer. (It would seem to this day that Tom, hoserdom's patron troubadour, loves his beer as much as his country.) Seeing the young man's guitar, the bartender asked Tom to sing for a drink, and the legend of Stompin' Tom Connors was officially under way.

The stompin', like the Connors mythos itself, has its origins in poverty: too poor for percussion, yet needing to hold the

attention of rowdy taverngoers, Tom took to stomping his left foot during up-tempo numbers. When one owner pointed out that Tom was stompin' his way through the wooden stage floor, the singer went to Beaver Lumber for the first of countless pieces of plywood he would use as his "stompin' board." A lot of stages were preserved that way. Touring and writing with breathtaking endurance, Connors, with little radio support, slowly built one of the most avid followings of any performer in the country's history: by the mid-1970s, he had a national fan base, his own recording label, more than two dozen albums (including two – two! – five-disc sets), a popular CBC-TV show, more awards than the country has provinces, and his own record label. And, to cop a phrase from border jumper Paul Anka, Connors had done it all his way.

He tanked it his way, too. Infuriated by what he perceived as the Canadian industry's inclination to reward people who'd done it the easy way (i.e., the American Way), he stomped away from it all in the late seventies, leaving nothing but a small pile of sawdust where once a legend had been. And gone he was. Until, that is, the calls started coming, the ones Tom could no longer ignore. He'd heard the call on CBC-Radio's *Morningside* before: on several occasions, Peter Gzowski's nation-binding voice had wondered what the hell had ever happened to Stompin' Tom Connors, and whether he'd come back to help his nation in this moment of supreme fractiousness and need. (It was kind of like one old gunslinger calling another out of retirement for a showdown with an old foe.) Tom had so far ignored the call,

He stomped away from it all in the late seventies, leaving nothing but a small pile of sawdust where once a legend had been.

despite the fact that, by his own admission, his boycott hadn't stemmed the southward lemming-flow much. He had also ignored the attempts to draw him back into the spotlight by Dan Aykroyd: a border jumper, to be sure, but a hoser nationalist and a major Tom fan. But then came the fulsome praise of another "border jumper," singer k. d. lang. She cited Tom's inspirational influence on her in both a Gzowski interview and a Juno Award acceptance speech. Not long after, EMI/Capitol Records re-released Connors's back catalogue, and the old albums sold as briskly as P.E.I. spuds. Finally, it happened. In 1988 Connors dusted off guitar, hat and plywood and wandered back into the heart of Canadian nationalism.

By the time of his return, Tom had become a larger-than-life symbol of messianic, balls-to-the-wall Canadianism. In downtown Toronto, Sam the Record Man promoted Tom's comeback album, *Fiddle and Song*, with an immense, mock-heroic wall mural which made the singer look like a pumped-up combination of Johnny Canuck, Quick Draw McGraw and Paul Bunyan. Legions of new Tom fans sprung up everywhere, and Connors himself took to the beefed-up

Tom had become a larger-than-life symbol of messianic, balls-to-the-wall Canadianism.

notoriety like a boxer – a boxer with maple leaves on his shorts – basking in pre-bout glory. Asked to contribute an essay on Canadian unity for a pre-referendum, anti-separatist publication called, inevitably, *If You Love This Country*, Tom weighed in with some of his most fulsomely patriotic sentiments yet.

Clearly, to Tom the threat of separatism was like a line drawn in the snow, and he made it abundantly clear in the essay that he was prepared to do whatever it took – *whatever it took* – to keep this nation together: "Why don't he (former Quebec premier Jacques Parizeau) and the rest of his separatist pals move to some other country like the former Yugoslavia, where everybody believes in separatism," growled Tom before evoking this chilling martial image as the likely aftermath of separation: "And of course, their own armed forces would be standing by to crush anybody foolhardy enough to revolt or rebel." Later in the essay, you could be forgiven for thinking Tom had traded in the plywood for the

evangelist's pulpit: "If this land is worth the blood and the death of even one French-Canadian soldier," he intones gravely, "it's at least got to be worth all the courage we can muster up to defeat this cancer called separatism." Before stepping down, Tom leaves separatist-sympathetic Quebeckers with this piece of diplomatically impeccable advice: "Get the hell off your ass and out of your backyards, and instead of flying to Florida to see palm trees, go to the west coast of Canada where the grass is green all winter."

Tom, of course, *would* advocate intraprovincial Canadian travel as the ultimate potent antidote to secessionary impulses. Not only has he learned to love the country by getting to know it from the underside of a park bench up, he believes that things change, and change profoundly, when Canadians jump that border: you lose something, become something different when you pass Customs. Shit, in Canada, Stompin' Tom Connors is nothing less than a precious national resource, the larger-than-life maritime cowboy of Canadian nationalism. And that's why he'll never go south.

Keep it Canadian Essential Stompin' Tom Tunes

1. "Bud the Spud" The agricultural hit that catapulted Connors into the Canadian imagination, and established three important patterns in his career: his ability to craft catchy melodies, his unwavering faith in the Canadian working class and his lyrical fixation on vegetables.

2. "Margo's Cargo" A sublimely strange narrative, in which Newfoundland couple Margo and Reg purchase a clock made out of varnished cow dung at a posh downtown Toronto department store. They then hatch a plan to get rich quick by supplying the store with raw materials to make more of these clocks: Margo and Reg load their cow into their truck, drive to Toronto and dump a steaming load of bovine shit in front of the store. One of Tom's most popular songs, probably because so many Hogtown-hating Canadians love the idea of dumping cow dung at the corner of Queen and Yonge.

3. "Sudbury Saturday Night" Playing bingo, gettin' stinko, forgetting Inco. A deliriously energetic ode to the joy of partying after an honest week's work in Nickel City.

4. "Big Joe Mufferaw" Tom tackles the historical legend of the baddest dude in the Ottawa Valley, a hoser outdoorsman who probably could have whipped Paul Bunyan's ass.

5. "Lady k. d. lang" Although lang doesn't exactly jump around like a "rangy-tang" anymore, she was absolutely thrilled by this musical tribute. Tom continued his tradition of championing certain Canadian performers, including Don Messer and Rita MacNeil.

6. "The Ketchup Song" Once again Tom turns to his vegetable/condiment muse, this time to deal with a love affair between a Leamington, Ontario, tomato, and a guy from Prince Edward Island called "Potato." Chorus contains the observation, "Ketchup loves potatoes."

7. "To It And At It" Tom demonstrates his verbal dexterity with some word-play so fast-paced and agile, it would leave most rappers gasping for air.

8. "Canada Day, Up Canada Way" Obviously not distressed by the loss of the term "Dominion Day," Stompin' Tom encourages all Canadians (as he does in every song) to celebrate Canada.

Go Boom Fall Down
The Tax-Shelter Film Follies

In 1979, a record 66 feature films were made in Canada with the benefit of government support. *Sixty-six.* Bear in mind that a scant five years earlier, that number was three (!) and that in per capita terms this meant that Canada, a country with one-tenth the population of the U.S., had outstripped Hollywood's rate of production, if only for one year, by a staggering 50 percent. If these statistics tax one's credibility, they should, because you probably didn't see any of the films (most of them were never deemed of sufficient quality to be released), nor would your memory likely be jarred by the invocation of some of that stellar year's titles. Anybody remember *Meat the Cleaver*? *Crunch*? How about *Under the Cover Cops*? Oh, come on, certainly you've seen *Read On*? *Hog Wild*? Not even *Mondo Strip*? Really?

Nineteen seventy-nine was the peak year of a period in Canadian movie production variously characterized as the Tax Shelter Boom, the Capital Cost Allowance Era and, possibly most poignantly, the time of Hollywood North. Whatever you call it, it is a cautionary tale of distinctly Canadian dimensions. From that vaguely satanic 66 peak, the number would plummet significantly after two years (less than half that by 1983), once the industry and the government that supported it realized that the annual production of dozens of films that no one wanted to release, let alone watch, could hardly be pointed to as a source of cultural health or pride.

As much as one might be inclined to bury the period's memory in much the same manner as the period buried the movies it produced, the national folly that was Hollywood North cannot be

forgotten, and for these reasons: first, because it reveals much about the inevitable schizophrenia that grips a country trying to produce commercial culture according to bureaucratic blueprints; second, because it stands as a particularly abject example of what tends to happen when Canadians attempt to be just like Americans, except without the history, money, population, promotional savvy or market base; and third, because it is a national farce of truly riveting dimensions. While it's fitting that the period almost inspired a movie of its own – called *Hollywood North* – it's even more fitting that the script was never actually produced.

To understand how it happened, one must recognize the historically dependent relationship Canadian movies have always had to forms of public support.

Ever since the national movie marketplace was largely consumed by American interests early in the century, thus laying the groundwork for the development of Hollywood's most lucrative out-of-country market, the only way Canadians could indulge the enormously expensive practice of making moving images was by begging government for money to do it. Indeed, there may be no more important fact in the history of Canadian moviemaking than this. It is what has made the greatest achievements in the national cinema possible – from Norman McLaren to Atom Egoyan, from animation to documentary, from Ivan Reitman to David Cronenberg, all that is noteworthy about Canadian movies was made possible through some form of government intervention in the industry. On the other hand, not only do governments (and

Canada's top box-office export: *Porky's*

government film policies) change like intemperate weather, they have proven notoriously reluctant to do anything that might upset the Washington-backed mega-industry to the south. If anything explains the frequent flights from reason taken by subsequent national film policies, it's this contradictory impulse to promote our own culture while not impeding that of the big guy to the south. Thus the fact that less than three percent of the national screen time in Canada is given over to Canadian movies. Thus the history of talented Canadian film-makers who have had to move elsewhere to make movies. Thus Hollywood North.

The story of the tax-shelter boom really begins with the opening of the doors of the Canadian Film Development Corporation (CFDC,

renamed Telefilm Canada) in 1967. The result of four decades of lobbying for some kind of government support to private-sector feature production, the founding of the CFDC is widely considered to represent the beginning of the feature industry in Canada. The problem was, the process of funding always took place in a supply-and-demand vacuum; that is, the CFDC could help get movies made, but it could – or would – do little to get them into more Canadian theatres. And every time someone suggested it ought to do so, through the introduction of policies that friends of Hollywood still like to demonize as "protectionism," the notion was usually beaten flatter than a seal pup on an ice floe.

By the early seventies, the government agency was, as ever, seeking ways to boost private-sector film investment and produc-

tion without disturbing the status quo. That's when someone suggested tax shelters: the dubious practice of offering tax write-offs for investments in productions the government would designate as "certifiably Canadian." The shelter was called the Capital Cost Allowance, and its early results were sluggish. However, things tended to pick up as the government raised the ceiling on the shelter, finally offering a full 100 percent write-off for investors in movies meeting a bureaucratic checklist of Canadian ingredients. This is when things started to go boom.

Attracted by the low-risk investment shelter, a veritable stampede of investors started forklifting money into Canadian production: between 1974 and 1978, the number of certified Canadian productions assisted by the government rose from three to 37. The problem was,

Recommended Viewing:

(Authors' note: The only task more difficult than finding two recommendable tax-shelter movies was keeping the list of lousy ones down to the same number.)

The Silent Partner (Daryl Duke, 1978) Crisply written, expertly executed little *noir* set in the newly opened Toronto Eaton Centre, involving a bloody cat-and-mouse game between a cynically ambitious bank teller (Elliott Gould) and the psychopathic thief (Christopher Plummer) he unwisely rips off. The all too rare, rule-proving exception of those dark ages: if more tax-shelter movies were as good as this – even on its modest commercial terms – the whole system might have been redeemed. Alas, most simply weren't.

Atlantic City (Louis Malle, 1980) Like *The Silent Partner*, *Atlantic City* is a loser's-eye account of greed's grim toll – as apt a metaphor for the entire Canadian tax-shelter episode as you're likely to find. The story of an unlikely couple – aspiring casino croupier Susan Sarandon and aging mob bagman Burt Lancaster – brought together by a botched dope deal, Louis Malle's bitter lowlife comedy is recommended for another reason beyond sheer quality: it features the entertainingly immodest Canadian broadcasting mogul Moses Znaimer as a despicably oily gunsel.

Risky Viewing:

Your Ticket is No Longer Valid (George Kaczender, 1979) An entire feature film about aging tycoon Richard Harris's chronically flaccid penis. Somewhere, sometime, someone actually thought this was a movie that needed to be made. Limp, limp, limp.

Phobia (John Huston, 1980) It speaks something of the sheer toxicity of the tax-shelter system that one of America's most distinguished and distinctive directors – John Huston, of *Maltese Falcon* fame – could produce the worst movie of a half-century career working within it. Nominally a thriller, but actually a tragic farce.

investments were (as they tend to be, Virginia) as often dictated by greed, opportunism and cynicism as they were a passionate commitment to the development of a distinct and vibrant Canadian film industry.

A host of producers from around the world flocked to Canada to cash in on the bonanza by making movies that were Canadian only in the checklist sense. As they were usually the result of doctors, lawyers, dentists and other upper-income professionals less concerned with art than a tax dodge, a number of commercially, not to mention culturally, hopeless productions were rushed into production which otherwise would rightly never have seen the light of script development. ("*Meat the Cleaver*? No prob: roll 'em!") Moreover, since the point-system process necessary to certify a production as Canadian was about as simple as astrophysics, a huge proportion of the budgets were sucked up by the various brokers, agents, lawyers and dealmakers who assembled packages for a living.

Sensitive to the enormous public expense of the tax-shelter production enterprise, while at the same time hamstrung when it came to doing anything about a commercial marketplace happily screening Hollywood movies for contented Canadian audiences, the CFDC started to invoke concepts like star systems, universal appeal and commercial competition as the justification for its if-you-can't-beat-'em-join-'em policies. The reasoning was as simple as it was mistaken: if we couldn't get our Distinctly Canadian movies into the marketplace, we'd make the kind of expensive, slick, culturally defoliated movies that would bring the marketplace to us. Of such logic

was the yellow brick road to a vibrant national film industry theoretically paved.

To counter this rising cost of tax-shelter productions, producers, with the full endorsement of the CFDC, sought to make movies they thought would be sure-fire bets on the international marketplace. In many cases, this meant churning out movies that were paler-than-pale imitations of whatever genre – slasher films, science-fiction fantasy, disco – was hot at the moment. It meant a lot of Canadian-made movies pretending to take place in other, more universally appealing (read "American") places than Toronto or Vancouver, but it also meant making movies with stars who had international appeal. This was a tricky one, as no one making movies in Canada could really afford stars with international appeal (and especially not if lawyers and investment brokers had already made off with a major chunk of one's budget); much dimmer celestial entities would have to do.

To look down the cast lists for Hollywood North productions is to glimpse a roll call of the once-weres, might-have-beens and whatever-happened-tos of American movies and TV: James Coburn, Richard Burton, John Cassavetes, Lee Majors, Elliott Gould, Suzanne Somers, Robert Mitchum, Karen Black, Tatum O'Neal, Sally Kellerman, Bruce Dern – all worked in Hollywood North at least once, none in anything that turns up prominently on their résumés.

Tax-shelter productions also meant the virtual strangulation of the once-vibrant Quebec industry, as the language of universal appeal is English, not French. If many of the province's most gifted film-makers, like Jean Pierre Lefebvre, Gilles Carle and Denys Arcand, simply went

Tatum O'Neal and Richard Burton emoting in *Circle of Two*

without work, others, like Claude Jutra, went to English Canada to make movies, with disastrous results. Needless to say, it was not a moment likely to fill the heart with national pride.

In retrospect, the tax-shelter system was not without its benefits. The fact is, the careers of David Cronenberg and Ivan Reitman were kick-started by the tax-shelter-production boom, and the sheer volume of movies made transformed Canada from a production backwater to a seasoned pro almost overnight. Some of the country's most successful export items, like 1979's *Meatballs* and 1981's *Porky's*, were tax-shelter productions, and people like Dan Aykroyd, Saul Rubinek, John Candy, Andrea Martin and Bill Murray all got their movie starts in Hollywood North productions. Moreover, the rare good

To look down the cast lists for Hollywood North productions is to glimpse a roll call of the once-weres, might-have-beens and whatever-happened-tos of American movies and TV.

tax-shelter movie did actually come along, like Bob Clark's *Black Christmas*, Daryl Duke's *The Silent Partner* and Louis Malle's *Atlantic City*. Not to mention all those great made-in-Canada George Kennedy movies.

By the early eighties, recognizing that it had helped make an international joke of the national film industry by facilitating the production of hundreds of lousy schlock movies, the government drasti-

cally reduced the tax shelter. The intention was to discourage what few investors hadn't already flocked elsewhere for fear of catching the stink of too many unreleased clinkers. People like Lee Majors, who even had a widely publicized fling with Canadian prima ballerina Karen Kain while filming some forgotten epic in Toronto, were returned to the televisual semi-obscurity from whence they came, and it was business as usual in over 90 percent of Canadian movie theatres, where American movies played to eager Canadian audiences who continued to live quite happily with the real thing, and without Canadian movies, Hollywood-slick or otherwise. Like a dream that fades with wakening, the false glitter of Hollywood North retreated to one of the darker corners of national memory.

A Piece of the Pie
The Triumph of Trivial Pursuit

Canada is a largely middle-class country full of people with time and change to spare in equal amounts: a country of avid golfers and cottagegoers, home to world-class consumers of movies and telecommunications technology and birthplace of a song performed by the gone, but nearly forgotten, Loverboy, called "Working For the Weekend."

Like so much Canadian pop culture, the story of the Canuck-born board game Trivial Pursuit begins with a surplus of spare time and a keen will to fill it. Not with something constructive, mind you. That might intrude upon the fiercely coveted Canadian notion of leisure time – the abiding national desire, as professional dumb Canuck Leslie Nielsen once expressed it, to "just loaf." Nope, Trivial Pursuit was created to enhance the pleasure of loafing, but god forbid without crossing the line between loafing and actual exertion. That said, Trivial Pursuit also began with something else which must be heeded for its influence on the national cultural temper: a small but utterly distinctive sound – the satisfying, gassy snap of a cool one being cracked open on a dull afternoon.

Which is where our story begins, on a miserable December day in Montreal in 1979. Chris Haney and Scott Abbott, friends, sports fans and fellow foot soldiers in the journalism trade, were "just loafing" in the way they favoured under the climatic circumstances: with a game of Scrabble and a few midday brews in Haney's kitchen. To beef up the suspense, the two had agreed on a best-of-seven championship with stakes set at a lofty $100 a game. Haney, a photo editor with the *Montreal Gazette*, noticed that his well-used game of Scrabble was missing a few pieces, rendering it pretty well useless.

Braving the elements and bolstered by the beer, Haney went out to buy a new game. When he returned, he threw it on the table in front of Abbott, a Canadian Press sports writer. The game cost $16, roughly the price of a twenty-four (or, in hoser-speak, "a two-four") pack in those days. "There must be a lot of money in games," Haney said, pointing at the box. Abbott agreed. That's when they decided to invent their own game and, as marketing legend has it, laid the groundwork for the game-industry neutron bomb called Trivial Pursuit in 40 minutes.

As guy's-guy baby boomers and infor-mation-industry workers, Haney and Abbott had a keen, overdeveloped interest in facts for facts' sake. Not the kind of stuff that enriches one's experience on earth, but the kind that enhances one's time spent loafing: sports scores, pop charts, prime-time TV schedules, news factoids – stuff like that. The shared media experience, in other words, which had become the defining currency of the postwar coming-of-age ritual, and the perfect intellectual snack food for minds semi-clouded by brew. How about a game that simply formalized what so many people they knew liked to do any-

way, that being to kill some of that loaf time by testing each other's knowledge of utterly useless information? That's how "Trivia Pursuit" started. It died shortly thereafter when Haney's wife suggested the name lacked a little something, and that "*Trivial* Pursuit" was better. *That's* how Trivial Pursuit was born.

The rest of the story became the stuff of up-from-nowhere entrepreneurial lore: how Haney and Abbott recruited two former hockey players to help invest in their idea – Haney's lookalike brother, John, and lawyer buddy Ed Werner; how Haney and Abbott used their press credentials to crash toy-industry conventions and grill experts on strategy; how the first edition's 6,000 questions were dreamed up during a sun-soaked

retreat to Spain; how the boys managed to make filthy-rich shareholders out of a few dozen friends by getting them to kick $1,000 each into the fledgling enterprise; the case of Carlsberg that accompanied the boys from pitch session to pitch session; and of course, the success–success beyond any loafer's most beer-fogged dreams: the tripling of the game industry's total take because of Trivial Pursuit sales alone; the one *billion* dollars in retail business generated by the game in the peak year of 1984, when 20 million copies were sold in the United States (in its best year ever, Scrabble sold three million copies); the 60 million copies sold by the mid-nineties. The most popular board game in the world, accounting for almost 40 percent of the

adult board-game market – a market which didn't exist before T.P. came along – and all because of the mighty Canuck B & B factor: Beer and Boredom.

Today, Haney and Abbott, beer-bonded multimillionaire adult-toy tycoons, continue their pursuit of the perfect loaf. Having turned in their press badges years ago, they've invested much of their genuinely jaw-dropping fortunes in bigger and bigger boomer playpens: two multi-million-dollar Toronto area golf courses, a Junior A hockey team and the racehorse farm whose luckiest product was a beast aptly named for the brown elixir of fortune itself, Charlie Barley. Needless to say, they're living the ultimate hoser dream: the permanent weekend, the ultimate loaf and the bottomless bottle of beer.

Rolling The Dice Canada's Other World Beaters

In the wake of Trivial Pursuit's unprecedented success, scads of would-be board-game inventors came crawling out of the woodwork. Having seen interviews with the Trivial Pursuit creators, these wannabes figured that it couldn't be too difficult to create another game that would garner millions. Of course, none of their mid-eighties efforts matched Trivial Pursuit's celestial sales figures. That said, those games that came closest to matching Trivial Pursuit's success were invented by – no surprise here – other Canucks. Yes, Canada is a board-game superpower. It must be all those hours we leisure-loving souls spend in cottages and rec rooms: we're definitely world-class when it comes to inventing best-selling ways to kill time. For your reference, here's a list of games invented in the wake of Trivial Pursuit:

Balderdash: Invented in Toronto by Paul Toyne and Laura Robinson, this is essentially a board version of the old "dictionary" game. Billed as "the hilarious bluffing game," Balderdash players win points for conjuring up credible definitions of obscure words. Since coming on

the market in 1984, the game has been successful as far afield as Germany, Saudi Arabia and New Zealand.

MindTrap: In 1983, Richard Fast decided he wanted to devise a board game that re-created the "whodunnit" appeal of an Agatha Christie novel. Joining forces with artist Garnett Plum and lawyer Tibor Sarai, the Kingston, Ontario, native came up with MindTrap, a game that challenges players with murder mystery scenarios and mind-bending puzzles. Released in the fall of 1991, it has sold 1.5 million copies and been translated into 12 languages.

Pictionary: In 1981, Vancouver native Rob Angel was living in Spokane, Washington. He jotted down some rudimentary ideas for a game that combined charades with drawing pictures, but never developed the concept. A couple of

years later, Angel was waiting tables in a Seattle restaurant. When Trivial Pursuit went nova, he decided to resurrect his idea. Pictionary was launched in Seattle in 1985, and has sold an astounding 35 million copies in North America.

Scruples: Invented in 1984 by Henry Makow, a part-time English professor from Winnipeg. Makow was researching an article on baby-boomer morality when he decided to come up with a board game based on ethical conundrums. Scruples poses tricky questions like "You're buying a house from an old lady, and she's asking too little. Do you tell her?" The game that keeps countless players arguing (six and a half million copies sold) has enabled Makow to retire from teaching.

From The Hip Pierre Trudeau's Rule of Cool

As an iconographically loaded image, Canada couldn't have asked for a more potent one than Pierre Trudeau as he floated through the mist in a canoe, gliding like a phantom across the glassy surface of a northern lake, resplendently adorned in fringed buckskin, his chiselled features as inscrutably handsome at 73 years as they were at 40. Collectively, a riveted nation gasped. The greatest media star it had ever produced was back, leaving Canadians with no choice but to do what we'd always done when the effortlessly charismatic Pierre Trudeau deigned to cross our perceptual field: just watch him.

Even more remarkable than the image was the historical context in which it loomed. The year was 1993, nearly a decade after the generation-spanning Trudeau era had ended, and nearly three decades since Lester Pearson's dashing and quicksilver-smart young minister of justice had first begun to turn the national head. The context was nothing short of what would turn out to be one of the most revealing domestic popcult phenomena of recent memory: the long-anticipated publication of Trudeau's *Memoirs*, an event that was carefully timed to correspond with the equally anticipated CBC documentary miniseries of the same name. The dreamy, *coureur-du-bois* chic of the canoe shot was the opening image of each episode, and it was nicely mirrored by the cover shot on the book itself, which also featured the country's most mesmerizing twentieth-century politician adorned in rustic style.

← Newly elected leader, 1968 Liberal convention

Trudeaumania, 1968

That we could still be seduced by this figure was abundantly and immediately apparent. Despite the glib, carefully managed insubstantiality of both series and book, the contents of which were rumoured to have been completely subject to the former prime minister's approval, Canadians ate them up like campfire hotcakes, making *Memoirs* the publishing and broadcasting event of the year. This, if nothing else, demonstrated the penetrating veracity of Stephen Clarkson and Christina McCall's assertion at the opening of their 1990 biography of the man, *Trudeau and Our Times*: he *does* "haunt us still."

As an evocative image, the canoe shot seemed every bit as carefully arranged and assembled as a corporate public relations commercial, or perhaps a campaign spot for someone running for the subconscious office of Supreme National Myth – the emergence from mist into sunshine like the return of a dream that resists repression. The serenely confident handling of the canoe reminded us of the enduring virility of the only Canadian politician for whom sexuality was as important as policy (and who was still fathering children in his seventies), as well as subliminally reinforcing the notion of Trudeau's seemingly god-given dominion over the nation itself.

The natural environment from which he emerged could not be mistaken for anything other than a metaphor for Canada, and his confident, solitary mastery of it. That, coupled with his ghostly visual materialization from it, once again found objective form for something our collective subconscious already knew: one could no more think of Canada without thinking of Pierre Trudeau than one could think of the American West without thinking of John

The serenely confident handling of the canoe reminded us of the enduring virility of the only Canadian politician for whom sexuality was as important as policy.

Wayne, rock & roll without Elvis or hockey without Gordie Howe. Which explains why he could compel us so despite the fact that, politically anyway, by 1993 Trudeau's Canada had more or less collapsed beneath the weight of a decade of Tory dismantling. More than a mere politician, Pierre Elliott Trudeau was the greatest pop star this country ever produced. If you doubt this assertion, attempt this simple test: try picturing Brian Mulroney in a canoe, and see how far the image floats.

This is why Pierre Elliott Trudeau is the only Canadian politician who warrants extended consideration in a book about Canadian popular culture. In recognizing the role that a carefully developed persona can play in the promotion of (or distraction from) political policy, and in cultivating that persona with the care and nurturing of a Hollywood-studio Svengali, Pierre Elliott Trudeau *was* pop culture. Swept to power on the crest of a wave of rock-star hysteria called "Trudeaumania," triumphant in the rainbow-coloured nationalist afterglow of 1967, Trudeau turned the country into spectacle itself, the glamorous movie it had only ever dreamed of becoming, with Pierre Elliott Trudeau both its director and its star.

What follows, therefore, can be interpreted in two ways: as an attempt to prove the Trudeau-as-pop-star assertion, or as a series of scenes from *Trudeau's Canada: The Movie.*

Birthday Boy Pierre Trudeau as Centennial Sprout

It's not that Trudeau, elected as Liberal prime minister in 1968, single-handedly got the cameras rolling himself. In many ways, the Centennial festivities of the previous year, the country's flower power–era birthday bash, had already done that. Looking back, in fact, 1967's year-long orgy of national self-love marks a key shift in the terms that the country imagined itself: from duty to fun, from a nation to an event, from a place to an attitude. The astonishing and sudden victory of Trudeau, with his historically unprecedented – for Canada, anyway – understanding of politics as public spectacle, and his savvy suturing of persona with policy, is at least partly accounted for by the shift in the national imagination made possible by 1967. Distinctive as he was, and remains, his arrival was also perfectly timed. As Larry Zolf noted in 1984, "Trudeau was our permanent Expo."

Fuddle Duddle Pierre Trudeau as Rebel

At a certain point on a February afternoon in 1971, Prime Minister Pierre Trudeau decided he had had just about enough of the Opposition's relentless needling about high unemployment rates. Fixing his oriental gaze across the floor at his tormentors, he silently mouthed an unmistakable ill wish: "Fuck off." Pandemonium broke out. Opposition member Lincoln Alexander stood and demanded that Trudeau repeat himself, which he gladly did, but silently. Shrugging off the outrage, the prime minister said to the House, "Mr. Speaker, I challenge any member opposite to say that they heard me utter a single sound." Following the prime minister's claim to

Elder statesman, 1984

reporters that what he'd really said in the House was "fuddle duddle," the nation briefly enjoyed a fuddle-duddle frenzy. T-shirts and buttons bearing the euphemism popped up everywhere, and a song of the same name – by a group called the "House of Commons," natch – briefly cracked the Canadian charts. A short-lived satirical comic magazine, featuring Trudeau as leading character, took the phrase for its title. If anything, the whole fuddle-duddle affair merely bolstered the prime minister's rep for irresistible irascibility. It was like having Jack Nicholson for prime minister. It was *not* like having Lester Pearson for prime minister.

Heavy PET Pierre Trudeau as Sex Symbol

The fact is, even the mouthing of the f-word in parliament contributed positively to the engineering of Trudeau's aura, for it suggested not only that the bachelor prime minister used it and knew what it meant, but that, unlike any suspicions we might have harboured of his jowly, waistcoated predecessors, here was a guy who actually did it. Where his prime ministerial forebears were, as far as public persona goes, hardly a studly lot, Trudeau seemed the very first Canadian leader to actually pack a loaded pistol. This is key: sex was as obvious an element in the Trudeau mystique as the rose in his Right Honourable lapel.

In 1967, Pierre Trudeau, then Lester Pearson's minister of justice, claimed the state had "no place in the bedrooms of the nation," and we soon began to sus-

> **Where his prime ministerial forebears were hardly a studly lot, Trudeau seemed the very first Canadian leader to actually pack a loaded pistol.**

pect the real reason why: he might well be caught sporting there. Not that Trudeau's *je ne sais quoi* was any subtextual secret, either. As early as 1968, the dawn of the Trudeau era, the new leader's hunkaliciousness was a matter of open journalistic interest: "An inescapable aspect of the Trudeau revelation has been his devastating effect on women," wrote Douglas Stuebing that year in *Trudeau: A Man for Tomorrow*. "There seems to be no middle ground in the feelings that women have for Canada's Prime Minister." In stark contrast to his political colleagues (say, House Opposition leader Robert Stanfield), Pierre Trudeau was a chick magnet. In their book *Trudeau and Our Times*, Clarkson and McCall claim that Barbra Streisand thought she loved him, and over the years the prime ministerial elbow was publicly clutched by such high-profile female companions as Margot Kidder and Liona Boyd. Lower-profile attention was not unprecedented, either. "Did the middle-aged lady running open-armed across the Yellowknife airport tarmac to hug and kiss Trudeau simply love the leader of our country to distraction," wondered Larry Zolf rhetorically at the Trudeau era's end in 1984, "or

was Trudeau the closest thing to a movie star offering sublimated sex, freely obtained and painlessly enjoyed, that the Northwest Territories had ever seen?" Make that the country itself and you've got your answer.

The Medium is the Message and The Message is Me Pierre Trudeau and Marshall McLuhan

According to Walter Stewart, whose 1971 book *Shrug: Trudeau in Power* marked one of the most thorough and penetrating early attempts at dismantling the Trudeau mystique, Trudeau learned about playing leader from no less an expert on media manipulation than Professor Marshall McLuhan. Even if the claim seems somewhat exaggerated, the affinity between the two men is not: not only were McLuhan and Trudeau frequent correspondents and dinner companions, they were definitely electronic-era soulmates. While McLuhan was one of the first communications experts to recognize that the content of the mass media was infinitely less meaningful than its form, Trudeau was one of the first Canadian politicians to make politics seem vastly less important than persona.

If Trudeau's artful fusion of persona with politics is what made his status as pop-cultural icon possible, it's also what made it possible to be seduced by his image but ignorant of what, in practical political terms, he actually stood for. While the cool, witty, unflappable and inscrutable prime ministerial persona remained more or less constant throughout his political career – except possibly for the misguided and flatly unconvincing global peace campaign of 1983-1984 – his policies were often erratic and contradictory. Don't forget, the man of whom John Lennon gushed in 1969, "If there

Shaking hands with nemesis Richard Nixon

were more leaders like Mr. Trudeau, the world would have peace," is the same man who would call on the tanks by invoking the draconian War Measures Act a year later, only to dismiss the truly disturbing implications of the action with the flip, almost Schwarzeneggerian tag line, "Just watch me." But this is the essence of persona's victory over politics in the electronic era: your politics don't need to cohere as long as your image does. Or, as McLuhan himself once said when asked about the key to understanding Trudeau's televisual savvy: "The medium can't take a real face. It has to have a mask."

Meet the Beatle Pierre Trudeau and John Lennon

On December 22, 1969, with just over one week remaining in the 1960s, Pierre Trudeau received two intensely well-known visitors. Not that there was anything new about this. Although little more than a year had passed of his reign, word of his novel and most unstatesman-like hipness had spread around the world. André Malraux had made a pilgrimage to Ottawa from France, Henry Kissinger from Washington, and Marshall McLuhan from the far reaches of the global village. Still, as far as counter-cultural credibility went, none of these were a match for John Lennon and Yoko Ono. Fresh from a Toronto summit with Marshall McLuhan, John and Yoko arrived in Ottawa a few days before Christmas to see Trudeau.

Possibly flush with McLuhanesque praise of the prime ministerial "message," the planet's most famous couple of the moment seemed practically giddy at the prospect of pressing Pierre Trudeau's

For the first time, Pierre Trudeau looked like a confused middle-aged guy who'd made a big, middle-aged mistake.

flesh. More than 50 photographers were on hand outside the prime minister's office that day, and the flashbulbs exploded as Trudeau shook the Beatle's hand then hugged the Beatle's wife. The three disappeared behind the doors to Trudeau's office, where the topics of conversation allegedly ranged from the Lennons' global peace effort to the generation gap and what life as a Beatle was really like. On emerging, Lennon was positively gushing with childlike excitement: "We talked about everything," he told reporters. "We spent 40 minutes – it was five minutes longer than he'd spent with heads of state!" Superficially strange as the Lennon-Trudeau summit seemed to many at the time, there was nevertheless a snug symmetry to the meeting as well: the politician as pop star welcoming the pop star as politician.

They'd Only Just Begun Maggie and Pierre

It must be taken as an early signal of Pierre Trudeau's popcult status that Dr. Joyce Brothers, the preeminent psychologist of choice for the day's TV talk and quiz shows, was once asked to comment on the prime minister of Canada's magnetic appeal to women. In part, this is what she said: "Vicariously they can watch and enjoy the nuances of his encounters with the ladies, be titillated by the rumours of romance, or – grand thrill of all – hope for the day the prime

minister falls in love and marries." That day came in 1971, when Prime Minister Pierre Elliott Trudeau exchanged vows with 22-year-old Margaret Sinclair, the daughter of veteran Liberal James Sinclair, whose own wife, Margaret's mother, was two years younger than the PM.

Initially, the union also seemed to seal the prime minister's bond with everything that was considered hip, youthful and exciting for its era. Margaret was a stunning upper-middle-class hippie princess who liked to dance, go barefoot, wear flowers in her hair and once claimed that her definition of culture was "rock music." In terms of the marriage's contribution to the Trudeau mystique, it was therefore every bit as important that she be seen to dig him as he her. If this gorgeous, free-spirited flower child could go for the PM – despite the chasm of age, experience, intellect and inclination that yawned between them – then we must indeed have the coolest and sexiest leader on the face of God's earth.

Neither the marriage nor what it initially represented was to last. Ironically, in fact, it proved a crucial development in the shifting of Pierre Trudeau's pop persona. It quickly became apparent that the two had little, if anything, in common, which merely emphasized Trudeau's age and remoteness from the generation and attitudes from whence his child-bride came. Moreover, as the marriage began to show public signs of breakdown (Margaret partying hearty with the Rolling Stones at the El Mocambo in Toronto), it seemed to us out there watching the very first thing our cucumber-cool leader seemed unable to control. And if Margaret wouldn't pay him

Meet the Beatle: with John Lennon and Yoko Ono

heed, what did that bode for his status as hippest head of state in the western world? In short, for the first time, Pierre Trudeau looked like a confused middle-aged guy who'd made a big, middle-aged mistake.

Margaret bore the prime minister three sons, and left them in his custody when they separated. Naturally, this resulted in a substantial shift in Trudeau's role as pop icon: a transformation from charismatically ageless stud to sober single father. It's hard to play the insouciant outlaw statesman with three kids to raise.

PET Today Trudeau As Elder Statesman

Proof of the man's impervious fascination as one of the country's most potent pop-culture icons was amply evident as

Suddenly, Meech Lake was Trudeau's show, and for the simple, inescapable reason that he had chosen to be in it.

late as 1993, when that canoe bearing Pierre Trudeau came looming like a ghostly vessel out of the morning mist, and once again we had no choice but to just watch him.

And we still watch, despite the fact that years have passed since we had any democratic responsibility to do so. But what's democracy got to do with stardom? We watch because it is impossible not to. And he knows it, this old lion, as his meticu-

lously orchestrated public moments make plain. When he chose to disapprove publicly with the Meech Lake accord, Prime Minister Brian Mulroney was quite palpably miffed. As all heads swivelled in Trudeau's direction, his charisma-challenged successor must have felt like one of those guests on the Johnny Carson show whose moment in the spotlight was rudely eclipsed by the sudden, unscheduled appearance of Bob Hope.

Suddenly, Meech Lake was Trudeau's show, and for the simple, inescapable reason that he had chosen to be in it. This, it would seem, is the apex of Canadian star power.

Death, Taxes, Wayne and Shuster

When Johnny Wayne, the winking half of the half-century-old Canadian comedy team of Wayne and Shuster died in 1990, it was like walking a hometown street and suddenly noticing that a building that had always been there was gone. While you might not have paid much attention to the damned thing in a long time, you couldn't help being touched and surprised by its sudden absence. Only then do you realize you thought it would always be there.

For many people growing up Canadian after the mid-fifties, it did seem like Wayne and Shuster, the Toronto comedy team who appeared on *The Ed Sullivan Show* a record-breaking 67 times (and how's that for a good Canadian number?) would always be there. That's why, like so much institutionalized Canadian popular culture, they were also easy to take for granted. Eleven years before Wayne's death, just as the duo were about to present the latest of the seemingly countless specials they produced for CBC over the course of three and a half decades, Bob Blackburn wrote in the *Toronto Star*'s *Starweek*: "They are the Death and Taxes of the comedy world. They have been with us forever. What is news, perhaps, is that they firmly intend to go on being with us – forever."

The very notion of the institutionalized permanence of Wayne and Shuster is of course an institution itself within Canadian popular culture. As proudly nationalistic performers enjoying both out-of-country familiarity and apparent tenure at the CBC, Wayne and Shuster must certainly be included in that category of home-grown entertainment which prided itself less on its popularity than its endurance. Like *Front Page Challenge*, Gordie Howe or *Mr. Dressup*, the mere presence of Wayne and Shuster acted as national succour in times of geopolitical turbulence. Symbolic stability. The world may change, and so may the temper of the country, but we rested easy in the knowledge that we'd always have schtick like this:

> **Wayne:** "I'll have a martinus."
> **Shuster:** "Don't you mean martini?"
> **Wayne:** "If I want two I'll ask for them."

Ba da boom. Cue Johnny's mugging turn to camera, the duo's trademark mode of bringing a gag home with the subtlety of a flying tomahawk. Their approach, which was honed by years doing broadly satirical sketches first at the University of Toronto, where they both studied English, and then as army performers during the Second World War, and then finally on CBC-Radio and television, was decidedly post-vaudevillian. They didn't do straight comedy à la Abbott and Costello, but always skits and sketches inspired by everything from Shakespeare ("Shakespearean Baseball," "Rinse the Blood Off My Toga"), to TV commercials.

Hard as it may seem to comprehend from this historical juncture, when popu-

At their peak of popularity during the late fifties and early sixties, there were no more visible ambassadors of Canadian popcult than Wayne and Shuster.

Wayne and Shuster: Global Canucks

Sight gag

Commercial parody

lar taste in comedy has generally shifted a brow or two either above or below the W & S approach, the fact is, the duo – who quit postgraduate studies in English to enlist in the Canadian army – were considered brainiacs among comics. Ed Sullivan, the famously humourless, frighteningly influential entertainment impresario who ranked the Canadian duo among his absolute fave performers, liked to call them his "Canuck egghead comics," and the *New York Times* once hailed the Harbord Collegiate high-school grads as "the harbingers of literate slapstick." Sid Caesar, move over.

At their peak of popularity during the late fifties and early sixties, there were no more visible ambassadors of Canadian popcult than Wayne and Shuster. Apart from the record-setting number of appear-ances on the Sullivan show (and they enjoyed an unprecedented contractual relationship with Ed which allowed them to do whatever they wanted on the show as often as they wanted on the show), they beat out the mighty Lucy herself in a North American critics' poll of best TV comic acts in 1962, had an American recording contract and were often called to perform on British television.

Despite clear evidence of being the most popular Canadian entertainment export since, well, Mary Pickford or the Dionnes, the team clinched its institu-tional status by never allowing the maple leaves to be torn from their chests: they never attempted an American series, turned down offers from Hollywood, Vegas and Broadway and made belliger-ent public displays of their proud nationalism. For them it was CBC – and Sullivan – or nothing. Yet for those grow-ing up Canuck in front of the television

during those peak years, the fact of Wayne and Shuster's ubiquitous export Canadianness was hardly a source of unconditional pride. As the sixties wore on, the pun-and-punchline approach of the team seemed increasingly square and literal, especially as the Sullivan show yielded to certain *zeitgeist* shifts by including guests like the Beatles, the Stones, Woody Allen and Richard Pryor. In this increasingly spicy cultural context, it wasn't always easy to feel the chest swell with national pride at the fact that these two guys were often the only Canadians you'd see on American TV.

Of course, those who felt that way were just too young, too colonized and too glamour-struck to realize that what Wayne and Shuster were really doing was sowing the seeds of what within two decades would become, arguably, the most influential contribution Canadians have made to North American popular culture ever – satirical sketch comedy. It's true: while we're currently so immersed in the comedic climate established by Canadians – SNL, SCTV, Carrey, Reitman, Kids in the Hall – as to be oblivious to it, the fact is it can all be traced back to Frank, Johnny and those excruciating egghead puns.

If the Canadian influence in contem-porary comedy is largely distinguished by its postmodern irony and obsessive fixa-tion on popular culture – not surprising for a small nation of couch spuds ren-dered terminally schizophrenic by the domination of foreign media – it's Wayne and Shuster who first introduced the practice to the world. Even very early on, before the Sullivan offer and the fact of institutionalization, and even before the introduction of *Mad* magazine, Wayne

The team clinched its institutional status by never allowing the maple leaves to be torn from their chests.

and Shuster would mix up their collegiate literary influences with the prevailing pop-culture references of the day: Shakespeare mingled with movies, Scheherazade with "Hertz-Rent-a-Carpet." Upon seeing a pioneering sketch exercise in postmodern juxtaposition called "Western Hamlet" – exactly the kind of thing *SCTV* pushed the envelope with years later – the Canuck eggheads received a fan letter from no less a fellow postmodern Canadian brainiac than Marshall McLuhan: "Your Western Hamlet was great!," he wrote the duo. "The parallel between the two art forms was most effective in throwing light on the play *Hamlet* too."

Now, of course, it's obvious: no marti-nus, no *Saturday Night Live*, no *SCTV*, no Kids in the Hall, no Jim Carrey. But, lest we think this legacy exists only in the airy realm of the intellect, there's a more direct connection, as well – Frank Shuster's daughter Rosie not only won multiple Emmies writing for *Saturday Night Live*, she was once married to Lorne Michaels, the Canadian-born brain-child behind that show, and a man whose own comedic career began with multiple CBC appearances as the straight half of a comedy team – Hart and Lorne – very much influenced by Wayne and Shuster. Ba da boom.

WAYNE AND SHUSTER 227

"Thou Shalt be in Thine Story"
Moses Znaimer Makes a Prophet

On Sunday, April 9, 1995, many Canadians got an extended glimpse into the psyche of Moses Znaimer. The showcase for the experience was a visually hyperkinetic, three-hour, first-person polemic broadcast in prime time by the CBC. Called *TVTV: The Television Revolution*, the show started with the announcement of the arrival of the day of wrath: "It's time," Moses said to the people. "Time to start the body count in one of the great battles of the second half of the twentieth century, the battle between the image and the printed word." Geez. And to think that most of us hadn't even heard the gunfire.

For those viewers familiar with Moses's distinctive broadcasting creations, say, MuchMusic ("The Nation's Music Station"), the recently launched "New Style Arts Channel" Bravo or the flagship Toronto station Citytv ("*Everywhere*") – the tone, style and content of *TVTV* came as no surprise: the camera darting around subjects like a hungry mosquito, the sudden jump cuts and shifts in perspective, the constantly churning McLuhanesque gumbo of words, slogans, images and on-screen text. If the message – something about print culture getting its antediluvian butt whupped by image culture – had a familiar ring, it's because *TVTV* was basically a distillation of what Moses had been saying in interviews, speeches and self-produced profiles for years: that television had remade the world in its image, in the process eclipsing the entire Gutenberg Galaxy with its pure ascendant brilliance.

Certainly there was no mistaking the messenger: if your TV fell within broadcasting reach of any of his expanding electronic outposts, you knew Moses: the man's tendency to appear as a prominent on-screen character in what he calls his "living movie" would have made sure of that. So if you watched any of Moses's media with regularity, sooner or later you watched Moses: he of the softly whispered ten-dollar words, the sermonist's steepled hands, black designer raiments and the lacquered microtail poking out just above the back of a buttoned-up, but perpetually tieless, collar. And, of course, the ear-catching, vaguely enigmatic slogans, that unabashedly McLuhan-influenced torrent of postmodern platitudes and electronic-era bromides endemic to his on-screen schtick: "TV is as much about the people bringing you the story as the story itself." "Print created illiteracy. TV is democratic. Everybody gets it." "Television is not a problem to be managed; but an instrument to be played."

That the nation, whether familiar with Znaimer or not, tended to tune out in droves (*TVTV* had some of the lowest ratings ever recorded for a CBC Sunday-evening special) should not blind us to the real message of Moses's long-coveted bid for national media attention. Most prophets go unlistened to in their own land anyway – it's part of the propheting package. The fact was, whether you listened to him or not, *TVTV* was proof that Moses Znaimer was, after three decades of warning us, now a figure to be reckoned with on a national scale: the most distinctive, flamboyant and media-smart private-broadcasting entrepreneur the country has ever produced, and someone sufficiently influential to lord over three

TVTV was proof that Moses Znaimer was, after three decades of warning us, now a figure to be reckoned with on a national scale.

hours of prime national public broadcasting time designed essentially to promote his vision, his product and himself. *TVTV* certified the fact that, like it or not, Moses Znaimer is as much a successful pop-culture product as he is a producer. Always a firm believer in the act of making the storyteller the story, Znaimer has worked every bit as aggressively to promote his vision before the camera as behind a desk or over a phone. When he developed a series profiling mould-breaking figures called *The Originals*, he featured himself in an episode, and aptly enough his registered term for the entire Citytv *zeitgeist* is "the living movie."

In the process of making a public spectacle of his own career, Moses has also become the first mogul in Canadian broadcasting history who's as much a TV character as a businessman. That's why it wasn't surprising to see him appear as a sadistic thug in Louis Malle's 1980 movie *Atlantic City*, nor to see Citytv so savagely parodied as the hilariously anything-goes Civictv in David Cronenberg's brilliantly discombobulating melding of McLuhan and media-era paranoia called *Videodrome* (1983).

Moses (born Moishe) Znaimer was brought into the world in the remote Soviet province of Tajikistan in 1942: his parents were fleeing Nazi pogroms when their first son was born. When the new family arrived in Shanghai and applied for refuge in Canada, young Moishe's mother

substituted another boy for official medical inspection, fearing her own son's childhood tuberculosis would prevent him from being allowed passage. The plan apparently worked, for Moishe – now Moses – is inescapably among us. Looking back at the close call of his early years, he told an interviewer in 1995 that "my first consciousness was there was this vast universe out there waiting to kill me."

As a revelation it seems to have seared itself on his sensibility, for much of Moses's professional life might be best explained as the actions of a man convinced that people were going to kill him if he didn't strike first. Whether the belief on the part of the prosperously grown-up, internationally renowned Moses Znaimer is delusionary is now beside the point. It's enough to understand that he believes it, and deeply so.

Growing up in the cultural mélange of Montreal's St. Urbain Street, Moses spent a lot of time taking care of his younger sister and brother while his parents worked, his opera-loving father as a bricklayer and shoe clerk, and his mother as a waitress. The Znaimers didn't make much, and what they did they invested in improving the lives of their children. One of the fruits of this determination was the Jewish parochial school where Moishe's Grade 7 teacher was poet Irving Layton, a man who managed to impart a life lesson to young Znaimer within moments of first strutting into the class. Picking up a piece of chalk, Layton wrote the numbers "99.9" over and over again before turning to the kids and proclaiming that 99.9 percent of people are philistines. Somewhere among those desks, young Moishe was bowled over: "I didn't even know what a philis-

Temple of the ultra-hip: Citytv at Queen and John

Beaming out the medium's message

tine was," Znaimer told an interviewer, "but I knew I didn't want to be one. The whole point was you want to be that one percent and you can't by being somebody else."

Throughout adolescence, Moses was smart and knew it: hustling pool was one formative way of lining empty pockets, and he's still known to boast about his street-tough youth. Still, his strong academic record earned him a scholarship at McGill, and it was while filling out the university enrollment forms that Moishe's name forever became Moses because, as he's said, it's "the ultimate power name." At McGill, in the early sixties, he prospered both emotionally and academically; not only did he meet his lifelong companion there, actor Marilyn Lightstone, his stellar academic performance earned him a scholarship to study government at Harvard.

Ever so briefly considering a career in print journalism, Moses quickly found himself more interested in what would luckily turn out to be the winner's side of the impending struggle for the late-twentieth-century mind. After successfully infiltrating the CBC in his early twenties, Moses developed his first truly interactive broadcasting experiment: the still-running national radio phone-in show *Cross Country Check-up*. But it was on TV that Moses really found his metier: by 1967 he had blown the dust off the old *Take 30* daytime talk show by playing a prominent role on and off camera, and in the process earned the reputation as one of the bright young lights at the CBC. The catch was, bright young lights aren't exactly welcome in the dim fluorescent corridors of the public

broadcaster, and a guy like Moses Znaimer was far more likely to be seen as a threat there than a saviour. Naturally, it didn't help when, in the midst of preparing a proposal for a TV version of *Cross Country Check-up* the impolitic young upstart told an interviewer that he'd like to run the CBC himself one day. Suddenly, Moses found the place a whole lot stickier. It became harder to push ideas across the thresholds of power, more difficult to slide concepts across the desks of influence. In 1969, shortly after proclaiming himself the man who would be king, Znaimer quit the CBC, a self-described "failed member of the church."

Still, the self-enforced excommunication was apt, as eventually any prophet worth his sandals has to start his own church. Which is what Moses Znaimer did in 1972 when he started the future "temple of the ultra-hip" – as named by San Francisco's *Wired* magazine – Citytv in Toronto. A bargain-basement operation designed to capitalize on changes in Canadian cable-television regulating policy, City was designed by Moses to be everything conventional TV (like the CBC maybe?) was not: fast, adventurous, noisy, multicultural and impolite. A little bit like it is today, that is, but even more deliriously vulgar. At first, Moses got more headlines than ratings for the cocky notion of programming soft-core porn for the notorious *Baby Blue Movies* series, but many headlines nevertheless. And no less a figure than Ivan Reitman produced a Citytv game show called *Greed*, in which contestants were given cash and prizes for performing oddball stunts.

Initially, despite such bold attention-getting strokes, converts to the temple were few. So few, in fact, City's viewers weren't of sufficient numbers even to register in the ratings. Disaster loomed until the mid-seventies, when Montreal's Bronfman family bought a 45 percent share of the debt-ridden station and hired an American broadcasting consultant named Jacques de Suze to sit in a Toronto hotel and watch local TV for three days.

De Suze's task was to find something City might do no one else was doing. Strange as it seems in today's overwired times, the "something" turned out to be a high-profile, completely local newscast. But not just another paper-shuffling-white-guy-behind-a-big-desk newscast. De Suze recommended a newscast with "a very street-oriented style," meaning mobility, accessibility, momentum, personality.

After the success of *CityPulse News*, as the broadcast was named, Moses's empire-building impulses went into overdrive. In the ensuing years, he would prove

A bargain-basement operation designed to capitalize on changes in Canadian cable-television regulating policy, City was designed by Moses to be everything conventional TV was not.

a tireless and apparently unstoppable force on the Canadian broadcasting scene: there have been very few CRTC (Canadian Radio-television and Telecommunications Commission) licensing hearings in the past two decades which Moses has not made an application to, and he has seemed utterly unfazed by the enormous amount of bureaucratic rejection he has experienced in the process. On the contrary, it seems to steel his maverick resolve, his inclination to bang even louder on a door if he suspects there's something going on inside to which he's not invited. What certifies a prophet's legitimacy if it isn't resistance? "If you want to make the CRTC nervous," he said, "force them to watch television... the one thing you don't have to prove when you apply for a television licence is that you know how to make TV."

He is inarguably the most influential figure in Canadian broadcasting today, and arguably one of the most influential in the world. The basic strategy concocted for *CityPulse News* – the portable video eye, the roving rainbow coalition of reporters, the ambulatory anchorpersons, the open non-studio, the breezily unprofessional sense of simultaneity and immediacy – are by now ubiquitous contemporary TV conventions, as likely to be deployed on stations in Europe or Australia as in Canada, where the influence of Moses is as inescapable as

sales tax. So much so, one must wonder if he takes any satisfaction from the fact that he's pulled off one of the most satisfying reversals a prophet can, which is to fundamentally alter the nature of the church from which the prophet was once banished.

By the mid-nineties, it was impossible to watch even the CBC without being confronted with the unmistakable, if embarrassingly derivative, impression of Citytv style: the jump cuts, the shaky-cam, text on screen, newsreaders with legs. Considering this, along with the publicly broadcast *TVTV* sermon and the fact that he had begun to make inroads into educational broadcasting with the acquisition in 1995 of the privatized provincial public network in Alberta called Access, one must acknowledge the veracity of Moses Znaimer's professional prophecy, the one which eventually forced his retreat from the church in the first place. By now, Moses *is* running the CBC, and just about everyone else in the business of making Canadian television.

When people go to work for Citytv, they are provided with a list of only half-joking commandments, one of which reveals as much of the smart kid who changed his named to Moses as it does his broadcasting philosophy – if, that is, the man and his media philosophy are in any way distinguishable anymore. It reads: "Thou shalt be in thine story."

Selected Bibliography

Baldwin, Douglas. "L.M. Montgomery's Anne of Green Gables: The Japanese Connection," *Journal of Canadian Studies* 28, no. 3 (Fall 1993), pp. 123-133.

Barris, Alex. *Front Page Challenge: The 25th Anniversary*. Toronto: CBC Enterprises, 1981.

Brooks, Tim and Earle Marsh. *The Complete Directory To Prime Time Network TV Shows, 1946–Present*. New York: Ballantine, 1995.

Clarkson, Stephen and Christina McCall. *Trudeau and Our Times Volume 1: The Magnificent Obsession*. Toronto: McClelland and Stewart, 1990.

Einarson, John. *American Woman: The Story of The Guess Who*. Kingston: Quarry Press, 1995.

Fulford, Robert. *This Was Expo*. Toronto: McClelland and Stewart, 1968.

Goddard, Peter and Philip Kamin, eds. *Shakin' All Over: The Rock n' Roll Years in Canada*. Toronto: McGraw-Hill Ryerson, 1989.

Gould, Ed. *Entertaining Canadians: Canada's International Stars, 1900-1988*. Victoria: Cappis Press, 1988.

Hofsess, John. *Inner Views: Ten Canadian Film-Makers*. Toronto: McGraw-Hill Ryerson, 1975.

Jackson, Rick. *Encyclopedia of Canadian Rock, Pop & Folk Music*. Kingston: Quarry Press, 1994.

Katz, Ephraim. *The Film Encyclopedia*. New York: Perigee, 1979.

Knelman, Martin. *Home Movies: Tales From the Canadian Film World*. Toronto: Key Porter, 1987.

____. *This Is Where We Came In: The Career and Character of Canadian Film*. Toronto: McClelland and Stewart, 1977.

McNeil, Alex. *Total Television*. New York: Penguin, 1984.

Manley, Frank. *Smash The State: A Discography of Canadian Punk, 1977-92*. Montreal: No Exit, 1993.

Melhuish, Martin. *Heart of Gold: 30 Years of Canadian Pop Music*. Toronto: McClelland and Stewart, 1983.

____. *Oh What A Feeling: A Vital History of Canadian Music*. Kingston: Quarry Press, 1996.

Miller, Mary Jane. *Turn Up The Contrast: CBC Television Drama Since 1952*. Vancouver: University of British Columbia Press, 1987.

Morris, Peter. *David Cronenberg: A Delicate Balance*. Toronto: ECW Press, 1994.

Morris, Peter. *The Film Companion*. Toronto: Irwin, 1984.

Partridge, Marianne, ed. *Rolling Stone Visits Saturday Night Live*. Garden City, N.Y.: Dolphin. 1979.

Romanowski, Patricia and Holly George-Warren, eds. *The New Rolling Stone Encyclopedia of Rock & Roll*. New York: Fireside, 1995.

Rutherford, Paul. *When Television Was Young: Primetime Canada 1952-1967*. Toronto: University of Toronto Press. 1990.

Stewart, Sandy. *Here's Looking At Us: A Personal History of Television in Canada*. Toronto: McClelland and Stewart, 1986.

Young, Scott. *The Boys of Saturday Night: Inside Hockey Night In Canada*. Toronto: McClelland and Stewart, 1990.

Photo Credits

Every effort has been made to contact copyright holders. In the event of an inadvertent omission or error, the editor should be notified at Prentice Hall Canada Inc., Professional, Trade and Reference Division, 1870 Birchmount Road, Scarborough, Ontario, M1P 2J7.

NAC   National Archives of Canada
CBC   Canadian Broadcasting Corporation
NFB   National Film Board of Canada

Cover Photos
Front cover, first row: Pamela Anderson Lee – Keystone Canada; *second row, left to right:* k.d. lang – courtesy of Warner Music Canada; Gordie Howe and Wayne Gretzsky – (c) *The Brantford Expositor; fourth row:* Pierre Trudeau – from 1968 Liberal campaign poster *Back cover, first row:* Joni Mitchell – courtesy of Warner Music Canada; *second row:* Pierre Berton – CBC Still Photo Collection, Toronto; *The Big Snit* – courtesy of the NFB; *third row:* Shania Twain – photo by Albert Sanchez, courtesy of Mercury Nashville, c/o Mercury/Polydor Records, a division of PolyGram Group Canada Inc.; William Shatner – Keystone Canada; *fourth row:* Mary Pickford (D & L Kaye Enterprises; *fifth row:* David Cronenberg – courtesy of Crash Post, Toronto; Mr. Dressup with Casey and Finnegan – CBC Still Photo Collection, Toronto *Opposite title page:* Wayne and Shuster, CBC Still Photo Collection, Toronto

Introduction
p.viii Safari/*The Globe and Mail;* **p.ix** *left:* CBC Still Photo Collection, Toronto; *centre:* CBC Still Photo Collection, Toronto; *right:* photo by Sandy Singer, courtesy of Academy of Canadian Cinema & Television, 1983 Genie Awards; *top right:* Canada Wide; *bottom:* Prentice Hall Archives; **p.xi** Smith/Stratford Festival Archives

With a Bullet: Bryan Adams Aims to Please
p.1 courtesy of A & M; **pp.2-3** Canapress

King of Cartoons: Canada's Animated Empire
p.4 courtesy of the NFB; **p.5** *left:* image from *The End,* courtesy of Chris Landreth, Alias/Wavefront; *right:* NAC/PA158835; **p.6** *top:* courtesy of the NFB; *bottom:* courtesy of the NFB; **p.7** NAC/PA160594

Paul Anka: Highway to My Way
p.9 *top left:* CBC Still Photo Collection, Toronto; *top right:* Canapress; *bottom:* Paula Thiessen; **pp.10-11** CBC Still Photo Collection, Toronto

Orphan Annie: Green Gables, Inc.
p.12 *bottom:* CBC Still Photo Collection, Toronto; **p.13** Barrett & MacKay, Cornwall, P.E.I.; **p.14** Metro Toronto Reference Library

Schwing Time: The Great Canadian Babewatch
p.16 NAC/PA137074; **p.17** *left:* Keystone Canada; *right:* Keystone Canada; **p.18** *top:* Keystone Canada; *bottom:* photo by John Barr, courtesy of Playboy Enterprises Inc.; **p.19** *top:* Marko Shark; *centre:* photo by Albert Sanchez, courtesy of Mercury Nashville, c/o Mercury/Polydor Records, a division of PolyGram Group Canada Inc.; *bottom:* courtesy of Warner Music Canada

Man Alive! The Export Boom in Canadian Beefcake
p.20 Keystone Canada; **p.21** *left:* CD cover photo by Nels Israelson, art direction by Henry Marquez, design by Michael Hodgson, reprinted with permission of Aquarius Records; *right:* CBC Still Photo Collection, Toronto; **p.22** *top left:* photo by Dominique Isserman, courtesy of Stranger Music, reprinted with permission of Dominique Isserman; *top left:* 1968 Liberal Campaign poster; *bottom:* photo by Andrew MacNaughtan, courtesy of CNN; **p.23** courtesy of Wolf-Kasteler

The National Dreamer: Pierre Berton
p.24 CBC Still Photo Collection, Toronto; **p.25** CBC Still Photo Collection, Toronto; **p.26** courtesy of Pierre Berton; **p.27** NAC/PA102387

The Man Who Fell to Earth: Jim Carrey Beams Down
p.29 *left:* CBC Still Photo Collection, Toronto; *right:* Keystone Canada

The Rock's Revenge: CODCO and This Hour Has 22 Minutes
p.31-33 all photos courtesy of Salter Street Films, Halifax

Emergent Evolutionary: David Cronenberg Breaks with Form
p.34 Cinematheque, reprinted with permission of Crash Post, *Dead Ringers* "The Mantle Clinic II Ltd."; **p.35** Keystone Canada; **p.37** courtesy of Crash Post, Toronto; **p.39** Cinematheque, reprinted with permission of Crash Post, *Dead Ringers* "The Mantle Clinic II Ltd."

Cronenberg's Brood: The Next Generation of Canadian Film
p.40 courtesy of Vos Productions Limited; **p.41** *left:* Eisen/Cinematheque Ontario; *right:* photo by Chris Buck, courtesy of Shadow Shows

Baby Boom: The Dionne Quintuplets
pp.42-44 all photos courtesy of the Dionne Quints Museum Collection, reprinted with permission of Annette, Cecile and Yvonne Dionne; **p.45** CBC Still Photo Collection, Toronto

Rock of Ages: The Endurables
p.47 *left top:* courtesy of EMI Canada and Jared Levine; *right top:* courtesy of Warner Music Canada; *left bottom:* courtesy of Leonard Cohen; *right bottom:* courtesy of Warner Music Canada; **p.48** *top left:* John Einarson collection; *top centre:* NAC/PA170175; *top right:* NAC/PA170173; **p.49** Landy/Canada Wide

When We Were Fab: Expo '67
p.50 NAC/PA185473; **p.51** NAC/C30085; **p.52** NAC/PA185506; **p.53** NAC/PA183653; **p.54** *left:* NAC/PA185484; *right:* NAC/PA185519; **p.55** NAC/C24559; **p.56** NAC/C26756; **p.57** NAC/PA183650

Rage of Aged: Front Page Challenge
pp.58-61 all photos from CBC Still Photo Collection, Toronto

The Sixty-Four Dollar Question: Canadian Game Shows
p.62 Michael Angel; **p.63** CBC Still Photo Collection, Toronto, reprinted with permission of Hatos-Hall Productions; **p.64** *top:* Shooting Star – Ponopresse Internationale; *bottom:* CBC Still Photo Collection, Toronto; **p.65** *left:* courtesy of CHCH-TV, Hamilton; *right:* courtesy of Bill Burrows

Life is a Highway to Hell: Goin' Down the Road
p.67 *left:* Cinematheque Ontario, reprinted with permission of Don Shebib; *right:* Cinematheque Ontario, reprinted with permission of Don Shebib

Doom Daddy: Lorne Greene
p.69 *top left:* CBC Still Photo Collection, Toronto; *top right:* Keystone Canada; *bottom:* CBC Still Photo Collection, Toronto

Pure Prairie League: The Guess Who/BTO Legacy
p.70 Michael Angel; **p.71** *top left:* John Einarson collection; *top right:* courtesy of Randy Fillipone's Guess Who memorabilia collection, Buffalo, NY; **p.72** John Einarson collection; **p.73** courtesy of Randy Fillipone's Guess Who memorabilia collection, Buffalo, NY

Canadian Shield: Who Asked Peter Gzowski to Save this Country, Anyway?
p.75 *left:* CBC Still Photo Collection, Toronto; *right:* CBC Still Photo Collection, Toronto; **pp.76-77** Slaughter/*The Toronto Star*

Honesty's Too Much: Dan Hill's Hit From Hell
p.79 CBC Still Photo Collection, Toronto

Obsession: Hockey Days and Nights in Canada
p.82 Prentice Hall Archives; **p.83** *top left:* CBC Still Photo Collection, Toronto; *top right:* Turofsky/Imperial Oil–Hockey Hall of Fame; **p.84** *top left:* courtesy of Brian McFarlane collection; *top right:* (c) *The Brantford Expositor; bottom left:* courtesy of Don Cherry; **p.85** courtesy of Combe Incorporated; **p.86** Cinematheque Ontario, reprinted with permission of Baton Broadcasting Inc.; **p.87** courtesy of Irwin Toy Limited; **pp.88-89** reprinted with permission of O Pee Chee Company Limited; **p.90** *top row:* Canapress; **p.91** Lennon/*The Toronto Star*

The 'EH' List: Canada's Hollywood
p.93 Prentice Hall Archives; **p.95** D & L Kaye Enterprises; **p.99** CBC Still Photo Collection, Toronto; **p.100** Cinematheque Ontario; **p.101** CBC Still Photo Collection, Toronto; **p.102** Keystone Canada; **p.103** D & L Kaye Enterprises

Sheer Hoser: Bob and Doug Take Off, Briefly
p.104 courtesy of Anthem/SRO Management, CD cover design by Martin Soldat; **p.105** *top:* courtesy of Anthem/SRO Management, CD cover design by Martin Soldat; *bottom:* from *The Hoser Handbook* (c)1984, A Prentice Hall/Madison Press Book; **p.106** courtesy of Anthem/SRO Management, CD cover design by Martin Soldat; **p.107** courtesy of ITV, Edmonton

Canadian Pinko: Norman Jewison
p.110 Allan/Shooting Star–Ponopresse Internationale Inc.

Fade to Black: Claude Jutra's Mon Oncle Antoine
p.113 Massenet/Cinematheque Ontario, reprinted with permission of the NFB; **p.114** photo by Norman Chamberlin, courtesy of the NFB, reprinted with permission of Mimi Jutra

The Friendly Giant: Canada's Boom in Kidkult
p.116 courtesy of TVOntario; **p.117** *left:* CBC Still Photo Collection, Toronto; *centre:* CBC Still Photo Collection, Toronto; *right:* CBC Still Photo Collection, Toronto; **p.118** *top left to right:* courtesy of Paul Sutherland, *Once Upon a Hamster* co-creator (with Dave Ellison) and executive producer; photo by Fred Phipps, courtesy of Playing With Time; courtesy of Playing With Time; courtesy of Showcase Television, Toronto; *bottom:* courtesy of Alliance, *ReBoot*, an Alliance/BLT Production; **p.119** courtesy of CHCH-TV, Hamilton

New Disorder: Kids in the Hall
p.120 Christenson/*The Globe and Mail*; **p.122** Keystone Canada

Blood on the Tracks: Gordon Lightfoot
p.125 Carstens/Canada Wide; **p.126** *top left:* Canada Wide; *top right:* courtesy of Warner Music Canada; **p.127** courtesy of Terry Whelan

PopCanLit: Canada's Pulp Mill
p.129 courtesy of Brian McFarlane collection; **p.131** courtesy of Brian McFarlane collection

The Circuitry of Sainthood: Marshall McLuhan's Northern Visions
p.133 *top left:* NAC/PA172794; *top right:* York University Archives and Special Collections/*Toronto Telegram* Collection; **p.134** York University Archives and Special Collections/*Toronto Telegram* Collection

Another Fine Messer: The Down-Home Tradition That Will Not Die
p.137 Mitchell/Canapress; **p.138** NAC/PA152025; **p.139** CBC Still Photo Collection, Toronto; **p.140** CBC Still Photo Collection, Toronto; **p.141** NAC/PA108419

Goin' Down the Middle of the Road: Canadian Easy Listening
p.142 courtesy of Sony Entertainment Canada Inc.; **p.143** *left:* courtesy of Hagood Hardy; *right:* CBC Still Photo Collection, Toronto; **p.144** photo by Alan Silfen, courtesy of Warner Music Canada; **p.144-45** CBC Still Photo Collection, Toronto

A Great Broad: Anne Murray
p.147 *left:* Leshnov/Canada Wide; *centre:* CBC Still Photo Collection, Toronto; *right:* courtesy of *Kitchener-Waterloo Record* Photographic Negative Collection, Dana Porter Library, University of Waterloo

Big News: The Real Canadian Star System
p.149 *left:* CBC Still Photo Collection, Toronto; *centre:* CBC Still Photo Collection, Toronto; *right:* CBC Still Photo Collection, Toronto; **p.150** *left:* Prentice Hall Archives; *right:* CBC Still Photo Collection, Toronto; **p.151** courtesy of ABC-TV

Leslie Nielsen Dumbs Down: The Case for a Canadian Hero
p.152 CBC Still Photo Collection, Toronto; **p.153** Phillips/Keystone Canada

The Great Outdoors: A Wilderness Worth Watching
p.154 photo by Ken Post, courtesy of Ralph Endersby; **p.155** *top:* courtesy of Susan Conway; *bottom:* courtesy of Susan Conway; **p.156** *left:* NAC/PA41306; *right:* CBC Still Photo Collection, Toronto; **p.157** CBC Still Photo Collection, Toronto

Apopalypse Now: The Nineties Sound Explosion
p.158 courtesy of K-tel International Ltd.; **p.159** courtesy of Warner Music Canada; **p.160** courtesy of EMI Music Canada; **p.161** courtesy of Warner Music Canada; **p.162** *left:* photo by Kharen Hill, courtesy of Blake & Bradford; *right:* courtesy of Warner Music Canada; **p.163** courtesy of Nettwerk Productions; **p.164** *top:* courtesy of MCA Music Entertainment, a division of MCA Canada Ltd.; *bottom:* photo by Trevor Hughes, courtesy of Jane Siberry; **p.165** Catherine Stockhausen; **p.166** photo by Ann Giordano, courtesy of Pandyamonium/William Tenn Artist Management; **p.167** *left:* courtesy of Larry LeBlanc, Canadian editor, Billboard; *right:* CBC Still Photo Collection, Toronto; **p.168** *top left:* courtesy of Rich and Mary Dodson; all other photos courtesy of Larry LeBlanc, Canadian editor, *Billboard*; **p.169** courtesy of Larry LeBlanc, Canadian editor, *Billboard*; **p.170** courtesy of Ralph Alfonso; **p.171** *left:* Canada Wide; *centre:* courtesy of Lou Blair Management; *right:* photo by George Whiteside, courtesy of True North Records, reprinted with permission of True North Records.

Porky's: Canada Pigs Out
p.173 *top left:* CBC Still Photo Collection, Toronto; *top right:* CBC Still Photo Collection, Toronto; *centre right:* CBC Still Photo Collection, Toronto; **p.174** *top left:* photo by Rebecca

White, courtesy of George Bridge, Elmira Maple Syrup Festival Committee; *top right:* photo by Lisa Scholten, courtesy of George Bridge, Elmira Maple Syrup Festival Committee; *centre:* courtesy of Molson Breweries; **p.175** York University Archives and Special Collections/Toronto Telegram Collection

Wheatfield of Dreams: How Canada Fertilized Reagan's America
p.177 *top left:* Crollalanza/Keystone Canada; *top right:* Keystone Canada; *bottom:* Prentice Hall Archives

The Reitman for the Job: Ivan the Vulgarian Storms Hollywood
p.179 Pelletier/Gamma–Ponopresse Internationale Inc.; **p.180** Bond/Shooting Star–Ponopresse Internationale Inc.; **p.181** Shooting Star–Ponopresse Internationale Inc.

Go Ahead, Make My Quota: The Royal Canadian Mounted Police
p.182 Glenbow Archives, Calgary NA2246-1; **p.183** *top:* photo by Jeffery Newbury, courtesy of Alliance Communications; *bottom:* courtesy of Ralph Endersby

Sonic Suburbia: The Rush Chronicles
p.185 photo by Andrew MacNaughton, courtesy of Anthem/SRO Management; **p.186** photo by Andrew MacNaughton, courtesy of Anthem/SRO Management; **p.187** *right and left:* design by Hugh Syme, reprinted with permission of Anthem/SRO Management

TV Nation: SCTV
p.188 courtesy of ITV, Edmonton; **p.189** photo by Hugh Wesley, courtesy of Second City, Toronto; **p.190** courtesy of Showcase Television, Toronto; **p.191** photo by Hugh Wesley, courtesy of Second City, Toronto; **p.192** photo by Hugh Wesley, courtesy of Second City, Toronto

Mr. Michaels Takes Manhattan: Saturday Night Goes Live
p.194 *bottom:* Keystone Canada; **p.195** CBC Still Photo Collection, Toronto; **p.196** Keystone Canada; **p.197** CBC Still Photo Collection, Toronto

Space Oddity: How William Shatner Learned to Stop Worrying and Love the Future
p.201 *top left:* CBC Still Photo Collection, Toronto; *top centre:* CBC Still Photo Collection, Toronto; *top right:* courtesy of W.D. Davidson and CTV; *bottom:* CBC Still Photo Collection, Toronto; **p.202** *left top:* Keystone Canada; *left bottom:* courtesy of MCA Music Entertainment Group and Lemli Productions; **p.203** CFCF-12 Television, Montreal

No Joke: The Canadian Sitcom Paradox
p.204 courtesy of Paragon International, Toronto; **p.207** CBC Still Photo Collection, Toronto; **p.208** CBC Still Photo Collection, Toronto; **p.209** CBC Still Photo Collection, Toronto

Sturm und Twang: Stompin' Tom Connors
p.211 *left:* photo by Alice Bixley, courtesy of Lena and Stompin' Tom Connors; *right:* CBC Still Photo Collection, Toronto; **p.212** photo by Jim Fishback, courtesy of Dave MacMillan, EMI Music Canada

Go Boom Fall Down: The Tax Shelter Film Follies
p.215 Keystone Canada; **p.217** Kahana/Ponopresse Internationale

A Piece of the Pie: The Triumph of Trivial Pursuit
p.218 Trivial Pursuit (R) is a registered trademark of Horn Abbot Ltd.; **p.219** *top left:* courtesy of Horn Abbot Ltd.; *top centre:* Trivial Pursuit (R) is a registered trademark of Horn Abbot Ltd.; *top right:* courtesy of High Game Enterprises Inc.; *bottom:* TM & (c) Gameworks Creations Inc., reprinted with permission of Gameworks Creations Inc.

From the Hip: Pierre Trudeau's Rule of Cool
p.220 NAC/PA111213; **p.221** NAC/PA117476; **p.222** NAC/PA184567; **p.223** *top:* NAC/PA139117; *middle:* York University Archives and Special Collections/Toronto Telegram Collection; **p.224** courtesy of NAC/PA113481; **p.225** courtesy of NAC/PA110804

Death, Taxes, Wayne and Shuster
pp.227 all photos from CBC Still Photo Collection, Toronto

"Thou Shalt Be in Thine Story": Moses Znaimer Makes a Prophet
p.228 Rosen/Canapress; **pp.228, 230-33** all photos by Paula Thiessen

Index

The text of this book is set in Adobe Garamond. This electronic version, designed by Robert Slimbach in 1989, is based on the original sixteenth-century design by Claude Garamond, a Parisian punchcutter.

The headlines, captions and call outs are set in Franklin Gothic. Designed by Morris Benton in 1906, it is one of the most enduring sans serif gothic typefaces spawned by the Industrial Revolution.

Acquisitions editor and editorial director: Sara Borins

Assistant editor: Paula Thiessen

Editorial assistance: Anne-Marie Sorrenti

Copy editor: Liba Berry

Creative services manager: Jan Coughtrey

Production coordinator: Julie Preston

Design: Concrete Design Communications Inc., Toronto